I0878573

Judgements of all Kinds

TE WHARE WĀNANGA O TE ŪPOKO O TE IKA A MĀUI
VICTORIA
UNIVERSITY OF WELLINGTON

VICTORIA UNIVERSITY PRESS
Victoria University of Wellington
PO Box 600 Wellington
http://vup.victoria.ac.nz/

First published 2013

National Library of New Zealand Cataloguing-in-Publication Data

McAloon, Jim.
Judgements of all kinds : economic policy-making in New Zealand,
1945-1984.
Includes bibliographical references and index.
ISBN 978-0-86473-897-4
1. Macroeconomics. 2. New Zealand—Economic conditions—1945-
1984. 3. New Zealand—Economic policy—History. 4. New Zealand—
Politics and government—20th century. I. Title.
339.50993—dc 23

Printed by Printstop, Wellington

Judgements of all Kinds

Economic Policy-Making in New Zealand 1945-1984

Jim McAloon

Victoria University Press

Contents

Acknowledgments

I have been working on this book for far too long and many people must be thanked for their assistance. I was prompted to begin writing on the postwar economy by the experience of teaching a course on postwar New Zealand to students at Lincoln University, when I found that much of what I wished to emphasise in the history of the New Zealand economy was not covered in other studies. Friends and colleagues at Lincoln, especially Harvey Perkins, Bob Gidlow, Greg Ryan, Nicky Murray, Lucy Baragwanath, Paul Dalziel, and Jane Higgins encouraged me to pursue this research, and Len Richardson, also in Christchurch, reinforced my hope that historical analysis might have a bearing on contemporary concerns.

I am grateful to Lincoln University for a period of sabbatical leave that enabled me to spend a lengthy period in Archives New Zealand's main branch in Wellington. The staff of Archives New Zealand and of the Alexander Turnbull Library were essential to this project's completion, as will be seen from the endnotes. The endnotes also reflect my debts to the work of dozens of scholars who have enlightened me and shaped my thinking.

In 2009 I moved to Victoria University of Wellington. I am grateful to Victoria for the leave that allowed me to write the final version of the book. I owe thanks for ongoing encouragement and frequent insights to colleagues in Victoria's History Programme and elsewhere, particularly Brad Patterson, Charlotte Macdonald, Kate Hunter, Brian Easton and Cybèle Locke. Glyn Parry thought it was worth doing, and Malcolm McKinnon deserves special mention for support at crucial moments as well as his generous reception of work that I hope complements his own magisterial study of the New Zealand Treasury. John Singleton (now at Sheffield Hallam University) was similarly generous even as we disagreed on some matters. I am grateful to Philippa Mein Smith and Peter Hempenstall (University of Canterbury) and to Chris Lloyd (University of New England and University of Helsinki) for inviting me to contribute papers to collections that they were involved in editing (and to Chris Lloyd, also, for his advocacy of the importance of historical political economy). More generally, the Economic History Society of Australia and New Zealand has provided a collegial forum for the exploration of these ideas as well as teaching me a great deal, and I am grateful to many participants at conferences of that association and the New Zealand Historical Association for allowing me to try out arguments.

An anonymous reader made valuable comments on the penultimate draft and I am very grateful for his or her thoroughness. At Victoria University Press, I particularly thank Fergus Barrowman for believing in the project and for some incisive criticism of the manuscript, and Amber Carter for a fantastic job in copy-editing.

Jenny Dawson is a theologian and a priest, not a historian and academic. But she has lived with and supported this project, and everything else I have done, and intangibly enriched the whole. This book is dedicated to her.

Preface

New Zealand economic and social policy in the decades before 1984 is often characterised – either implicitly or explicitly – in simplistic and negative terms. In contrast, the drastic reshaping that occurred in the years after 1984 receives much more focus and continues to influence political debate. The New Zealand Treasury, for instance, notes that 'Over the last quarter of a century, the New Zealand economy has changed from being one of the most regulated in the Organisation for Economic Cooperation and Development (OECD) to one of the least regulated'.[1] A former governor of the Reserve Bank referred to the post-1984 changes as 'one of the most remarkable economic liberalisations of modern times' and likewise maintained that 'New Zealand has been transformed from one of the most regulated economies in the OECD to arguably the least regulated'. Moreover, he expressed the opinion that 'the decline of New Zealand after World War II displayed the baleful logic of Hayek's road to serfdom', if 'bureaucratic' serfdom rather than 'police-state'. Serfdom, in this view, amounted to 'protective trade barriers and price, wage and capital controls in an attempt to insulate itself from changes in the world economy and to suppress inflation. But each intervention created distortions that spawned new interventions. By the early eighties, almost all prices, interest rates, rents, wages, and dividends were controlled by government – to say nothing of the import controls and the foreign exchange controls'.[2]

The experience of the early 1980s – which, I maintain, was an aberration rather than representative of the postwar decades – is still enlisted in political debate. In 2010, with the New Zealand economy suffering under the impact of the global financial crisis, the Labour Party suggested that the focus of monetary policy should be broadened from price stability to other measures of economic welfare and that more generally state policy might take a more activist role in shaping economic growth. A right-wing Australian think-tank, the Centre for Independent Studies, responded by observing that in 1984 'New Zealand was known as the "Polish shipyard of the South Pacific" for its inefficiency and protectionism. Since then, the political consensus has largely moved towards open trade and markets where possible'. The Labour Party was criticised for espousing 'interventionism and arbitrary government,' and seeking a return to 'an explicitly protectionist, xenophobic, 1970s Keynesian fortress'.[3]

These accounts conflate the complex history of 40 or more years into a few catchphrases. Periodisation is important: the 1970s were, to state the obvious, very different from the late 1940s, and to characterise four decades with terminology appropriate to the specific circumstances of the late 1940s or the early 1980s is quite misleading. A subtler periodisation is helpful to understanding; I suggest that while the economy was tightly controlled in the 1940s and early 1950s – necessarily so, in the circumstances – there was from the mid 1950s an increasing engagement with the outside world. While this was driven by circumstances, policymakers took initiative as well as merely responded. Growth as well as security was emphasised, and indeed the balance shifted over time. Of course there are some themes that stretch across the decades. As in most western democracies, a historically distinctive policy regime was built in New Zealand as a result of the Depression and the Second World War. Maintaining and adapting that postwar settlement is the first of two major themes underpinning this book. The second, and more important, is that the particular circumstances of New Zealand as a small settler (or post-settler) economy are often not given the attention they deserve; external circumstances shaped, and often constrained, economic policymaking.

This book is not a work of broad synthesis, but of detail. Much more remains to be written about, among other topics, social policy, the changing nature of work (or 'labour markets' if one prefers) and the development of farming, manufacturing and service industries. What this book does do, rather, is offer a perspective from the 'engine-room'. I hope to shed some light on the perceptions, ideas, and competing interests that shaped the views and actions of ministers and officials in managing a small, externally dependent economy. Many able scholars have written about the postwar decades in light of what happened after 1984; I have tried to avoid that hindsight in favour of understanding the context of the time. Neither of this book's two basic themes, of the postwar settlement and a settler economy in transition, are original of course, but I aim to at least indicate the complexity of the history of postwar economic policymaking and the ways in which policy changed profoundly over four decades.

Denis Healey was Chancellor of the Exchequer in the British Labour governments between 1974 and 1979. In his memoirs he quoted one of his 12th-century predecessors, a certain Richard son of Nigel: '"Non enim in ratiociniis sed in multipliibus iudiciis excellens scaccarii scientia consistit" – or in English, "for the highest skill at the Exchequer does not lie in calculations, but in judgements of all kinds"'.[4] Judgements, as Healey emphasises, are not merely technical. Economic policymaking is a profoundly political affair, and policymakers' judgements are influenced by their political values, the power of interest groups and external factors. Policymakers in past decades may have been astute or misguided, right or wrong, but very seldom did they have the luxury of making policy in circumstances of their own choosing. We do them a disservice if we do not at least attempt to understand the context in which they lived and worked. My one hope in writing this book is that our judgements of the past may be better informed.

Chapter One

Contexts and Considerations

In 1935 New Zealand was, as Keith Sinclair once remarked, 'one of the least populous independent states, the most dependent on world trade, and hence least in control of its economic fate'.[1] Incorporated into the British Empire in 1840, the colony was settled by tens of thousands of immigrants from the British Isles and elsewhere. Like other settler colonies, New Zealand enjoyed rapid economic growth, but depended not only on exporting a 'narrow range of foods and raw materials' to Great Britain but also on British capital for development.[2] Extensive loans funded state-owned infrastructure, especially from the 1870s. Like other settler colonies, too, white New Zealand's prosperity was based on the more or less rapid dispossession of the indigenous population, who were comprehensively outnumbered within a few decades. Primary sector exports underpinned a growing manufacturing sector from the 1880s, although Britain remained the dominant source of imported manufactured goods. After the First World War, former settler colonies experienced considerable economic difficulty, and the Great Depression of the 1930s threw the problems with their particular economic structures into sharp relief. The Great Depression also had profound effects on industrial economies in the United States and Europe, and in broad terms resulted in significant reshaping of economic and social policy, particularly after 1945. That reshaping – a new settlement based on state oversight of demand and investment, some redistribution of income through tax and benefits, some recognition of organised labour as a partner in economic policymaking, and a general commitment to full employment – was supported by a managed international monetary regime dedicated to stable exchange rates and expanding world trade. It was a settlement that set the boundaries of economic policy but certainly did not remove ideological conflict between left and right.[3] Economic policymaking in New Zealand after 1945 developed in the context both of the postwar settlement that influenced the entire western world and of the particular issues affecting a small settler economy.

Historical discussions of postwar economic policy in New Zealand vary widely in their assessments. Although the merits of postwar policy are contested, the more influential accounts are strongly critical. These critical accounts are often related to the radical restructuring of economic and social policy after 1984 and maintain that the course of economic development and state policy since the war had become unsustainable in its focus on security rather than competitiveness or growth. Even with a Labour-led government after 1999, which was in many respects eager to distance itself from its predecessor of the 1980s, the *New Zealand Official Yearbook* declared, in 2000, that:

> In an attempt to avoid international determination of local living standards, the New Zealand Government turned to 'insulationism'. For 50 years, security often overshadowed growth as a policy objective . . . But gradually, it became evident that living standards in New Zealand were not as high by international comparison as they had been, and dissatisfaction grew. Structural problems emerged in the economy . . . From 1984, a new Government reorientated policy towards encouraging the use of New Zealand resources to service international demand.[4]

The New Zealand Business Roundtable, an invitation-only organisation of chief executives from New Zealand's largest companies, indulged in outright caricature – as one might expect of a lobby group. In 1992 its chairman, the brewing magnate Douglas Myers, claimed that 'for the first time in more than fifty years, New Zealand is an attractive place to operate an internationally oriented business'. In the early 1960s, according to Myers, New Zealand was

> hyper-regulated. . . . we had a British-style trade union system with all its horrors. . . . chronic labour shortages and a cradle to the grave welfare system. There were plenty of jobs for low-skilled workers in protected industries producing over-priced goods for captive consumers. This bizarre structure was supported by more or less guaranteed access for our products to the United Kingdom. New Zealanders were content with their colonial dependence and abysmal levels of productivity growth. You would need to hurry to Albania before it changes to understand what New Zealand was like in those days.[5]

Eastern European parallels – variously Albania or a Polish shipyard – suit political rhetoric and are, to say the least, glib.[6] Serious scholars have also been critical in their judgements. In their excellent study of Australasian economic relations with Britain during the quarter century after 1945, John Singleton and Paul L. Robertson point out that Australia and New Zealand were usually contending with difficult circumstances, particularly as the close economic relationship with Britain weakened. Nevertheless, domestic policy did not help. Scarred by memories of the Depression, 'New Zealand made slow progress in the field of economic development after 1945. An emphasis on stability rather than growth was part of the legacy of the 1930s'. Even if 'other countries emphasized stability and full employment after the Second World War', this was 'not to the same degree as either Australia or New Zealand'.[7] Public policy was inconsistent, misdirected, and 'driven by the short run imperatives of full employment and high consumption'.[8] Any reform agenda 'to encourage savings, competition, and the efficient allocation of resources . . . was precluded for political reasons'.[9] This unfortunate lack of political will resulted in 'the squandering of domestic capital on the protected sector' and 'domestic capital . . . being drawn by the lack of import competition into the production of expensive junk'.[10] Governments did encourage some foreign direct investment but this only 'attracted overseas firms keen to exploit the rent-seeking potential of an insulated economy'.[11] In short, unavoidable circumstances and policy delinquency were combined.

> Growth was constrained by the weakness of overseas markets for temperate agricultural commodities, domestic policies that suppressed competition and encouraged rent-seeking, and sheer isolation. . . . Protection lowered the incentive for firms to strive for efficiency. Wage and price controls that had been introduced to achieve stability and fairness encouraged further erosion of the competitive spirit. . . . [and] almost inadvertently constructed a sclerotic environment. . . . Australia and New Zealand were dealt poor hands and played them very badly'.[12]

Sclerosis is also implicit in James Belich's account of New Zealand's twentieth century. Belich uses the word 'recolonisation' as a summary description for the economic, cultural and political domination of New Zealand by Great Britain, a domination that was driven by refrigeration and 'narrowed the New Zealand economy massively'.[13] Recolonisation amounted to 'a cultural as well as an economic system, and it had important social dimensions too. It reinforced imperatives for social, moral and racial harmony. . . . the system survived challenges and outflanked exceptions sufficiently to dominate New Zealand history in the century after 1882'.[14] Neither the first Labour government nor its National successors challenged recolonisation. The Muldoon administration from 1975 to 1984 was 'recolonisation's last stand', and regime change only came with the Labour government after 1984. Recolonisation is 'the master variable of modern New Zealand history' and the key problem is failing to confront it.[15] For Belich, the 40 years after 1945 were decades of continuity, and dependent continuity at that.

The independent Marxist scholar Bruce Jesson argued along similar lines. For Jesson, like Belich, the dominant influence on New Zealand society was dependence on Britain, cemented in by refrigeration and the associated networks of finance and shipping. Manufacturing was dependent, much of it owned by British firms setting up behind the import-licensing wall. Thus 'the colonial relationship continued in a new form', and businessmen were happy to accept this regulated economy. 'New Zealand in the 1950s and 1960s was suffused with self-satisfaction'.[16] The economy was 'relatively unsophisticated . . . in some respects . . . a generation or more behind the United States and Britain. Business in New Zealand had a provincial and rural orientation'.[17] By the 1970s, the:

> business oligarchy showed no capacity for leadership. Muldoon's policy of borrowing money and subsidising exports was making the situation worse, not better. But the business oligarchy was too much part of the dependent, protected economy to reform it. By the late 1970s it was obvious that the elderly men at the commanding heights of New Zealand business had ceased to serve any useful purpose. The oligarchy was a product of earlier phases of New Zealand's economic history, but had no role to play in this one.[18]

Jesson's critique, which on economic policy is ironically close to Myers', was also cultural. New Zealand society was 'thin', with 'nothing much in the way of institutions between the individual and the state. . . . a hollow society, a society without texture, a society without centres of resistance, as 1984 and its aftermath have demonstrated'.[19]

In an earlier generation, the economist and public servant W. B. Sutch had argued along similar lines. Sutch saw New Zealand trapped in a conformity mediated through 'the political representatives, the press, and the economic groupings that had traditionally resisted social reform – farmers, financiers, importers, merchants, retailers, manufacturers, most professional men'. One wonders who is not included in this list of delinquents. 'These groupings, the press, and most of the trade unions had been strong enough to confine the Labour movement to a programme of social amelioration and not one of modification of the colonial economy'.[20] Sutch reserved particular criticism for the dominant figures in the first Labour government, Peter Fraser and Walter Nash: 'the weight of [Fraser's] considerable influence was placed alongside the forces in New Zealand and abroad shackling change and development. . . . Fraser and Nash did not look beyond the modification of a colony'.[21] Less surprising, for Sutch, was the National Party's unquestioning acceptance of the same regime; none of the party's constituencies had much interest in industrial development, and the party continued to assume that 'New Zealand did not need to alter its colonial economic structure and could live well by encouraging the grass to grow'.[22] Redemption only came in 1958 when a balance of payments crisis prompted the new Labour government to suddenly accept the virtues of crash industrialisation along the lines long advocated by the new Secretary for Industries and Commerce – Dr W. B. Sutch – and 'for the first time in New Zealand's history, the government set about actively developing a somewhat broader industrial base.'[23]

To suggest that these negative characterisations are influential is not, of course, to ignore other more judicious assessments, which generally highlight the efficiency and productivity of the country's primary producers at least until the 1970s and their success in earning the foreign exchange necessary to sustain a growing population. In these accounts, as Geoff Bertram has suggested in a recent essay, difficulties became more pronounced from the late 1960s and policy only became seriously misguided after 1975.[24] Philippa Mein Smith suggests that the 1935–49 Labour government rewrote the settler contract by remaking and extending the Liberal farmer–labour coalition of the 1890s, and guaranteed security and opportunity to organised workers and farmers, especially male breadwinners and smaller-scale dairy farmers.[25] Against those who imply that New Zealand was uniquely delinquent, Mein Smith usefully notes the common policy ground with Australia. She also stresses that the policies of the 1930s and 40s emphasised wages backed by social security and 'a variant of "protection all round": a controlled economy to manage the core problem of economic instability and safeguard the ideal society, this time in the form of a universal welfare state'.[26] Echoing Keith Sinclair's biography of Walter Nash, Mein Smith argues that industrial development was a key part of the strategy from the late 1930s, and on this 'New Zealand met strong British disapproval at the prospect of aspiring to be anything other than the empire's farm. The Australasian model of state development survived, however, because Britain soon needed all the food that New Zealand could produce to sustain its people through another world war'.[27] To Mein Smith, this was by no means recolonisation; even if the National Party adopted slavishly anglophile rhetoric in the 1950s 'in practice it continued the Australasian model of state development, whose core business involved managing the economy in an increasingly uncertain and confusing post-war world'.[28] Britain's reduced economic power from the late 1940s provoked a long-run reorientation of the New Zealand economy, and Mein Smith's account, which is congenial to this book, is of an inevitable diversification managed with at least passable success.[29] As well, the rapidly changing world economy after 1973,

New Zealand's difficulties were exacerbated by many of Muldoon's policies; his approach to economic policymaking amounted to 'the abuse of executive power'.[30]

Writing in the early 1980s, Gary Hawke also emphasised change in the decades after 1945 and stressed that 'the economic system which prevailed after the Second World War did produce economic growth, at least until the 1970s'.[31] While the import controls of 1938 were decisive in creating an insulated economy, he noted that insulationism was less a fundamental reorientation than a shift in emphasis 'away from traded goods so that foreign exchange was a less direct determinant of total economic activity'.[32] New Zealand would and did remain a trading economy, and 'from the mid 1950s, emphasis was turned towards relaxing the foreign exchange constraint through increased exports rather than insulating the economy'.[33] Even if the state influenced economic activity, 'the economy remained a decentralised one and any notion of a politician "running it" was always ludicrous. . . . At no time did government usurp the prime place of private decisions'.[34] John Gould, in a book published only two years before Hawke, took a more pessimistic view. While Gould saw improved efficiency in farming and considerable growth in manufacturing during the 1950s, the climate became more difficult after 1966.[35] Gould criticised 'the aimless drift which had characterised [National's] economic management' during most of the postwar period and lamented the decline of the work ethic and the rise of tax evasion, crime, and trade union bloody-mindedness, as well as the invariable public demand for election-year spend-ups. Some or all of these amounted to 'a national disgrace'.[36] The back of the book described a postwar economy 'characterised . . . by adhocery . . . temporary solutions to long-term problems. New Zealand has staggered from crisis to crisis and sunk slowly into the mire of its current economic situation'. A couple of years later Gould published an account of the Muldoon years which was much less severe in its criticism; by then he saw a mixed record but considerable success in adapting to changing external circumstances.[37] At the end of the 1980s, the journalist Colin James shared ground with Belich in seeing postwar economic history as the transition from colonialism to independence, although like Mein Smith and Hawke he was less critical of the period before 1984. James characterised the crises of the 1970s and 1980s as due more to changing external and internal circumstances than to a long-term failure.[38]

In 1997, Brian Easton's account of the New Zealand economy since 1945, *In Stormy Seas,* appeared.[39] Easton's was an accessible quantitative study, well informed by political economy, dealing with the results of policy more than its formation and stressing the country's dependence on external trade: 'all of our political economies were about the interaction between New Zealand and the outside world'.[40] For Easton, generally fortunate circumstances prevailed until the mid-1960s, and as external conditions changed, so policy and economic activity diversified, but diversification became more difficult as the world economy hit recession in the mid-1970s. Easton later published an insightful collection of biographical essays, *The Nationbuilders*, on influential figures from the 1930s to the 1970s, whose combined intention was 'increasing national sovereignty by consciously repatriating powers and institutions (including businesses) from the metropolis to New Zealand'. Economic growth, in Easton's view, 'requires some active involvement from the government'.[41] Indeed, 'New Zealand went into a period of exceptional prosperity from the mid 1930s' precisely as governments accepted such a responsibility.[42]

Among Easton's 'nationbuilders' were four Prime Ministers, and we also now have solid biographies of most of the Prime Ministers and Ministers of Finance between 1935 and 1984, although the extent to which these works discuss economic policymaking varies considerably.[43] Easton also included one Secretary of Commerce and Industry and two Secretaries to the Treasury. In 2003 Malcolm McKinnon published an excellent history of the latter department (there is no similarly detailed discussion of Industries and Commerce, or Trade and Industry as it became in the late 1960s).[44] McKinnon naturally emphasised Treasury's position in the institutional structure: the background, character and approach of senior officials, and the changing relationships between the various branches of the department. McKinnon is particularly concerned to trace the evolution of Treasury's role from expenditure control to economic management. If expenditure control was the primary concern under Bernard Ashwin (secretary from 1939 to 1955), economic management came to dominate after 1960 and the 'central goal of economic management since the early 1960s [was] increased growth. This goal drove the development and planning conferences of the 1960s, the calls for liberalisation in the 1970s, Think Big in the early 1980s, and the substantial liberalisation of the mid- to late 1980s'.[45]

The history of economic policymaking is therefore highly contested terrain. What considerations allow one reading of the past to prevail over another is a topic beyond the scope of this book, but the more critical accounts seem to enjoy more influence, perhaps because they reflect the agendas of the major business and farming lobby groups, of dominant newspapers, and indeed of articulate and influential economic policymakers of the present day and the last 30 years. The relationship between history and policmaking is explicit in in Michael

Bassett's study of the state in New Zealand over the whole period from 1840 to 1984. Bassett, a historian and a key figure in the 1984 Labour government, discerns 'a nostalgic hankering after those earlier days of big government' permeating 'academic writing about New Zealand's welfare state' and he maintains that no one 'has examined whether incremental interventionism, whatever its short term benefits to particular groups, was a reliable basis for long-term prosperity'.[46] Bassett states quite baldly that 'New Zealanders spent the years from 1945 to 1984 trying to keep Labour's welfare state operational' which is a rather simplistic account of the postwar economy.[47] Where he emphasises the extent to which the state's role expanded after 1945, this is seldom with any sense that similar developments were evident in most western democracies.[48] The general style of Bassett's discussion tends to pile on impression after impression, scarcely ameliorated by his admission that there was considerable and consistent liberalisation after the end of the war.[49] Bassett's overall argument is that:

> Constant improvisation became a problem with New Zealand's state edifice. Endless tinkering eventually produced diminishing returns and brought statism into disrepute with many New Zealanders. . . . by the 1980s some layers of well-intentioned intervention conflicted with others and . . . an over-regulated, over-legislated society had become virtually ungovernable

He also maintains that after 1945 New Zealand's relative decline was 'even faster' than Britain's. New Zealand had become 'one of the developed world's economic laggards'.[50]

'Virtually ungovernable' is a gross exaggeration, and the general tone of Bassett's work, and some of the other literature reviewed here, places it in the tradition of what the British historian Jim Tomlinson has called 'declinism'.[51] Declinism, 'the assumption that [the nation's] economic performance was inferior to its competitors, and that this was a symptom of a secular malaise, dominated much of both popular and academic discussion of the economy, even if prescriptions for curing this malaise continued to be violently disputed'.[52] As Tomlinson notes, 'varying political forces have found declinism a congenial way of understanding Britain. . . . as a result, declinism has been a major influence on post-war British politics; not only an idea widely accepted, but one that has motivated a great deal of political programme making and political action'.[53] Declinism was associated with the British political left in the early 1960s, and it emphasised the allegedly archaic attitudes of economic and political elites during the long period of Conservative rule from 1951 to 1964. The social democratic version was summed up in Harold Wilson's phrase about the white heat of technological revolution; the Marxist version in Perry Anderson's summary dismissal of Britain's supine bourgeoisie and subordinate proletariat.[54] By the late 1970s, 'declinism' had become the ideological justification of Thatcherism, which maintained the left's criticism of gentlemanly dilettantism and added to that a profound hostility to trade unionism and to the whole edifice of the post-1945 welfare state.[55] In New Zealand, the right-wing version is of course that of Bassett and others of like mind, and the left-wing version is that of Sutch and Jesson.

Declinism, therefore, explains many accounts of New Zealand's postwar economic history. As Tomlinson notes it is 'an ideology, a set of ideas and assumptions which are popular and largely unquestioned, articulated in both elaborate and more cursory treatments'.[56] When it is not simply wrong, it is a profoundly ahistorical approach, imposing as it does the luxury of perfect hindsight on the postwar world. Declinism also largely disregards context, especially the international context (a surprising omission in trade-dependent New Zealand) and implicitly postulates some unattainable ideal, often in terms of the superior performance of Other Countries.[57] Declinists, as Tomlinson observed, shared a 'political investment in pathologising . . . society in order to make the case for revolutionary change'.[58] While much of the Treasury briefing to the incoming 1984 government underscored poor handling of the situation since the 1973 oil shock, Roger Douglas, finance minister in the 1984 Labour government, frequently claimed that the whole record since the early 1950s had been one of taking soft options: 'New Zealand is at an economic crossroads. Further tinkering will be disastrous for our future. The time has come for bold innovation, for taking the tough options we have ducked for thirty years'.[59] Similarly, the report of the summit conference of economic interest groups, convened by the newly elected Labour government in the spring of 1984, claimed that 'the failure to match resources and performance has not been a short term problem but rather a feature of the New Zealand economy for the last 30 years'.[60]

For Roger Douglas and his ministerial allies, then, profound economic crisis after 1974 did not merely require new policies; it brought into question the intrinsic merit of the Keynesian postwar settlement. Keynesianism is a convenient shorthand term for a broad and general approach to economic policy, and inevitably the use of shorthand obscures more than it explains unless definitions are made clear. Keynes – John Maynard Keynes, Baron Keynes of Tilton (1883–1946) – has often been described as 'the twentieth century's most influential economist'.[61] The central corpus of Keynes' writings appeared during the 1930s, the decade of the Great Depression, and maintained that while in the long-run markets might be 'fundamentally stable and will tend to move the economy toward equilibrium at the highest practical rate of employment', there were too many variables in the real world that might 'render the private economy fundamentally unstable and liable to prolonged stagnation and unnecessarily low levels of employment'.[62] Thus, governments could, and should, intervene in recessions by spending and increasing demand, borrowing to do so if necessary. Increased demand for goods and services would create a virtuous circle or multiplier throughout the economy, as demand, production and employment fed on themselves. Although this is not always appreciated, Keynes' insights inevitably meant that if demand was excessive, the government should move to control inflation by raising taxes or interest rates and thus taking money out of circulation. It is, therefore, quite wrong to suggest that traditional Keynesians were unconcerned about inflation.[63]

More generally, Keynes' approach implied that governments inevitably affected the economy for good or ill. Whereas classical economists regarded an economy as self-correcting in the long-run, for Keynes the long-run was too long: 'in the long run we are all dead'. Even if 'Keynes was by no means responsible for the expansion of the welfare state that is sometimes linked to his name, his theories placed increasing responsibility for economic performance on the government's shoulders, and his attacks on the priority which classical economics attached to a balanced budget helped loosen a fiscal constraint that stood in the way of more generous social programmes'.[64] Conservative and progressive parties came to share Keynesian approaches after 1945, and although Keynesian approaches were more congenial to parties of the democratic left, Keynes himself was never a socialist, and more or less explicitly aimed to save capitalism from itself by mitigating inequality and hardship.[65] Perhaps Keynes' central insight was that a modern economy is not simply a collection of individuals but a system in itself, and as such can be influenced by an activist public policy. The business cycle fluctuates between boom and slump, and those fluctuations can be eased by public authorities applying counter-cyclical policies: increasing spending and investment during a downturn to compensate for falling demand and tightening when demand is excessive. Dominant for over 30 years, Keynesianism fell into disrepute in the 1970s and 1980s, but Keynes' reputation appears, in the wake of the recent financial crisis, to have undergone something of a revival.[66]

Keynesianism was, obviously, not unique to New Zealand. This country's path in economic policy after 1945 was a local variant of the dominant postwar settlement, which in its broad outlines prevailed in democratic states from Scandinavia to Australasia. There is now a considerable literature on 'regimes of capitalist regulation' concisely defined as 'the system of conventions, rules, laws and institutions that regulates an economy, including regulation of employment relations, monopoly and competition, public/private ownership and investment, rules and styles of organizational management, financial structure and control, international exchange and trade, and taxation'.[67] Such 'regimes' are usually relatively long-lasting, enduring for some decades at least, and frequently emerge from profound crisis. A number of scholars have argued that the periodic major crises of capitalism – the 1870s and 80s, the 1930s and 40s, and the 1970s – resulted in major shifts in the regime of capitalist regulation and in the political economy of individual states. How crises and regime changes play out in particular societies is by no means predetermined, of course; developments in any society are profoundly influenced by the characteristics and relative strength of what Peter Gourevitch calls 'societal actors' and others call interest groups or classes.

The enduring solutions to the crisis of the 1930s and 40s shared a fundamental characteristic: a compromise between capital and labour. Whether individual nations resolved this crisis earlier or only later, after 1945, depended on their political configurations: the strength or weakness of the 'societal actors', their interests, their and their country's place in the international division of labour, and the decisions they made, influenced by ideology.[68] The contrasting ways in which a crisis may be dealt with are indicated, for instance, in comparing the United States and Nazi Germany after 1933. As Gourevitch has observed in general terms for the 1930s:

> [if] labor-allied parties and trade unions were drawn into coalitions, economic policy innovation could take place, and in a constitutionalist context. Where organized labor was repressed but another source of mass support was tapped, policy innovations occurred, but under fascist dictatorship. Where organized labor was excluded but not repressed, as in the United Kingdom and in France . . . policy changes were more limited.

In New Zealand and in Sweden, labour parties were the dominant partners from the mid 1930s; in the United States, Roosevelt drew organised labour into his political coalition. Innovation in these – very different – societies foreshadowed wider developments elsewhere after 1945, when 'the policy debate resumed, augmented by the titanic consequences of the war itself'. The result was a degree of convergence in liberal capitalist societies based around a historic compromise.[69] Underpinning this convergence were fresh memories of distress, unrest and catastrophic war; the desire to avoid a repetition was a powerful incentive for many years.[70] A fundamental part of this compromise was the understanding that organised labour would abandon the ambition to socialise industry and accept the logic of capitalism. In return, industry and commerce – employers, generally – would to a significant degree recognise the right of labour to organise and bargain. The historic compromise aimed at universalism in social services, some redistribution of income and a much more activist fiscal or budgetary policy to achieve these ends and stable growth. Capital also accepted a level of state involvement in macroeconomic planning (not least in public spending to maintain demand at low points in the business cycle) that prior to the 1930s had been largely rejected out of hand.

In many countries, agriculture was an important element in the compromise: farmers' organisations accepted the managed economy in return for price support schemes, and labour, conversely, accepted that this meant relatively dear food.[71] Again, of course, this played out differently from one society to another. In Sweden, for instance, the accommodation was explicit: a proportional electoral system meant that farmers were directly represented in parliament through the Agrarian party, which broke ranks with other non-labour parties and struck a deal with the Social Democrats. With a simple plurality ('first past the post') electoral system, New Zealand farmers had to throw their lot in with one or other of the three, and later two, larger parties. New Zealand farmers provided the bulk of the country's export earnings to a degree unusual in Europe. Consequently, they enjoyed great influence, had less interest in domestic purchasing power than small farmers in Scandinavia or the United States, and were less likely to feel the need to strike a deal with organised labour in the long-term. Their attachment to non-labour parties was reinforced by a long tradition of pragmatic state intervention to support rural interests. There was only a temporary flirtation between Labour and some dairy farmers in the late 1930s before the Second World War caused a major change in the relationship between New Zealand farmers and the state.

Generalisations about a postwar historic compromise are instructive, but New Zealand is one of a distinctive group of democratic Western states: former settler colonies, sites of rapid British colonisation in the nineteenth century, with economies based chiefly on primary exports, for many decades mostly to Britain. Scholars differ over which societies should be included in this group. If only nation-states qualify, then New Zealand, Australia, Canada, Uruguay and Argentina are generally counted (although the latter two are included within 'informal empire', where British investment and influence but not political control prevailed). A definition including regions such as the American Mid-West would enlarge the list.[72] While settler societies enjoyed considerable prosperity in the nineteenth century, the Great Depression highlighted the dangers of narrow specialisation in primary exports, and after 1945 developmentalist agendas were emphasised. Developmentalism was not unique to the settler economies, of course, but given the importance of diversifying the economic base, public investment was of particular significance in New Zealand, as in Australia. In South America, particularly the Southern Cone – Argentina, Chile, and Uruguay – where modernisation and economic nationalism went hand in hand, the state was, if anything, even more important than in Australasia. South American developmentalism could be personalised, as under Juan Perón in mid-century Argentina, or driven by military governments in ways alien to Australasian political culture. An important difference between the Southern Cone and Australasia was that developmentalism in the former region was constrained by a semi-feudal or corporate agrarian sector, whereas Australasian family farming combined the rhetoric of capitalism and individual opportunity and did not give rise to a dispossessed peasantry (except an indigenous minority).[73]

By the later 1940s, policymakers in Australia and New Zealand were seeking to modify at least some dimensions of the inherited structures of dependence. The general postwar concern with economic growth and social consensus had a specific focus in settler societies: breaking out of the staples trap of colonial dependence on exporting a narrow range of primary commodities to Britain. Policy in the settler societies was concerned with ensuring export earnings were sufficient to pay for domestic development and that import spending did not reach undesirable levels – what would be later theorised as the balance of payments constraint.

A distinctive dimension of developmentalism in some settler societies after 1945 was the explicit encouragement of population growth. While population growth had been very rapid and sometimes explosive up to 1914, the Depression had seen stagnation, and after 1945 Australian and New Zealand governments emphasised immigration and natural increase. New Zealand's population was well under two million in 1945 (and therefore below a meaningful threshold for some economists); it doubled in the 40 years to 1985.[74] The two Western European countries most like New Zealand in their combination of relatively small populations and dependence on agricultural exports to Britain were Ireland and Denmark, but the demographic histories were very different. Denmark's population increased by 25 per cent between 1945 and 1984, and that of Ireland was almost exactly the same in 1970 as in 1945, having declined through the 1950s and 60s (as it had done through most of the nineteenth century and after independence for 26 counties in 1922). High levels of Irish emigration are usually seen as an indictment of Irish economic policy, at least until the end of the 1950s.[75] In the combination of recent European settlement, significant dependence on primary sector exports to Britain and rapidly growing population, New Zealand was more like Australia, Argentina, and Uruguay, and in terms of the scale of population most like the latter. Even so, New Zealand's population growth from 1945 to 1984 was greater: it doubled, whereas Uruguay's population in 1945 was two million, and in 40 years increased to three million. Argentina and Australia also doubled, the former from 15.3 million to 30.6 million, the latter from 7.4 million to 15.8 million. Population growth in Australia and New Zealand was seen as a strategic imperative in the aftermath of the Pacific War, and more generally reflected the expansionist rhetoric that had been so common in nineteenth-century settler societies.[76] The extent of population growth after 1945 obviously had some very significant implications for the development of infrastructure.

Table 1.1: Economic growth and population growth, selected countries 1945–73

	GDP per cap Average annual growth 1945–73 %	Population (000) 1945	Population (000) 1975	Population increase 1945–75 %	Population increase 1945–75, annual average %
New Zealand	2.8	1688	3118	84.7	2.73
Australia	3.1	7389	13771	86.4	2.79
Denmark	6.3	4045	5060	25.1	0.81
Ireland	4.6	2952	3177	7.6	0.25
Argentina	3.0	15390	26082	69.5	2.24
Uruguay	1.1	2081	2842	36.6	1.18

Source: Maddison, The World Economy: Historical Statistics

The historic compromise that shaped economic policy in Western Europe, North America and Australasia after 1945, then, was about modernisation and economic growth as well as distribution. Indeed, to be workable and accepted by capital and labour alike, the historic compromise required growth and emphasised 'high investment, rapid export growth, and wage moderation'.[77] In the quarter century after 1945, American growth, based on abundant resources and technological leadership, was remarkable enough, but Western Europe and Japan, starting from behind, grew faster.[78] Their growth, in Barry Eichengreen's words, was extensive and 'based on capital formation and the existing stock of technological knowledge . . . the process of raising output by putting more people to work at familiar tasks and raising labor productivity by building more factories along the lines of established factories'.[79] The international monetary regime established at Bretton Woods in 1944 was of critical importance in a number of respects. The system centred on stable exchange rates; in simple terms, currencies were pegged to the United States dollar, which in turn was valued at $35 to the ounce of gold. The system was secured by the American commitment to exchange dollars held by governments and central banks for gold at that price. Stable exchange rates also implied restrictions on short-term speculative movements of capital, which 'insulated countries seeking to protect their currencies from destabilising capital flows and provided the breathing space needed to organise orderly adjustments'.[80] Competitive devaluations to grab an advantage against trading rivals were frowned on. Stable exchange rates encouraged trade and long-term investment rather than speculative returns from short-term investment, and 'let countries run monetary policies in line with their own conditions', addressing inflation, unemployment or investment as circumstances required.[81] Capital controls and tariff protection, moreover, meant that the profile of international investment changed after 1945. Before 1939, the dominant form of foreign investment had been loans (New Zealand, like other settler societies, had been an enthusiastic borrower of money from the rentiers of Britain). After 1945, foreign investment was increasingly a matter of multinational corporations establishing operations abroad, particularly in manufacturing. From the 1950s, many American firms invested intensively in Europe and elsewhere. This engine of growth was less evident, though far from absent, in Australia and New Zealand, and was of some importance in Canada.[82]

By the early 1970s, much was changing. In many countries, organised labour became less willing to accept wage restraint, and industrial conflict became more noticeable. Western European growth faltered as it now 'became more difficult to grow by building more factories along the lines of existing factories and by purchasing blueprints, licenses, and operator's manuals from the United States'. Growth now required 'investing in new products and unproven technologies', which did not fit well with a relatively high degree of planning and centralisation.[83] As the massive United States balance of payments surpluses of the early 1950s became large deficits by the late 1960s, the exchange rate stability established by Bretton Woods faltered and failed. There were a number of causes of this instability. American policy had been inflationary, not least in running a disastrous war and relatively generous domestic social policies without significant tax increases.[84] Once large dollar balances were held outside the United States the risk, or perceived risk, of the exhaustion of American gold reserves provoked instability and eventually the unilateral termination of the fixed rate for gold.[85] What emerged after 1971 was a regime in which currency markets had much more influence, in which unpegged currencies 'stood in their own right, backed only by the resources of the issuing country and by investors' confidence in the determination and ability of its government to maintain the purchasing power of the monetary unit'.[86] The transition was, however, a very difficult period and the final blow to the long postwar boom came with the Yom Kippur War in the Middle East, in October 1973, and the rapid increase in oil prices that followed. Rising unemployment, falling growth and increasing inflation all characterised the rest of the 1970s. Increasing internationalisation of production and the greatly expanded influence of financial markets, especially for short-term currency trading, combined to reduce the autonomy of national governments in economic policymaking, although to what extent is debated.[87] In short, an unusually favourable combination of circumstances prevailed for the quarter-century after 1945 but much less so thereafter, and the ability of New Zealand policymakers to influence the external context was minimal.

If Keynesian approaches dominated policy in democratic states after 1945, this was never inevitable, and Keynesian hegemony had never been unquestioned. Even as western governments moved towards the mixed economy and the welfare state in the aftermath of the Second World War, exponents of classical liberalism quietly organised for the day when the pendulum would swing.[88] A key text for classical liberals was Friedrich Hayek's 1944 *The Road to Serfdom*. In this, Hayek argued that an economy managed by state planning was ultimately incompatible with liberty. These debates were not entirely absent from New Zealand. Some National politicians expressed Hayekian ideas in the 1940s, and by the 1970s criticism of the postwar consensus was becoming more frequent here, as elsewhere. Michael Bassett's account of the New Zealand political economy is representative of many who had once been more or less orthodox Keynesians but who responded to the deformations of late Muldoonism and a changing external environment by becoming ardent deregulators. Again, though, deregulatory policies after 1984 were hardly unique to New Zealand; as in the 1930s and 40s, specific characteristics varied from country to country according to circumstance, but the policy direction was broadly similar and evolved in the context of a changing global economy. For some New Zealand policymakers, the heady experience of radical change perhaps made revolutionaries out of reformists, as it sometimes does. For others, and indeed for many revolutionaries at first, the argument was, simply, that times and circumstances had changed. The 1984 general election took place in an atmosphere of unusual economic difficulty, not least because Robert Muldoon, who would lose the election, was resisting strong pressure to devalue the currency and running the foreign exchange reserves down as a result. Richard Prebble, a key minister from 1984 until 1988 who was intimately associated with the privatisation of state-owned assets, was two days after the election 'shown a copy of the Treasury's briefing papers and recalls being "stunned" by the magnitude of the crisis. As he turned the pages he concluded that none of the old political solutions would work'.[89]

Treasury's briefing was a piece of advocacy, based on certain assumptions about economic policy. Perhaps 'the old political solutions' would not have worked (although a simple reference to 'the old political solutions' is excessively generalised). It does not follow that they did not work in their day, and even less does it follow that policy in the 40 years from 1945 was an undifferentiated monolith. Most of those who do not regard the record since 1945 as an unmitigated disaster and who would still place themselves on the social democratic left at least accept that the environment from the mid 1970s was very different from that of the 1950s or 60s. It did not follow that the policies adopted after 1984 were the only possible or sensible policies to adopt, and the extent to which the 1984–90 Labour government adopted policies of deregulation and, eventually, privatisation, had well-known political consequences. As the Labour Party, in opposition after a crushing defeat in 1990, sought to rebuild itself, much was heard of that loose body of thought known as the 'Third Way', in which even nominal social democrats explicitly or implicitly characterised the postwar settlement as outmoded. The approach was an attempt to give programmatic coherence to the balancing act between market-friendly policies and the progressive, redistributionist heritage that characterised a number of governments in the 1990s, notably the Clinton administration in Washington and the 1997 Labour government in London. The term itself has probably been brought into disrepute by Tony Blair's enthusiastic espousal of it, but perhaps it deserves better than that. As expounded by the eminent sociologist Anthony Giddens in the early and mid 1990s, the Third Way approach recognised that circumstances had changed fundamentally after the early 1970s, particularly, as we noted above, in the increased globalisation of production and finance.[90]

Giddens argued that adherence to the policies of the postwar consensus made British Labour unelectable. This was partly because the realities of political economy had changed, partly because the right-wing, inside and outside the Conservative Party, was in a newly militant phase. However, Giddens conceded a great deal of ground to the right. 'The welfare state, seen by most as the core of social democratic politics, today creates almost as many problems as it solves'.[91] One need not agree, even if there is merit in Giddens' observation that the Keynesian postwar settlement made certain assumptions about male breadwinners, mass production, a relatively large blue-collar working class, cultural uniformity, and largely self-contained national economies – all of which were changing rapidly by the 1970s.[92] In other respects, the Third Way approaches caricature; the postwar consensus is implicitly regarded as profligate. Giddens suggests 'as a prime motto for the new politics, no rights without responsibilities. . . . Old-style social democracy . . . was inclined to treat rights as unconditional claims'.[93] This is simply untrue; neither Peter Fraser in New Zealand nor his counterpart Clement Attlee in the United Kingdom ever regarded the welfare state as absolving citizens of the duty to work.

The Third Way is also based on accepting that there is no alternative to capitalism (which is what Giddens means by observing that the terms 'left' and 'right' have lost their meaning), but classical social democracy also involved a compromise with capitalism. It can be debated elsewhere whether the Third Way amounts to a loss of political confidence by the social democratic left. In any event a group of scholars in economics and public policy attempted to foreshadow a Third Way programme for an incoming New Zealand government in 1999. Some of these contributions were heavily influenced by Giddens, but one might have wondered which parts of the postwar regime other contributors now regarded as problematic. Peter Conway, for instance, identified 'a core idea that marks out the Third Way: people need jobs' as if full employment had not been a basic principle of the postwar settlement.[94]

New Zealand economic policy in the postwar decades, then, is not susceptible to the simplistic analyses of either demonisation or nostalgia. New Zealand policymakers were operating, like those elsewhere, in the general context of the settlement forged out of depression and world war, but in a modernising settler society like New Zealand there were also distinctive features in economic policy, notably around issues of development, capital investment, population growth and trade dependence. Nor, in fact, should the strength of the consensus be exaggerated. The historic compromise did set some limits, but the differences between political parties in philosophy and support bases remained important. The external environment was far from static; the British market for pastoral exports weakened, the dominant position of the United States in the world economy was moderated by European and East Asian growth, the stable international monetary regime created at Bretton Woods fell apart in the early 1970s, and the 'thirty glorious years' of world economic growth after 1945 were followed by a recession of severity unprecedented in half a century. Within New Zealand, the population grew rapidly through immigration and natural increase until the early 1970s. As farming became more efficient, the population became, even more than it had been in 1935, urban and working in secondary and tertiary industries. Social change was a constant, and the pace intensified from the mid 1960s. All these dimensions shaped the perceptions and the ideas of policymakers, and as in other parts of the world, one cannot understand New Zealand economic policy in the postwar years without discussing the wide-ranging consequences of the Depression and world war. The Great Depression highlighted the problems of a settler economy very sharply, and we will therefore first examine the political economy of New Zealand in the 1920s and 30s, and the policies that the Labour Party developed before and after 1935 in an attempt to address those problems and give some effect to the labour movement's long-cherished ambitions for economic and social transformation.

Chapter 2

Depression and War: The Labour Party and the New Settlement

The crisis years between the late 1920s and the late 1940s profoundly changed the world economy and the relationship between states, national economies, social classes and economic and social policy. If a new settlement emerged in democratic western states after 1945, it was arrived at only after great difficulty, indeed catastrophe. It was a settlement that organised labour played a central role in shaping, particularly its political wing in social democratic or labour parties. However, of equal importance was the response of other organised classes and factions. How this settlement developed differed from country to country and depended on many factors, including the structure of the economy, the organisation and ideologies of the main classes or 'social actors', and the political and institutional framework. In New Zealand, as in other settler societies, the inter-war decades' economic difficulties took on a particular form as the limits of the nineteenth century framework became clear. It was becoming increasingly difficult to maintain prosperity and rapid growth based on exporting primary produce to Britain, importing capital from there for development, and encouraging a manufacturing and service sector oriented to domestic needs and servicing the dominant export activities. While Labour never had a monopoly on innovative thinking, the party's development of policies on central banking, public infrastructure, industrial development, and social services and transfer payments anticipated what would in many countries become the norm after 1945.

Labour's restructuring of the New Zealand political economy after it won office in 1935 has been described as creating a consensus that persisted for 40 or 50 years.[1] If the basic thinking underlying Labour's approach had been developed by 1935, the experience of governing, and especially of meeting the challenge of global war, extended the party's thinking. Labour politicians were driven by two major considerations in developing the party's policies: electability and New Zealand's entrenched economic problems after 1918. The Labour Party had been established in 1916, unifying a number of labour and socialist groups that had emerged in the preceding 15 years. Labour's original platform advocated essentially radical socialist policies, including substantial public ownership. While this approach appealed to many – but by no means all – working-class voters, it was quite unhelpful in constructing an electoral majority. Through the 1920s and early 1930s Labour moderated its approach. The Depression was a crucial influence in that policy development, along with international trends in democratic socialist thought, and an analysis of New Zealand's distinctive situation as a small settler capitalist economy. To a considerable extent, the Second World War would reinforce the direction of Labour's policies, while naturally imposing considerable challenges in economic management.

Economic Difficulty in the 1920s and 1930s

From the mid 1890s until the First World War, New Zealand had experienced sustained economic expansion, driven by a combination of rising demand in Britain for refrigerated foodstuffs, a growing domestic population, intensive land development, and generally abundant capital for investment (by no means all of it imported). One consequence of this long boom was greatly increased activity in the land market, with rapid turnover; rural land prices doubled in real terms between 1895 and 1913.[2] The increase in net values for cultivated land accounted for 'around 70 per cent of the rise in aggregate income per capita' between 1890 and 1914, although productivity growth was more than respectable in dairy and meat processing factories, and probably also in transport and distribution.[3] During the war, farmers benefited from the commandeering of their exportable surplus for Britain at fixed prices.

The New Zealand government had been controlled from 1891 until 1912 by the Liberals, initially a broad coalition of urban and rural wage-earners, smaller business, small and moderate-sized farmers, and those who aspired to farm ownership. In time this coalition fractured, with independent labour parties emerging after 1905 and farmers increasingly supporting a more conservative Reform Party. From 1912 until 1928 Reform governed. While the Liberals had dominated the New Zealand electorate until 1908, Reform's parliamentary majorities were usually fragile, and often depended on split votes in three-way contests with Labour and the Liberals. Although Reform rhetoric was conservative, the activist state remained strong. Many have attributed the wide range of activities that state organisations undertook in New Zealand and Australia – land development, agricultural marketing, transport, energy, insurance, banking, telecommunications, pensions, labour exchanges, factory regulation and industrial arbitration – to pragmatic judgements about the necessities of colonial development. The approach also reflected a global renegotiation in the wake of the economic crisis of the 1870s and 80s. In a variety of forms, government intervention in economic processes had become common by 1910, particularly in supplying or regulating services and moderating some of capitalism's more egregious inequalities. In democratic states, a social liberalism was more or less influential; even in authoritarian ones, like the German Empire, governing oligarchies could see the merits of ameliorating some of the more obvious grievances and maintaining the regime by reducing popular insecurity.[4]

The Great Depression is commonly dated from 1929, but it has long been clear that New Zealand's economic fortunes fluctuated throughout the 1920s. Most accounts have highlighted the general weakness of the British economy during the decade and the fall in export prices in 1921 when the immediate postwar boom ended. After 1921, New Zealand exporters faced 'increasing competition in a [British] market which was growing only slowly'.[5] British industry's competitiveness was severely compromised by wartime inflation, and the return to the gold standard in 1925 and the accompanying over-valuing of sterling, unemployment and high interest rates reduced demand and investment.[6] Greasley and Oxley have argued that another major constraint on New Zealand's rural prosperity in the 1920s was the significant fall in land values. An increasingly speculative market crashed and farmers' 'spending was constrained by a reduction in their net wealth and by their inability to sustain their accustomed route to financial success: selling land. . . . If the land market collapse depressed New Zealand's real GDP per capita through the long depression of the 1920s, it also depressed real wages, and the troubles of the farm sector spilled over to the urban economy'.[7]

Until 1935 economic policymaking in New Zealand combined state-led colonial developmentalism with the British orthodoxy of balanced state budgets and free trade.[8] Monetary policy was left to the banks and New Zealand did not have an independent currency; banks circulated their own notes, usually at par with sterling. Sterling itself had historically been freely convertible into gold at a fixed rate, but this 'gold standard' was abandoned between 1914 and 1925, and again permanently in 1931. The gold standard had prevailed across much of the world until 1914.

> Adherence to gold forced national economies to adjust when they spent beyond their means. If a nation ran a trade deficit, importing more than it earned, it spent more money – that is, gold – to pay for imports than it earned for its foreign sales. As gold left the

> country, the domestic supply of money declined, and the nation's purchasing power also declined. This reduced demand and made it hard for national producers to sell their goods. Producers had to cut prices and force wages down. . . . As local wages and prices dropped, foreigners would buy more of the country's goods and nationals would buy fewer imports. Thus imports would drop and exports would rise, returning the country to balance.[9]

The gold standard thus required a degree of 'insulation from domestic politics'.[10] The exclusion of the working classes from political participation meant that 'the common laborers who suffered most from hard times were poorly positioned to object to increases in central bank interest rates adopted to defend the currency peg. Neither trade unions nor parliamentary labor parties had developed to the point where workers could insist that the defense of the exchange rate be tempered by the pursuit of other goals'.[11] Democratisation in many countries after 1918 'raised the possibility of challenges to the single-minded priority the monetary authorities attached to convertabililty'.[12]

In the strict sense New Zealand, rather than operating a gold standard, ran a sterling exchange system 'with the trading banks' reserves of sterling held in London determining the Dominion's money supply. New Zealand trade surpluses increased the sterling reserves in London, which made possible increased advances in the Dominion. Money supply, therefore, was governed by the export surplus'.[13] The effect, however, was similar to the gold standard. Export earnings were indifferent for much of the 1920s and credit was tight. What made this situation worse after 1929 was the fact that most banks operating in New Zealand were either Australian or Anglo-Australian (the partially state-owned Bank of New Zealand was the principal exception). The banks therefore found it convenient to pool Australian and New Zealand earnings in London. 'Primarily as a result of Australia's financial weakness, the trading banks' sterling reserves in London collapsed, notably between June 1929 and March 1930' and New Zealand's own economic difficulties were intensified by wearing the consequences of the Australian depression as well.[14] As a Treasury official, Bernard Ashwin, put it in 1930:

> the London credit balances built up by these banks from the good trading years of New Zealand have apparently been used to support the Australian exchange. This arrangement . . . works out quite unfairly to the people of this Dominion, and at a time like the present it is clearly seen to be prejudicial to the interests of the country.[15]

Ashwin's remarks, although presented as an academic paper, were 'also the text with only minor changes of a Treasury memorandum explaining to Niemeyer why the government wished to consult him' on banking and currency. Otto Niemeyer was a senior official in the British Treasury and a director of the Bank of England; his New Zealand excursion followed his invitation to advise the Australian government. Strictly speaking, it was Niemeyer who proposed creating a Reserve Bank of New Zealand, but Treasury and at least some ministers were receptive.[16]

Ashwin's paper was an attempt to address the problems of monetary policy and central banking in a settler economy. Primary producing countries like New Zealand were in a difficult position. Because of export and market specialisation, such countries were:

> subject to exceptionally large goods-market shocks. Many specialized in the production and export of a narrow range of commodities, exposing them to volatile fluctuations in the terms of trade. Countries at the periphery also experienced destabilizing shifts in international capital flows. . . . a decline in commodity export receipts would render a capital-importing country a less attractive market in which to invest. Financial inflows dried up as doubts arose about the adequacy of export revenues for servicing foreign debts. And as capital inflows dried up, exports suffered from the scarcity of credit. Shocks to the current and capital accounts thus reinforced each other.[17]

With the simultaneous shocks of falling commodity prices and falling capital inflows, peripheral countries 'had few options': they could continue to service debt, or they could keep foreign exchange reserves high by restricting imports. Either way, domestic growth and domestic employment would be sacrificed.[18] The combination of circumstances does much to explain a widespread distrust of banks and 'the money power' in New Zealand and other settler societies after 1918. The most extreme expression of this view, at least in Australasia, was when the New South Wales state Labor Premier, J. T. Lang, openly advocated repudiating the interest on debt in 1931. More generally it was reflected in the popularity of social credit ideas, an eccentric variant of underconsumptionist thinking. Underconsumptionist theories emphasise the shortage of demand as a cause of economic difficulty; where Keynesians would advocate public investment to stimulate demand, social crediters thought that the inability of citizens to purchase all they wished could be addressed by printing more money. Social crediters also espoused hostility to banks, modern corporate capitalism, and the bureaucratic state.

The Depression was a major trauma in New Zealand as elsewhere. Between 1929 and 1931, export receipts fell by 37 per cent.[19] One economic historian has been tempted 'to wonder whether [the Depression] could really have had profound social, economic and political implications,' as the shrinkage of the New Zealand economy was not 'outstandingly big on an international scale'. The five years from 1930 saw a fall in per capita income of 'somewhere between 10 and 20%'. Nor was unemployment of 'about 12% of the [white, male] labour force. . . . outstandingly severe in an international perspective,' given British unemployment around 20 or 25 per cent, American and Australian 25 or 30 per cent, and German, 44 per cent. All the same, New Zealanders of the time 'would rightly take little comfort' in comparisons, particularly in view of the experience of the long boom after 1890. Of course 'the average experience was not the individual experience, still less the fate that people could reasonably fear might soon be theirs'.[20] In 1931 the government imposed an across the board wage cut of 10 per cent, and even though prices fell between 1930 and 1933, the cut was long remembered, as was the relief work regime, which required arduous work in roadmaking, tree-planting and the like, often in remote areas at low pay. More damaging still to many of those who remained in work was the general sense of insecurity, and the generation that experienced it never forgot it.[21]

Politicians, perhaps particularly Labour MPs, encountered many circumstances that were much worse than whatever average it may be sensible to refer to.[22] The 1928 election had produced a surprising result: the Liberals (revived under the name United) defeated the Reform government and formed a minority administration with Labour support. Although the United government initially espoused expansionist policies, as the Depression worsened, United and Reform joined in coalition from 1931. The generally critical view of the coalition is summed up in Keith Sinclair's remark that George Forbes, the United leader and Prime Minister, was 'a good, honest man whose political merits will doubtless, one day, be uncovered by some dogged researcher'.[23] Gary Hawke, however, has argued that the government as a whole displayed 'willingness to tackle problems as they were recognised, followed through in actions that were sensible and sometimes imaginative'.[24] Certainly the coalition asked committees of various sorts to consider responses to the Depression. The most notable was the 1932 Economic Committee of economics professors, which recommended devaluation, along with wage and interest rate cuts and a move to a balanced budget within three years. With the exception of devaluation, this was entirely orthodox.[25]

The Development of Labour Policy

Labour politicians were not so constrained. The party's policy development in the years before 1935 had common ground with social democratic parties elsewhere. At the party's foundation in 1916, and for some years afterwards, Labour policy focused on wholesale public ownership. That traditionally socialist view had never been the only influence in Labour's thinking, and the impossibility of securing an electoral majority on that basis reinforced the appeal of a more heterodox approach, combining full employment, a measure of wealth redistribution, expanded social services and an activist approach to economic policy. If not utopian, this approach still amounted to a radical transformation.

The Labour Party's founding platform of 1916 reflected both the political strength of militants within the party and the polarisations of the First World War. The militants, who supplied the party's first parliamentary leader, Harry Holland, had thought the war was capitalism's terminal crisis and that revolutionary transformation was not distant. Most Labour voters, although by no means all, had more immediate concerns.[26] Labour advocated for wholesale nationalisation as well as significant and incremental reforms to health, education, pensions, wage regulation, accident compensation and industrial law, and from 1919 the party firmly committed to pursuing these objectives through the parliamentary process. Land policy remained a problem, with a commitment to gradual nationalisation being dropped only in the late 1920s. By 1928, although policy development was erratic, Labour was placing more priority on economic stimulation through public spending, redistributive policies and selective industrial development; some were beginning to talk of repositioning the party as a farmer-labour party, appealing particularly to struggling smaller-scale dairy farmers.[27]

Labour had little economic expertise in its parliamentary caucus during the 1920s. Harry Holland, the party's leader from 1919 until his death in 1933, was an old socialist evangelist, who in his Australian youth had been a member of the Salvation Army. Self-taught, no stranger to poverty and political imprisonment, his certainty in the inevitability of socialism was at once an asset in motivating the converted and the wavering, and a liability in alienating more moderate voters. Holland's thinking, until nearly the end of his life, reflected the orthodoxies of pre-1914 Marxism.

> No one could come near to Holland in his scarifying denunciation of capitalism, in identifying its poisonous agencies in government, or in championing with both rage and compassion the plight of

> the worker. He was the ideal leader for a party seeking to attack the status quo and to champion the cause of the deprived, the powerless and the embittered.[28]

Most historians have suggested that as Labour sought wider appeal, Holland's austere radicalism became a liability. Certainly Labour did not attain a majority under Holland; his successor as party leader, Michael Joseph Savage, would take the party to victory in 1935. Also Australian-born, also with a militant background, an astute parliamentarian and propagandist, Savage's greatest asset was his avuncular image, which the party exploited to the full. Savage's deputy and successor, Peter Fraser, was outstandingly able. A Scottish radical by upbringing, Fraser had like Holland and Savage experienced poverty and done his political apprenticeship in militant trade unionism (like Holland he had also served terms of political imprisonment). Like them, too, he was self-educated, and he dominated social and later foreign policy, leaving finance to Walter Nash, with whom he formed a close political relationship of enduring importance.[29] Nash, a shopkeeper and commercial traveller from the English Midlands, was one of a growing number of middle-class recruits into the Labour Party and exemplified the Christian Socialist strand in Labour thinking. Nash's socialism combined a strongly ethical approach to economic policy, a belief that rational planning offered more satisfactory outcomes than unregulated markets, and a sense of fiscal responsibility.

Savage and Fraser, and Nash outside parliament until 1929, took a leading role with Holland in developing Labour policy after 1925.[30] The English socialist and historian R. H. Tawney was a major influence on their thinking, particularly his ethical argument that remuneration should be based upon service and that the motivation for work should be to give service to the community rather than to enrich oneself. There were echoes of this idea in Nash's frequent observation, from 1922, that the 'first charge on all wealth created shall be the care of the aged, the ailing, the young'.[31] Also influential was the underconsumptionist analysis of J. A. Hobson, who had argued that wealth should be redistributed in order to increase mass purchasing power and thus, by increasing demand, reduce unemployment. Hobson's thinking anticipated Keynes (who in the late 1920s was advocating increased public spending although not redistribution as such) and suggested that 'enhancing the economic power of the working-class consumer was . . . a constructive and transformative measure, not a cause of further economic disorder'.[32] Nash would quote Hobson in his maiden speech. Labour took it for granted that New Zealand was a land of plenty, and only deficient or poorly distributed purchasing power prevented general prosperity. Redistributive taxation policy, expanded monetary benefits, centralised wage fixing, and industrial development for economic diversification and employment creation all followed as proposed remedies.[33]

Labour politicians also thought hard about the state of the New Zealand financial system during the 1920s. Because of the extent to which the private banks controlled monetary policy according to London reserves and – as Labour would frequently argue – considerations of private profit, in 1925 Nash wrote an influential pamphlet on the topic. He elaborated Labour's criticism that the private banks 'control the productive and distributive system of the Dominion' and the party's scepticism that private banks would ever be willing or able to direct credit where it might be most productively employed.[34] Nash advocated a state bank, which would include an agricultural credit department to aid farmers by providing cheap loans and 'marketing our primary produce throughout the world'.[35] Nash also argued that the modern economy was highly centralised in any event and it followed that centralised control exerted by the democratic state was more beneficial to 'the community'.[36] Although Nash's exposition was moralistic rather than technical, it reflected proto-Keynesian thinking on the importance of the state in encouraging investment and thereby stimulating demand and consumption. It also represented an attempt to engage with the specific difficulties confronting a small and isolated settler capitalist economy, dominated by primary sector exports to Britain and dependent on external sources of finance and manufactured goods.

Not that Labour's engagement was uncomplicated. The party's parliamentarians produced a minority report from the 1931 all-party parliamentary committee that had been convened to consider the worsening Depression. While Reform and United went into coalition, Labour called for 'a bold policy of . . . primary and secondary industrial development, with systematized productive effort and definite planning of output in the respective industries' as well as a much greater role for the state in monetary policy.[37] As Holland later explained, the quantity of money in circulation should increase to match the quantity of goods available, an exposition of underconsumptionism that was almost indistinguishable from social credit (a less naïve approach might have been to advocate redistributing income to increase mass purchasing power or stimulating demand through investment).[38] Nash's small-business background gave him useful insights into the commercial world, and he was all too aware not only of the country's dependence on pastoral exporting to Britain but also that this dependence could not in the short-run be wished away. There were some repudiationists and some advocates of social credit and of total price control in the caucus, against whose seductions Nash had to argue severely. This faction seemed to imagine that New Zealand could set its own standard of living regardless of outside influences, a mistake that Fraser and Nash never made.[39] Savage was occasionally less disciplined in his thinking; in 1936, for example, he maintained that there would be an inexhaustible demand for public works funded by 'the public credit' as society moved 'onwards and upwards'. It was all very well to declare that 'we have got to organize and protect our own economy in New Zealand'.[40] Nash and Fraser realised that this had to be negotiated, particularly as the Imperial Conference at Ottawa in 1932 had bound the dominions to reduce discrimination against British manufactured imports as the price of 'a complex set of British import quotas' for their primary exports.[41]

If Nash and Fraser were pushing the Labour Party towards a measure of economic realism, the Minister of Public Works and Reform leader, Gordon Coates, was driving the Coalition's monetary policy away from orthodoxy.[42] Coates's first major initiative was to devalue the currency by 20 per cent in January 1933. Although the economists' committee had recommended this step some months earlier, Coates pushed it through Cabinet against the reluctance or incomprehension of his colleagues, aided by a good deal of militant language from farm lobbies and farmer politicians.[43] Devaluation compensated exporters to some extent for the disastrous fall in prices they had experienced. Labour, Treasury, and the banks were unlikely allies on devaluation. Labour was opposed because of increased prices for imported basic commodities. Treasury was opposed on principle and because it would add to the costs of repaying government debt, and to business and living costs, and would reward farmers for their enthusiastic and debt-financed speculation in land in the 1920s. The banks opposed devaluation as it amounted to the government taking control of the exchange rate from them.[44] The Minister of Finance, Downie Stewart, a Dunedin lawyer, also opposed devaluation and resigned, to be replaced by Coates.[45]

Coates's second major initiative was the creation of the Reserve Bank, 'intended to disassociate monetary conditions in New Zealand from those in Australia'.[46] On this initiative, there was some agreement between Labour and the more progressive elements in the Coalition, although the Reserve Bank as Coates designed it did not go nearly far enough for Labour. As Niemeyer had recommended it in 1931, a central bank insulated from political influence was positively desirable; 'the Bank of England promoted central banking in the dominions because it wanted to underpin international monetary stability and cooperation, and to erect institutional bulwarks against monetary unorthodoxy'.[47] Legislation had been drafted in 1932, and Coates was provoked to finalise the matter, in part, because the Bank of New Zealand had been unwilling to comply with his wishes on devaluation despite being part-owned by the state.[48] Coates, however, entirely agreed with Treasury and the Bank of England that the Reserve Bank should operate at arm's length from ministers and to that end should include a private shareholding.[49] Labour's intention was that the Bank should be a state entity and subject to ministerial direction. This was precisely the pressure from democratic politics that had been avoided by central bankers in the decades before 1914 and by the Niemeyer-Ashwin-Coates approach of the early 1930s. Coates was a pragmatic conservative and, within that context, an economic nationalist; he was not an embryonic social democrat. As well as insisting on a depoliticised monetary policy, he had little enthusiasm for loosening fiscal policy to stimulate demand and production and thus was no Keynesian.[50] The policies which Coates developed, although a departure from orthodoxy, have been described as 'protection mixed with a type of mercantilism. . . . devaluation . . . tariffs . . . market regulation'. This approach was 'neo-orthodox in that it derived from remedies to disorder suggested by classical economic theory and it preserved private property' and it is contrasted with the second, more radical option of 'demand stimulus. . . . through deficit spending for public works, transfer payments, and other targets. Demand stimulus was the new scheme of the thirties. . . . demand stimulus coalitions . . . were *cross-sector, cross-class* alliances of groups whose patience with market solutions had run out'.[51] Although Labour had moderated its own policies by 1935, those policies were still a radical departure from orthodoxy.

Labour in Power

Labour convincingly won the general election at the end of 1935, with 53 seats to the Coalition's 19 (the popular vote was 46 per cent to 33, with the remaining votes and 8 seats going to independents and smaller parties). Labour moved rapidly to give effect to its intentions. The new parliament's first Act nationalised the Reserve Bank. Where the 1933 legislation gave the bank 'control . . . over monetary circulation and credit . . . to the end that the economic welfare of the Dominion may be promoted and maintained,' the 1936 Act required the bank 'to give effect . . . to the monetary policy of the government as communicated to it from time to time by the Minister of Finance. For this purpose, and to the end that the economic and social welfare of New Zealand may be promoted and maintained, the bank shall regulate and control credit and currency . . . '.[52] Nationalisation was far from a meaningless gesture; it challenged the monetary orthodoxy that Niemeyer, Ashwin and Coates had espoused. The new Act implied that no longer would domestic economic activity be automatically dictated by overseas earnings, and it gave the government power to direct the operations of private banks. The government could also direct the Bank to extend credit for government purposes, particularly public works. If this prescription for central banking – 'priority to domestic economic stability and the promotion of economic development' and the intention that 'monetary policy should insulate economic activity from external shocks and not amplify those shocks' – was a departure from orthodoxy in 1936, it soon became more widely accepted internationally.[53]

The government swiftly increased wages and benefits, and increased spending on public works (including a much-publicised state housing programme), to which were also devoted more modern construction machinery. All this increased purchasing power set off Keynes's multiplier and gave an impression of confidence and vigour. As the world economy was improving in any case, Labour was fortunately placed. Developmentalism and underconsumptionist thought met in the often-quoted phrase from Labour's manifesto, that the party's objective was 'to utilise to the maximum degree the wonderful resources of the Dominion'. Policy was gendered, of course, with much directed to the male breadwinner 'to provide him and his dependents with everything necessary to make a "home" and "home life" in the best sense of the meaning of those terms'.[54] The basic wage would be set at a level to provide 'an adequate standard of living for a man, his wife, and three children'.[55] Labour believed that an unmanaged economy would not meet the needs of the people. Economic individualism was said to have failed: 'its spirit – the spirit of acquisitiveness – has perished'.[56] Labour's belief that the overall 'purpose of the Government is to bring security to all our people' is well known. Security however was not an end in itself; it would improve the moral tone. Labour politicians hoped that:

> [workers'] skill and energy [would] be beneficially used not exclusively for themselves, but for the Dominion as a whole. These foundations are difficult to lay because acquisitive instincts affect the actions of all of us to such an extent in present circumstances. . . . [but] when there is security for all who are willing to work the fear of poverty and depressions will disappear, and with it the dominant acquisitive instinct will gradually be eliminated'.[57]

Security and co-operation for the common good were also implicit in the government's labour legislation. Labour amended the Industrial Conciliation and Arbitration Act to provide a 40-hour week, make membership of trade unions compulsory for those workers under the jurisdiction of the Arbitration Court and to allow the formation of national as well as regional unions. The government also supported the formation, in 1937, of the Federation of Labour. The tightly organised FOL would, during the war, become a key partner in the government's economic planning, but more generally the FOL's formation fitted the government's ideas about the inevitable centralisation of the modern economy.[58] As he had a decade earlier, Nash wrote that centralisation was inevitable, and therefore management of the economy by a democratic government was preferable to private monopoly. Accepting cyclical recessions and depressions as inevitable was 'to deny all conscious progressive purpose'.[59] Security and planning also justified guaranteed prices, which would encourage 'stability and efficiency' in the dairy industry by government purchase and marketing of the whole export output. Guaranteed prices would be not merely an equalisation across years but also somehow reflect the farmer's needs and usefulness to the community and 'ensure for Producers an Adequate Remuneration for the Services rendered by them to the Community' (in the event, only dairy farmers were interested in the scheme; sheep farmers, generally, had sufficient resources to survive price swings).[60]

Industrial development, similarly, ought in Labour's view to be planned not only to increase production and living standards but also to provide employment for a growing population, public works not being intended as a permanent employer on a large scale.[61] As Nash put it, 'progress towards full employment must be made through the extension of our secondary industries and development of new industries and services'. Full employment was not negotiable: 'under any rational economic order every person willing to work is entitled to the things necessary for a reasonable standard of living. If science, power, and the machine displace human labour, then social, economic and financial procedure must be adjusted to the new conditions'. [62] Labour ministers believed in state-led modernisation, so that industry policy would proceed on the basis of eliminating 'wasteful competition' and 'giving a conscious direction to the productive energies of the country' for the 'maintenance of existing industries at the highest pitch of efficiency, the encouragement of new industries that can be established with reasonable social advantage, and the best use of our undoubted resources of raw materials that are yet in the primary stages of development'. There was no thought of 'the bolstering-up of uneconomic enterprises by subsidies or tariffs'.[63] The Industrial Efficiency Act, 1936, codified Labour's approach. The Minister of Industries and Commerce, Dan Sullivan, argued that the question was 'whether the old law of free competition – may I say free cut-throat competition – the law of the jungle, and the survival of the fittest is to be the principle that is to obtain in the future, or whether we are to have organization, ordered industrial life, and the application of the best principles of civilization to the conduct of industry'. Planning was contrasted with wasteful use of natural resources, inefficiency, and surplus capacity.[64] In the event, wartime would mean that these plans would effectively be put on hold, and industry policy would be driven by more immediate concerns.

The ultimate expression of the government's commitment to security was the 1938 Social Security Act. Preparing legislation took much of the government's first term, and led to some fractious debates between ministers and backbenchers. Nash had the unenviable task of working out how the party's aspirations for comprehensive security in old age, unemployment and sickness, and free or low-cost medical treatment were to be paid for; not all backbenchers appreciated that there were financial and institutional constraints on the party's vision. The Social Security Act 1938 provided for increased monetary benefits and subsidised medical treatment (Labour MPs had wanted free treatment, but the doctors would not accept this), funded by a dedicated social security tax. With this legislation enacted but not taking effect until 1939, Labour won a decisive victory in the 1938 general election.[65]

The government's policies combined with an improving world economy to produce a significant recovery by 1938. During that year, however, while import spending remained high, export earnings fell markedly. This was the first of many periodic balance of payments crises after 1935, and the government's response had far-reaching implications. From the end of 1938, all imports had to be licensed, and the quantity of any particular imported commodity could be varied by regulation. Exporters, likewise, required a license, and had to convert their overseas earnings into New Zealand currency through a New Zealand bank. The purchase of foreign exchange was subject to Reserve Bank approval. In short, the government took significant power to manage the balance of payments. The government was also forced to seek renewal of significant loans on the London market, and in the middle of 1939 Nash engaged in protracted and acrimonious negotiations with the British government and the Bank of England. Both objected to the New Zealand programme of autonomous industrial development and relatively generous social welfare and services; for all his mild-mannered demeanour, Nash bitterly resented being lectured by the British as if he were an errant schoolboy. In the end, with war imminent, the British conceded the loan.[66]

Even before this, the Labour government had struck the fundamental problem with the British relationship. In 1932 the imperial conference at Ottawa had attempted to secure the empire's economic position by reinforcing it as a defensive trading bloc, with preference to members and discrimination against others. The New Zealand Labour government wanted to underpin guaranteed prices with a bilateral trade agreement with Britain but there were two obstacles to this. Ottawa had provided for more or less equal treatment for all the dominions, which meant that New Zealand could not expect additional access; and even before the war British farmers were being subsidised in order that strategic vulnerability on food imports might be reduced. On the other hand, by entrenching their position as markets for British manufactured goods, Ottawa had limited the dominions' ability to industrialise. When Nash sought to develop a bilateral trade agreement, in lengthy negotiations during 1936 and 1937, and again when he was negotiating loan renewals in 1938–39, he found unrelenting hostility to any suggestion of expanded industrial development in New Zealand, which necessarily would have involved a measure of protection. Nash hoped that industrial development could proceed alongside a commitment to import British manufactured goods, if Britain accepted a cap that would allow New Zealand manufacturers to take advantage of rising demand. Agreement on this point was unlikely.[67] Nash struck the worst of both worlds. He 'had been struggling to achieve a vision of imperial trade which might have produced a high standard of living, but which would have confirmed New Zealand's colonial economic status [but] Britain's needs and British attitudes at once blocked any guarantee of the expanding markets New Zealand needed, while being inimical to the industrial development which might make the Dominion less dependent'.[68] The results of Nash's successive visits to London before the outbreak of war made it 'obvious to the Labour ministers, as it had been to Coates, that the British market was limited. New Zealand was being thrust into economic development and independence'.[69] In many respects, the war would put that process on hold, while at the same time reinforcing and reshaping Labour parliamentarians' views on the means and ends of economic policy.

The Wartime Economy

The Second World War began in September 1939, and the New Zealand government moved quickly to declare war on Germany. Savage, whose health was failing, died in March 1940 and Fraser became Prime

Minister. Wartime, of course, meant the diversion of as much of the country's resources as possible to the Allied cause. The economy was necessarily tightly controlled, and two and a half years' national income, including two years' export earnings, was diverted to wartime purposes.[70] Wartime economic management shaped Labour's view of postwar possibilities, broadened the government's international perspective and led to hopes for a new world of multilateral co-operation.

In the first wartime Budget, in 1940, Nash declared that the government thought it 'infinitely better for everybody' to finance the war out of taxation and saving, rather than Reserve Bank credit or external loans. Therefore, and to control inflation by reducing the quantity of money in circulation, the government intended to 'tax to the economic limit for war purposes and borrow for essential productive works and for any balance of war requirements'.[71] This approach closely followed that advocated by Keynes in his February 1940 pamphlet on 'How to pay for the war', and adopted in the British budget in 1941.[72] It was a textbook example of 'demand management in an inflationary boom' and demonstrated that Keynesian approaches implied restraint as well as stimulation.[73]

Comprehensive controls on wages and prices, and many other aspects of the wartime economy including stringent rationing, were broadly identified with the policy of economic stabilisation.[74] The Economic Stabilisation Commission, created in 1942, had a wide range of methods open to it: 'subsidies, standardisation, simplification, zoning, rationalisation, government importation and selling below cost, absorption of part of the costs by traders, and loading non-essential items with the increased cost of essential goods'.[75] In particular the commission relied on subsidies, which by the end of the war amounted to £8.9m. Thus 'subsidy payments were equivalent to over 2½ per cent of the national income and had become a significant component of the New Zealand pattern of financial transactions'.[76] The commission's chairman was Bernard Ashwin, and it was at 'this time that . . . Ashwin [became] the individual who, above all others, was at the centre of the New Zealand political economy of the day' being on the key primary produce marketing bodies and the Reserve Bank board as well as, since 1939, Secretary to the Treasury.[77] In addition to the Economic Stabilisation Commission, the government established numerous industry control committees, manpower councils and the like, and liaised closely with primary producer organisations, not to mention organised labour. The profusion of consultation was no doubt useful in securing consent for the highly managed economy.

In agriculture, the government prioritised supply of food and raw materials to Britain and to armies in the field. Britain quickly arranged a bulk-purchase agreement, and the government stabilised farm incomes by creating special Reserve Bank accounts into which went the proceeds of any overseas price increases above the December 1942 level.[78] Wartime did not slow the mechanisation of agriculture; if anything, the pace intensified as labour became scarce. Tractors doubled in number, with thousands supplied by the United States.[79] The male labour force in farming fell by a fifth between 1936 and 1951, most of the reduction being in dairying.[80] A good deal of manufacturing capacity was diverted to military purposes in what might be described as extraordinary import substitution. This was noticeable in the engineering, metal, and electrical trades, clothing and footwear, but construction too was significantly diverted to defence.[81] The import and exchange controls of 1938 meant that 'manufacturing entered the war with a very high degree of protection against outside competition', but the extraordinary requirements of wartime were as important in the development of manufacturing, even though it was difficult to import new plant.[82]

The government took wide powers to direct labour, including conscription for military service. At the beginning of the war there were still 20,000 unemployed, but by the middle of the war a quarter of the male labour force was in the armed forces.[83] Married women, young women, students and older workers were encouraged or required to fill the gaps. From 1942, under comprehensive requirements to register with the National Service Department, workers could be directed to remain in or move to specified occupations. By the end of the war almost as many workers had been directed in terms of civilian employment as were in uniform.[84] There has been debate over the extent to which gender roles changed, but there is no doubt the war had a significant effect on female employment.[85] Whereas manufacturing employment had accounted for around 15 per cent of both the male and female paid workforce between the wars, by 1945 it was 19 and 24 per cent respectively. Public administration also increased markedly, from 6 per cent of the male workforce and 16 per cent of the female in 1936 to 15 and 27 per cent respectively in 1945. The 1945 figures were unusual, in that many thousands of men were still overseas with the armed forces, but the trends were not reversed.[86] Wartime, then, accelerated the trends towards a population that was predominantly urban and employed in non-farming occupations, while farming remained the key export earner.

Incorporating the trade unions into the state apparatus was essential to the government's approach. Wage-fixing became centralised, the Arbitration Court being empowered in 1940 to bring down comprehensive General Wage Orders. The 1936 amendment to the arbitration legislation had encouraged the formation of a number of unions, such as the Clerical Workers, whose membership was large but whose scope for mass mobilisation relatively small. An erstwhile Communist from the Seamen's Union, Fintan Patrick Walsh, quickly increased his powerbase in the new unions and the FOL, particularly by allying himself with Fraser.[87] As the country's most powerful trade unionist, Walsh was essential to the success of wartime economic policy, and he was appointed to the Economic Stablisation Commission. At the same time, the FOL president, Angus McLagan, was put in the Legislative Council and appointed to Cabinet. Walsh, in particular, developed considerable skill in wartime economics.[88]

Stabilisation, as both Gary Hawke and Michael Bassett have emphasised, required a high level of solidarity to function.[89] Solidarity and the common good were key elements in Labour's economic thinking and, implicitly at least, the success of wartime economic management encouraged Labour ministers to believe that the postwar economy could be as successfully planned. This was something of a commonplace in social democratic rhetoric overseas as well. As Fraser told the 1943 party conference: 'If millions can be spent in order that we may win the war, then the people of the Dominion have every right to expect that money will be provided for the costs of peace. If democracy can organise itself to wage war successfully, it should organise itself equally well to give work and security to every citizen.'[90] An immediate expression of this view was the comprehensive, and largely successful, programme for the rehabilitation of ex-servicemen and women. The Rehabilitation Act 1941 was based on a determination to avoid the perceived mistakes of 1918, where farm settlement (often on highly marginal land) had been the dominant provision. The Motueka MP, C. F. (Jerry) Skinner, was brought back from active service in 1943 to be Minister of Rehabilitation. In the years following, demobilised troops would receive subsidised training across the whole range of trades and occupations, from apprenticeship to university. They would receive preference in state housing, assistance to establish themselves in farming or self-employment, and gratuities based on the length of time overseas.[91]

The idea that wartime sacrifice had to be justified by a better postwar world informed New Zealand's emerging economic diplomacy. Fraser shared this view with John Curtin, Ben Chifley and H. V. Evatt in Australia, Mackenzie King and Lester Pearson in Canada and with Roosevelt in the United States. At the 1944 Commonwealth Prime Ministers' meeting the dominion leaders 'kept stressing the four freedoms of the Atlantic Charter as the basis for any post-war settlement'. All present except Churchill shared a 'strong determination to press ahead with social and economic development'.[92] To the Canadian parliament, later in the year, Fraser noted that the Charter principles – of freedom of speech and of religion, from want and from fear, as well as national self-determination and global economic co-operation – 'must be honoured, because thousands have died for them'. There had to be a better world: 'not only political democracy, but educational, economic and social democracy'.[93] Under no circumstances would 'the forces of reaction' be tolerated, that sought 'the return of the privilege-dominated pre-war conditions'.[94]

The allied nations attempted in the numerous and lengthy international discussions about the shape of the postwar world to address the problems that, they believed, had caused economic instability and depression, and had thereby precipitated fascism and war. The United Nations was to provide effective means for dialogue, security and the resolution of disputes; through its own various agencies it would also promote economic and social development. The international monetary system was to be reformed through the measures agreed at Bretton Woods. These included stable exchange rates, pegged to the United States dollar, which was fixed in terms of gold at $35 to the ounce. An International Monetary Fund would provide temporary cover for balance of payments deficits, and the International Bank for Reconstruction and Development (the World Bank) would provide development finance. The question of free trade was more difficult. Most agreed that it was desirable in principle. At Bretton Woods, allied nations also agreed on an International Trade Organisation, but negotiating the detail took some time and although the ITO charter was finalised in Havana in 1948, the organisation was never established.[95] As we shall see in the next chapter, 'free trade' meant different things to different governments, and the General Agreement on Trade and Tariffs emerged as the partial substitute for the ITO.

The Labour government was determined that New Zealand's voice should be heard in those discussions. Despite some trans-Tasman tension, much of New Zealand's wartime diplomatic effort was run in conjunction with Australia; that Labor governed in Canberra from 1941 was a distinct advantage. Nash frequently represented New Zealand on economic matters, and the succession of international economic conferences, from the Food and Agriculture conference in 1943 to Bretton Woods in 1944 and beyond, 'represented the zenith of Labour's aspirations – to do for mankind what social security, full employment, guaranteed prices and other measures had, they believed, done for New Zealand'.[96] There was a measure of agreement between the labour governments in Canberra and Wellington that the new economic organisations should adopt full employment as an explicit and fundamental principle. This was not merely idealism. 'Were Australia to adopt unilaterally a policy of full employment, imports would rise as domestic demand expanded, and exports would decline as local costs rose and resources flowed out of export industries into those catering to domestic demand. Consequently, Australia's international economic policy should be to promote the full employment objective amongst the major world powers'. Otherwise, full employment could only work in a tightly controlled economy.[97] As Nash expected, the major powers were unwilling to enshrine what they saw as a matter for domestic policy in international agreements. There was also some difference of opinion between the Australasians (and other small states) and the major powers over whether full employment preceded and would facilitate free trade or the other way around. The end result was general reference to the desirability of high employment in a number of the relevant declarations, an outcome with which Nash was happy enough.[98]

Conclusion

Looking beyond the end of the war, Nash's reflection on the attempts to shape a new international economic order linked them with the government's domestic aims: 'expansion of the whole world economy to provide the purchasing-power sufficient to maintain an adequate diet for all . . . full employment in all countries, enlarged industrial production, the absence of exploitation, an increasing flow of trade . . . , an orderly management of domestic and international investment and currencies, and sustained internal and international economic equilibrium'.[99] Even by 1945 the Labour government had made considerable progress toward realising these ambitions, and in doing so had shaped a new regime. Naturally, the new order was not a complete break with the past, but there were major differences.[100] The commitment to full employment – albeit shaped around the ideal male breadwinner – was a radical departure and it implied that demand and investment would be managed to that end. Managing investment was an important dimension of political control of monetary policy, which is among the reasons Labour took power to direct the Reserve Bank; demand management also meant an activist fiscal policy. Maintaining purchasing power and thus demand was a key reason – along with ethical considerations – for Labour's comprehensive approach to transfer payments. Full employment was closely related to Labour's ideas about modernising and extending industry, which in turn were shaped by the government's view that New Zealand's economic future needed to involve more than exporting primary produce to Britain and receiving capital and manufactured goods in return. Infrastructure development was also a key part of Labour's plans for modernisation, although there Labour was following an established colonial tradition. Actively encouraging population growth was likewise an older policy in Australia and New Zealand, but there was an increased sense of urgency in this after 1945.

Labour was able to profoundly transform economic policy for a number of reasons. A social democratic party's willingness to embark on fresh thinking in response to the Great Depression, as Sheri Berman has persuasively argued, significantly influenced its electoral success. Labour certainly displayed that sort of creative thinking and like the Swedish Social Democratic Party was an early leader in the reshaping of social democracy.[101] There is more to the story than good ideas, however. Labour generally displayed a high level of cohesion and discipline in 1935 (if not always afterwards). The relatively centralised New Zealand state also assisted Labour's cause. Where the Australian Labor government of 1929–31 had been fatally obstructed by the Senate and the banks, the New Zealand parliament was effectively unicameral (the upper house had little power and would be abolished in 1950). Partial as they were, Coates's innovations served Labour well. If Coates's Reserve Bank was more orthodox than Labour would have wished, at least he had established a central bank that Labour could direct by new legislation. Labour was also fortunate in the quality of its opposition: both Reform and United had lost almost all their ministerial talent long before 1935. More broadly, the general success of a highly managed wartime economy made plausible the argument – and not just within the Labour Party – that planning could effect a more prosperous and more just postwar economic order.

The public service was changing too; the fresh thinking provoked by the economic and social crises of the interwar years was not confined to politicians. Treasury was the guardian of economic orthodoxy, but Bernard Ashwin, the key figure in Treasury, worked alongside the new administration, however reluctantly. Ashwin, Secretary from 1939, had 'a robust sense of the virtues of fiscal responsibility and the merits of his department in guarding it'.[102] While many in Treasury had been unenthusiastic about Labour, Ashwin was a consummate bureaucratic warrior and realised that if Treasury was to retain its influence then obstructing the new government would be counterproductive as well as improper.[103] Wartime experience as Director of Stabilisation arguably made Ashwin a Keynesian in spite of himself, for he had been obliged to think about the economy as a whole.[104] Nash, for his part, was neither a social crediter nor a repudiationist; there was common ground as well as difference between the two men, and Nash speedily confirmed Treasury in its oversight of all spending proposals. The combination of Labour's developmental agenda and the demands of wartime management elevated not only Treasury but also the Public Works Department and the Department of Industries and Commerce, particularly as the latter took responsibility for price and wage control after 1942. The latter department, in a sense, always played second fiddle to Treasury, but some remarkably talented civil servants in these departments and elsewhere would be involved in shaping postwar policy.

As the war ended, Labour politicians hoped and believed that the hardship and sacrifice of war should be justified by a more prosperous society, one which would ensure development at home and peace abroad. Neither politicians nor civil servants expected that the postwar transition would be uncomplicated, but on many points the early postwar years were far more difficult than anticipated. Domestic circumstances would be complicated enough; the international environment greatly intensified the difficulties for policymakers in what was and would remain a small and trade-dependent economy.

Chapter 3

Reconstruction: Economic Policy in the Later 1940s

Walter Nash presented his 1945 Budget on 9 August 1945, the day Nagasaki was destroyed. The Second World War ended a week later, but with unprecedented destruction and severe disruption of international trade and production, the effects of the war dominated economic management for years to come. Labour ministers generally thought that economic planning could deliver both social justice and prosperity. Ministers, key officials and many economists expected that the end of hostilities would be followed by a short boom and then a more or less severe recession. This, after all, was what had happened in 1918. In managing the transition to a peacetime economy, the government sought to avoid boom and bust, control inflation, ensure the reintegration into civilian life of ex-servicemen and women, develop infrastructure and expand social services at the same time as meeting commitments to Britain. In the circumstances of the later 1940s, this all implied continuing strict economic controls, but the extent and nature of those controls was, to a degree not often appreciated, driven by British demands rather than by Labour's ideology or domestic circumstances.

New Zealand was, out of sentiment and self-interest, committed to assisting Britain's recovery to the maximum extent. This meant not only continuing to supply as much food as possible but also stinting the country's own importing in order to assist British industrial recovery. While political rhetoric emphasised Commonwealth loyalty, behind the scenes New Zealand ministers and officials became increasingly irked by London's demands. To an unwelcome degree, the colonial economy remained entrenched, and not only because of British pressure. The new international order negotiated at Bretton Woods and elsewhere had relied on excessively optimistic assumptions about a rapid transition to the peacetime order. Free trade was contentious, not only because the ambitious plans for industrial development that governments of former settler colonies like New Zealand had prepared relied on a degree of protection but also because so far as the United States and other major powers were concerned, free trade did not extend to agricultural products. The most important influences on New Zealand policy in the second half of the 1940s were, therefore, quite beyond the control of the New Zealand government. New Zealand policymakers were certainly not alone in having to reconcile postwar desires for liberalisation with the necessity to protect a fragile economy.[1] While the government eased controls in many instances, the increasing unpopularity of continued stabilisation was the major factor in Labour's electoral defeat in 1949.

Domestic Agendas

After a decade in office at the end of the war, Labour ministers were experienced but tired. Peter Fraser and Walter Nash continued to dominate the ministry as they had since 1935, but both were now over 60. Fraser's health worsened, through the combined effects of overwork, loneliness and a less than ideal diet (he would die in 1950).[2] Nash remained robust, but his predilection for procrastination and centralising the smallest decisions in his office became more pronounced. The party culture prized loyalty over talent; apart from Fraser and Nash, five other ministers had been in office continually since 1935. Too often ministerial vacancies were created by death rather than retirement, although two able younger ministers had been appointed during the war: C. F. (Jerry) Skinner to Lands and Rehabilitation, and Arnold Nordmeyer, initially to Health and then, from 1947, Industries and Commerce. A Presbyterian minister before parliament, Nordmeyer was one of the most intellectually able of the younger Labour MPs; like Nash he espoused Christian socialism, but unlike the older man he was incisive and disciplined in the management of paper and public business.[3]

The immediate priority was an orderly demobilisation, not only of servicemen and women but also of the whole economy. The government, and probably most citizens, viewed rehabilitation of servicemen and women as a national obligation. In the nine months from 1 July 1945, 75,000 men and women were demobilised (the potential eligible total was 167,000). Servicemen received a gratuity of half a crown for each day of overseas service; £23m was paid out (a significant boost to spending power). With subsidised apprenticeships, university study, farm settlement, and concessionary loans for business and housing, rehabilitation expenditure peaked at close to £21m in 1947 and averaged £19m between 1946 and 1952.[4]

More generally, the public wanted wartime constraints to be relaxed. Ministers and officials, however, had vivid memories of the period after 1918, when rapid relaxation of wartime controls had provoked a brief boom, runaway inflation and a slump in rapid succession. Bernard Ashwin, Secretary to the Treasury, thought that there would be a critical period through to about the end of 1948. The money supply had nearly trebled during the war, and production would have to expand as fast as possible to meet the high demand for goods and services, and thus reduce inflationary pressure.[5] The business press, if not the daily newspapers, shared the government's assessment of the economic situation.[6] Dan Sullivan, Minister of Industries and Commerce, had noted in July 1944 that revoking wartime controls was both inevitable and desirable, and his officials developed a timetable for progressive relaxation. Appreciating the tension between liberalisation and security, Sullivan pointed out that theoretical liberty might exist without economic controls, but there were practical constraints on liberty if one had not enough to eat. He contrasted an older, individualistic, economic theory with 'the "social service" State which has positive economic obligations to its members' that was now emerging 'throughout the civilised world'.[7]

The greatest positive obligation was full employment. The Employment Act 1945 empowered a new employment service to gather information and to do 'all things necessary or expedient for the purpose of promoting and maintaining full employment, whether by facilitating the better location or availability of employment or otherwise howsoever'.[8] The Prime Minister took the legislation through the House himself. Fraser argued that it was 'undoubtedly true, that in a country run on untrammelled capitalistic, profitmaking lines, unemployment is inevitable. We are moving on from that conception very rapidly'.[9] The legislation realised an old Labour dream, 'an essential and foundation part of the policy of the Labour movement, industrial and political, ever since it was founded'. Fraser's advocacy drew on William Beveridge's text, *Full Employment in a Free Society*. Beveridge, an architect of the British welfare state, had argued that a number of policies were necessary for full employment: transfer payments to increase and stabilise consumption; budgetary policy that maximised consumption; moderately priced housing; price stability for necessities; a national health system; encouraging and regulating private investment to develop plant and infrastructure; expanding public sector industries to stabilise investment and bring monopolies under public control; control over the location of industry to ensure regionalisation; controlled marketing of primary produce; and organising the mobility of labour to match demand and supply.[10]

The Labour government had anticipated many of Beveridge's conditions in its pre-war legislation, and stressed that full employment would be in a mixed economy, co-ordinated by the government. Nash quoted Beveridge's observation that 'the main attack on unemployment must consist of ensuring high stable demand at all times for the products of industry. That means high stable spending,' which was quite compatible with private control of most industry.[11] While at a general level Labour's policy was based on the male breadwinner, ministers made it clear that full employment also applied to women (although the implications for women were not addressed in detail). Gender was an ambiguous dimension in social policy, which often emphasised the imperative of family formation. The universal family benefit, introduced in 1946, was a key part of this. The benefit consolidated previous maternal endowments into a universal weekly payment to mothers of 10 shillings per child, which amounted to 16 per cent of the median family income, assuming two children. As well as its undoubted appeal to mothers, not least because of its recognition of their economic role, many employers appreciated its potential for moderating wage demands and opposed abatement against other (male) income because of the disincentive to overtime. After the sharp fall in the birth-rate during the Depression, reproduction came to be represented as a national duty.[12] As in many other countries, and for reasons which probably had little to do with ministerial exhortation, the birth-rate began to increase after 1943, and rapidly so from 1947. From 1947, moreover, the government resumed an active immigration policy, offering subsidised passages to young single Britons who would be directed in employment for two years. Many other immigrants funded themselves, and although significant numbers of New Zealand residents emigrated at the same time, the net gain from migration in the later 1940s increased from 3038 to 6989.[13]

The government's expansion of social services went well beyond keeping up with population growth. In education, for example, between 1944 and 1949 the number of students in primary and secondary schools increased by 16 per cent and students in technical and university education increased by 51 per cent, but spending per student increased by 52 per cent in real terms.[14] Similarly, the total spending under Vote Health increased in real terms by 160 per cent between 1945 and 1949.[15] There was an explicit trade-off in that taxation increased substantially to fund increased social services and transfer payments. In the last full peacetime year 1938–39, per capita taxation was (in 1949 values) nearly £33. It peaked at £76 10s in the last year of the war, and fell to £71 3s 6d in 1949–50. The proportion of tax revenue levied on incomes increased from just under 40 per cent to around 60 per cent.[16] It bears drawing attention to the fact that Labour ministers believed that this social contract was justified in terms of solidarity.

The government was, therefore, pressing ahead with a reform agenda in difficult circumstances. As J. B. Condliffe observed many years ago, 'the New Zealand economy emerged from the war taut with suppressed inflation', and the government continued strict price control, subsidisation, and rationing of many commodities.[17] Rationing, of course, was variously to deal with import shortages and the government's investment priorities, as well as the export commitment to Britain. As Ashwin noted, the end of the war meant 'increasing public impatience with controls, coupled with a general feeling that such controls were unnecessary and should be taken right away'.[18] Incredibly, newspapers complained that the 1945 Budget was not a peacetime budget and denied 'relief from the oppressive war burdens'.[19] Ashwin thought that acceptance of continued stabilisation would require 'solid support of the best elements amongst all sections of the community', which meant keeping the sector groups informed and conciliated.[20] The sector groups, however, were focused on their own interests to an unconstructive degree. Retailers complained about import shortages. Farmers complained about public housing expenditure, workers' shorter hours and high wages, and continued controls on building and investment.[21] There is some truth in Michael Bassett's observation that 'Materialism, not socialism, was on New Zealanders' minds. Keeping faith with stabilisation, the regulated economy and the needs of the British increasingly seemed outdated. . . . Many expected from the state as of right what they had once dreamed about or accepted gratefully'.[22] On the other hand, there is an enduring view, not moderated by the nationalisation of coalmines and the Bank of New Zealand, of Fraser as having lapsed a long way from socialist principles.[23] Certainly Fraser became much more vocally anti-communist in the late 1940s (not entirely without reason so far as the international context was concerned).

The government had particular problems with its putative allies in the trade union movement. Full employment, however desirable, was problematic, as the Polish economist Michal Kalecki had pointed out a few years earlier.[24] Without a level of unemployment, organised labour could push wage claims to an unhelpfully inflationary level. Some economists (notably, in this part of the world, Australia's Director of Postwar Reconstruction, Nugget Coombs) argued that an incomes policy, in which unions and employers agreed to managed wage growth in return for the maintenance of other desirable economic and social policies, was therefore essential. Incomes policies were a key part of Scandinavian social democratic strategy.[25] Fraser's government preferred to continue with an informal approach, relying on the close relationship with Fintan Patrick Walsh and his iron control of the Federation of Labour. This did not deter strategically located unions from taking industrial action. Watersiders, seafarers, miners and carpenters were particularly restive, as were some public servants. In many cases, militant unions objected not only to wage control but also to Walsh's argument that the unions' historic concern with wages and conditions had largely been met; the postwar era required economic co-operation and unions needed to take a share of responsibility for economic progress in a capitalist economy.[26] Walsh's opponents felt that this conflicted with unions' proper role, whether as a socialist vanguard or advocate of their members' immediate interests. The government responded sternly, not only with rhetoric and regulation but also sometimes with legal sanctions, including deregistering the Auckland carpenters' union.[27] There was an enduring, and perhaps inevitable, tension between the whole-economy perspective of a Labour government and the more specific concerns of trade unions. This tension was evident in other countries as well, of course, and was on one level also about the limits of the postwar settlement. If the historic compromise had ensured significant economic benefits for workers, this was at the expense of maintaining capitalist control over the great majority of trade and industry. More generally, the government's focus on discipline and restraint was often unpopular.

Infrastructural Development, Industry Policy and Stabilisation

Before the war, Labour had looked forward to economic development through modernised infrastructure and stressed the importance of public housing. From 1945 an extensive agenda emphasised housing, hydroelectricity, highways, and railways in that order.[28] Treasury was less convinced, repeatedly warning of the inflationary dimension of public works expenditure. Importing raw materials and plant meant fewer consumer goods; competition for labour reduced the workforce in consumer goods and also contributed to the imbalance between the money supply and immediately available goods and services (by paying wages to workers not immediately producing consumer goods). Capital works therefore should be 'restricted as far as possible to those such as hydro-electric development which are essential to increase production for the home market or for export'. On that argument, housing was less of a priority.[29]

However, Treasury's 'expertise was financial rather than economic'.[30] Depression and war had resulted in a significant backlog in development (as well as in replacing and upgrading capital goods in private industry). The government's intention to make up lost ground as swiftly as possible was constrained by shortages of many basic construction materials. Local cement production accounted for less than two thirds of the national requirement, and steel imports were

40 per cent of the immediate pre-war average.[31] Domestic production of building materials – and of the consumer goods that Treasury advocated – was restricted by shortages of power. Even if Labour had wanted to give housing less priority, both the reality of overcrowding and the dominant rhetoric of nuclear families living in domestic bliss in detached houses made a high level of housing provision imperative.[32]

Ambition had to be balanced by reality. From 1938 to 1950 the cost of completing a 'typical four-roomed State dwelling' increased 86 per cent.[33] There was a severe shortage of construction workers. In the first full postwar financial year (to March 1947) the total construction workforce was 36,000, from an estimated strength of 47,000 in 1939. Almost all the decline had been in the public sector. One reason was that much public sector work was in remote areas and this was less attractive to workers than urban living. The Minister of Works estimated in 1947 that 4000 construction workers could be immediately employed; they would have to be immigrants recruited on the basis that they would spend a specified period working on construction projects as assigned.[34] The development agenda and the desire for population growth thus intersected.

It was not only pronatalist policy and electoral appeal that made the government concentrate on housing; given available raw materials, houses were easier to build than dams. There had been a burst of activity in state housing construction as the war drew to a close, with over 3200 completions in the year to March 1945. This number fell to about 2800 in each of the following two years before increasing first to 3000 again and then to nearly 5000 in the Labour government's last financial year (private completions were two or three times as numerous).[35] Electric power was an instrument of industrial modernisation as well as domestic, and hydroelectric construction had been continued during the war as far as possible, with generating capacity increasing by more than a third.[36] Plans announced in 1946 called for 10 new stations on the Waikato river in the North Island and new or expanded stations on the Clutha, Tekapo, Cobb, and Waitaki rivers in the South Island. Between 1945 and 1950, North Island generating capacity increased by 63 per cent and the South Island's by 7 per cent (North Island capacity was expanded much faster because of the higher population and higher demand; the Cook Strait cable was many years in the future).[37]

Labour had emphasised industrial development since before 1935 for a combination of reasons: employment, modernisation and saving overseas funds. As S. R. H. Jones has suggested, the government had not developed the import and exchange controls imposed in the exchange crisis of 1938–39 into a coherent industrial strategy. The

Industrial Efficiency Act 1936 had also been relatively limited in its application.[38] That is not to say that Labour ministers were short of ambitions or hopes for a more diversified economic structure. Industry policy did not consist of one overarching strategy but was spread across the budget, taxation policy, import and exchange controls, investment policy and employment policy. Autarky was not on the agenda; goods that could not be manufactured economically in New Zealand would continue to be imported. Where necessary, industrialisation would involve overseas companies establishing branch plants in New Zealand; the government would give British firms preferential treatment in that regard.[39] While the business press ritually denounced import control and complained that 'scarcity has been given the status of high policy' some commentators admitted the merit of protection 'along commonsense lines' to encourage efficient and quality local firms and protect them against 'unfair foreign competition'.[40]

Industries and Commerce Minister Dan Sullivan noted in his last departmental report that industrial development policy was not separate from the need to actively increase the population and 'to enable the Dominion to hold an effective place among the nations bordering the Pacific'.[41] Sullivan, who died in April 1947, noted that there was little difficulty in stimulating industrial development immediately after the war; many firms had plans for expansion. What was necessary, he thought, was to move beyond import substituting industrialisation and develop manufactured exports out of New Zealand raw materials. While not excluding the processing of imported raw materials, Sullivan instanced the potential of fruit and vegetable processing, textiles, chemicals and forest products. He thus anticipated the 'manufacturing in depth' approach of the late 1950s, and also the competition from mass producing low-wage countries, urging a focus on quality as New Zealand's industrial signature.[42] His successor, Arnold Nordmeyer, held similar views.

Although within the bailiwick of the Department of Agriculture rather than Industries and Commerce, primary production was just as much a subject of industry policy. The Department of Agriculture was on safe ground in assuming that markets for all exportable produce were 'assured for the next few years' and probably thereafter, 'if the great industrial countries can maintain full employment'.[43] The imperative was to make production more efficient. While more mechanisation was implicitly a decision for individual farmers, better feeding to improve production and reduce livestock mortality, higher-yielding crops and lessening plant and animal disease were all the focus of publicly-funded scientific research by the Department and the country's two agricultural colleges.[44] While increased use of fertiliser was also a decision for individual farmers, it could be encouraged by subsidy, although the extent to which this was done varied considerably over time.

Industry policy could be influenced through fiscal policy; for instance, sales taxes could channel consumer demand. In 1946 Nash abolished sales tax on building materials, clothing and household furniture among other items. The priority given to household formation was clear, and a pronatalist agenda was evident in Nash's rider 'including perambulators'.[45] Nash reduced income tax in 1946, intending to provide incentives to work, and he abolished the wartime excess profits tax as a direct encouragement to industry.[46] Infrastructure development and house building meant that public expenditure directly stimulated the construction and building materials industries, as did concessionary loans for private house building. Capital works, particularly hydroelectric development, not only stimulated the engineering trades but also general industrial expansion in the longer run, by providing modern sources of power.[47] Import and exchange controls could be used to encourage industrial development and encourage efficiency: when Nash revalued the currency in 1948, one consequence was to cheapen imports, thereby increasing the pressure on local manufacturing to operate more efficiently. Depreciation allowances, of course, were used to encourage investment in new plant.

While the Industrial Efficiency Act gave the government wide powers to encourage industrial growth, in practice the government used only one part of those powers: the power to limit entry to specified industries by licensing. Licensing required officials and those involved in the industry to devise a plan for its expansion; there was therefore considerable scope for established parties to prevent competition from new entrants. Of the nearly 30 industries subject to licensing in 1946, many were distributive trades such as pharmacy and petrol, but manufacturing industries included some construction materials, radios, and food canning. The licensing system was also attractive because it allowed the government to prioritise returned servicemen for establishment in designated businesses.[48] Allied to industry licensing, but not dependent on it, was an official preference for dispersing manufacturing across provincial towns. Although such dispersed investment was inefficient, in the early postwar years buildings and machinery were available in such areas and not elsewhere; pressure on housing in the main centres was eased, and dollar shortages made the importing of new plant very difficult. Industries and Commerce also justified dispersal on strategic grounds, and by notions of balanced regional development and 'help[ing] to preserve the home life' in the provinces.[49] By 1947 Treasury was questioning the policy, as the inefficiencies meant higher prices for consumers, but dispersal was evident until the end of the 1950s.[50]

Industry policy included the control of investment, which had been very strict during the war. From 1940 the Minister of Finance had to approve the establishment of any new company or an increase in the capital of an existing one (a power delegated to the Registrar of Companies in 1945); from April 1946 these capital issues controls were eased and issues below £10,000 did not require approval.[51] The Reserve Bank advised the trading banks on what classes of loans should be allowed. The business press thought such control was 'fundamentally sound as it provides an avenue of productive investment for the very considerable sums in the hands of the public' while being 'designed to contract spending for speculation and consumption and to conserve bank credit for capital investments which will result in national efficiency and, consequently, will broaden the field for employment'. In particular, the Reserve Bank discouraged loans for sharemarket speculation, intending to deter short-term investors who during any sort of trouble would sell quickly and push the market down. 'Speculation has its place in the community, but when large sums of money are available to the public, speculation can take on an anti-social complexion'.[52] Subject to capital issues controls, then, a large part of the government's industry policy amounted simply to standing back and letting investors take up share offerings, of which there were many. The high level of wartime savings provided ample funds for equity investment. At the end of 1945, for instance, a Feltex issue immediately attracted £1m, and the New Zealand sharemarket rose considerably in the early postwar years.[53]

Modernisation in infrastructure, industry and primary production, then, was integral to the Labour government's postwar agenda. Through a variety of means – direct encouragement, subsidised services, fiscal policy – as well as its own emphasis on construction, the government shaped the direction of, and directly supported, private enterprise in primary and secondary industry. The focus in secondary industry was largely domestic, but of course primary industries dominated exports, and in the 1940s the British market was supreme. There was, however, much more to New Zealand's economic relationship with Britain than supplying pastoral exports.

External Context: Britain and the Balance of Payments

Britain's economic position in 1945 was dire, and because the New Zealand economy was so closely integrated with the British, the British situation was a major constraint on New Zealand policy. While

Fraser, Nash, and other public figures made frequent, and sometimes extravagant, professions of loyalty to Britain, the reality was more complex. The relationship between New Zealand and Britain had a number of separate if overlapping dimensions. At the rhetorical level there was a continuing sense of kinship, and admiration for the British people's wartime sacrifices. From the middle of 1945 Britain was governed by a Labour administration; one might therefore have presupposed some identity of interests between Wellington and London (and Canberra for that matter). There was common ground between the three governments in their hopes that the Commonwealth would develop as an economic and diplomatic third force, holding a middle ground between Moscow's Stalinism and Washington's brash materialism, although 'there was little economic or political basis for such a way'.[54] However, where Australia and New Zealand shared desires of industrial expansion and economic maturity, British ministers imagined that the Australasian dominions' function was to facilitate British economic recovery.

The Ottawa conference of 1932 had attempted to strengthen the Empire and Commonwealth as an economic bloc, with mutually preferential treatment for dominion primary exports to Britain and British manufactured exports in return. By the end of the 1930s, the New Zealand government's desire to encourage industrialisation provoked considerable hostility in London. On one hand, the New Zealand government put economic independence on hold during the war, supplying Britain with food and wool to the maximum extent at guaranteed prices. On the other hand, manufacturing was remarkably stimulated by wartime conditions. The war also strengthened the Sterling Area, which had developed out of Ottawa; Sterling Area countries were those that did most of their trade with Britain and consequently held their overseas reserves in sterling. During the war, members agreed to pool in London whatever US dollars they earned by exporting; the American trade surplus with the Sterling Area (and the rest of the world) meant that dollars were increasingly scarce.

After the war, unresolved economic tensions between Britain and New Zealand re-emerged. The Labour government in London ran the Sterling Area as an instrument of British economic recovery (if for no other reason than the sheer pressure of circumstances). For New Zealand, this meant continuing to supply Britain with the maximum possible quantity of food. New Zealand's membership of the Sterling Area meant that Britain did not have to pay for these supplies with scarce dollars, and to that extent the dollar pool was conserved. The New Zealand government's willingness to assist Britain arose from sentiment and economic interest alike, the latter reflecting the fact that Britain was New Zealand's largest market and likely to remain so for many years to come. Yet New Zealand agendas for domestic economic development made the British view of the Sterling Area quite problematic. This was especially because the United States would be a preferred source for many imports, particularly machinery and industrial plant essential to the development agenda. The New Zealand government had to negotiate in London for permission to draw on the dollar pool.

Britain had paid for the war by comprehensively liquidating overseas assets and had relied on extensive American assistance. The Americans had at first required cash upfront, but in March 1941 they instituted the Lend-Lease programme, by which war materials were supplied on generous terms. However, neither President Roosevelt nor his successor, Truman, were inclined to allow the US Treasury to fund the British Empire's return to its former glory after the war, and congressional opinion was even less well-disposed. Lend-Lease finished in August 1945, as soon as Japan surrendered.[55] Few in Britain, or elsewhere, had anticipated that the Pacific war would end so quickly.[56] Having lost the lifeline of American aid, Britain needed a major export recovery and an American loan.

Keynes led the British delegation in the loan negotiations, even as his health was failing. Against the American agenda of free trade and the end of formal imperialism, Keynes was equally committed to restoring the City of London's financial supremacy.[57] He had a profound influence on British policy towards the Sterling Area, not only because of the commanding position that he had in the British Treasury but (after Labour took office) also because he had taught the Chancellor of the Exchequer, Hugh Dalton, economics.[58] Keynes was a liberal committed to saving capitalism, while Dalton still hoped for socialist transformation, but the American loan was essential if the social reforms which Dalton and his colleagues planned were to be carried out. Thus for Dalton the priority was managing the postwar transition, and any approach that could facilitate the American loan, and reduce British liabilities to the rest of the Sterling Area, would be helpful.

Keynes indulged in much wishful thinking about Britain's financial relationship with the United States.[59] While he accepted the fact of American financial power, a substantial loan would give the United States excessive influence over British policy. If that power were to be mitigated, the United States and the Sterling Area would have to be persuaded of the nobility of Britain's wartime sacrifice. Overall, Keynes hoped for 'a retrospective contribution to the [British] costs of the war of £750 million ($3 billion) from the United States and of about £880 million from the sterling area'.[60] The American contribution would be 'a sort of retrospective lend-lease' waiver of the money spent in America before December 1941, which, as Keynes argued, had crash-started American wartime industry.[61] Sterling Area countries should be asked to surrender part of the sterling balances held in London and informed that otherwise their balances would be frozen. The Indian government's sterling balance was by far the largest, at nearly 37 per cent of the total (Keynes hoped for £500m from them), but New Zealand and Australia could, he hoped, be picked off first, even though their holdings together amounted to only 5.4 per cent of the whole. He argued that New Zealand and Australia, having built up significant sterling balances during the war by exporting to Britain, were profiteering at British expense.[62] In fact New Zealand and Australia's long-term debt to Britain exceeded their sterling balances, so they were hardly profiteering and there 'would . . . be a certain embarrassment in suggesting that they should agree to scale down the balances held by them in the UK while leaving the long-term debt to the UK untouched'.[63] It was an embarrassment that Keynes speedily overcame. His insistence that Britain alone had suffered financially has been described as 'the plaintive note of ethical superiority with which the British customarily preface their begging letters'.[64] In any case, whatever the morality of the war against fascism, it had also reflected Britain's strategic interests.[65]

The loan negotiations began in September 1945. Unsurprisingly, the Americans were not receptive to the suggestion that they should grant the British three billion dollars. Although it has been remarked that the later Marshall Plan was nothing more than that sort of enlightened self-interest, in 1945 American officials tended naïvely to assume that the postwar transition would be brief and uncomplicated.[66] Only with the entrenchment of the Cold War would American attitudes change. 'The British empire finally ceased to be an obstacle on the road to progress and instead became a bulwark against the Communist menace'.[67] British ministers, affected by Keynes's earlier optimism, only reluctantly abandoned hopes of a large grant or an interest-free loan. When it was confirmed, the loan of $3.75 billion came with stringent conditions, including an understanding that some sterling balances would be surrendered as 'a sterling area contribution to the Mutual Aid system of wartime finance' – a commitment made without the Sterling Area being represented.[68] The British, in fact, had approached the loan negotiations hoping that the issue of sterling balances would be fudged; the Treasury, in particular, did not want the matter out in the open and feared the prospect of 'an acrimonious multilateral conference of major creditors'.[69] The

American negotiators, however, insisted on a specific commitment to dealing with the sterling balances.[70]

One reason the Americans insisted on reducing sterling balances was to weaken Britain's preferential trading arrangements with the Sterling Area, and that point was important if a reluctant Congress were to ratify the loan.[71] Dalton and his colleagues disliked the terms, but thought, probably correctly, that the alternative was continued austerity, and abandoning much of the government's domestic programme.[72] The United States had, indeed, pushed hard for the end of the Ottawa system of imperial preference, but 'suggested that they would make few compensating tariff cuts'.[73] As one British negotiator observed, in 'linking imperial preference with a loan the US was exploiting Britain's economic weakness'. Equally, though, 'the British were so entirely preoccupied with securing financial assistance from the US that they had no patience for the dominions' interest in the negotiations'.[74] In other words, the British refused to concede imperial preference because preference suited them, not out of concern for the dominions' economies. On neither preference nor sterling balances were dominion or colonial governments consulted.

After the loan was approved, Keynes developed more detailed proposals for reducing the sterling balances. Each Sterling Area country's balance would be divided: some to be available immediately for conversion into dollars, some released in instalments through to 1951, and some to be surrendered.[75] These proposals were not universally supported in London. The Bank of England regarded the balances as commitments pledging the honour of the United Kingdom and feared that resiling from them would provoke a banking crisis. The Board of Trade emphasised that sterling balances facilitated the purchase of British goods (which was precisely why the Americans wanted the balances reduced). The Foreign and Commonwealth Offices had no wish to drive an independent India out of the Commonwealth by massive reductions of that country's credit in London.[76] Keynes, however, mindful of American expectations, was determined that the balances would be reduced. He admitted that this would be 'highly distasteful to, and strongly resisted by, the other parties concerned. There is no means . . . by which . . . we can avoid political difficulties of a high order'.[77] Some scenarios proposed the immediate release of less than 10 per cent and spreading out the non-surrendered remainder over many decades. Thus 'through the operation of compound interest, deferments of payment, especially if no interest is allowed, can be so arranged as to provide the equivalent of cancellation, without that ill-sounding word having been actually mentioned'.[78] The essential point was that if Sterling Area countries did not comply with British demands, their sterling balances would be frozen. Thus 'whilst cancellation must remain, in accordance with our pledges, a matter of voluntary agreement, the ultimate terms and rate of repayment must be in the last resort imposed, – which is, if you like, a distinction without a difference'.[79] One condition of the American loan was that sterling would become freely convertible into dollars by about mid-1947. Keynes advised that this should be represented to Australia and New Zealand as a benefit of waiving some of their balances – disingenuously, for Keynes and British ministers feared, correctly, that convertibility would lead to a run on the pound.[80] The fact that very little of the accumulated balances would be available for conversion at any one time would be glossed over, but balances not waived 'will not be available for expenditure *anywhere*. It is important that this should be understood'. In other words, unless the Australasian governments agreed to sacrifice a portion of the accumulated balance, none of the balance would be available to them.[81]

The Costs of the Sterling Area for New Zealand

Fraser was in London, mostly on United Nations business, in the first weeks of 1946 and met with Keynes and Dalton late in February. They pressed Fraser to cancel half New Zealand's net sterling balance of nearly £55m, suggesting that export earnings would soon rebuild the New Zealand balance. Fraser expressed New Zealand's willingness to assist 'even to the point of sacrifice' but reminded the British that there was a huge backlog of development to be made up in New Zealand, which required overseas funds. In turn, the British emphasised that the whole Sterling Area depended on British recovery.[82] Fraser deliberately procrastinated on cancellation.[83] There was no advantage in being the first to cancel without guarantees others would follow suit; the problem required a multilateral approach, which the British had never tried to develop.[84] In July, it was Nash's turn to meet Dalton, and a British Treasury official wrote to Ashwin, again arguing that while Britain had been economically shattered by the war, New Zealand was in a very good position. The British Treasury now claimed that Britain had borne all the financial overheads of the war, and had not charged New Zealand for such expenditure as the supply lines to the New Zealand forces in the Mediterranean theatre. Dalton again asked New Zealand to write off £20m, which he described as 'some slight redistribution of the burden inherited from the war'. The whole matter would 'require careful presentation in its relation to the New Zealand public'.[85] The British had perhaps forgotten that the continued deployment of the 2nd New Zealand Expeditionary Force in the

Mediterranean after Pearl Harbor had been at the strenuous urging of the British government, and that at least the great majority of the costs associated with the New Zealand forces, some £60m, had been a loan from Britain to New Zealand, two thirds of which New Zealand repaid by March 1945 and the rest by the end of 1946.[86] In any event, New Zealand's accumulation of sterling during the war had been offset by very heavy expenditure of foreign exchange, later estimated at 'close to £150 million, equivalent to New Zealand's export earnings for about two years'.[87] There was in the British Cabinet and elsewhere a 'persistence of outdated views over the reliability and cohesion of the sterling group of countries after the war'.[88]

Only in March 1947 did Fraser announce a 'gift' to the United Kingdom of £10m sterling, to be written off New Zealand's London balance (Australia wrote off £25m at the same time).[89] For public consumption, of course, Fraser described the write-off as 'recognition of the magnificent and unprecedented effort of the United Kingdom and her people in maintaining freedom'.[90] Having been blackmailed by Keynes and Dalton, Fraser was less than pleased when the National Party leader, Sidney Holland, carped that the money was the 'least practical' form of assistance and that more food, instead, should have been sent.[91] Holland's hypocrisy was breathtaking, for he would campaign relentlessly against food rationing in 1949. New Zealand's London balances were further reduced by Nash's enthusiastic repayment of debt. Between 1945 and 1949, New Zealand's public debt held in London fell from £200m to £80m.[92] Although this meant a reduction in theoretical importing capacity, one can imagine that Nash saw little option: given the British attitude there was precious little else that he could do with the London balances, and the desire to reduce dependence on London must have been compelling.

Convertibility of sterling, by which holders of sterling could exchange pounds for US dollars, was restored on 15 July 1947. As British ministers had feared, the continuing weakness of their economy resulted in an immediate and disastrous fall in London's dollar reserves, and convertibility was revoked after six weeks. The crisis had serious consequences for New Zealand. As well as the continued all-out supply of food by New Zealand, the British Prime Minister, Clement Attlee, urged New Zealand to further restrict dollar expenditure, and to accept delays in imports not only by eschewing more readily available dollar goods but also by accepting that Britain needed to prioritise exports to dollar countries. New Zealand would thus be caught both ways: unable to earn dollars herself, nor even to substitute British capital and consumer goods for American. Attlee lectured Fraser on how to run the New Zealand economy, urging 'careful consideration of the immediate essentiality of capital works programmes particularly those involving dollar expenditures or such heavy calls on the productive capacity of this country as would affect our efforts to earn dollars by exports to hard currency countries'. Attlee well understood that his requests were almost unacceptable, as he offered a version suitable for public consumption.[93] Fraser warned Attlee that Britain would have to guarantee essential supplies to New Zealand and that continued controls on prices and imports would be necessary. 'In following a policy of not embarassing the United Kingdom Government by seeking world market prices for our produce the terms of trade position must be taken into account in order not to impair our own internal stability'.[94]

The New Zealand government's immediate response was the stage-managed Aid to Britain Conference, held in Wellington in mid-August 1947, involving representatives of the major economic sector groups. The conference's resolutions followed Attlee's public request, and for some time afterwards an Aid for Britain committee exhorted citizens to intensify production and economise on domestic consumption.[95] What was said in public was one thing; in private, New Zealand ministers and officials were becoming increasingly exasperated. Early in September 1947, Attlee's Commonwealth Secretary, Lord Addison, met Fraser and the Australian Prime Minister Ben Chifley in Canberra. Addison made a 'strong request' that the Australasians 'may so conduct their external economy that they will need to make no new claim on the United Kingdom for dollars during the next six months': that is, confine dollar expenditure to their own current dollar earnings, which were meagre precisely because of the diversion of dollar-earning commodities to Britain. Chifley and Fraser told Addison that this was 'quite impracticable' but that every effort would be made to save dollars.[96] New Zealand annoyance was intensified when Addison suggested that Britain might not be able to supply sterling area countries with iron and steel semi-manufactures, capital goods, textiles and so on because they would be needed for trade negotiations with 'difficult' countries like Argentina. Fraser protested that New Zealand needed those items to maintain production of food and supplies of consumer goods, and reminded Addison that without New Zealand supplies, Britain would have to spend dollars on food.[97]

Later in September 1947, London called an urgent conference of Commonwealth Sterling Area states. The British Treasury repeated the demand that Sterling Area countries that had a rough balance in their dollar requirements and earnings should not make any net claim on the dollar pool for the next nine months. The New Zealand delegation, led by the civil servant Leicester Webb, pointed out that talking of individual countries could be 'most misleading' given the diversion of dollar-earning commodities to Britain. He warned the British not to push their luck; dominion patience was not unlimited and excessive severity would 'lead to a weakening of Commonwealth economic connections. It would . . . oblige us to seek much closer economic relations with the United States'.[98] As they had before, and for the same reasons, the Commonwealth Office and the Bank of England 'understood, what apparently the [British] Treasury failed to understand, that the formula would bear heavily on some Dominions and would, if rigidly applied, damage Imperial economic relationships'.[99]

Yet the British pressure continued. In January 1948 Nash reduced the year's import licenses at Attlee's request. The British Board of Trade then complained about the difficulty of access to the New Zealand market.[100] In May, Nash froze import licenses for British cars and all nonessential goods for the rest of the year.[101] This meant continued controls on imports and domestic rationing of export commodities.[102] The July 1949 Commonwealth Finance Ministers' Conference tightened the screws again. With recession and diminished demand for imports in the United States, ministers agreed to reduce dollar demands and consequently imports by 25 per cent (and when the British government devalued sterling by 30 per cent in September 1949, New Zealand and most other Sterling Area countries followed suit, which meant that imports paid for in dollars became more expensive). A recipe less helpful to Labour's chances of winning the 1949 election could hardly have been imagined, as the National Party made much political capital out of ongoing austerity.[103]

Continued British pressure caused some tentative rethinking in the New Zealand Treasury. In November 1947 Ashwin noted that if Britain, because of their own dollar-earning priorities, was unable or unwilling to meet New Zealand's needs then New Zealand would need to reorient trade towards earning dollars independently.[104] In April 1948 he warned Nash that New Zealand's own dollar trade was in deficit and that Britain was asking New Zealand to increase dollar earnings for the benefit of the Sterling Area. The commodities that offered the best chance of this, meat and dairy, were precisely those of which Britain took the whole exportable surplus. Ashwin thought that manufactured exports should be encouraged and that a 'vigorous campaign to provide shipping, hotel, and tourist facilities for visitors from the American continent would have scope for increasing our dollar earnings substantially, and would at the same time develop one of New Zealand's most valuable national assets'.[105] Ashwin's deputy, Edward Greensmith, was distinctly hostile to the Sterling Area, raising the question of what margin of preference should be given to it, and within the Sterling Area what margin should be given to Britain, since New Zealand was selling to Britain at lower than market prices and paying higher prices for imports through giving preference to British goods.[106] Greensmith warned of a long-run decline in prices for primary exports, which reinforced the need for market diversification; Britain could be expected to seek further concessions as world prices fell. He bluntly recommended going after dollar markets and diversifying into processed exports, such as wool tops instead of greasy wool, leather rather than scoured hides, and timber, pulp, and newsprint as well as tourism.[107]

The Department of Industries and Commerce seemed to be of two minds. On the one hand it echoed Treasury, suggesting that a new policy of trade promotion and market diversification was required, which would have to 'remove any direct or indirect restricting influence on the production and export of goods capable of finding a market in USA or Canada'.[108] On the other hand, the Secretary, G. W. Clinkard, observed that:

> in large measure, the greater the proportion of our exports sent to the United Kingdom, the more we are economically part of the United Kingdom in considering questions of this nature. It follows that we cannot judge whether or not we have been unduly prejudiced . . . without being in a position to assess the pros and cons from the point of view of the United Kingdom, not only in its individual capacity, but as the central unit of the British sterling areas as a whole. It is considered that it is not possible, in all the circumstances, for us to judge these issues.[109]

Ashwin and Greensmith's bold arguments were rather speculative in the late 1940s. World trade was still thoroughly disorganised, and in any event, 'Australia and New Zealand had no realistic alternative to participating in the Sterling Area during the mid 1940s. Leaving this group would not have helped either of them to overcome US agricultural protectionism', which severely constrained any short-term possibility of developing alternative markets.[110] The grand International Trade Organisation vision of global free trade had 'no logic in the unstable circumstances of the 1940s' and the more limited General Agreement on Trade and Tariffs emerged as 'more adaptable to the demands of wartime sustenance, recovery, economic restoration, and, above all, the Cold War'.[111] The New Zealand government's position was that it had to retain considerable control over imports in order to support domestic industrialisation. Infant industry protection was, after all, a common justification for protection.[112] The United States objected in general terms to such policies but could hardly expect New Zealand and other dominions to accept free trade after the Geneva ITO negotiations in 1947. During the ITO negotiations, not only did the US Congress refuse to reduce protection on wool; it actually passed legislation providing for severe additional duties. 'The Australians spoke for most of the delegates when they described the wool legislation as "quite fantastic having in mind the whole understanding on which the Geneva negotiations were based" . . . [and] immediately convened a Commonwealth meeting to consider the implications'.[113] President Truman vetoed the new restrictions but then secured compensatory legislation giving subsidies to an American wool industry that was 'neither efficient nor competitive', while reducing tariffs only minimally.[114] It had become abundantly clear that in the American lexicon 'free trade' meant whatever the Congress wanted it to mean.

Circumstances meant therefore that New Zealand participation in the international economy after 1945 was never straightforward. It was not only external pressures that complicated matters. Despite Nash's involvement in the Bretton Woods negotiations, he was unable to secure New Zealand's accession to the International Monetary Fund. Inevitably, Nash had some reservations over the details of the arrangements but 'he understood and made it clear . . . that the IMF's ability to underwrite a more prosperous world after the war outweighed any misgivings New Zealand might have about the detail'.[115] Unfortunately there were plenty of conspiracy theorists at home who railed against 'dollar imperialism', and they were by no means all on the left. There was opposition from within the Labour caucus and the wider labour movement, but also from the Farmers' Union and the National Party. Sidney Holland and his future foreign minister, Frederick Doidge, beat the imperial drum loudly, denouncing Bretton Woods and the ITO as treason to the British Empire.[116] New Zealand could not join the IMF before Britain did, and British accession only came after the end of the New Zealand parliament's 1945 session. Although Fraser and Nash managed to get the Labour caucus to agree to join, Fraser was not prepared to allow the matter to intrude into the difficult 1946 election campaign; the question went back to caucus in July 1946. Nash argued hard for getting inside the tent, but 'Fraser sat on the fence. In the end the discussion was suspended with no decision reached'.[117] Thus, despite Dalton's earnest request for New Zealand to join (and, as he hoped, reinforce British voting power) New Zealand stayed out of the IMF. Nash openly maintained that the British delay had lost New Zealand the chance of joining and securing access to development capital.[118] New Zealand only joined in 1961.

Stabilisation Continued

By 1948 it was clear that hopes of a rapid transition to a less controlled peacetime economy were illusory. Shortages of essential materials persisted, and the Sterling Area's dollar reserves were low. The convertibility fiasco had brutally demonstrated the weakness of sterling, and New Zealand had little alternative but to comply with the British agenda, if under protest. Strict stabilisation policies would therefore need to continue. For all these reasons, in 1948 parliament passed the Economic Stabilisation Act, by which the government took wide powers to promote economic stability not only by regulation, particularly in terms of price and wage control, but also by any other means deemed necessary or expedient. While the potential for regulation was very wide, there was a sense in which the Act should be seen as providing reserve powers rather than a detailed prescription.[119] The National Party criticised the wide powers conferred by the legislation but did not reject the principle.[120]

More generally the Act reflected the government's determination to manage the economy so that the broad agenda of price stability, industrial development and full employment could be secured. Given the inflationary potential of a full employment policy, the government saw 'the necessity for permanent price-control to ensure that the benefits of a full-employment policy, with its consequent sustained pressure of purchasing-power on production, are enjoyed by the community as a whole'.[121] The Control of Prices Act 1947 confirmed the existence of both the Price Tribunal and the Price Control Division of Industries and Commerce. The Tribunal was a quasi-judicial body; while it retained the right to set prices in all cases that came before it, it would delegate much work to the Division. The Division would, through a comprehensive network of industry sections and regional offices, collect statistical and qualitative information, and present reports to the Tribunal. Introducing the legislation, along with a little populist rhetoric about saving 'the people' money, Nordmeyer argued that price control had existed since 1915, and was resorted to in one way or another by most countries.[122] Nash would have hoped for liberalisation, but thought that continued shortages and severe inflationary pressure made the continuation of price control 'clearly justified'.[123] Nordmeyer indicated that prices would be set on a 1939 baseline, and any increase above that level had to be approved if the goods in question had been available in that year. For new commodities, the Tribunal would set a base date.[124] The National Party, again, criticised socialist regulation, but Holland was astute enough to reserve his position on the principle of price control.[125]

The Act left much to be worked out by ministerial directive. Nordmeyer thought that 'the Tribunal should endeavour to fix formulae, price ceilings for all industry, and industry margins, both wholesale and retail, leaving to the Director the detailed administration affecting individual firms and cases'.[126] The legislation was enacted without a firm idea of the basis on which decisions should be made. Although Nordmeyer hoped that the Tribunal would confine itself to issues of principle, its function as an appellate body for administrative decisions raised the possibility of greatly increased compliance costs for business. It was, indeed, 'practically impossible to say at what point the price structure of an individual enterpriser comes within the jurisdiction of the Tribunal, if only because the established formulae . . . are never precisely applicable in a given case'.[127] Some might have said that was an irremediable flaw. Certainly in the first year or two of operation, the Act generated a great deal of work. Late in 1948 the Director of Price Control stated that permanent price-control 'required the replacement by easily administered "whole-industry" formulae, of individual price approvals, laboriously determined after investigations into the accounts of individual traders'. Clearly, they were a long time coming.[128] Nor was the price control system integrated with wage fixing. In October 1947 the Arbitration Court increased minimum wages by nearly 18 per cent. Five months later a senior official in price control noted that it was 'urgently necessary' to get ministerial direction on how increased wage costs should be reflected in the price control system. The practice had been largely to allow price increases based on increased wage costs, which to say the least risked institutionalising a wage-price spiral.[129]

The government also used budget policy against inflation. Nash continued wartime national savings schemes both to absorb surplus funds and to pay for development works and rehabilitation without borrowing overseas. Budget surpluses also absorbed surplus funds and gave room for tax reductions, which in turn would encourage a 'general all round increase in production [which was] an urgent, if not vital necessity' not only to reduce inflationary pressure but also to maintain full employment and public services.[130] Nash surrendered some £21m in tax between the end of the war and the 1946 Budget.[131] Privately, Nash had told Fraser in 1946 that 'taxation must be reduced to the limit', and by 1949 per capita taxation fell by six per cent in real terms.[132] Nash also sought to reduce spending demands where possible, particularly cutting subsidies. In 1946 he increased railway rates by 15 per cent; they had not been changed since 1938.[133] In the 1947 Budget Nash adopted a general principle that if a subsidy did not address an anomaly arising from the circumstances of wartime or reconstruction, it would be removed. Thus, while bread, butter, milk, tea and coal remained subsidised, Nash abolished many other food subsidies including those for fruit, meat and sugar. He increased rail charges again and abolished a 25 per cent subsidy on shipping freights. The overall effect was reducing a projected subsidy expenditure of £19.6m to £13.5m.[134] Nash cut a further £2m from subsidy expenditure in 1948 and again reduced taxation by £4m as compensation for increased consumer prices, and no doubt also in the hope that some more militant unions would moderate their wage demands if take-home pay increased.[135] By 1948, Treasury's warnings of the perils of inflation were becoming more forceful and Ashwin thought the 1948 tax cuts were unwise.[136] Nash was far from opposed to reducing public spending in certain areas, but against Treasury's single-minded focus on fiscal rectitude, the government also had to balance its development agenda and citizens' legitimate expectations of a higher material standard of living.

Conclusion

Circumstances in the second half of the 1940s were extremely difficult. The dominant constraint, of course, was the legacy of war. From that followed the requirements of the Sterling Area, or more precisely British insistence that the Sterling Area was a vehicle for British recovery (the British Labour government displayed almost as little sympathy for their antipodean comrades as the Conservatives had in 1939).[137] The term 'insulationism' is often used to describe New Zealand policies after 1945, but that word obscures as much as it illuminates. Fraser and Nash did not advocate autarky; they sought a progressive and managed development of world trade. Unfortunately, industrial powers, particularly the United States, were wedded to agricultural protectionism. With British demands, American obduracy, worldwide and local shortages of material, and the need to prioritise reconstruction, a controlled economy was inevitable. Developing infrastructure, especially electricity, was essential not only for consumption but also for primary and secondary industry. While the manufacturing industry was a priority, the government's approach was considered and realistic.

The Labour government believed in a managed economy, not in austerity as a good in itself, and aspired to the economics of plenty as well as redistribution. Labour liberalised as well as controlled in the postwar years and was as committed to controlling inflation as to full employment and extending the welfare state. So far as the politics of economic management were concerned, it has long been recognised that a crucial element in Labour's defeat at the end of 1949 and its replacement by long-running National administrations was that party's acceptance of the broad outlines, and much of the detail, of Labour's approach to policy. Like many other western conservative parties, the National Party adopted much of the new consensus once its electoral popularity and economic workability were demonstrated. Certainly there were differences of emphasis. In particular, National was always more inclined to focus on the perspectives of an idealised consumer, and campaigned vociferously against continued rationing. But Mark Twain and Bob Semple, the Minister of Works, in their respective and inimitable fashions, provided useful summaries of the meaning of 1949. Twain, years before, had written that 'the radical invents the views. When he has worn them out the conservative adopts them'; Semple, with considerable if understandable bitterness, is said to have observed that 'the bastards walked barefoot to the polls to vote us in in 1935, and they drove to the polls to vote us out in 1949'.[138]

Chapter 4

Consolidation: The First National Government and Economic Policy

The general election at the end of 1949 inaugurated a long period of political domination by the National Party, lasting until 1984. Like other mainstream western conservative parties, National moved towards accepting the managed mixed economy. National came to office promising liberalisation and consumerism while maintaining and even extending the public works, social services and welfare measures that Labour had enacted. The broad outlines of the postwar settlement, if not particular emphases, were thus entrenched in National's first government, which lasted until 1957.

New Zealand changed rapidly during these eight years.[1] The population increased by 374,691, or 20 per cent, to 2.26 million. The high birth-rate accounted for three quarters of the increase and immigration for the other quarter (in fact, of course, the two causes were connected, for many immigrants began to have children as well). In 1949, 28 per cent of the population were aged under 15, and in eight years this increased to 32 per cent. Even more striking were the sheer numbers: 547,705 under-15-year-olds in 1949 and 722,284 in 1957. The population was therefore young and urban – about 60 per cent living in urban areas – although the very rapid growth of urban and suburban areas after 1949 was due more to the increase in absolute numbers rather than a greatly increased percentage of urban dwellers.[2]

Employment patterns were changing. The workforce increased by 15.5 per cent. Primary production's share fell by 3 per cent (3.5 per cent for men, 1.8 per cent for women), a slight fall in absolute numbers. Of course these figures reflect certain assumptions; many thousands of women in primary production would not have been counted because they were classed as 'married women'. Much of the shift for men was into building and construction (up by over 2.5 per cent). Among women, the share in distribution and finance increased by 3.5 per cent, and administration and professional numbers increased by more than 2 per cent, twice the increase for men. The share in manufacturing industry was almost static at 24 per cent for both men and women; most manufacturing industry serviced domestic demand and grew with the population.

New Zealand remained dominated by white settlers and their descendants. Even though the Pākehā birth-rate was high enough at 25 per thousand, the Māori rate was almost twice that, at 46 per thousand. With falling rates of infant mortality, Māori comprised 6 per cent of the population but accounted for 14 per cent of the natural increase. High immigration from Europe, however, meant that the Māori share of the total population did not increase, and as yet two thirds of the Māori population lived in rural areas. Only in the decade after the 1956 census would settler New Zealand see some profound changes as Māori moved into towns and cities and sustained immigration began from tropical Polynesia.

Rapid population growth brought social and economic challenges. The social history of the 1950s is underexplored, and must remain so in this book, but economically it is notable that the rapid population growth was accommodated. In part, this reflected an active political commitment to supporting population growth, but the rapid increase in primary sector outputs and exports, as some scholars have highlighted, underpinned the viability of the New Zealand economy. National would moderate some dimensions of the controlled economy, but external circumstances would make it more difficult to do so than the party had expected. The party's bold rhetoric in Opposition rapidly encountered several reality checks both internally and externally.

The early 1950s were overshadowed by the Korean War. The outbreak of war increased already severe international tension; rearmament meant increased demand for raw materials. High export prices and inflation, followed by a balance of payments crisis when the demand for raw materials eased, were the immediate domestic consequences. Although there was then a quick recovery and a generally favourable balance of payments, the settler economy remained vulnerable. Britain continued to exert pressure on New Zealand economic policy through the Sterling Area, even as the end of bulk purchase of New Zealand exports approached in 1954. From that date onwards, the British market could not be taken for granted. The balance of payments and inflationary pressure dominated Treasury's perspective; the National government was as committed to developmentalism as Labour had been. The party's industry policy supported continued expansion of pastoral production and a shift in focus from import substitution towards a tentative orientation to exporting in manufacturing. Before the first National government lost office in 1957, the necessity of trade diversification would be evident. Economic policy was not about security but rather dealing with a changing settler economy, modernising infrastructure and managing population growth.

Perspectives: The National Party

The National Party had been established in 1936 out of the Coalition government defeated in 1935, combining the Reform and United (previously Liberal) parties, which, philosophically, had become virtually indistinguishable. Some smaller right-wing groups that had emerged during the Depression also joined the new party; in the face of Labour's strength, conservative unity was imperative.[3] The party's objectives did not betray much interest in political philosophy. The first referred to loyalty to the monarch and Empire, the second to national defence, and the third and fourth to 'policies designed to benefit the community as a whole, irrespective of sectional interests' and 'progressive and humanitarian legislation'.[4] The latter phrase claimed the Liberal heritage; the former was a staple of bourgeois class consciousness. There were three broad factions: pragmatic rural conservatives, urban right-wingers championing the virtues of minimalist government, and, especially after 1945, urban liberals who professed a desire to think for themselves and were put off Labour by its cloth-cap image.[5] Factionalism was intense under the party's first leader, Adam Hamilton, a rural Southland conservative; in 1940 he was replaced by Sidney Holland, a Christchurch right-winger who had flirted with the quasi-fascist New Zealand Legion in 1935.[6]

Holland was a small manufacturer; his family had a Primitive Methodist background (Sidney later became an Anglican) and his father had been Mayor of Christchurch and later a Reform MP.[7] Holland was not much of a theorist, but 'got his education by listening and not by reading'.[8] He was an outstanding political organiser and a vigorous, if simplistic, debater with 'the physical presence, the bluff ebullience, and the confident arrogance to inspire his caucus colleagues at a time when the caucus was weak in numbers, morale and speaking ability. . . . Tenacious and robust, he fused the various factions in the National coalition into a united party and hammered Labour unmercifully by castigating socialism, bureaucracy, restrictions on the individual, and militant trade unions'.[9] Only in 1943 did Holland attempt to 'explain what the National Party stood for rather than simply what it opposed'.[10]

This exercise began by accommodating conservatism within the emerging social democratic settlement: 'having conquered our foes upon the battlefield, we must set the seal upon our victory by the conquest of want, ignorance, prejudice, squalor and disease'.[11] Holland's rhetoric emphasised independence and self-reliance, which he attributed to the national character. 'Most people want to be free and independent, thrifty and self-reliant. . . . New Zealanders are at heart individualists, never happy as mere cogs in a wheel, where every choice concerning their lives is made by someone else'.[12] The precondition for those values was private ownership. 'Nothing gives a greater urge to independence and self-reliance than private ownership. . . . everyone, no matter how humble his station in life, should be able to OWN something – a home, a shop, a piece of land, a factory or a share in one . . . Every New Zealander should strive, by saving, to buy his own home, or to have a share in the private ownership of the means of production, distribution and exchange'.[13] Class co-operation went without saying, but was partly justified by social mobility: 'many of our so-called capitalists have graduated from the ranks of manual workers' and 'in New Zealand we do not know extremes of wealth and poverty as experienced in other countries'.[14]

There was more common ground between Labour and National on rights and obligations than either might have admitted. National, like Labour, accepted the right to 'useful and creative employment, and fair pay adequate to command the necessities and amenities of life' including shelter, food, medical care and education.[15] Nor would Fraser have dissented from the observation that the corresponding obligations were 'to work for the common good of all . . . to give of one's best in service, ideas and loyalty to one's job'.[16] Holland argued that prosperity could only be achieved by work, and security without obligation 'can only result in moral decay' (again, Fraser would not have disagreed).[17] The differences, however, were also clear. Holland added the right to be free from state dictation, and the obligation 'to be thrifty, independent, self-reliant and trustworthy'.[18] Artfully, Holland collapsed wartime regulation into a generalised denunciation of socialism whereby 'what occupations [people] shall follow, what they may buy, where they may buy it from, how much they may have of this or that – are subject to dictation by the State' and claimed that 'the war is being used as an excuse for imposing State socialism'.[19]

The National Party brought a number of able politicians into parliament in the 1940s. Holland's deputy and eventual successor, Keith Holyoake, came from a small farming family in Nelson. He had represented his home electorate between 1932 and 1938, and was assisted to a safe rural seat in the lower North Island in 1943. Holyoake, like his mentor Coates, espoused a pragmatic rural conservatism, combining state support for agriculture and industry with a rhetoric of self-reliance and hostility to bureaucratic intervention.[20] There were two more ideologically committed lawyers, Jack Watts from Christchurch and John Marshall from Wellington. Watts, who would be Minister of Industries and Commerce and then of Finance, thought that if economic planning were anything other than 'general foresight and willingness to look ahead' then it would become an incoherent patchwork of regulation.[21] Labour, he said, had achieved security at the cost of 'stagnation and decline'. Centralised planning obstructed enterpreneurship, which by its nature was decentralised. It was, in the postwar world, counterproductive to protect the producer because there was no shortage of spending power; rather the reverse, and 'we must place the consumer right in the centre of our economic system'.[22] On the right of the party, Hayekian ideas sometimes showed. One MP complained, 'many of our young people have been taught to be drones, that the State will look after them and their destinies. . . . education to dependence on the State has been evident in all Socialist countries. . . . Beneficient socialism must in the end turn to totalitarianism, because under the beneficient Socialist State people become effete and they need compulsion to stir them if production is to be maintained'.[23]

We should, therefore, not overstate the degree of ideological convergence. Where Labour rhetoric stressed rewards for service, or fair shares, National ministers:

> want[ed] to see our farmers, traders, and manufacturers enjoying prosperity acquired through their own efforts and the maximum possible freedom from unwarranted interference or dictation by the State. We want a State in which hard work, industry and enterprise, thrift and independence will receive encouragement with just rewards and compensations.[24]

Where Labour would use regulation to ensure fair or desirable outcomes, National argued that private enterprise was the engine of economic growth 'and the benefit will not merely be shared by a few, but will be spread throughout the community in the form of full employment at good wages. At the same time, social services will ensure that the conditions of security are available to all'.[25]

National's major problem was that many voters associated it with harsh Depression-era policies. Even though he had qualified the observation, Holland was dogged for years by his description of the Social Security Act 1938 as 'applied lunacy' (a riposte, of course, to Savage's 'applied Christianity'). In 1949, he said: 'I always hope that I shall remember the slump as something to avoid, and the way it was handled, too' and explicitly accepted that the state should spend to mitigate a recession.[26] Holyoake frequently got annoyed at suggestions that Labour had a monopoly on social welfare legislation and pointed out that much social legislation had been improved incrementally over decades. Holyoake, more than Holland, exhibited a calm and cheerful optimism. In 1951 he derisively observed that:

> The Labour party said that if ever we became the Government we would slash, we would cut, we would smash and we would grab. Oh, the terrible things that we would do! [yet]. . . . New Zealand has never been more prosperous. There is no unemployment; wages, salaries, and incomes are higher than they have ever been before; social security is higher than it has ever been before; the standards of living of all sections of our people are higher than they have ever been before. . . . [Labour MPs] are slump-minded. They have talked slump for the last fourteen years. They have preached it; I think they have even prayed for it. . . . the National party simply refuses to be plunged into a slump.[27]

National's 1949 campaign was compelling, promising social security with less regulation and more consumerism, and the party defeated Labour with 46 seats to 34 and a majority of the votes. The new government would begin with a strong commitment to liberalisation, but the pressure of events, particularly industrial conflict, and a continuing shortage of dollars within the Sterling Area, as well as the short-lived commodity boom that accompanied the Korean War and the subsequent crash, all combined to moderate the government's ideological fervour.

A Burst of Liberalising Zeal

Holland took the finance portfolio himself and held it until the 1954 election. His associate minister was Charles Bowden, an accountant and stock-and-station agent, who was a capable and pragmatic administrator. During the 1940s Nash had dominated economic policy; Ashwin's influence reflected not only his position as Secretary to the Treasury but also his membership of most of the ad-hoc bodies that the Labour government had established during the war. After 1949, there was some discussion about the merits of a new body to co-ordinate economic policy, but establishing a research division in Treasury reflected Ashwin's determination to keep his department at the heart of things, and there was no other departmental head who might have convincingly put forward an alternative model. Foss Shanahan, in the Prime Minister's department, created orderly subcommittees of ministers and officials, the key ones being managed by Treasury.[28] By 1952 Ashwin's personal influence had subtly become Treasury's institutional dominance, although it should be noted that on most major issues the subcommittees heard directly from all relevant departments.

New ministers and experienced officials no doubt took a little time to get the measure of each other. Senior Treasury officials, Malcolm

McKinnon has suggested, were slightly ambivalent towards the new government. Holland had complained loudly about Labour's high public spending, and his belief in fiscal rectitude matched Treasury thinking. Wartime and postwar experience had increasingly caused Treasury to regard inflation as the major problem in economic management. Inflationary pressures during the 1940s were considerable, and they did not abate in 1950. Ashwin's post-election briefing was rather old-fashioned in its austere scepticism about public spending. Inflation had 'been causing . . . grave concern' along with 'shortages of labour and materials in essential industry, of recurring general wage increases, of pressure on imports, and to some extent of balance of payment difficulties'. Ashwin attributed the problems to 'investment in capital works well beyond that portion of the country's resources available for the purpose'.[29] The spending departments were undisciplined, and the nation's moral fibre had weakened: the 40-hour week had been accompanied by 'people working no harder, if as hard, as previously'.[30]

Holland had also advocated rapidly easing import controls, but on this he and Ashwin did not agree. Ashwin, anticipating balance of payments difficulties, warned that overseas reserves would need to be increased before there could be substantial import liberalisation 'except in appearance'.[31] A series of events – the 1938 balance of payments crisis, a highly constrained wartime situation, postwar shortages and the demands of the Sterling Area – all combined to reinforce awareness of the continuing vulnerability of a settler economy to its balance of payments. The automatic adjustments of the pre-Reserve Bank era, by which a decline in overseas reserves was met by deflation and a credit squeeze, had been unacceptable to the Labour government and were no more acceptable to National. With a heavy developmental agenda, moreover, New Zealand governments had a significant interest in ensuring that there were sufficient overseas funds to pay for the necessary imports.

Some weeks after taking office, Holland addressed the nation on the public finances. He warned that continued inflation would have very serious consequences. There had been, he said, 'reckless national extravagance' and expenditure had to be strictly prioritised, 'introducing into the Government's financial administration business methods and plain commonsense that is so badly needed'. On the other hand, 'sound development of the country's resources should proceed as fast as practicable' without inflation. 'The Government believes in expansion of production and full employment with the highest possible standard of living. We can maintain full employment and social security benefits and wages by spending annually what we earn [but not more.]'[32] In his first Budget, therefore, Holland announced continued public works spending, which he said would be funded to a much greater extent by internal loans. These, by absorbing available money, would be less inflationary than using Reserve Bank credit. The rhetorical purpose was to cast Labour as profligate, yet Nash had been as enthusiastic a raiser of internal loans.[33] Defence spending increased significantly to cover compulsory military training and New Zealand's commitment in the Korean War. Some weeks before the Budget Holland had cut subsidies by just over £9m, as well as increasing rail charges.[34] The impression of a greater reliance on the market in economic policy was reinforced when improved world supplies allowed Holland to take the last commodities – petrol and butter – off ration in June 1950 (although Nash had reduced subsidies and rationing too).[35]

The government promoted its first internal loan, of £20m, very heavily, using not only newspaper and radio advertisements but also planted opinion pieces in the newspapers and personal approaches from bank managers and stockbrokers to their clients. National had the advantage of close links to newspaper proprietors and the commercial sector.[36] Cabinet directed the Post Office to provide facilities for a network of local organisers who canvassed for support by telephone and personal visits.[37] However, subscriptions were unspectacular, and the target was only reached after repeated broadcasts by the Prime Minister, intense phone canvassing, and a substantial, and non-repeatable, conversion of Treasury Bills held by the Wool Board.[38] One provincial newspaper was uneasy that 'the Government made something of a patriotic issue of what should have been a purely business proposition in time of peace', particularly as the rhetoric risked impugning the patriotism of those investors who chose not to support the loan. A 'citizen has a fundamental . . . right to decide where, when and how he will invest his capital. . . . An investor in normal times, is under no obligation to lend his money to the State'.[39] The whole exercise, indeed, was as much about the National Party's political profile and the party's criticism of Labour's alleged profligacy as it was about sound public finance.

Exposure to the realities of government would diminish Holland's ideological fervour (one very detailed history of taxation in New Zealand refers to the onset of 'Tory fatalism').[40] Treasury perspectives, too, became more nuanced even as inflation and the balance of payments remained the principal concerns. Even given his predilection for austerity

> Ashwin and his colleagues had been tempered both by wartime and post-war experience . . . and by Keynesian ideas of economic management. . . . The former made senior Treasury officials alert

> to the dangers of an ill-thought-out loosening of controls. . . . The latter fostered a belief in the long-term merits of "economic management", albeit not the directive variety favoured by . . . Labour . . . but something more subtle, drawing on the insights of Keynes and his followers into the working of a national economy.[41]

There was a shift towards the language of economics, rather than simply accounting, in the Economic Surveys, which from 1951 were published annually to accompany the Budget. Written in Treasury, they appeared under the authority of the Minister of Finance, and were thus both analytical and political documents.[42] If Ashwin's first briefing to Holland had underplayed the external context, the first Survey made it clear that while inflation was 'the most urgent problem,' the major inflationary pressures were external: 'the worsening of international relations and the expansion of rearmament and stockpiling programmes'.[43] The New Zealand government could not influence those circumstances and could only hope to moderate the domestic consequences. New Zealand had, however, done better than some other countries. Inflation since 1937 amounted to 59 per cent, compared to 69 in Canada, 74 in the United States, and 88 in Australia.[44] In domestic policy, public spending on infrastructure, however necessary, was inflationary under conditions of full employment because wages were paid out but the stock of goods and services on which they could be spent did not increase proportionately; in an already full labour market, wage costs were driven up and prices with them.[45] Redistributive policies increased purchasing power among those with less capacity to save. In short, it 'might not be an over-simplification to say that the welfare state postulates a mild degree of inflationary pressure'.[46] In this exposition, inflation was a complex technical issue and not a moral problem.

Ideas about economic management became more nuanced in the light of experience. Internally, industrial relations remained tense and the government's approach combined repression and accommodation; the postwar settlement would be maintained but its limits would be policed. Externally, New Zealand's own balance of payments and that of the Sterling Area demonstrated a small settler economy's vulnerability. The need to reduce that vulnerability combined with rapid population growth to reinforce the developmental imperative.

Industrial Conflict: Policing the Settlement

Like the Labour government before it, National had difficulty containing wages when demand for labour was high. National politicians' language on industrial relations reflected both a dislike of militant trade unionism and the party's adhesion to the rhetoric of class co-operation; thus, 'responsible' trade unionism was acceptable. As in the later 1940s, this meant co-operation between the government and the Federation of Labour, whose leading figure, Fintan Patrick Walsh, had no intention of allowing rivals to emerge in the trade union movement. Within the movement, opposition to Walsh was led by the waterside workers, who with their allies were not inclined to accept wage restraint and whose preference was for a trade unionism based upon mass mobilisation rather than agreements in the corridors of power and a judicialised wage-fixing system in the Arbitration Court. In February 1950 the watersiders, drivers, freezing workers, carpenters, labourers, and some other unions walked out of the FOL conference and established a rival Trade Union Congress.[47] To an extent, the militants challenged the parameters of the postwar settlement.

The Arbitration Court adjudicated the claims of unions in particular industries, and also made general wage orders that applied across the board, but its powers were limited to setting a minimum. It had little power to control ruling rates (the level of wages paid in practice). In giving general wage orders the court was required to have regard to economic stability and the relative shares of income received by wage and salary earners, farmers and other occupational groups, and, from 1953, to price stability and general economic conditions.[48] An inconsistency was that the 1936 Industrial Conciliation and Arbitration Act specified that male wages should support a male breadwinner with a dependent wife and three children, but the general wage order regulations took no account of that principle.[49] The court's president, Arthur Tyndall, well knew that stability required that all parties accept the wage-fixing process as legitimate, which meant regular and moderate increases at least at the level of the cost of living. Tyndall's political acuity, along with Walsh's undoubted grasp of economics, contributed in no small measure to the Court's success during the 1950s.[50]

When the rival labour federations applied for general wage orders later in 1950, the Court warned against justifying such orders by reference to the male breadwinner. Because only 22 per cent of male wage and salary earners were supporting a wife and three or more children (and 29 per cent were supporting no children), such a justification amounted to 'provision for . . . four and a half times as many children as are dependent upon workers'.[51] Noting the importance of the family benefit, the Court felt that 'any further adjustment in the economic status of the family man as compared with that of other adult male workers should be left for the . . . legislature'.[52] Even so, the Court made a general order of 15 per cent. Substantial wage increases concerned the government because of their inflationary potential and because of state sector relativity with private sector wages. Ashwin suggested that the Prime Minister convene a high-level meeting between industry organisations and the unions in the hope of moderating the situation.[53] Little came of this. Holland was, for the moment, less interested in negotiating co-operation than in destroying the watersiders' union and its militant allies, which he and his government did in the industrial confrontation from February to July 1951.

That confrontation has been extensively discussed by historians, and need be only briefly noted here.[54] Waterside work was arduous, frequently unpleasant and dangerous; those characteristics as well as the importance of the waterfront in New Zealand's trade-dependent economy gave rise to a powerful culture of mass trade unionism on the wharves. In the years after 1945, there had been frequent industrial disruption as watersiders sought to use their strategic position to secure higher wages. A generally toxic relationship developed between the union's leadership and the Cabinet, who wanted wage restraint in the interests of macroeconomic stability. This did not change with the National government, but a party of manufacturers, farmers, and retailers had much to gain by demonising militant workers. A dispute over the application of the General Wage Order to waterside workers' wages in February was rapidly escalated into a lockout and a state of emergency.

The state of emergency provoked a number of other unions to strike in solidarity with the watersiders, but after five months the militants were comprehensively defeated, at least in the short-term. Walsh and the Federation of Labour actively worked with the government; whatever the merits of Walsh's argument that the FOL should be a partner in economic growth, preserving his personal power was a more compelling motive for assisting Holland to destroy the militants. In the election campaign that followed the dispute, Holland rediscovered the virtues of subsidies. Bassett goes so far as to say that the 'Government triumphed over a section of the trade union movement that National supporters most detested at the price of virtually ceasing its attempts at macroeconomic reform'.[55] Certainly Holland now argued that despite subsidies' disadvantages, without them wages and benefits would increase to match higher prices, and inflation would increase 'at the very time when the greatest care should be taken to keep a firm grip on it'.[56] However, subsidies were hardly indiscriminate. In 1951 subsidies on dairy produce, wheat and flour accounted for 62 per cent of all subsidy expenditure, increasing to 85 per cent in 1953 and 96 per cent in 1957 (clothing was subsidised in 1951 and 1952).[57] In subsidising milk, butter and bread, no doubt the government wished to demonstrate to wage-earning voters that militant action was not only futile but also unnecessary. There was much more to the retreat from liberalisation than political expediency, though. International tensions were making the economic climate much more difficult than Holland and his colleagues had imagined in 1949.

The Balance of Payments and the Sterling Area

The Korean War broke out at the end of June 1950. The war, and the international tension that preceded it, generated a boom in commodity prices, including wool, as major powers increased their stockpiles. The boom, and the subsequent bust, had a major impact on New Zealand, but these were not the principal reasons why National reimposed import controls in 1952. Once again, New Zealand policy was driven by British demands of the Sterling Area.

The boom saw 'terms of trade for raw materials against manufactures improved by 30 per cent between the first halves of 1950 and 1951,' reinforced by the fear that the war could spread far beyond the Korean peninsula.[58] Shortly before the war, when the trade balance was already favourable, Treasury warned that conditions would be unlikely to permit 'a substantial easing up of import control'. Liberalisation would lead to indiscipline, and almost certainly a return to controls.[59] As wool prices continued to increase, the government reduced but did not abolish controls against Sterling Area imports; those from North America remained strictly controlled.[60] Once the war settled into a stalemate, early in 1951, the commodity boom crashed, but importing had surged and, as Treasury had feared, the large current account surplus rapidly became a large deficit; importers lacked the experience to judge the market and over-ordered.[61] Wool exports had realised £46.5m in 1949, £74.6m in 1950 and £128m in 1951, falling back to £82m in 1952. Meat and dairy exports almost compensated for wool's fall, but import spending increased from £143.5m in 1950 to £187.7m in 1951 and £229.4m in 1952. Overseas receipts had exceeded payments by £14m in 1950 and £16m in 1951 but were in deficit by £23m in 1952.[62] Overseas reserves dropped 44 per cent, from £123.5m in July 1951 to £69.5m a year later.[63]

In 1952 the government reversed course and severely tightened import controls, but rather than reducing allowable quantities, the government reduced the amount of foreign exchange allowed to importers, through the Reserve Bank, to 80 per cent of their 1950 allocations.[64] Most accounts attribute stricter controls to a loss of nerve after the import blowout in the wake of the wool boom and bust. As Bassett puts it, when wool boomed, 'the Government . . . was so generous with import licences that when the price of wool fell sharply over the summer of 1951–52, imports flowed into the country at an unsustainable rate. Ministers took fright'.[65]

The main reason for stricter import controls, however, was not the domestic consequences of the Korean crash, but the politics of the Sterling Area. The diversion of New Zealand's earning capacity to service the wider Sterling Area interests (or, some might say, the narrower British interest) had been a major problem in the later 1940s. In the wake of the devaluation of sterling, British exports recovered after 1949. This in turn relieved pressure on sterling balances, which was one factor allowing the Holland government to ease import controls. The Korean war prompted a much greater Anglo-American military commitment to NATO and the defence of Western Europe, 'where it was feared the Red Army might strike at any moment' while attention was distracted in Korea. This was scarcely likely, but the perception of imminent European danger 'caused the Attlee government to rearm so furiously, expensively, and (in an economic sense) ruinously'.[66]

Rearmament meant that Britain had again to earn and save dollars in order to finance the required imports from the United States. Once again, New Zealand had to constantly seek British agreement to an increased allowance of plant and raw materials, even from within the Sterling Area. In June 1951 Bowden asked the British Board of Trade for special consideration with respect to metal, paper, machinery, and chemicals, to keep imports at 1950 levels. This was 'vital to continuance of our economy and that to extent that United Kingdom was unable to supply we would endeavour to obtain supplies from other markets', that is, dollar sources.[67] The British claimed that their own position was desperate; in the second half of 1951 they would lose $1500m of their dollar reserves. New Zealand newspapers waxed eloquent on the need for a 'Family Approach to a Family Crisis. . . . every country in the Commonwealth and Empire must play a part in meeting the challenge'.[68] The Commonwealth Finance Ministers' Conference in February 1952 obliged New Zealand to increase the trade surplus with non-sterling countries by between £7m and £12m, to a total surplus of £25m.[69] This amounted to a severe import cut, and it was imposed principally because of British demands of the Sterling Area and only secondarily because of New Zealand's balance of payments.[70] Despite the disadvantages of the Sterling Area, there were few, if any, alternatives. For New Zealand, as for other Sterling Area countries, 'the persistence of using sterling as a reserve asset was the result not just of symbolic or emotional allegiance but of a rational understanding that diversification would disrupt the entire sterling system of exchange rate stability and damage the British economy (and perhaps the global monetary system) in ways that were not in the interests of its trading partners'.[71]

By 1953, both the domestic balance of payments and that of the Sterling Area were easing, and Holland ended exchange controls for importers in 1954, hoping that importers and traders would 'use this restored freedom wisely and with discretion, and will avoid embarrassing themselves, their banks, and the national economy'.[72] Over the next three years, the government further eased quantitative controls. Although the Holland government's direction was towards liberalising imports, the crises of 1951 and 1952 had demonstrated the continuing vulnerability of New Zealand's small settler economy to forces beyond this country's control.

The Modernisation Imperative

Labour had seen modernising infrastructure as essential to developing the New Zealand economy and making it more robust. Despite Holland's electioneering rhetoric about waste and extravagance, the National government had no wish to abandon infrastructural development. 'National remained, as Reform and United had been in the past, a party of developers as well as of fiscal conservatives'.[73] Advertising for national development loans in the early 1950s was all of a piece with nineteenth-century settler boosterism: 'New Zealand where the riches of the earth are our prosperity . . . where the burden of the orchards, the products of the soil, the wool, meat, butter and cheese that we export are our wealth . . . where our progress depends on the development of our land'.[74] Holland opened one loan campaign proclaiming that 'There is a dazzling vision before us'.[75] National was not about to let Labour monopolise the rhetoric of nation building.

While Ashwin had sometimes expressed scepticism about public works, infrastructure development was a matter of necessity. The wartime investment deficit was still largely unrecovered by 1951, even though investment had increased from 16 per cent of GNP in 1947–48 to 19 per cent in 1950–51. Conversely, personal consumption accounted for 70 per cent of GNP in 1938–39; in 1943–44 it had fallen to 47 per cent and in 1950–51 had only returned to 58 per cent.[76] Although infrastructure spending contributed to inflationary pressure, 'any reduction in the rate of Government investment large enough to cause any significant decrease in inflationary pressures could not be made without abandoning or postponing projects for which a good case can be made on social and economic grounds'.[77]

Infrastructure development was driven both by a rapidly growing population and by agendas of economic modernisation. Population growth was partly justified by racial fears in 'the outlying and precarious footholds of the Western World in Australia and New Zealand. . . . we cannot expect the peoples of Australia and New Zealand to remain in undisputed possession of these favoured lands without outside help and self-help. . . . The population urge and the menace of Communism may merge and that is our problem'.[78] Immigration was thus about more than meeting the demand for labour, although that was a major dimension. Assisted immigrants (almost entirely from the United Kingdom) were selected according to occupation and bonded to work for two years. Between 1949 and 1957 these accounted for around 30 per cent of the net migration gain.[79] The population was correctly projected to reach three million by 1973, and this 'must be taken into account when considering how much should be spent on such items as schools, hydro-electric construction, or housing.'[80] Housing attracted considerable public spending; in the five years to March 1955, £21m was spent on school buildings (in 2012 terms, around a billion dollars). Hospital works and development in the later 1950s were put at £30m.[81] There was a waiting list in 1955 of 33,000 for telephones, and long-distance connections were well below international standards, with 90-minute delays frequent. Electricity consumption increased by about 40 per cent between 1948 and 1953 and demand would continue to grow, not least because household electrical appliances became more common.[82]

No part of the infrastructure was as capital-intensive, or required so much long-range planning, as electricity. In 1956 the government commissioned a major review of hydroelectric capacity and the anticipated need through to 1975. With existing development due for completion in 1962, the North Island generating capacity would be 1.13 gigawatts, and the South Island half that at 613 megawatts. Assuming that demand increased at the existing rate, by 1970 the North Island would need another 800 megawatts and the South Island nearly 200. There was little more scope for development within the North Island; fortunately, engineers from the Swedish state power board advised that a Cook Strait Cable was feasible. Therefore, major development could be planned in the South Island.[83] The projected cost would be £235 million to 1970, and the government intended to fund development as far as possible from electricity revenue rather than loans.[84]

In short, as the 1955 Economic Survey put it, 'the planned programme of Government works has been at the minimum necessary to keep pace with population growth. A reduced level of expenditure on basic development projects would hinder farming and industrial production'.[85] What had been 'reckless national extravagance' in 1950 was no more than necessary development in 1955.

Industry Policy

Industry policy and infrastructure modernisation were closely connected. In the most immediate sense, the latter both created the conditions for private enterprise to develop and influenced the direction of that development. More generally, National had come to office accepting the principle of price, import and investment controls. The extent of National's liberalisation in these areas is contentious. Bassett has argued that while the government began with enthusiasm, reform stalled after 1951 under the pressure of interest groups' vociferous lobbying and Holland's fear of the electoral consequences. National did not like the controlled economy, but they 'were grappling with a tar baby . . . they could not figure out how to escape from it'.[86] There is certainly evidence to support Bassett's view, but Gould, writing 30 years ago, suggested that by 1956 'imports into New Zealand were more nearly "free" than at any time between 1938 and at least the late 1970s'.[87] As we have seen, the balance of payments was a central concern in economic management; combined with a heavy development programme and a commitment to full employment – which meant that an external imbalance could not be resolved by allowing recession – a measure of control was inevitable.

National politicians were well aware that their electoral success depended not only on wealthier farmers and urban business but also on the lower middle class, including many independent traders.[88] It was a reasonable apprehension that radical deregulation would threaten some of this support. The new Minister of Industries and Commerce, Charles Bowden, was well aware of the perspective of provincial small business and wanted 'to protect adequately the worthwhile units and prevent any violent disruption in the present pattern of our economic life'. He warned that a comprehensive review of industry policy would be 'fraught with great difficulties . . . especially in the face of established interests of both capital and labour'.[89] Even so, he eased import controls during 1950 and 1951, and the Board of Trade consulted with local manufacturers before recommending decontrol of imports that competed with locally produced goods.[90] Perhaps because of the consultation, there did not appear to be widespread protest, although some unhappy manufacturers lobbied Nash, by now Labour leader; he considered issuing a pamphlet that raised the spectre of industry being destroyed by imports made by 'COOLIE ASIATIC LABOUR'.[91] This was not Nash at his most idealistic.

After the 1951 election, Jack Watts, a more enthusiastic liberaliser than Bowden, became Minister of Industries and Commerce and further eased import controls. In March 1953 he stated that the interests of consumers and primary industries should be taken into account alongside those of manufacturers in setting levels of protection.[92] The Board of Trade noted that many industries prospered without protection from licensing and import competition was an incentive to efficiency. Some manufacturers had not realised 'how relatively strong they are in the New Zealand market'; industries that needed much more protection than relatively modest tariffs 'may be of doubtful economic worth'.[93] Watts had hoped to see quantitative controls replaced by tariffs; this, however, did not happen for many years.

The government's approach to price control similarly reflected the conflict between aspiration and circumstance. Bowden noted in 1950 that 'strict price control over a wide but diminishing field will be necessary so long as effective demand continues to exceed the quantity of goods available'.[94] The government did take some major commodity groups off price control in its first year, including many household appliances and some items of machinery and industrial tools, as well as many foodstuffs, and some others came under a simplified regime.[95] The pace slowed after mid 1951, as export earnings fell and the government became more concerned 'to retain stability in the internal economy'.[96] In 1953, though, Watts decontrolled softgoods and many categories of clothing. In 1954 there was a general review, after which the approach was that price control would be confined to those situations where there were shortages; prices were subsidised; free competition was impeded by exchange or import control, tariffs, licensing, monopoly, restrictive practices, capital issues or credit control; or prices were unfair. The emphasis shifted to a positive list, whereby gazetted lists specified controlled (as opposed to uncontrolled) commodities.[97]

Capital issues controls allowed fairly detailed management of investment. These had been administered by the Registrar of Companies from 1945 to 1952 and then by a committee including senior public servants and lay representatives. Most applications were allowed until the Korean boom ended, as money was plentiful and it was thought desirable 'to mop up fluid funds'. The exceptions were finance and hire purchase companies and 'a few speculative ventures'. After the Korean bust, the government tightened the criteria, wanting to channel investment to 'the most essential industries', and to ensure a free field for large government loans.[98] The priority was now cases where no new finance was involved (such as a share issue on takeover), where exports would increase or imports decrease, or where a shortage of essential goods would be met.[99] Perhaps paternalistically, the committee itself thought that that the main virtues of control were not in prioritising investment but in protecting the investing public from questionable schemes and making companies think carefully about plans for expansion.[100] Even so, until the 1957–58 downturn, most sectors got most of what they applied for, the exceptions being wholesale and retail trade, hotel development, and brewing (Treasury's enthusiasm, in the late 1940s, for tourism development did not seem to have come to much, although it recognised that hospitality, retail and entertainment would eventually have to be allowed to grow).[101] One dimension of capital issues control was the regulation of overseas investment, which, without a great deal of publicity, grew under National, particularly in 1956 and 1957. This investment was mostly British and Australian and tended to concentrate in larger concerns and, in manufacturing, in the more capital-intensive industries.[102]

The government influenced the direction of private enterprise in many other ways alongside direct controls. The country's pastoral exports were the main source of foreign exchange, and although the National Party enjoyed very substantial support from farmers, there was little disagreement between the parties that farming should increase its efficiency and output. Between 1949 and 1957 the area of land under cultivation decreased very slightly (from 20.2m acres to just over 20m acres) but farm production volumes increased significantly. The number of sheep increased by almost half. The output of wool increased by a third, and butterfat and meat production each increased by a fifth.[103]

State support for farming took many forms in addition to tax and depreciation allowances for machinery and development. Publicly funded scientific research expanded during the 1950s in the two agricultural colleges, the Department of Agriculture, and the Department of Scientific and Industrial Research, a commitment 'reflected in the development of improved and higher yielding varieties of plants, in their more effective handling'. Mineral deficiencies in soils had been identified and treated. Cereal diseases had been eliminated. Many 'serious insect pests have been brought under control'. New pasture crops and management, including 'the use of chemical sprays, have done much to control the noxious weeds that [once] seriously reduced farm production'.[104] All this effort was reinforced by the producer boards – the Wool Board, the Meat Board and the Dairy Board were the dominant ones – which were funded by levies on producers, were involved in marketing and development, and enjoyed statutory recognition and preferential interest rates at the Reserve Bank.[105] In addition to the considerable public scientific effort, the air force had experimented with aerial topdressing in 1948. Private aviators took up the opportunity with enthusiasm, and a decade later, of the 9.2m acres of grassland that had been top-dressed, four million had been done from the air. This was an increase from only 5.7 million acres top-dressed in 1949.[106]

The approach to guaranteed prices, or export price stabilisation, changed in subtle but important ways. After 1950 farmers felt that industry reserve accounts, which were jointly overseen by government and producer organisations, could get too large and that it would be better as a rule to pay out in full and allow individual farmers to develop their businesses as they saw fit. Although the contrast with Labour's regime was most evident in the dairy sector (where, in 1956, amending legislation removed the reference to ensuring a reasonable standard of living for farmers), the general principles came to apply to all farm exports. Price support remained an important consideration, but the reserve accounts were also expected to contribute to the development of the sector.[107]

Few other industries were the beneficiaries of such close and detailed support as farming. This is not to say that National was indifferent to industrial development, or that the party believed that the whole economy amounted to processed grass. Generally, National ministers, and most officials, assumed that industrial growth would service domestic consumers and substitute for imports rather than diversify exports. In general, National ministers relied on price, import and capital issues controls rather than the more detailed approach to industrial development allowed by the 1936 Industrial Efficiency Act. By 1957 the Act had been repealed and only three industries remained licensed: pulp and paper, paua shell for sale, and tyres and tubes.[108] Yet the government's spending decisions, and particularly its commitment to infrastructure development, had major implications for the building industry and its suppliers, and enterprises in these sectors prospered considerably during the decade.

Housing was a major spending item, even if National had a greater preference for private-sector housing than Labour. Following a review by an ad-hoc committee, Housing became a separate Cabinet portfolio in 1953 and the first Minister, William Sullivan, made it plain that the government had 'discard[ed] the belief that the housing problem can be satisfactorily overcome by building vast numbers of State houses. Encouragement of private building appeals as more likely to provide a sensible and permanent solution'.[109] Mindful, however, that banks would usually only advance two thirds of a house price, Sullivan announced a Mortgage Guarantee Scheme: State Advances would underwrite the difference so that private lenders could advance 90 per cent up to the then reasonably modest price of £2200. As Sullivan noted, people who could afford £2000 were not rich but did not meet the criteria for a state house. In addition, State Advances lent directly to many individuals under National, with the total in housing loans increasing from less than £500,000 in 1950 to £7.8m in 1955. Spending on state house building dived from £7.1m in 1950 to £4.3m in 1952, and then increased to £6.3m in 1954.[110]

Even more significantly, the housing committee had recommended, and Sullivan introduced, a Group Building Scheme. A builder who wished to construct a group of houses registered with State Advances. That office would approve the plans and assist the builder to get bank finance. The builder was at liberty to sell the houses on the open market, and the government undertook to purchase any that were unsold.[111] Unsurprisingly, the scheme proved popular among builders; it was a one-way bet (Sullivan himself was a substantial building contractor).[112] Labour's state housing model was equally beneficial for large construction firms, as 'the government cheque arrived each month according to a negotiated schedule'.[113] Whatever form it took, the considerable public spending on housing underpinned the fortunes of the construction industries.

While much National support for industry did not take the form of direct involvement, there was one significant exception. The 1952 Commonwealth Economic Conference had encouraged Sterling Area countries to diversify their economies, and particularly to expand export markets and commodities. This directly encouraged the New Zealand government in its ambitious plans for a pulp and paper industry, a matter that has been discussed by a number of scholars.[114] Governments, the Forest Service, and Industries and Commerce had all been considering a pulp and paper industry since the late 1930s, and by the 1950s many of the radiata forests were nearly ready for harvesting. A new company, Tasman Pulp and Paper, included a major state shareholding along with British interests and the leading New Zealand construction firm Fletcher; Tasman was granted a monopoly of the New Zealand newsprint market until 1960. There were clear reasons for state investment, particularly to encourage industrial transformation based on processing indigenous raw materials and to develop a more diversified range of export commodities and new export markets.[115] Although some scholars have been sceptical, Astrid Baker has emphasised the development's importance, not only in encouraging industrialisation but also in prompting closer engagement with United States and Australian sources of finance, machinery, and markets. The development 'marked an important step in New Zealand's economic disengagement from Britain'.[116]

Towards the Reorientation of Trade Policy

'Economic disengagement from Britain' was inevitable, and the signs were evident much earlier than is sometimes appreciated.[117] In 1952 the British guaranteed unrestricted access for New Zealand meat until 1967. Consequently, the New Zealand government was optimistic that 'long-term market prospects for our primary products overseas seem sufficiently strong to support an intensive effort to increase production in New Zealand'.[118] This was illusory, for the British bulk purchase agreement expired in 1954, and thereafter New Zealand's position steadily worsened.[119] New Zealand was increasingly competing in the British market with producers in South America, continental Europe, and Ireland. The British government was also committed to significantly expanding domestic food production and reducing dependence on food imports, an understandable desire after the Battle of the Atlantic, if not appreciated in New Zealand.

Despite the sentimental gush about the British connection in which newspaper editors and Sid Holland traded, some commentators and officials had expressed concern about the British market before 1954. Edward Greensmith, as we have seen, had been particularly concerned; he succeeded Ashwin as Secretary to the Treasury in 1955 and warned in 1956 that manufacturing would have to expand to employ the growing population, and primary export earnings would have to increase in order to pay for the required imports of capital goods and raw materials. That meant new markets would have to be developed, which in turn would require a review of domestic protection in order to facilitate bilateral trade agreements.[120] At the same time the Minister of Agriculture, Keith Holyoake, was emerging as the near-certain successor to Holland, a succession that could not be long delayed (it took place 10 weeks before the 1957 election). Holyoake, steeped in farming politics and a shrewd and practical minister, was ahead of most of his colleagues in grasping that the trading environment was changing irreversibly. Ministers of Industries and Commerce and their officials tended to be pessimistic about the possibility of diversifying into new markets or commodities.[121]

Australian and New Zealand ministers were experiencing increasing 'disenchantment . . . with the Commonwealth economic network. . . . [and] decided to seek the revision of the Ottawa Agreements', reducing preferences for British imports while maintaining guarantees for their own exports.[122] Australia led off in June 1956, and New Zealand ministers soon followed, with Watts visiting Britain in October 1956.[123] Trade negotiations necessarily involved the producer organisations, but Greensmith thought these had little idea of the situation and

Watts and Holyoake felt that they got little useful advice from those sources.[124] The Dairy Products Marketing Commission maintained that 'the United Kingdom is and will remain our principal market for dairy products and assured right of free entry . . . is of fundamental importance'.[125] J. D. Ormond, a Hawkes Bay sheep farmer and Meat Board chairman, told ministers that even with increased Argentinian and Australian production, 'New Zealand had a right to the British market and, in fact, should claim a greater percentage than was talked of in the old days. . . . they should have it out with the British Government as to where they stood. New Zealand had increased production terrifically'. Ormond thought New Zealand was in a strong position because of 'racial affinity', British consumers' liking for sheepmeat, and because Britain was the only large importer of meat in the world.[126] A frustrated Holyoake observed that the producers apparently expected the government to 'tell the people in London the story with all the embellishments, and say that it was in the spirit of Ottawa that they had come. . . . insist[ing] now that the spirit of Ottawa which postulated an expanding market for New Zealand for all primary produce at remunerative prices must be ensured'. Holyoake's sarcasm was lost on his audience; one prominent Canterbury farmer 'thought the Minister had expressed what was in their minds, except perhaps that their thinking was not perhaps quite as loose as his'.[127]

Early in 1957, Holyoake and Watts told the producer organisations to work out what exactly they wanted. The ministers felt that the producers were unable or unwilling to move beyond making speeches about what the British owed New Zealand.[128] Within the civil service, too, there were divisions: Treasury, and now Industries and Commerce, favoured a carefully developed and comprehensive approach, whereas Agriculture (contrary to Holyoake's approach) tended to echo producer views.[129] Ormond's attitude – that the 'New Zealand Trade Mission to the United Kingdom had a straightforward question to ask and that was whether the Commonwealth or the foreigner was going to take the meat market' – was hardly helpful.[130] Holyoake led the New Zealand delegation to London in April 1957. His opening statement was restrained, stressing New Zealand's economic dependence and commitment to the Sterling Area in the early postwar years, which had deeply affected the pattern of trade.[131] Understandably, the swiftness with which the British had changed the rules provoked considerable annoyance in New Zealand. New Zealand's problem was that even if unrestricted access to the British market continued, the British would be unlikely to give guarantees about market share. Most importantly, New Zealand wanted revision of Ottawa preferences for British goods in the New Zealand market so that New Zealand could develop bilateral trade agreements elsewhere.[132] The eventual agreement secured free dairy and pork access (with no guarantee on price) on the same basis as sheep meat and beef until 1967, annual consultations on trade and agricultural policy, and consideration of remedial action if New Zealand's meat position was seriously threatened. This was more than might have been expected, but it was conditional on New Zealand not immediately revising tariff preferences for British goods, which Holyoake had threatened to do.[133]

Britain was now quite unwilling to guarantee New Zealand's position, and Holyoake became highly critical of Ottawa, not least because New Zealand preferences for British imports into New Zealand were based on value, so the British position was inflation-proofed, whereas the protection for New Zealand in the British market was largely quantitative, and thus not protected against price fluctuations.[134] There was now disenchantment with the British economic relationship at the highest levels of the New Zealand government, but New Zealand was in a weak bargaining position. It was easy enough to talk of finding new markets, but developing them would take time and effort. Privately, New Zealand officials' assessments of alternative potential markets were not optimistic. The Ministry of Agriculture saw some scope in Italy, the Federal Republic of Germany, and Japan. Little information was available on the Soviet Union, and the ministry felt that there were political obstacles to developing much trade with Eastern Europe.[135] For all that, there was a growing awareness of the 'urgent need to diversify our trade' and, as the Minister of Industries and Commerce put it, that 'our manufacturers must begin to think in terms of exporting'.[136] The old settler economy was changing irreversibly.

Conclusion

Managing the settler economy in the 1950s was not straightforward. The National government had accepted the principal elements of Keynesian management, as most other western conservative parties had done, and this was undoubtedly the key to its long-run political success. Yet there was much more to National's approach than electoral calculation. In accepting the managed economy, National was accepting the conventional wisdom of the day. As Jack Watts put it in 1954, 'Think how different was the period following the first World War from the years which have followed the second. This time there has been no world-wide pestilence or vast trade convulsions. Disease has been checked by new medical discoveries and Governments have learned to manage their economies'.[137] Certainly,

National tilted towards private enterprise in some matters, and liberalised and deregulated in others. This was within the boundaries of the postwar settlement, although arguably National sought to shut down more radical versions of the settlement through the industrial confrontation of 1951. National accepted full employment, not least because manufacturers, traders and farmers benefited along with workers, although it had become evident before 1949 that there was no shortage of jobs. If the settler economy was to change and diversify, infrastructure had to be developed, and that required high public spending. If development shaped opportunities for private enterprise, it was also a source of inflationary pressure, as was full employment more generally. Until 1955, with the exception of the Korean bust, primary exports generally sustained infrastructure development, a rapidly growing population, importing and manufacturing.

The British connection remained utterly problematic. In 1951 and 1952, the British again forced constraint on New Zealand importing because of British balance of payments problems. After 1954, the British market could not be taken for granted and some ministers and officials realised this before the National government lost office. External dependence remained the most important constraint on New Zealand economic policy. When National lost office in November 1957, export prices had been falling for well over a year. Labour came to power just as a balance of payments crisis broke, and although Labour would be in office for only a single term, the crisis would provoke a significant modification of the parameters of economic policy in the direction of more diverse development.

Chapter 5

Transition 1958–66

The decade from 1957 was one of rapid social and economic change. The weakening of the British market after the end of bulk purchasing in 1954 and the balance of payments crisis in 1957 prompted much reflection about the fragility of the settler economy. While the Holland government had overseen a consolidation, the decade after 1957 was one of cautious transition towards a more diverse, modern economy.

The Labour government, elected at the end of 1957, dealt with a short, sharp downturn and sought to expand industry and diversify exporting. National defeated Labour at the end of 1960, and continued with much of Labour's approach, although National tilted somewhat more to consumption and somewhat less to restraint. The Treasury's dominant position in economic advice was increasingly complemented by the Reserve Bank and a more assertive Department of Industries and Commerce. The 1957–58 crisis provoked intensified import and exchange controls, but the longer-term response was an increased focus on industrial development. As the British market weakened and British membership of the European Economic Community seemed increasingly likely, trade policy became even more important. There were a number of new trade agreements, notably the 1965 trade agreement with Australia. Industry policy increasingly emphasised developing manufactured exports alongside pastoral, the language of growth supplanted that of stability, and growth increasingly became a matter for public discussion.

In many ways the first half of the 1960s seemed a continuation of the 1950s. The population continued to grow fast, increasing by 20 per cent, to 2.7 million between 1957 and 1966. Eighty per cent of the growth was due to natural increase; while immigration remained high, it contributed a fifth of the population increase rather than a quarter, as it had between 1949 and 1957. Māori, who were counted as 6 per cent of the population in 1957, accounted for 15 per cent of the natural increase. While immigrants continued to be predominantly British, increasing numbers began to arrive from tropical Polynesia and with the increasing number of Māori, a more diverse population was foreshadowed. As it had been in the earlier 1950s, the population was relatively young. Although the birth-rate was falling (significantly so for Māori), marriage was occurring at younger ages. In the second half of the 1950s, 43 per cent of men and 68 per cent of women who married were under 25. In 1966 the proportions were 59 per cent of men and 78 per cent of women, and 45 per cent of women who married in that year were under 21. High marriage rates meant rapid growth of urban areas; in 1966 nearly two thirds of the population lived in the 18 largest urban areas; what was particularly notable was the very rapid movement by Māori into urban areas over the decade from 1956.

Changes in the workforce reflected continuing urbanisation, and women, who had accounted for 24 per cent of the paid workforce in 1957, comprised 27 per cent in 1966. Primary sector employment continued to decline, from 17 per cent to 13 per cent of all workers, even as farm production kept rising. Adminstrative and professional occupations increased slightly and became significantly more female, with proportionally three times as many women as men in such positions. Whereas building and construction had increased as a proportion of the workforce during the earlier 1950s, the sector's share remained stable from the late 1950s. Manufacturing increased from 25 to 27 per cent, but the increase reflected a greater proportion of men in such occupations.

In the decade after 1957, then, employment, consumption and population growth all remained high and for much of that decade export earnings sustained the growth. The basic elements of the postwar settlement, including transfer payments, publicly funded social services and full employment, were maintained and to a degree expanded. These strong continuities in domestic policy perhaps obscured the fundamental changes that were occurring in the structure of the settler economy.

The Nash Government

Walter Nash led the Labour Party to victory at the end of 1957. Although the party won 48 per cent of the popular vote, it accumulated most of its support in already safe Labour electorates, and its parliamentary majority was only two (one, after appointing a Speaker). Nash was two months short of his 76th birthday when he became Prime Minister. There was a high level of public affection for him, but his best political days were in the past. His inability to move paper, always notorious, became even more pronounced. As Prime Minister, he took more pleasure in the grand themes of foreign affairs than in domestic issues and did not provide the active and strategic leadership that the government needed. Arnold Nordmeyer, the Minister of Finance, was the dominant figure in Cabinet and had the principal responsibility for dealing with the serious decline in the balance of payments while delivering Labour's social policies and avoiding unemployment.

Nash had distributed the promises during the election campaign with enthusiasm and without much co-ordination with Nordmeyer.[1] Labour's promises included a significant expansion of the welfare state, increased pensions, housing loans at the concessionary rate of three per cent, and allowing families to capitalise – that is, to anticipate – their family benefit up to £1000 (about $45,000 in 2012 values) for housing. Labour had now accepted National's state funding of private house ownership and sought to extend it. Pay As You Earn (PAYE) for income tax was imminent; since the existing system required payment at the end of the tax year, taxpayers would have to be compensated for effectively being taxed twice. Both parties promised rebates; Labour's maximum of £100 became a notorious symbol of election-year auctions, even though National's proposal was more expensive.[2] To the stock question of how these and other initiatives would be funded without increasing taxation, Nash responded with blithe optimism.[3]

Although both parties maintained a commitment to the welfare state and the managed economy, it would be unwise to overstate the degree of consensus. Where National appealed to economic individualism and consumerism, Labour was if anything even more influenced by Christian Socialism than in 1935. Nordmeyer explained that the Labour Party:

> regards the development of a decent and just social order as the expression of that command 'Love thy neighbour as thyself'. It believes service is more important than self-seeking; that the profit motive is not the chief driving force in the hearts of men. . . . It repudiates the notion that the search for dividends and the desire for profit is the proper end of man. It denies that private enterprise will of itself ensure equity and fairness for the community as a whole. It believes that man is something more than a cog in the industrial machine. It believes that he can contribute his best efforts only as he is given an increasingly effective voice in the determining of the conditions under which he works and lives. It believes that extreme poverty and extreme wealth are alike indefensible.[4]

The state had an essential role in ensuring 'equity and fairness' and also in co-ordinating economic growth for the long-term, even if this required short-term restraint. 'More rapid economic growth could be accomplished if our rate of capital formation were raised. The rate of capital investment is still less than in a number of other countries. A prerequisite for a higher level of investment would be a willingness on the part of the community to save more and consume less of our rising national income.' Yet the public works of the 1940s and 50s were about to pay off; there was now 'a sound structural basis for accelerated expansion of directly productive plant, buildings and capital equipment in the years ahead.'[5] Nordmeyer, therefore, was giving more emphasis to economic growth, and moving beyond the agenda of 1938.

The upper levels of the public service changed too. Bernard Ashwin had retired from Treasury in the middle of 1955. His successor as Secretary, Edward Greensmith, is regarded as less dynamic than Ashwin, less successful as a bureaucratic warrior and 'Ashwin's departure may therefore have enhanced the influence of the Reserve Bank', which under its Governor, E. C. Fussell, 'saw its ambit reaching well beyond monetary policy'.[6] The Bank generally agreed with Treasury on the merits of fiscal and monetary restraint. It believed more strongly than Treasury that infrastructure should be funded by overseas borrowing. From 1958, too, Greensmith was complemented by Henry Lang, the Treasury's chief research officer, who had returned from a three year posting in London. Lang's thinking would become increasingly influential, particularly in advocating a less insulated economy and a more diverse export strategy. Lang's 'was a cosmopolitan world in which nations succeeded by engagement, rather than avoidance'.[7] If Greensmith was self-effacing, no one ever said that of W. B. Sutch, Secretary of Industries and Commerce from 1958, who immediately set out to establish his department as a quasi-Ministry of Economic Affairs.

Early in December 1957, as soon as the new government had been sworn in, Greensmith reviewed the public finances. Treasury expected a budget deficit of £24m (and had earlier calculated that Labour's proposals to increase universal superannuation and the family benefit would cost about £20m).[8] Overseas reserves were dangerously low.

> Another 'post-Korea boom' can hardly be counted upon and any return to a satisfactory situation must therefore be more gradual. Immediate and firm corrective measures to repress demand for imports are needed if there is to be the requisite early and significant reversal of trends and if the fears, leakages and losses arising from a weak exchange situation are to be avoided.[9]

Spending had to be reduced and revenue increased, but 'on a broad front and over a moderate period' so as to avoid shocks. Treasury therefore suggested making more use of internal loans, reducing immigration, stabilising or reducing development programmes, increasing rail and postal charges, and rigorously reviewing expenditure.[10] Imports needed to be reduced by about £30m, which was 'difficult, but not impossible' to do without threatening employment.[11]

On 1 January 1958 Nash announced emergency measures, revising the import licensing schedule to prioritise imports of food, machinery and raw materials and restricting all other imports by allocating a fixed sum of foreign exchange to each tariff item.[12] The government borrowed £45m from Australia, Britain and the United States, a step that went against the grain for Nordmeyer.[13] Most newspapers accepted that some severe measures were necessary and that import control was the best or only option.[14] In the event, the January measures were only a stopgap. The Minister of Industries and Commerce would soon warn his colleagues that if the trend continued, New Zealand was facing default on import payments.[15] In March Greensmith advised that the situation had worsened, and that action should be 'adequate and rigorous rather than lenient or chance-taking'. Greensmith suggested that the government could immediately increase its own charges and make 'rigorous' economies in expenditure. Taxes should be increased, particularly on tobacco, alcohol, gambling and new cars.[16] Greensmith assumed that these taxes would not lower consumption of tobacco, beer and gambling, but that they would reduce demand for new cars and spirits. The overall effect would be to double the revenue from all these sources, reduce imports, and if the new taxes could direct import spending towards capital goods for industrial development, so much the better.[17] The Reserve Bank thought there was no alternative, short of heavy borrowing, to significantly reducing consumption.[18]

With increasingly pessimistic advice, the framework for Nordmeyer's first Budget was laid out. It would forever after be known as the Black Budget.[19] Nordmeyer wrote the Budget himself, but there are conflicting accounts of whether Treasury expected some of its advice to be rejected and therefore overbid in order to get what it really wanted, or advised only what it believed to be necessary.[20] Henry Lang recalled that Treasury overbid and were horrified when Nordmeyer accepted all the recommendations; McKinnon suggests that while that may have been true 'the figures . . . left little room for choice'. The market for farm exports was slowing as world stockpiles grew. The current account was in deficit by nearly £40m for the year to March 1958, having been barely in credit for the previous year and in deficit by £16.5m in 1956.[21]

Nordmeyer intended to 'ensure that any reduction in living standards arising from lower overseas prices for our exports is spread fairly throughout the community without hardship or unemployment'.[22] As he noted, before 1936 a fall in export earnings had been matched by a fall in imports simply because farmers spent less and the banks adopted tighter lending policies. While that worked to maintain the external balance over the medium term, 'Governments are no longer willing to suffer the fluctuations in employment, business activity, and living standards that used to arise from the free interplay of economic forces'.[23] The Budget increased consumption taxes as Treasury had recommended and tightened hire-purchase requirements; the intention was not only to deter imports and raise revenue but also to avoid inflation by reducing domestic spending power in line with reduced imports. The government's family-oriented approach to social policy meant decreased tax exemptions for single taxpayers and increased exemptions for dependent wives, and the family benefit was increased by 50 per cent. These measures were also intended to substitute for wage increases, relieving employers of increased costs, but they necessarily meant increased taxes.[24] However, Labour had been explicitly committed to greater redistribution by transfer payments in any case. By 1960, age and superannuation benefits taken together increased by a quarter (age benefits had been income-tested since 1938 whereas superannuation was universal; spending on the latter had more than doubled). Family benefit payouts increased by half, and the new provision for capitalising that benefit for housing costs was widely taken up.

Nordmeyer maintained that the economic problems were entrenched and long-term. The balance of payments crisis demonstrated that 'over a long period of time New Zealand has been living beyond her means'.[25] While full employment and high demand made balance of payments difficulties more likely, this was compounded by the expectation that the terms of trade for agricultural products would continue to worsen. New Zealand's economy would have to diversify, and that meant continued spending on development. Nordmeyer and Treasury were unwilling to borrow for development, and that meant having to 'choose more carefully between current consumption and the provision of capital assets'.[26]

Where to strike that balance was a matter of economic and political judgement. Even conservative newspapers admitted that 'New Zealand cannot live for ever on borrowed money'.[27] Treasury continued to warn of the 'low level of reserves and the sheer impossibility of correctly estimating export prices a year ahead' and feared that premature relaxation could mean a much worse crash.[28] The import allocations for 1959 were even tighter than 1958. Nordmeyer, Treasury, the Reserve Bank and W. B. Sutch, the new Secretary of Industries and Commerce, all agreed on the need to build a large reserve of overseas funds so that import allocations could be more stable. However, Sutch's minister

Philip Holloway and the departments of Statistics and Customs thought the existing allocations were far too tight.[29] Export prices recovered in 1959, not least because the British budget was decidedly expansionist, but given the government's industrial and infrastructural development priorities, Nordmeyer argued for continued restraint and a priority for investment, while easing fiscal and import policy, especially in 1960.[30]

The 1958 crisis had dominated the second Labour government's term, although it served to reinforce Nordmeyer's inclinations towards longer-term planning and gave teeth to commonplace rhetoric about deferring consumption in favour of investment. The government also extended social provisions, expanded transfer payments, and taxed accordingly. Nordmeyer has received high marks from some scholars for 'courage and responsibility', but the Labour government never recovered from the Black Budget.[31] With a compliant press, Keith Holyoake was easily able to portray Labour as a party of austerity and, in light of the generous promises of 1957, of irresponsibility, and Labour lost the election in November 1960.

The Second National Government

Holyoake is now regarded as one of New Zealand's more effective Prime Ministers. He had been a successful Minister of Agriculture during the 1950s and grasped the realities of the British market before most farmers did; like Nordmeyer, therefore, he sought to diversify trade and the economic structure. Holyoake's approach to economic management emphasised farming as the main export industry, encouraging private enterprise, restraint in public spending, and balancing competing sector interests through informal negotiation. He recognised the inevitability of change but sought to manage crises and change quietly, often piecemeal rather than in dramatic Budgets, so that the voters were reassured rather than challenged.[32]

Holyoake's choice of Minister of Finance indicated that he would keep the real oversight of economic policy himself. Harry Lake, a Christchurch accountant, was likeable, unambitious and capable. In appointing Lake, Holyoake over-rode the claims of a more senior minister, the combative and talented Marlborough farmer Tom Shand, who became Minister of Labour. The other major economic portfolio, Industries and Commerce, went with the newly enlarged portfolio of Overseas Trade to the Deputy Prime Minister, John Marshall, who had under Holland earned a reputation as an authoritarian conservative. During the 1960s a more urbane and cultured Gentleman Jack emerged, and he travelled the world tirelessly, arguing New Zealand's case for special consideration with current and prospective members of the Common Market and developing new markets for New Zealand exports.[33]

The new government, like its predecessor, was met by a balance of payments crisis, a more sudden one than in 1957. Nordmeyer's biographer suggests that the import spending was on capital goods and raw materials for industry rather than consumer goods.[34] Nordmeyer also maintained that the fall in overseas reserves had been sudden and unexpected, although he and his colleagues had no doubt had an eye on the election during 1960.[35] Surpluses of £26.4m and £11.8m in the years to March 1959 and 1960, respectively, had been replaced by a deficit of £47.5m. While the figures were worse than had been expected, the situation was 'not critical but difficult'. Overseas reserves were higher than in 1957, but export prices and internal inflation were relatively worse. Holyoake, mindful of what had just won him the election, was not inclined to a dramatic Budget. The Reserve Bank advocated reducing demand through a credit squeeze and tax increases, but advised care so as not to depress confidence or reduce businesses' plans for expansion.[36] Treasury, too, supported gradual adjustment rather than shocks. 'Policy should be smooth but very firm in its application and inflation should be curbed as soon as evidence of it is seen'. Tightening and liberalisation should both be applied cautiously and gradually.[37] Implicitly, Greensmith admitted that the 1958 Budget and his own advice had been too severe.

The 1961 Budget was a muted copy of 1958. Lake increased Government charges and tightened rules for consumer borrowing, but Holyoake professed himself 'determined to avoid the panic measures and crash tactics of three years ago' even while heavily reducing import allocations.[38] It is difficult to avoid the conclusion that the newspapers gave Holyoake a much easier time than they had allowed Nordmeyer. Restraint continued in 1962, with both Treasury and the Reserve Bank warning against premature relaxation.[39] The world economy grew more rapidly in 1963, and New Zealand's current account improved with high wool prices. Treasury and the Reserve Bank continued to argue that investment rather than consumption should be encouraged.[40] The Reserve Bank advised frankly that the 'opportunity to escape the three-year "stop-go" cycle that has plagued the economy in recent years, and inhibited long-term policy formation, is sufficient reason in itself for a firm approach to budgetary policy in 1963/64'.[41] Perhaps such advice influenced Holyoake's approach to transfer payments; while not revoking the increases that Nordmeyer had made, the National government did not greatly increase such spending. The government's major election-year sweetener was allowing more car imports and making some income and estate tax concessions.[42]

Holyoake calculated, correctly, that with its own comfortable majority and the fact that Nordmeyer was the Labour Party's new leader, the government could afford to be reasonably relaxed about the election and, indeed, the result reflected little shift in political opinion.

A consequence of Holyoake's own preference for undramatic policymaking was the government encouraging more public discussion around economic issues. In 1961 the government established a small, quasi-independent advisory group, the Monetary and Economic Council, chaired by a rising young university economist, Frank Holmes. The Council's regular public reports generally reflected the orthodoxy of the day and, indeed, echoed Treasury advice to successive ministers.[43] The first report recommended greater stability rather than 'unnecessarily abrupt changes in national expenditure' in a short cycle, in which boom was almost as bad as bust.[44] The Council thought that poor public understanding contributed to expansive electioneering and 'triennial elections have, not surprisingly, been a source of triennial economic crises'.[45] At the same time, though, there was little room for significant cuts in public spending: education was important for a skilled workforce, foreign affairs for trade promotion, capital expenditure for development, and subsidies for keeping prices down.[46] Consumption should be restrained in the interest of saving and investment, and importing should prioritise capital goods and raw materials so that industrial development would provide commodities that would be 'efficient substitutes for imports or earn more overseas exchange'.[47] None of this would have been particularly uncongenial advice, but official advice was confidential and the Council's reports contributed to greater public discussion of economic issues in a period of transition.

Industrial Development

Balance of payments crises in 1957–58 and 1961 were sharp reminders of a settler economy's fragility and, with the evident problems in the British market, influenced industry policy. Industrial development, trade development and shaping a public consensus around growth were closely related over the decade after 1957 and beyond. None of this was uncontentious. The interest groups – farmers, manufacturers and retailers – had conflicting agendas, and within the public service, Treasury's views contrasted with those of Industries and Commerce. Labour and National had a degree of common ground in encouraging manufacturing, but the parties differed in important respects.

Manufacturing had grown significantly since 1940, and Labour ministers in particular had emphasised the importance of export diversification. The novelty of developments after 1957 can be exaggerated. Much of the exaggeration is due to the continuing influence, in the literature, of W. B. Sutch, who became Secretary of Industries and Commerce in 1958. Sutch's extensive writings indicated that industrial development had hardly been thought of until that date, and that the entire political and economic elite had complacently accepted a colonial economy based upon the export of processed grass to the United Kingdom. In his account, the 1957–58 balance of payments crisis prompted the Labour government to suddenly accept the virtues of crash industrialisation, and 'for the first time in New Zealand's history, the government set about actively developing a somewhat broader industrial base'.[48]

There have been few critical assessments of Sutch's thought. Much of Brian Easton's account highlights Sutch's relative orthodoxy and his insistence that social and economic development went together, and he defends Sutch against posthumous suggestions by certain National politicians that he was a Marxist or worse.[49] A. M. Endres has shown the extent to which Sutch's thinking evolved. In the late 1930s Sutch shared Nash's hope that trade agreements with Britain would allow room for domestic industrial development. In his thinking about development Sutch came to espouse the view, associated with the Argentine economist Raúl Prebisch, that relying on primary produce exports trapped a peripheral country in declining terms of trade, and that industrialisation was required for import substitution and foreign exchange savings. Only after 1960 did Sutch emphasise 'manufacturing in depth': a much more extensive processing of exports. From then, too, he became an increasingly strident critic of economic colonialism and its collaborators.[50]

Sutch was an articulate exponent of the policy of industrial development, but he did not invent it. It was hardly news in 1957 that the 'agriculture and service sectors would not grow sufficiently to maintain full employment'.[51] Nash had said as much more than 20 years previously, and it remained a consistent theme in Labour Party thinking. Similarly, Sutch did not invent the idea of 'manufacturing in depth'; Dan Sullivan and Nordmeyer had been thinking in those terms in the 1940s. The Holland government had overseen major developments in pulp and paper – surely that counted as 'manufacturing in depth'– and National's interest in developing a steel industry is often forgotten. Sutch's 'view on industrialisation to 1960 was unsophisticated particularly in overstressing import substitution'.[52] When he did advocate for export-oriented industrialisation, he was hardly alone, but, as we shall see, his views on that question could be thoroughly contrary, even perverse. Where he was 'right and original' was in emphasising the high skill-level of New Zealand workers and the importance of developing that asset so that exports could compete on quality not bulk – what in later jargon would be called a 'knowledge economy'.[53]

The Labour government's industry policy was driven by Nordmeyer and the Minister for Industries and Commerce, Philip Holloway, who had had a varied career in business and risen to Cabinet, aged 40, after only three years in Parliament. Given the crisis atmosphere of 1958, Holloway was rather overshadowed by Nordmeyer, who had held the portfolio himself at the end of the 1940s.[54] Holloway was a committed moderniser who supported rationalising plant and production for greater efficiency, technological development, continuous training for skilled workers, and import selection not merely to defend the balance of payments but also to encourage local manufacturing. He saw a protected domestic base as essential to developing manufactured exports, and appointing overseas trade commissioners as essential to finding markets.[55] After 1960 John Marshall held the portfolio. He shared many of Holloway's views, although he preferred to gradually reduce import controls, which the government did steadily and unspectacularly. Marshall stressed ministerial encouragement, 'bringing . . . manufacturers kicking and squealing into a new era of competitive, export-oriented private enterprise'.[56]

If Labour and National differed in degree on import controls, they agreed on liberalising conditions for investment. Nordmeyer largely abolished capital issues controls in 1960. All that remained were ceilings on the level of interest that could be offered and requirements for approval where overseas capital was involved or where the sum involved exceeded £10,000 and was intended to finance business in hire purchase or credit sales.[57] Lake removed almost all the remainder in 1962. Nordmeyer provided more generous depreciation allowances on machinery, and Holyoake and Lake extended Nordmeyer's allowances. Believing that pastoral production needed to expand further, National also extended tax allowances for farm development and reduced gift and estate duties, seen by farmers as a disincentive to expansion.[58]

As farming continued to expand output, so did the urban economy grow and diversify. Between 1960 and 1967 the number of companies listed on the stock exchange grew by more than a quarter (this of course included retail, distribution, financial services and other non-manufacturing enterprise). There was particular growth in food processing, metal and plastic manufacturing, chemicals, clothing and household wares, with an enthusiastic wave of mergers and takeovers in the first half of the decade, and the stock market embarked on a long bull-run. Foreign investment had much to do with the acquisition of new technology, but locally owned enterprises also actively sought licensing agreements for overseas technology.[59]

Development continued to require extensive borrowing. Before 1957 this had been through domestic and British loans, but thereafter it became harder to source loans in London, partly as British officials came to feel that investment funds were needed at home. Tentative forays onto the New York market in the mid 1950s had been expensive.[60] Fraser and Nash had procrastinated on joining the International Monetary Fund and the World Bank in 1946, but the question was revived in the late 1950s. While some National politicians had vociferously opposed joining in the 1940s, 'conservative opinion . . . had now moved decisively towards an international rather than an Empire framework for capitalism and finance'.[61] In 1961 the National government joined both organisations.

The application became controversial. Critics, many presenting a left-wing nationalist argument, claimed that the IMF would dictate New Zealand policy and impose unemployment. The socialist economist Wolfgang Rosenberg was particularly trenchant and pointed out that the IMF had pushed 'an iron austerity' on Peru in 1959–60. Rosenberg warned that the IMF would expect balanced budgets as a general rule, thus undermining the Keynesian approach of deficit spending during recession. Similarly, the IMF disliked exchange and import controls, which Rosenberg, like many in New Zealand, believed essential to maintaining full employment.[62] Harry Lake naturally emphasised the advantages of loans to cover temporary balance of payments difficulties and encourage development, and he maintained that there was little evidence of major powers dictating the IMF agenda.[63] Nash's early enthusiasm for Bretton Woods had been replaced by his party's scepticism of foreign, and particularly American, money (not that he had refrained from borrowing dollars in 1958).[64] Many Labour members shared Rosenberg's concern and the party demanded a referendum.[65] Yet there was a touch of naïvety in some Labour rhetoric. The future leader, Norman Kirk, thought that without the IMF, 'over the years New Zealand has built up a social order which is unique'. The price of abolishing unemployment and achieving economic security had been 'a problem of balance of payments. I would sooner have every year a balance of payments problem than an unemployment problem', he said, blissfully unaware that by following that course he might get both before very long.[66] Nordmeyer's speech was strangely muted; perhaps he privately supported accession or at least believed the risks were worth it.[67]

Early IMF and World Bank reports caused the government little discomfort. An IMF mission in 1962 reinforced Treasury and Reserve

Bank advice on the importance of avoiding swings in economic policy and investment rather than consumption and accepted that full employment should remain a priority. With the exceptions of quantitative import controls and exchange controls, the mission did not think that the New Zealand economy was excessively controlled given its circumstances.[68] Yet those exceptions were precisely what Rosenberg, among others, had regarded as key to full employment, and while the New Zealand embassy in Washington reported that the IMF regarded its advice as only a guide, if heavy borrowing was contemplated 'it would be advisable if some effort was made to meet the wishes of the Fund'.[69] By 1965, the government would borrow $80m from the World Bank, mostly for electricity and port development.[70]

National and Labour had a measure of agreement on fostering a more diverse economic base through state support for major industrial developments. The parties agreed on technologically sophisticated metal industries, but not on textiles. During 1960 the Labour government became interested in establishing a cotton mill at Nelson as a joint venture between New Zealand, British and American interests. Officials drew the plans up rather hastily in 1960; they were vague on the basis of pricing, which was no small matter given the near-monopoly position envisaged for the mill. Nash's precipitate announcement of the project, in the 1960 election campaign, caused the American partner to withdraw. Clothing manufacturers objected to the prospect of buying a limited range of cloth from a monopoly supplier; textile importers and Federated Farmers (the latter always suspicious of protected industries other than their own) likewise complained vociferously, and after considerable internal debate, the government cancelled the mill and paid compensation to the British partner. Marshall would later recall that the episode was salutary in encouraging the development of more systematic criteria for new industrial projects.[71]

Monopolies were less objectionable in metal refining because of the necessary scale of such industries. Aluminium smelting had been discussed for decades, and in 1960 the Labour government announced a firm plan for a smelter at Bluff. A power station would be built at Lake Manapouri; the smelter's bauxite would be imported and most of the aluminium exported. The initial plan was that the Australian company Comalco would build the power station and the smelter; in 1963 Comalco withdrew from the power station and the National government took over that part of the project, the smelter opening in 1971. Opposition was most intense to the proposal that the lake, in Fiordland National Park, be significantly raised. The resulting campaign, extending over a decade, was a watershed in the modern history of environmental politics. Opponents also criticised the relatively cheap electricity that the government allowed Comalco. A potent mixture of environmentalism and economic nationalism was thus foreshadowed.[72]

Iron and steel had also been talked about for decades, as New Zealand has abundant supplies of ore. A 1920s ironworks at Onekaka, in Golden Bay, did not last in the face of Indian competition. Dan Sullivan, Minister of Industries and Commerce from 1935 to 1947, hoped to develop a national iron and steel industry based on the ironsands on the west coast of the North Island. These however contained titanium, and smelting them required advanced technology. The Department of Scientific and Industrial Research devoted considerable effort to resolving this problem in the 1950s and early 1960s.[73] From the mid 1950s the leading construction firm Fletcher had been interested in seeing a domestic steel industry develop and discussed the matter with ministers in both National and Labour governments.[74] The National government began a cabinet-level investigation in June 1957.[75] In January 1958 Nash and Holloway discussed the matter with the British Prime Minister, Harold Macmillan. The British wanted confirmation that the project was commercially and technically feasible before committing any capital.[76] In the meantime officials and ministers also pursued the development of a merchant-bar mill in South Auckland, recycling local scrap metal. Pacific Steel, developed relatively quickly as a joint venture between Fletcher, British interests and other New Zealand companies, began production in 1962.[77] The Labour government set production and distribution conditions, guaranteed protection and market share, and established an embargo on scrap metal exports, despite some scepticism on the part of Industries and Commerce officials.[78]

The Iron and Steel Industry Act 1959 established a Steel Investigating Company with a 51 per cent state shareholding and the other shares allocated by ministerial decision. In the event, the government's chosen Australian partners withdrew and the investigating company became wholly state-owned. One historian suggests that Holloway and Sutch excluded Fletcher from consideration because they were reluctant to see the company dominate steel as well as pulp and paper.[79] As well as the technical issues of smelting the ironsands, electricity supply was a major consideration, with sufficient power only available in 1965 at the earliest.[80] The major argument for the mill was, as Marshall put it in 1961, saving overseas funds by import substitution, for there was little evidence of potential for exports.[81] Sutch, a strong advocate, argued that a steel mill was similar to the successful forest products industries 'with their high capitalisation, complicated production, demand for technical and managerial skills and use of domestic raw materials'. Sutch would also cite 'studies abroad' of industries contributing to economic maturity. 'At the head of the list of such industries are iron and steel, non-ferrous metals, and paper and paper products in that order'.[82] That was a rather simplistic approach to economic development, implying that one model was universally applicable, although economic thinking was less critical of such approaches then than later.[83]

The Investigating Company reported favourably in December 1962. Based on current prices, New Zealand-produced steel would be competitive if it supplied half the local market; several months later, some Industries and Commerce officials expressed uncertainty about whether that would be achieved. A New Zealand car was constantly talked about but would require major government intervention, particularly by restricting consumer choice in order to ensure viable production runs. There could be demand from the manufacturers of truck chassis, vehicle bodies and forklifts, and from boatbuilders in light of the expansion of fishing, but there was little certainty about the demand for structural steel. New Zealand steel users were at present 'able to draw their iron and steel supplies from world supplies in as much variety as they wished'.[84] A group on the right of the National Party, the Constitutional Society, criticised the government's involvement in 'what is essentially a private undertaking'. Holyoake's reply was blunt: 'If this industry, which measures up so well to the criteria for development, were not allowed to proceed, there would be virtually no case for industrial development of any kind in New Zealand'.[85] The government established a Provisional Board in May 1963 and New Zealand Steel was incorporated in 1965 with a 30 per cent government shareholding, a 20-year monopoly of processing ironsands and a 10-year monopoly of the New Zealand market so far as it could supply that market.[86] The mill began production in 1968.

There was of course much more to industrial development than the high-profile issues of cotton mills, aluminium, iron and steel, and the IMF. In 1960 the Labour government organised an Industrial Development Conference. Nash declared that 'it is time to shift the emphasis from security and stability – we shall take these . . . for granted – and to direct our efforts towards growth'.[87] Sutch's imprint was evident in much of the conference documentation, which stressed diversifying the country's economic structure and heavily committing to import substitution along with in-depth manufacturing.[88] Many of the briefing papers focussed on technological development and productivity growth. Some observers thought that the discussion was 'dominated by the opposing points of view of farming and manufacturing'.[89] Federated Farmers emphasised the importance of their industry, complained about an excessively controlled domestic economy and, indeed, saw little need to develop manufacturing. Given their orientation to exporting, farmers perhaps saw little reason to be concerned about domestic consumption.[90] The Manufacturers Federation thought that industrial development required permanent protection against overseas cheap labour.[91] The Treasury kept a low profile, but Frank Holmes argued that manufacturing growth would be best assisted by 'a framework of appropriate conditions for . . . efficient expansion' particularly including low inflation, and 'a reasonably competitive market in New Zealand [which] implies . . . resistance to claims by domestic industries for excessive protection'.[92] Where farmers wanted import controls reduced to tariffs, manufacturers maintained that would be no protection against cheaper foreign imports, and the resolution attempted to strike a balance by referring to 'a properly designed and adequate tariff, supplemented in special circumstances by import licensing'.[93]

The National government therefore attempted to reconcile the contrasting agendas of farming and manufacturers. Holyoake himself, whose self-description as an 'old farmer' was a considerable asset, accepted the importance of manufacturing while maintaining that farming would be the dominant export industry for many years to come. Farm production continued to grow as it had in the 1950s. In 1963 the government convened an Agricultural Development Conference to consider, in light of fast domestic population growth and the 'likely continued heavy dependence of the economy on . . . farming', what increases in output were desirable and practicable and how to achieve them.[94] The conference – really a small working party – concluded that export prospects to 1972 warranted a target of a two per cent cumulative annual growth rate in pastoral exports and an increase in livestock of more than a third, and by 1967 the targets were being met.

The debates that had dominated the Industrial Development Conference also played out in the Tariff and Development Board, which Parliament unanimously established in 1962. The Board began with a major review of industry policy. Industries and Commerce's observations unsurprisingly reflected Sutch's well-established views in favour of import-substituting heavy industry: steel, copper, motor vehicle components, machine tools, chemicals, and synthetic fabrics. With the partial exception of the timber industries, manufacturing for export was only in principle of equal priority to import-substituting industrialisation.[95] Treasury's paper reflected the department's growing scepticism about import substituting industrialisation, a view which 'stressed the benefits of participation in the international division of labor' and indicated Henry Lang's influence.[96] Industrialisation was not an end in itself, but 'one aspect of the expansion of the total New Zealand economy' and it should emphasise exporting rather than import substitution. 'To base policy on the assumption that we shall not be able to increase exports and that local production should be encouraged almost regardless of cost is not only a policy of despair but it is also doomed to failure. . . . New Zealand cannot be self-sufficient and if it is to prosper it must export'. Protection should be reduced; 'to compensate the New Zealand producer for every individual difference between his cost structure and that of the overseas supplier would be to deny completely the principle of comparative advantage resulting from international specialisation'. New Zealand would do better to leave labour-intensive manufacturing to those countries with plenty of labour, and compete by efficient mechanisation.[97] The Reserve Bank agreed with Treasury that the priority had to be maximising export earnings, although it was less definite about comparative advantage.[98]

Unsurprisingly, the retailers, chambers of commerce and British interests found Treasury's argument for reduced protection congenial.[99] Federated Farmers rehearsed their well-worn views, being quite opposed to officials or politicians making administrative decisions about industrial development. They rejected the rhetoric of employment, import substitution and development in depth (the farmers did not include state land development policy, agricultural advisory services or trade diplomacy in their strictures against official engagement with the economy).[100] Equally unsurprisingly, the manufacturers thought a relatively high level of protection would be needed for some time in order to allow industrial development, and certainly to the point of protecting against imports from cheap labour countries.[101]

The Board's report tilted toward the manufacturing lobby. Government should ensure economic stability and provide leadership and a suitable environment for enterprise. Earning foreign exchange was the most important consideration in industry policy, with saving through import substitution secondary. Here, Treasury's view had prevailed. On low-wage competition, however, the Board thought that while low-cost imports would sometimes have to be accepted as the price of a bilateral trade deal, generally New Zealand industry should be competitive only with 'similar countries', which meant restrictions against low-wage manufactured goods. Shifting from quantitative import controls to tariffs should not disrupt existing industries. Foreign investment should be welcomed to some extent at least. There was a case for infant industry protection, subject to overall criteria of economic efficiency. In general, the Board expected that the primary sector would remain vital and that there was increased scope for minerals, forestry, and more processing.[102] Generally, the Board advocated tax and other incentives for development in farming and manufacturing and for exporting, and Budgets from 1963 made these more generous.[103] The Board also recommended, and the government established, the Development Finance Corporation in 1963 as a public-private partnership, operating, in Marshall's words, as a lender of last resort.[104] This approach to the development of manufacturing and farming – of incentives for increased exporting, and for investment in plant and machinery – demonstrated a clear understanding that the diversification of both markets and commodities was essential.

Again, though, we should not exaggerate the degree of consensus. Labour's approach was one of active state involvement in industrial growth. While National accepted this in the case of steel and aluminium, as earlier in forest products, Marshall in particular much preferred the state's role to be confined to setting a framework in which private enterprise could develop. The difference might be described as that between involvement and encouragement. Within the public service, Industries and Commerce leant towards the former, Treasury the latter, although the visibility of the differences diminished after the government compelled Sutch to retire in 1965. Sutch and his minister, Marshall, had profound differences of opinion; Easton has also suggested that Sutch's views about protected industrialisation clashed with the National Party's farming constituency and their associated financial institutions.[105] Writing long afterwards, Marshall implied that Sutch was untrustworthy, as well as philosophically uncongenial and given to trying to dominate his minister.[106] The intensity of the debates around cotton, steel, and the IMF indicate that there were significant differences of opinion about the direction and the means of development. At the same time, there was a growing awareness that the old settler economy had to change, indeed was changing whether anyone liked it or not.

A New Trade Policy

Change in the settler economy was driven by its weakening foundation in the British market. Of necessity, the years after 1956 saw a fundamental reorientation of New Zealand trade policy. Nordmeyer observed in 1958 that 'the time has arrived for a new approach. . . . A greater effort must be made to produce goods for export which our potential customers want, rather than to produce the commodities which we think they ought to want,' and this would require more flexibility in production and marketing.[107] Two years later, he used words that any finance or trade minister in the next fifty years might have used: 'every effort must be made to enlarge and diversify markets for our export products and to persuade other countries to moderate their policies of agricultural protectionism'.[108]

In a world of bilateral trade agreements, access for New Zealand primary exports to new markets had to be paid for by importing commodities produced by those countries. The Ottawa obligation to give tariff preference to British manufactures was therefore an obstacle. New Zealand's High Commissioner in London thought that the British had only recently understood this and the extent to which New Zealand had adopted policies to suit Britain in the early postwar years.[109] Whether the British understood it or not, they continued to argue for preferential access for British goods as the price of New Zealand's unrestricted access to the British market for dairy produce.[110]

In April 1958 the new Minister of Agriculture, Jerry Skinner, led negotiations in London. The New Zealand government wished Britain to address the difficulties faced by New Zealand dairy exporters from subsidised British production and competition, or dumping, by Ireland, Sweden and Finland. The British eventually agreed only to quietly request the two Nordic countries to reduce their exports by 25 per cent, with countervailing duties held in reserve.[111] Because of their trade agreement with Ireland, the British offered simply to consult with Dublin if future exports threatened New Zealand's position. Politically, it was easier to immediately reduce imports of Polish butter.[112] Even though New Zealand had sought tougher action rather than a quiet word, the Commonwealth Secretary, Lord Home, lost no opportunity to stress that even this concession would require New Zealand to maintain preferences for British manufactures.[113] From Wellington, Nash fruitlessly reminded Macmillan of New Zealand's major increases in food exports to Britain after the war, even at the cost of continued domestic rationing.[114] Macmillan, for his part, bore domestic criticism both for denying the British consumer cheap European butter and for pushing New Zealand to the point that British manufactured exports were threatened.[115] At one point, indeed, the New Zealand negotiators threatened to abandon Ottawa entirely.[116] The Anglo-New Zealand trade agreement of August 1959 guaranteed entry for unlimited quantities of New Zealand primary produce to Britain, but without any commitment on price or excluding other suppliers. Britain would keep free of duty those New Zealand goods currently free of duty. New Zealand would keep but reduce preferences for British imports and only give tariff protection to those industries that had good prospects of success.[117]

Trade patterns, naturally, did not change immediately: 'Revision of the Ottawa Agreement did not enhance New Zealand's economic independence'.[118] Of course that would not have happened overnight, but things changed considerably during the next decade. The significance of the 1959 negotiations was that New Zealand ministers openly challenged the assumptions that had governed economic relationships with Britain since at least 1932, and arguably for 75 years. Yet even as the British market weakened, engagement with other trading partners was slow. While Industries and Commerce deployed a growing number of trade commissioners, the Department of External Affairs continued to think that New Zealand's fundamental orientation was to Britain. Although the United States was keen to encourage Australia and New Zealand to increase trade with Japan, this was largely due to the American agenda of 'keeping Japan in the capitalist fold'.[119] Additionally, so far as Australasian food and wool exports were concerned, 'the Americans hoped that Japan would develop into a substitute for the protected US market'.[120] Geopolitics and pandering to the protectionist American farm lobby thus coincided. Discussions about a New Zealand–Japan trade agreement began in 1953, but New Zealand manufacturers and the British government objected, the former suspicious of low-wage competition, the latter objecting to any weakening of their country's own protected position in New Zealand. A draft trade agreement with Japan therefore did not proceed to signing in 1955. However, when Australia signed an agreement with Japan in 1957, there was renewed interest in New Zealand, despite Nash's lack of enthusiasm. The New Zealand agreement, negotiated between July and September 1958, secured access for New Zealand meat and wool in exchange for machinery and textiles.[121]

The most important development of the early 1960s, of course, was the first British application to join the European Economic Community. Many scholars have dealt with New Zealand's response to British efforts to join the EEC.[122] The EEC's Common Agricultural Policy would have entailed prohibitive discrimination against New Zealand farm exports to Britain, and National ministers inevitably spent a great deal of time on the matter. From the beginning, the negotiating position was that New Zealand must keep open access to the British market.[123] In July 1961 the British Secretary of State for Commonwealth Relations, Duncan Sandys, visited Wellington. He was generally emollient and accepted the distinctiveness of New Zealand's position in being very largely dependent on the British market, but he pointed out that Britain's own negotiating position meant this could not be said in public.[124] One member of Sandys' delegation reminded New Zealand ministers that this country would have to find markets for its increasing volume of pastoral exports regardless of the Common Agricultural Policy. This was reiterated in the trade consultations between the two countries later in the year.[125] The British remained committed to increasing their self-sufficiency in food and while expressing polite appreciation of 'the efforts made by New Zealand in the past to meet the requirements of the United Kingdom market' now simply said that 'circumstances had changed' and no commitment could be made beyond 1967.[126]

Ministers understood that a good deal of attention would need to be paid to publicising New Zealand's case throughout Britain and the Six in the Common Market.[127] It was important to neither be so intransigent as to negate such goodwill as the British had nor to create the perception among the Six that New Zealand's problems were insoluble.[128] The new reality had been made unpleasantly clear in March 1962, when Britain asked New Zealand to limit butter exports by quota. Greensmith felt that this unpleasant precedent should be accepted because the world butter market was saturated and British goodwill had to be maintained.[129] The British had proposed that their accession to the EEC be accompanied by an agreement that Commonwealth nations be guaranteed the same relationship with the EEC as they had with Britain before accession. This was scarcely likely to appeal to the Six, and the French indicated that they were not at all committed to any special arrangement for New Zealand.[130] When negotiations on British accession broke down in February 1963, it was clearly only a temporary respite. The British government had made the EEC so significant a policy that they could not resile from seeking to join; and in any event, as all now knew, the British market was becoming increasingly difficult, so there could be no letup in the search for other markets.[131]

At the same time as ministers and officials were dealing with the EEC, they were also moving towards a trade agreement with Australia. Apart from the beneficial aspects of a nearby and relatively large market, New Zealand's balance of trade with Australia was greatly in the larger country's favour. Preliminary discussions had occurred in 1956 and 1958; New Zealand industrial growth, particularly in newsprint and pulp, very largely depended on the Australian market and therefore more liberal trade agreements were essential. In February 1961 John McEwen, the Australian trade minister and Deputy Prime Minister, invited his New Zealand counterpart, John Marshall, to Canberra. Australian officials had suggested 'discussion of long-term arrangements for the coordination of the Australian and New Zealand economies'. New Zealand ministers were willing, but would not 'agree . . . to a "division of labour" whereby New Zealand would undertake the simpler processes and Australia the more advanced processes of manufacture'.[132]

The ensuing discussions took more than three years. Some ministers and officials thought that access to the Australian market could give New Zealand manufacturing economies of scale but others, including Sutch, were sceptical. Sutch was so sceptical, in fact, that he did not lead the New Zealand negotiations, being replaced by his deputy, Jim Moriarty.[133] Treasury, of course, thought that the trade imbalance was better remedied by increasing New Zealand exports than by limiting Australian imports.[134] Sutch thought that arguments for free trade in forest products with Australia relied on a 'hypothetical and highly optimistic assessment'; he thought there was no guarantee of an Australian market (which was rather the point of a trade agreement) and that any agreement would lead to 'destructive competition'. Contrarily, he then argued that the forest products industry 'must and will expand dramatically'; ministers may have asked to where, if not to Australia, given Australia's lack of both radiata pine and manufacturing capacity. Australia was a net importer of forest products and would in all conceivable circumstances remain so until the end of the century. Even if Australia did achieve self-sufficiency in forest products by 2000, that would give New Zealand a third of a century and a strong continuing position once securely in the market.[135]

Negotiating the New Zealand Australian Free Trade Agreement was tortuous. On both sides there was considerable attachment to protection and equally a wish to achieve an agreement for political as well as economic reasons. In New Zealand, at least, Marshall devoted much time to persuading manufacturers of the virtues of competition even as he later admitted that their obstinacy had strengthened his negotiating hand.[136] The agreement, when signed in 1965, contained some exemptions, but overall covered 85 per cent of New Zealand exports to Australia and 51 per cent of Australian exports to New Zealand. Even given some ongoing haggling, 'it cannot be denied that NAFTA was a milestone in the development of trans-Tasman cooperation'.[137] Marshall, introducing the agreement in parliament, emphasised both that New Zealand industry and primary producers needed access to this larger and nearby market and that consultation processes and exemptions would prevent New Zealand industry from being swamped by Australian. The Labour Party professed scepticism about the agreement, but did not condemn it outright.[138]

Changing entrenched trade patterns was a long process, but the necessity – indeed the inevitability – had become clear by the late 1950s. If the decline of the British market was regretted by some and not entirely understood by others, generally ministers and officials attempted to manage that decline by negotiating what were in effect transitional arrangements and by rapidly increasing trade promotion activities. At the same time, manufacturers were exhorted and encouraged towards exporting. Holyoake's preference, as we have seen, was for steady and unspectacular policy development, and Marshall would later describe industry and trade as undergoing a 'quiet revolution' during the second National government. While external realignment was proceeding slowly, until 1965 the balance of payments did not cause undue concern and domestic demand remained high.

Conclusion: Overheating and Crashing

The decade from 1957 was one of transition. Renegotiating the British market began, and trade agreements with other states were signed, notably with Australia and Japan. Manufacturing and service industries modernised and grew, and the diversification of export commodities was widely accepted as important. With differences in emphasis, both political parties agreed that growth, rather than security, was the imperative in economic policy. By mid 1964, there was a general climate of prosperity. Farm earnings, business confidence and imports were all high. Holyoake's preference for steady and undramatic policymaking seemed to have paid off. This approach was not in itself incompatible with officials' preference for disciplined and consistent fiscal and monetary policy. It did mean, though, that Budgets tended to be stable or expansionary, with restrictive measures announced gradually and quietly. In 1964, with export earnings high, Treasury and the Reserve Bank advised moderate measures to control demand and avoid inflation.[139] Instead, the 1964 Budget delivered considerable spending increases in education, defence and public works, particularly electricity.[140] With the exception of defence, these increases reflected National's ongoing development agenda, but some weeks after the Budget, Treasury warned that demand was being excessively stimulated and the government would have to borrow to cover its budget deficit.[141] Late in September 1964 Cabinet agreed to slow the increase in public spending and tighten monetary policy by reducing lending for consumption.[142]

The familiar pattern, of strong growth followed by a balance of payments crisis, was repeated as export prices, particularly for wool, fell in mid 1965, while import demand remained high. Again, the moderately expansionist 1965 Budget was followed by a quiet tightening of credit.[143] In October 1965 Lake increased sales tax on many commodities and reduced import allocations for cars, and in December 1965 and February 1966 he increased other taxes and tightened public spending. Treasury had advised more stringent measures to reduce liquidity, particularly increasing consumption taxes and a direction to the Arbitration Court to hold the line on wages.[144] A voluntary and gradual approach – however congenial it might have been to Holyoake in terms of not alarming the voters – was hardly adequate, and in March 1966 the IMF bluntly warned that 'correction of the balance of payments position now deserves the highest priority'. Taxes and interest rates both needed to increase if demand were to be reduced. [145] The IMF indicated that the budget deficit would have to be reduced before further loans were contemplated. In May, Treasury told ministers that 'New Zealand is facing the most serious balance of payments difficulties since 1938. Adequate remedial action now is imperative if a major crisis is to be avoided'.[146]

Just as it was in 1957, so it was again in 1966. With an election due in November, restrictive fiscal and monetary policies were off the National Party's agenda, even if, arguably, National could have taken advantage of the Labour Party's inexperienced new leader, Norman Kirk, who had rolled Nordmeyer at the end of 1965. Cabinet sought to achieve the desired result by expenditure reduction rather than taxation increases. It is now well known that Tom Shand, the Minister of Labour (who had always wanted Finance), warned Holyoake that tax increases were essential and that Treasury advice had to be heeded. Shand considered resigning, but his own sense of party loyalty prevented him from taking such drastic action, and 'Holyoake and Lake . . . persuaded Cabinet to reject Shand and Treasury's advice'.[147] The political agenda for the 1966 budget was to focus on past expansion and imminent prospects for future rapid growth, underplaying the extent of overheating.[148] National comfortably won the election at the end of November, retaining all but one of its seats (the vote tally was less impressive, since both National and Labour shed tens of thousands of votes to the small-time right-wingers of the Social Credit Political League). Two and a half weeks later, on 14 December 1966, wool prices collapsed. Brian Easton has described that day as the end of the long postwar boom.[149] The next seven years would be characterised by considerable instability as the pace of internal and external economic change intensified.

Chapter 6

Instability, 1967–72

After the wool crash of December 1966, New Zealand's economic circumstances became less stable; the world economy was changing and the postwar settlement was beginning to fracture. The settler economy had been changing since the mid 1950s, but the pace of change intensified after 1966 and the patterns of the years since 1945 began to alter. Population growth slowed; for the first time since the Depression the natural increase was, in the second half of the 1960s, less than in the preceding five years, and this trend continued into the early 1970s (the average age at first marriage continued to fall, reaching an all-time low in 1971). The net gain by immigration was almost negligible between 1966 and 1970 but surged strongly from 1970. The population continued to urbanise, and even as Māori birthrates fell from very high levels, the Māori share of the population increased to exceed eight per cent by 1972. The proportion of the workforce in primary sector occupations continued to decline. After 1966, however, the proportion in secondary industries also fell. As well as becoming more urban, then, the population was increasingly working in service and administrative occupations. There was, and perhaps more so in retrospect, a general climate of modernisation and prosperity, even affluence.

Pastoral exports continued to account for the great majority of overseas earnings, but after 1966, ministers and officials alike placed even greater emphasis on diversifying export markets and commodities, not least because British membership of the EEC seemed imminent. When Britain finally joined the EEC in 1973 there was almost a sense of anticlimax. The 1966–67 balance of payments crisis caused ministers and officials to seek an acceleration in the shift to a more export-oriented, diverse economy, but this was contentious as it effectively involved a redistribution of income and wealth to exporters. For these and other reasons, wage-fixing also became much more disputed than it had been for some years. The postwar settlement was beginning to fray, although the National government remained broadly committed to the welfare state. The international economic context became much more challenging as the long postwar hegemony of the United States cracked and the stable exchange rates of Bretton

Woods abruptly ended in 1971. For New Zealand, the instability was most pronounced in erratic export earnings; there would be a measure of recovery at the end of the 1960s, and a pronounced commodity boom in 1972, contributing to an illusion that the difficulties had been successfully negotiated.

Managing the Wool Crash

The wool crash on 14 December had, as the Minister of Finance, Harry Lake, put it, 'turned a very difficult external financial position into a crisis'.[1] It was a crisis, however, that the government would seek to get through with a minimum of alarm. Shortly before the crash, Treasury had warned of serious excess demand and urged tight controls on spending.[2] The wool crash made those arguments compelling, although the immediate problem now was managing a loss of revenue rather than reducing excess demand. Early in February, Holyoake announced a number of measures: abolishing free school milk and subsidies on flour and butter, increasing state house rentals and postal charges, reducing concessionary loans to house buyers, imposing more stringent hire-purchase rules, temporarily reducing overseas travel allowances, and ending no-remittance import licenses, which had allowed New Zealand residents who owned overseas funds or shares to use them to pay for imports above normal allowances.[3] The measures were, as McKinnon points out, 'the toughest since Nordmeyer's 1958 "Black Budget"'.[4]

Lake died in February 1967. His successor was Robert Muldoon, an Aucklander who grew up in modest circumstances and who had been in Parliament since 1960. After war service Muldoon had achieved professional success as an accountant, and he rapidly made his name as a forthright parliamentarian, uncompromising and with a terrier-like intelligence. His political views were an unusual mixture of the liberal and the authoritarian conservative: often intolerant of nonconformity, he had been one of 10 National MPs who broke ranks to abolish the death penalty in 1961. Muldoon expected Cabinet rank immediately after the 1966 election, but Holyoake made him wait because of tactless comments he made about the election campaign. Early in February 1967 Holyoake gave him the then distinctly unglamorous portfolio of Tourism, as well as Associate Minister of Finance.[5] Muldoon only succeeded Lake as Minister of Finance after Marshall declined (once again, Holyoake refused to appoint Shand).[6] Holyoake would later champion Muldoon's career, but initially 'was concerned that Muldoon appeared to be unwilling to take advice from anyone, seemed to think that he knew everything, and had in the past made trouble for his own ministers'.[7] Muldoon would be Minister of Finance for more than 14 years, and it must be emphasised that he 'came into a crisis situation and despite some initial apparent success never got out of it'.[8]

Holyoake continued to dislike sudden and radical changes in economic policy, believing that they caused undue alarm and cost the National Party votes. Therefore, and because of Muldoon's inexperience, Holyoake closely watched Muldoon's performance through 1967.[9] Muldoon's first, uncompromising advice from Treasury was 'that further measures to reduce demand are urgently necessary'.[10] Treasury preferred targeted increases on items such as cars, petrol, alcohol, and overseas travel, both to deter importing and because broad increases in indirect taxation would increase the cost of living and provoke the trade union movement to demand high wage increases.[11] This advice was unpalatable for National ministers because of the risk that they, in their turn, would be abused for bringing down a Black Budget. Holyoake, and many MPs, preferred increasing direct taxes.[12] Treasury warned that the alternative to stern fiscal measures was devaluation, and that action needed to be swift, otherwise currency 'speculation and lack of confidence will continue'.[13] Holyoake nevertheless had the party caucus spend two months working through various options. Apart from avoiding the appearance of crisis, Holyoake wanted to ensure that National MPs were tied to whatever measures were implemented; it had been too easy for Nordmeyer's less-than-loyal colleagues to maintain that the 1958 budget had been his alone. It was not until 4 May 1967 that Muldoon delivered the first of what would become a trademark device: the mini-Budget.[14]

The mini-Budget was of course a political document as much as an economic. In it, Muldoon professed optimism about the future: 'Plans are well advanced for the development and expansion of great industries based on indigenous resources such as forestry, the iron and steel industry, and the proposed aluminium industry using power from Manapouri. A new surge of interest is apparent in the fishing and mining industries and in tourism'.[15] Following Treasury advice, Muldoon significantly increased sales taxes and duty on petrol, spirits and tobacco, and he required banks to reduce advances and overdraft limits. The positive side of the mini-Budget was increased export incentives.[16] By June the restrictive policies were beginning to show results, with public spending hardly increasing and revenue, mostly indirect tax, growing significantly.[17] Treasury felt that while the full Budget need not be tough it should underline the significance of the wool shock. Muldoon broadly followed the advice, indicating that while public spending had increased by nine per cent per annum in the previous three years, it would now be restrained to less than four per cent growth.

Devaluation

Budgetary policy, however, could only do so much. Consistent pressure on the balance of payments meant that devaluation was increasingly discussed as a means to shift income to exporters and encourage increased investment in exporting. Ministers and officials had briefly considered devaluation in February 1967, but it was unpalatable.[18] Apart from the perception that devaluation was an admission of failure, the government needed the International Monetary Fund's consent, and the views of the British government still carried great weight. Devaluation would cause import prices to increase, and the increased cost of living would prompt the trade union movement to seek wage increases. Without reduced domestic demand, however, more expensive imports would simply encourage an expansion of manufacturing for the domestic market, rather than investment in exporting. If devaluation 'were to work as a measure to restore the balance of payments, it would require a domestic deflation of substantial scale,' which many people would resent.[19]

In June 1967, Treasury officials prepared a paper on devaluation for the Cabinet Economic Committee. On many points the discussion reflected the strong views of Henry Lang, now a Deputy Secretary, in favour of managed and export-oriented liberalisation. The IMF allowed exchange rate alterations only to correct 'fundamental disequilibrium,' and a change had to be sufficient to resolve the problem in one hit.[20] The basic question was whether New Zealand was in fundamental disequilibrium (the meaning of which the IMF had left 'carefully unspecified').[21]

Treasury did not think that the wool crisis in itself amounted to that; wool prices had always fluctuated and it was 'difficult to detect any long-term downward trend'. New Zealand's real problem was a 'chronic shortage' of overseas exchange, due not only to the long-term trend for pastoral commodities but also to excessive domestic demand for resources and labour. Domestic inflation reduced the competitiveness of New Zealand exports and pushed money incomes up, which meant that excess demand flowed into import spending. Direct import controls meant inefficient use of overseas earnings on equipment and raw materials for import-substituting industries, while agricultural protectionism overseas made export markets difficult. In short, fundamental disequilibrium was much more to do with the structure of protection and demand management than with wool prices. Devaluation would, other things being equal, give farmers an incentive to increase output and would also make manufactured exports more competitive. This in turn would allow reduced spending on farm support (making the shift of income to farmers more politically palatable). Treasury did not, however, yet recommend devaluation. The trend in export prices was difficult to read; even if devaluation were justified on principle, the quantum would depend on that trend. Devaluation would only really work if it was accompanied by other liberalising measures, particularly in imports, subsidies, and wage policy, and the IMF would be likely to want such liberalisation in any event. Treasury thought that the government should take those steps before devaluing, if it was necessary, some time in 1968.[22] The argument was about what would later be called the sequencing of reform.

By August 1967 wool prices were looking decidedly unpromising. If December 1966 were to be repeated, ministers feared that devaluation would be inevitable, and Muldoon warned the IMF accordingly. On 27 September, the first day of the Dunedin wool sales, prices were again very bad.[23] Meat and dairy prices were also low. On Sunday 1 October senior ministers and officials met. Muldoon and the Secretary to the Treasury, N. R. Davis, were both overseas at the IMF, and Shand, the Minister of Labour and a frustrated maker of economic policy, had been told the meeting was about wool, no doubt so that he would not prepare a detailed argument for devaluation. Treasury suggested that a devaluation of 20 per cent had to be considered, although officials were divided. Lang did not express a firm view. The Reserve Bank (and Davis, commenting later) thought it premature and suggested that previously announced measures had reduced inflation and should be given more time to work through the system. Of the ministers, Shand, Marshall and the acting finance minister, David Seath, were in favour, but Holyoake apparently refused to commit himself.[24]

On 4 October the officials – Davis and Noel Lough from Treasury and Reserve Bank governor Alan Low – reviewed the arguments with Marshall and Seath. Marshall suggested that devaluation should be done at the beginning of the export season, even though he 'realised all the difficulties involved, including the political point that it would be contended that all the benefits would go to the farmers while the additional costs would have to be met by the consumers'. Ministers agreed to plan for an announcement on Saturday 14 October.[25] The next day, however, ministers hesitated, partly because of a suggestion that the IMF would expect a commitment to exempt 80 per cent of imports from licensing instead of the existing 30 per cent, and include cars in that exemption. The officials recommended accepting these conditions, but Holyoake and Marshall would only commit to liberalisation in a general sense, and certainly not to percentages (later that day it emerged that the IMF would drop its insistence on percentages but 'would require a pretty definite commitment in general terms').[26]

On Sunday afternoon, 8 October, Muldoon, now back from the IMF, met with officials. Muldoon thought the devaluation discussion should be delayed for six months, as he was not convinced of the advantages and 'doubted whether his political colleagues would support the kind of policies needed to make devaluation effective'.[27] Muldoon was himself hardly an enthusiastic exponent of such policies. He was feeling his way into the finance portfolio, and he was politically close to many manufacturers, who feared and disliked the prospect of import competition.[28] Later that evening Muldoon and the officials joined Marshall, Shand and Holyoake. Muldoon developed the case against devaluation. As Muldoon put it, the IMF's initial reaction was that 'if what we had been telling them to date was correct, then there would appear to be no case for devaluation at this stage' and that overseas borrowing could get New Zealand through the downturn. The real question was whether devaluation was a short-term expedient or an instrument of structural reform that would increase the emphasis on exporting. Muldoon agreed that it 'could be argued that devaluation is necessary to alter the structure of the economy, but if this is right it is still questionable whether this would be the best time'. Unless the government had the resolve to follow through with the consequential liberalisation 'we would be wasting our time'.[29]

Officials emphasised the continuing weakness in the wool market. Low argued that 'we have been in a state of fundamental disequilibrium for years, as indicated by our widespread restrictions in imports and use of foreign exchange, our borrowing programme and the weakening in our reserve position'. Delay only made matters worse. Shand agreed and 'did not think the proposition that we can hang out or scrape through is good enough. . . . devaluation would be preferable to a period of stagnation. . . . Devaluation was one way of rebalancing the economy. While we could wait till later in the season he felt that now was the time to do it. His wool had been sold last Friday so he could speak without a personal interest, but he was now more firmly convinced that we should devalue'.[30]

Muldoon warned that British ministers and officials 'would take devaluation . . . very badly'. Devaluation would present a barrier to British exports to New Zealand, which was one reason the British had recently made a £15m loan conditional on the understanding that there would be no devaluation.[31] The British Treasury feared the implications for sterling: 'people would say that if it could happen to New Zealand after 30 years [sic: actually 20] of stable rates, it could happen to sterling'.[32] The Labour government in Britain had inherited a shaky balance of payments in 1964 and had been under sustained pressure to devalue since then (and under almost equally strong pressure from the United States government not to devalue; Washington feared the contagion spreading and putting pressure on the dollar).[33] While Muldoon agreed that the time was past when Britain should dictate New Zealand's economic policy, it was still important to keep London as happy as possible for trade reasons. More important for Muldoon was the anticipated public reaction. Farmers would resent the removal of incentives (even though, as he might have said, they would be the principal beneficiaries). Manufacturers would resent the removal of import controls. Unions would object to increased prices. Generally, 'the 1958 Budget would fade into insignificance compared with the upheaval of devaluation'.[34]

Despite Muldoon's reservations, Lang gave formal advice from the Treasury and the Reserve Bank that New Zealand should devalue by 20 per cent on 14 October because monetary and fiscal policy alone could not remedy matters. A current account balance could not be expected until late 1969 at the earliest and required continuing tight import and exchange controls. A 20 per cent devaluation would be 'one of the most revolutionary economic measures taken by any Government in New Zealand's history', affecting all parts of the economy. It would make reorientation toward exports 'increasingly attractive'. With the associated liberalisation, it would allow a more efficient reshaping of the economy such that 'Market forces rather than Government fiat will determine allocation of resources'. Moving sooner rather than later would terminate the speculation that uncertainty invited.[35] The major problem, as Holyoake put it, was the political difficulties.[36] It was evidently for that reason that, on 9 October, Holyoake sided with Muldoon against Marshall and Shand, and rejected devaluation in the meantime, agreeing to review the matter four weeks later.[37]

In the event, the British forced the New Zealand government's hand. In early November the British Treasury and the Bank of England became convinced that poor trade figures made a British devaluation imperative and finally persuaded Wilson and the Chancellor, James Callaghan.[38] On Saturday 18 November, Wilson and Callaghan warned their New Zealand counterparts that they would announce a British devaluation of 14.3 per cent during the British Sunday.[39] That evening, Holyoake and Muldoon met officials. Davis advised that matching the British devaluation would be insufficient. Discussion firmed around 20 per cent.[40] The next day, Muldoon again expressed discomfort at the liberalisation he expected the IMF to require. Lang advised that the 20 per cent would allow reduction of quantitative controls on imports in any case. Cabinet formally decided on 19.45 per cent, for parity with Australia, a parity that had been lost when Nash revalued the New Zealand currency in 1948.[41] The announcement on 21 November 1967 placed the most weight on the British devaluation and also referred to a continuing fall in export returns and continuing balance of payments problems, despite tight fiscal and monetary policies. Given the benefits exporters could expect, the government foreshadowed a review of all export assistance (as it turned out, export assistance would become more generous by 1972, not less), and noted that devaluation would 'facilitate the progressive liberalisation of import licensing and exchange controls'. Anticipating the trade unions' reaction, the government declared that incomes would not be allowed to rise so far as to fully compensate for the increased price of imported goods.[42]

The devaluation saga reflected Holyoake's preference for avoiding dramatic shifts in policy. The cumulative effect of all the measures adopted during 1967 was a significant reorientation of the New Zealand economy in the direction of export-led growth. For public consumption, the government portrayed the British decision as the sole reason for New Zealand devaluation, although afterwards ministers emphasised the potential for a major and necessary economic reorientation.[43] The 1968 pre-Budget Economic Review noted that devaluation could prompt 'a major structural change' that would relieve persistent balance of payments problems. Given 'suitable measures of restraint. . . . [it will] tend to divert domestic and overseas expenditure towards New Zealand produced goods, thus helping to achieve balance of payments equilibrium, at an adequate level of economic activity' and would 'encourage the reallocation of resources of capital and labour to the import-saving and export sectors of the economy'. Import substitution on its own was now seen as a trap; 'at a certain stage . . . [tending to] retard rather than to advance the rise in living standards' by spreading labour and capital excessively across too many small units with little scope for economies of scale, with the small domestic market representing a cap on output.[44] The influence of Lang, who would become Secretary to the Treasury at the end of 1968, was clear in these arguments.

The government, despite the clear advice from Treasury and the Reserve Bank, had hesitated to devalue. A more experienced finance minister than Muldoon was in 1967 might have been able to make a stronger case for devaluation (or, indeed, against it). Muldoon correctly understood that the consequences would be major but, echoing Holyoake, used their magnitude as an argument against devaluation rather than addressing how those consequences might be managed. Treasury did not consider managing the consequences either. Devaluation implied constrained domestic demand, particularly by limiting wages, and neither ministers nor officials gave much thought to discussing the matter with the trade unions. Holyoake might himself have shown more leadership, given his firm oversight of economic policy, and might have reflected on the precedent set by his mentor, Coates, in 1933, when a devaluation that year secured the beginnings of a recovery from the Depression. Perhaps the worst dimension of 1967 was that whatever advantages there were in devaluation were reduced because Holyoake refused to take the initiative, ended up being pushed by the British, and thus lost an opportunity to shape the discussion about reorganising the New Zealand economy.

The Failure of Incomes Policy

Devaluation's consequences contributed to long-lasting tension between the government, employers, and trade unions. The tension, more generally, reflected differences over the future of the postwar consensus. Industrial militancy and wage growth were an international phenomenon in the later 1960s, and New Zealand was not immune. Organised workers in many countries became tired of limiting wage increases in the interests of economic growth, particularly as profits grew and memories of the Depression receded.[45] In New Zealand, export-led growth implied diminished attention to domestic demand, and unions resisted the resulting constraint on wages.

Some economists had drawn attention to the inflationary consequences of full employment, particularly through labour's high bargaining power in such circumstances. In certain countries, especially Scandinavia and elsewhere in Western Europe, incomes policies were the favoured response. The term itself generally means an agreed policy that limits wage increases for both actual and minimum rates, and which is overseen or brokered by the government, whether directly by ministerial involvement or indirectly through a judicial or administrative body. It may include negotiated compensations or trade-offs such as social services, investment strategies, or price control. The reason for controlling money wages by limiting collective bargaining in this way is to 'bring about a reasonably rapid fall in the rate of wage inflation without suffering the deleterious consequences – in terms of lower output and employment – [of] the main alternative approach . . . a reliance solely upon restrictive monetary and fiscal policies'.[46] Incomes policies had never been much favoured in New Zealand, partly because of an apparently workable informal consensus between employers, unions, and government.

The trigger for wages militancy in New Zealand was the Arbitration Court's decision in June 1968 that no general wage order would be granted, a decision directly related to the devaluation and the monetary and fiscal tightening during 1967. The consequence was a general weakening of the Arbitration Court and a considerable increase in second-tier bargaining, that is, where unions took the Arbitration Court's award minimum and then engaged in direct bargaining for higher rates. The government had hoped that a general wage order would not undermine the 1967 measures. Tom Shand and Noel Woods, the Minister and Secretary of Labour, informally said as much to the new Arbitration Court judge, Patrick Blair. Blair indicated that he could be relied on to give weight to issues of economic stability but would prefer an amendment of the regulations covering the general wage order to require him to do so. This, however, the government declined to do, no doubt in order to avoid a fight with the Federation of Labour.[47] Thomas Skinner, the FOL president, has been described as a very conservative man in his approach to institutions; his over-riding priority had been to reunify the FOL after the divisions of the Walsh presidency, to which he had succeeded in 1963.[48] He had little desire for a confrontation but, after the Court had given minimal increases in a couple of cases, the FOL reluctantly joined with the Public Service Association in applying for a general wage order of 7.6 per cent.[49]

To widespread surprise, by a majority decision the Court made no order. The Court accepted that the cost of living would justify an order but noted that there were additional criteria, and quoted the Treasury's submission that a healthy balance of payments 'is not merely a desirable policy objective – it is something that we must achieve'.[50] The Court observed that 'forced by circumstances the country is passing through a period of transition from which it may emerge with marked changes in its pattern of trade and the structure of its economy. . . . if the opportunities [of devaluation] are grasped New Zealand will have some international cost advantages which may enable us to cure or minimise our persistent balance of payments problem and also our undue dependence on primary exports'.[51] While, as Skinner complained, devaluation privileged exporters, that was the whole point. The Workers' Representative on the court, Archie Grant, thundered his dissent; the unions 'are entitled to say, as did Isaiah they, "looked for justice, but behold, oppression; for righteousness, but, behold, a cry"'.[52] Morality aside, Grant argued that the order would intensify the recession, quoting the Government Statistician's view that demand had already been pushed too low.[53]

Grant correctly predicted that the order was 'an open invitation for further and more serious industrial dissension'.[54] The FOL worked to get the matter re-heard.[55] The Employers' Federation (dominated by larger, capital-intensive industries) was as keen as the FOL on a political solution, although threatening industrial disruption was part of Skinner's tactics. Skinner's commitment to arbitration was as great as Shand's, and was based on the belief that direct action was viable only for a minority of well-placed unions. Although Shand was persuaded that the credibility of arbitration required a re-hearing, he could not convince Cabinet. Treasury, Muldoon, Marshall, and Holyoake were opposed either on principle, or because of unwillingness to appear to have given in to threats, or because of the weight of farmer opinion. Thus, the only way for a renewed application to succeed was if the employers' and workers' representatives on the Court voted against the judge. The result of this – famously described by Muldoon as an 'unholy alliance' – was a five per cent order. In fact the order was capped so that it only applied up to a threshold, and it was justified on the basis of more up-to-date economic figures having become available. This was not entirely specious; the judge indirectly suggested that he might have accepted a lesser figure than five per cent.[56]

The fiasco of the nil order could have been avoided. Ministers and officials had anticipated criticisms of the devaluation. An early decision to compensate wage earners to some extent might have avoided a great deal of trouble; put bluntly, on this issue the National government looked after the class interests of its business and farming supporters and abandoned consensus. Muldoon later wrote that the government could have lived with 2.5 per cent at the first hearing.[57] Assuming that 'the government' was not Muldoon's version of the first person singular, as it later became, it is a pity that this had not been made clear. Shand's backdoor approach to the judge had politicised what was supposed to be a judicial body, and the government could hardly complain if the FOL later did the same thing.

The nil order was only the immediate cause of more sustained conflict over wages. More fundamentally, as the government sought to privilege exporters by increasing their returns, constraining the domestic economy and seeking slower wage growth, the argument was about the future of the postwar consensus.[58] Without limiting wage increases, Treasury feared 'a return . . . to the chronic balance of payments difficulties experienced in the past' and warned that 'our competitive position in export markets will be undermined and demand for imports will rise to unmanageable proportions'.[59] Wage fixing since 1951 had been managed by a general, if informal, consensus brokered by a very small number of powerful men. Through the 1950s the key figure had been the Federation of Labour president, Fintan Patrick Walsh, whose control of the FOL and cordial relationship with National ministers generally ensured industrial tranquillity. As Minister of Labour from 1960, Shand cultivated strong personal relationships with the trade union leadership and generally ensured that consensus continued. Walter Nash apparently thought no other National MP had so good an understanding of the New Zealand economy.[60] There were, however, strict limits on Shand's enthusiasm for trade unions; any that became too assertive for ministerial tastes were threatened with the full force of the law, with major disputes involving drivers and others in 1962 and 1965.[61]

By the later 1960s a number of more militant unionists were rising to prominence (some of them veterans of 1951). Even before the nil order, wage growth was lagging behind GDP.[62] Some unions made enterprise agreements, with larger employers 'bidding for labour and paying the price of industrial peace', and the higher ruling rates then dragged up Arbitration Court awards.[63] The 1969 Auckland electrical contractors' dispute was a good example. The Arbitration Court had given a rise of 7.5 cents to a minimum of a dollar an hour; the ruling rate was already $1.12, the employers offered $1.20 and the workers demanded $1.50 and struck for seven weeks. A Committee of Enquiry then recommended $1.28, and while the dispute settled on that figure, the worst thing from the employers' point of view was that the new ruling rate was so far above the award minimum and that the 28 cent premium rapidly spread to other industries.[64]

Shand died at the end of 1969, and Holyoake gave the labour portfolio to a 'surprised and unenthusiastic' Marshall. Marshall's diligence could not be faulted, but as he himself noted, he was 'already fully committed as Minister of Overseas Trade [with the EEC becoming critical], Attorney-General, Deputy Prime Minister, chairman of half a dozen cabinet committees and Deputy Leader of the Party'. The cynical might think that it suited Holyoake to tie the pretender to the throne down with 'the most demanding, frustrating and thankless job in cabinet'.[65] Marshall's belief in markets meant he was averse to the government imposing solutions, or doing much more than facilitating agreements between capital and labour.[66] Inflation, however, became a more serious problem after 1967. Whereas inflation had not reached five per cent since 1952, it would seldom fall below that figure until the late 1980s, becoming more severe after 1974.

Despite his philosophical preference, Marshall began to explore the possibilities of a more formal incomes policy during 1970. In April he met with the economic sector group leaders in an attempt to develop a consensus. Marshall emphasised that the gains that had followed tough policies in 1967 and 1968 should not be wasted, and devaluation was a one-shot weapon.[67] Marshall's hope, also, was to secure a deal with Skinner rather than 'the radical element within the union movement which was snapping at the heels of the FOL executive', but Skinner was no more interested in limiting free-wage bargaining than were the 'radicals'.[68] As an incentive, the government brought down a two-month price freeze in November 1970 and in January 1971 intensified monitoring of retail prices.[69] The Employers' Federation indicated that they would accept price surveillance in return for wage stability and in particular a ban on strikes and wage movements during the life of an award.[70] Skinner occasionally seemed willing to consider the last point but more often insisted that the FOL would accept no restrictions on wage bargaining.[71] During 1970 the number of strikes reached a post-1951 record, and the Secretaries of the Treasury, Industries and Commerce, and Labour observed that 'the attitude of employers and unions towards each other is worse than it has been at any time in our experience'. The officials advised that whether an incomes policy was achieved by agreement or decree, there had to be one clear method of determining wages; second-tier bargaining had to end and agreements have a reasonable life. They advised Marshall to make one last attempt at consensus before imposing a solution but feared that the latter course would 'be successful only if it were broadly acceptable to the unions or if it could be enforced. Both of these possibilities seemed remote'.[72]

Marshall convened another conference on 3 February 1971, which spent more time arguing over percentages than addressing broad issues. The conference provisionally agreed, however, to a guideline of a 30 per cent increase over 1 January 1970 in award rates and 15 per cent in actual rates. Skinner repeated that the FOL simply would not accept limits on the free negotiation of wages; the most they would accept would be 12-month agreements with cost-of-living adjustments. Any compulsion would mean 'Government would be buying a fight up and down the country'. The employers said little except to underline their requirement of fixed rates during the currency of an agreement. Marshall put a brave face on very little progress.[73] When the conference reconvened five days later, the employers now also became unhelpful, asking for a six-month wage-freeze followed by new guidelines for future settlements.[74] Marshall, near the end of his patience, said that the government was determined to resolve the situation one way or another and if his suggestion of 30 and 15 per cent was not accepted, the government would impose a solution.[75]

Thus the government introduced a Stabilisation of Remuneration Bill.[76] All rates that had not increased by 15 per cent since the beginning of 1970 would increase. All new agreements would be for 12 months, subject to twice-yearly cost-of-living adjustments (which would be discretionary if wages were above the minimum). New agreements were not to exceed seven per cent without being referred to a new Remuneration Authority.[77] The latter point arose from officials' advice that 'an absolute ceiling on wage increases' was not only 'impracticable' but also unenforceable, and would lead to a major confrontation with state services unions and 'major difficulties are imminent with waterfront workers. . . . unless one has a reasonable chance of winning one should not enter into this sort of battle'.[78] The Remuneration Authority hardly fulfilled the government's hopes. It proved vulnerable to threats of industrial action, and did not disturb the principle of relativity.[79] Further, the Stabilisation of Remuneration Act did not bind the Arbitration Court, which proceeded to award the Clerical Workers 16 per cent.[80]

The Act was only intended as an interim measure, and officials and ministers were anxious to develop a more comprehensive approach.[81] To this end, Cabinet agreed to a 60-day wage and price freeze from the end of January 1972.[82] In the event, the freeze was announced on 14 February and was to last until 31 March (a largely symbolic move as the new Prime Minister Marshall indicated, because few awards expired before then). At the same time, the government froze its own rail and postal charges for 12 months and undertook to maintain butter and sugar prices at current levels. It also pledged to recall the 1968 Royal Commission on State Services to consider relativity with the private sector.[83] During the freeze, officials and the Cabinet Economic Committee discussed a future regime. Lang argued that wage and price controls were undesirable in the long-term but in the shorter-term high-wage increases were damaging.[84] No long-term solution emerged. At the end of March the government brought down regulations that repealed the Stabilisation of Remuneration Act and gave the government the power to control wages, prices, dividends, and farm incomes.[85] During the rest of 1972, price and wage increases slowed, probably because the economy was slowing anyway.[86] Prolonged negotiations had achieved relatively little; while in the end the government was willing to compel a short-term solution, neither employers nor unions were prepared to compromise sufficiently. None of the key actors – interest groups, ministers, or officials – showed much interest in developing an enduring tripartite approach to incomes policy. Employers and unions both sought to maintain freedom of action, officials thought it compromised the established pattern of confidential advice and simply gave pressure groups another forum, ministers regarded it as a constraint on parliamentary sovereignty and Marshall, at least, disliked the idea as an interference in the market.[87]

Yet, if the profound economic reorientation that National sought was to be achieved, a new consensus had to be somehow developed.

Consensus-Building, the EEC, and Export Incentives

The wool crisis at the end of 1966 had reinforced the importance, for the government, of increasing exports and diversifying markets and commodities; changes given urgency by the likelihood of the EEC expanding to include not only Britain but also Ireland and Denmark, both major dairy producers. From 1967, as well as attempting to control wages and, however reluctantly, devaluing, the government increased the encouragement available to exporters and continued its efforts to shape public opinion.

In February 1968 Holyoake convened a National Development Conference for later that year, involving representatives of all the sector groups, individual manufacturers, farmers, civil servants, academics, and so on, in order to shape a consensual indicative plan. As always, Holyoake eschewed sudden change. While planning had to be export oriented, it also had to be incremental and 'build on the institutions and administrative arrangements that have grown up in New Zealand'. An indicative plan was a set of guidelines, which were 'not to be regarded as a strait-jacket'. It should 'indicate the best lines of growth while leaving wide elements of choice to the company, the organisation, and the individual. . . . [who will] take into account the inducements offered to them'.[88] The conference, of course, was the latest and largest of a number of initiatives of the kind since 1960, and it eventually adopted the goal of doubling export earnings over the coming decade, with manufacturing and tourism becoming more prominent and farming remaining dominant with a declining share. More investment would be required, and that meant increased saving. While manufacturing would become more export oriented, efficient import substitution would have to continue. Since 'price expectations for some traditional exports [were] poor' it might have seemed a little strange to continue to rely on them, but this was seen as necessary in the medium term while alternatives developed.[89]

In Muldoon's words, 'devaluation . . . gave us an opportunity to restructure the New Zealand economy, and the National Development Conference has charted for us the methods by which this can be achieved'.[90] The 1969 and 1970 Budgets implemented many NDC recommendations. Farmers got more generous tax allowances for development, especially to encourage conversion from dairy to beef (an explicit response to changing overseas markets) and into larger units. Manufacturing exports, forestry, fishing, tourism and aquaculture were similarly encouraged, which anticipated some of the major developments of the next 20 years.[91] None of this was without cost. The revenue foregone through incentives to farmers and manufacturers had to be made up by other taxpayers, and the equity of such arrangements is still debated.[92]

Farmers were particularly favoured by the National government. More generous support in 1970, including increased fertiliser subsidies and exemption from land tax, was justified as compensating farmers for drought and rising costs, a combination which, it was said, had given rise to something approaching a crisis of confidence in farming (and that despite the financial gains from devaluation). Treasury, while agreeing that production needed to increase, thought that across-the-board subsidies were palliatives that encouraged waste and distorted investment decisions while doing little to address real problems.[93] Despite this generous support, the farming lobby remained vociferous in its demands. In 1971 prices for farm exports were high, but the farming organisations expected further compensation for the two less-remunerative years immediately before.[94] Treasury warned that meeting all the farmer demands would mean tax increases, but it would 'obviously be difficult for the Government to get farmers to accept that the prospects for the coming year are so good that any further assistance is unnecessary'. The extent to which further assistance would be justified depended on the outcome of the EEC negotiations. If New Zealand secured a poor deal, 'the manufacturing sector may have to make a much greater contribution to earning foreign exchange' and farming assistance should not entrench existing patterns of production. The Budget needed to play for time and include 'assistance to farmers only where it is necessary to maintain the viability of the industry. It is clear for example that there is no longer a case for any assistance to the dairy industry'.[95]

The EEC negotiations, although fraught and lengthy, resulted in a reasonable deal for New Zealand exporters. Whereas New Zealand ministers had expected Britain to seek long-term guarantees for New Zealand access, London was disinclined to do so by the time of the second British application in 1967. The most that could be expected was a transitional arrangement, and the British would negotiate even that with reluctance. The French vetoed the second British application as they had the first, but in 1970 there was a new president in the Élysée and a new Prime Minister in Downing Street. Georges Pompidou was far less resistant to EEC enlargement than de Gaulle, and Edward Heath was fully committed to British membership. For New Zealand, Marshall continued to take the principal role, and led the final round of negotiations in Luxembourg in 1971. Brinkmanship was the order of the day. In the face of persistent British refusal to push for a transitional level for dairy produce acceptable to New Zealand, Marshall stated:

> that regretfully he would have no option but to take the first plane to London and to say to the media on arrival that Britain was letting New Zealand down. Rippon [the chief British negotiator] said: 'You wouldn't dare'. Marshall, with the well-known urbanity no longer masking the steel, said simply, 'You try me'.[96]

Marshall got satisfactory five-year transitions and Britain, Ireland and Denmark joined the EEC on 1 January 1973. In 1975, the terms of British membership would be renegotiated in Dublin at the insistence of Harold Wilson, who had returned to office in 1974. The Dublin Declaration would allow continuing access for New Zealand farm producers to EEC markets, although price remained a matter of negotiation.

British EEC membership was of great symbolic significance for New Zealand. This symbolism has formed the core of some subsequent accounts. In 2001 James Belich observed that '[i]f a single year has to be chosen as the turning-point [of decolonisation], it would have to be 1973, when Mother Britain ran off and joined the Franco-German commune known as the . . . EEC'.[97] Belich stressed the extent to which New Zealand negotiators portrayed this country as dependent and vulnerable, to the point of infantilisation.[98] It is true, as Singleton and Robertson have emphasised, that 'New Zealand was a supplicant with little leverage. . . . [and] was lucky to enjoy 10 years of respite before Britain finally obtained entry into the Common Market in 1973'.[99] But, as Singleton and Robertson show, there is more to it than that. The British market for New Zealand exports was weakening from the mid 1950s. As Marshall told Parliament, even if Britain had not joined the EEC, the trade agreements with New Zealand would have been renegotiated, and both Ireland and Denmark were providing stiff competition in dairying. New Zealand would not be in a sellers' market.[100]

As some British officials and the Foreign Secretary admitted, open New Zealand opposition would have reinforced the anti-EEC lobby, possibly defeating British membership in the House of Commons.[101] If New Zealand had done that, Britain could hardly have remained sympathetic to this country's exporters. It would have been a doomsday option. An amicable British accession was the best result all round. That said, the British had to be pushed very hard by New Zealand diplomats and ministers; senior British figures, and the British High Commissioner in New Zealand, regarded New Zealand as both a nuisance and as a captive market for manufactured goods. There was great annoyance in London when in 1967 the New Zealand government, after prolonged lobbying, rejected British jets for the domestic airline NAC in favour of cheaper and (as it proved) far more successful American-manufactured Boeing aircraft.[102]

Privately at least, Holyoake had some sympathy for the British view that their EEC membership would cause New Zealand to grow up economically.[103] In fact the prospect provoked that process. In 1950, Britain took 66 per cent of New Zealand exports, and that proportion was maintained until the 1957–58 balance of payments crisis. In 1959, Britain took only 56.6 per cent of this country's exports, and the proportion fell below half in the June 1963 year.

Table 6.1 Destination of New Zealand exports, percentages by value

June year	UK	EEC	US	Aust	Other
1963	47.44	17.57	16.78	4.40	13.81
1964	47.38	18.6	14.70	4.64	14.68
1965	50.81	16.19	12.27	4.69	16.04
1966	44.51	15.74	14.12	4.78	20.85
1967	43.7	11.65	15.86	4.89	23.90
1968	43.31	10.53	17.01	7.11	22.04
1969	39.12	12.32	17.45	7.65	23.46

(Source: NZOYB, 1970, p 643.)

The British share continued to fall rapidly; in 1971 it was only 34 per cent. Dairy exports, however, which were 15 per cent in 1969 of all New Zealand exports, were overwhelmingly concentrated in the British market.[104] Export diversification had been of fundamental importance since the mid 1950s. The 1966 wool shock had reinforced the importance, and rapidly increasing export earnings after 1970 suggested that the transition was proceeding well. In reality, the commodity boom of the early 1970s was linked to instability in the international economy.

The Fracturing International Settlement 1971–72

By 1971 it was becoming clear that some fundamentals of the international postwar economy were fracturing. The most significant was the end of the Bretton Woods regime of stable exchange rates based around a peg to the US dollar, which in turn was pegged to gold at $35 per ounce. Although some economic historians argue that the transition to more flexible or floating exchange rates was accomplished relatively painlessly, there was at the time considerable anxiety in treasuries and central banks.[105] Whereas the United States trade surplus had meant a scarcity of dollars in the early postwar years, by the late 1950s American investment and military bases overseas had resulted in a sustained outflow of dollars. Increasingly, these dollars were held by private institutions, which were immune to 'regulation and control by government bodies in general and American regulatory and other decrees in particular'.[106] Exchange rate stability was increasingly difficult with 'the growth of capital mobility and increasing porousness of capital controls'.[107]

The key to exchange rate stability was the guarantee that dollars could on demand be redeemed for United States gold. But there was an implicit dilemma. For the dollar to work as a reserve currency and international liquidity to remain high, dollars had to be plentiful outside the United States. But that meant US balance of payments deficits, which undermined confidence in the dollar and gave holders of dollars an incentive to redeem them for gold before anyone else did.[108] Indeed, if the dollar was to be a long-term reserve currency then 'the United States could maintain the convertability of the dollar only through internal deflation' – much as Gladstonian orthodoxy had been integral to sterling's long reign as the premier reserve currency a century earlier. But if the United States tightened monetary and fiscal policy to strengthen its balance of payments and reduce the pool of overseas-held dollars, then deflation might spread from the US to all countries and, with balance of payments worsening in many countries, general protectionism might ensue. American political circumstances meant 'a demand for both social spending at home and military spending abroad' and these demands were satisfied without tax increases in the mid 1960s; thus policy became more inflationary. Many European countries, and Japan, had no wish to see the dollar devalued, since that would undermine their own export strategies.[109]

There had been intermittent alarms during the 1960s, which American and European central banks dealt with by establishing a gold pool in which they bought and sold their own gold reserves as necessary in order to maintain the price at $35 per ounce. By the end of the decade, in the wake of the Six Day War and the sterling devaluation of 1967, the pool was falling apart as individual central banks and private buyers traded their dollar reserves for American gold. The pool ended in March 1968.[110] In subsequent months the United States managed to replenish its own gold reserves, but during 1971 West European governments, fearing another shortage of gold, cashed dollars in. It was the classic problem: collective self interest was in stability, individual self interest was in maximising one's own position.[111]

What turned a problem into a crisis, in the view of some scholars, was the attitude of the Nixon administration. President Nixon judged that 'the United States could no longer afford the luxury of supporting the Western economic system as a whole. He would do what was best for the domestic economy and his own political future and let the international economic system adapt to the United States'.[112] Nixon's Treasury Secretary, John Connally, summarised the administration's attitude with admirable clarity: 'Foreigners are out to screw us. Our job is to screw them first'.[113] Catherine Schenk has shown that Nixon was actively contemplating smashing Bretton Woods for two years before August 1971, egged on by Connally, who persuaded the president 'that America's global political and strategic dominance depended on economic hegemony and that economic nationalism would deliver political gains at home'.[114] Thus, Nixon destroyed Bretton Woods because he 'wanted no systemic restraints on his power over the domestic economy. Placing little value on international economic and monetary policy, Nixon believed that increased global competition made a healthy balance of trade a nation's chief international economic priority'.[115]

Other scholars place less emphasis on the wickedness of Richard Nixon and more on the long-term dilemma that the United States faced. One does not have to be an admirer of Nixon to accept that he had a point in regarding domestic deflation and austerity, or increasing interest rates, as too high a price to pay for maintaining the dollar at \$35 to the ounce of gold, although Nixon's approach was to maximise American interest rather than negotiate a resolution of the problem.[116] In 1971 first the Low Countries, then Germany, then France cashed in their dollars for gold, and finally on Friday 13 August Britain requested gold for \$3 billion of its dollar holdings.[117] On 15 August Nixon suspended convertibility of dollars into gold. In November the United States persuaded other western powers to accept, in the Smithsonian agreement, an 8.5 per cent devaluation of the dollar against gold and the permanent end of convertibility into gold. In anticipation of another US devaluation, the free price of gold continued to rise. In June 1972, under pressure to devalue, the British government allowed sterling to float; with anticipation of another devaluation of the dollar in early 1973, other major currencies were also floated.[118] 'The Bretton Woods international monetary system was no more'.[119]

Muldoon described the monetary crisis of 1971 as 'potentially . . . the most dangerous international economic threat since World

War II' but also as an adjustment that had been long overdue.[120] The end of Bretton Woods signalled another dimension to the end of New Zealand's close economic relationship with Britain. In December 1971 New Zealand followed Australia in changing the intervention currency from sterling to US dollars. This meant that when currency dealing was required in order to maintain the New Zealand dollar at the specified value, the dealing would be in terms of US dollars rather than sterling. It was a tacit recognition that Britain no longer dominated New Zealand's economic relationships. Six months later, with the pound permanently floated, Britain reduced the Sterling Area itself – once so great an influence on New Zealand economic policy – to Britain and Ireland.[121] With continuing instability, not least in the US dollar itself, a new exchange rate regime was worked out over the following months. From July 1973, following discussions in both Canberra and Wellington, and in accordance with Reserve Bank advice, the value of the New Zealand dollar was managed 'in relation to a weighted basket of currencies. This marked a compromise between the desires for greater flexibility in the new environment of floating, and for a stable rate to reassure producers'.[122]

International commodity markets boomed between 1971 and 1973 as many governments unleashed 'a last "dash for growth" and other objectives were forgotten in the process'. This was partly a response to inflation, on the principle that expanding the supply of goods and services would control prices, and 'the freeing of exchange rates was seen as a green light'.[123] There were also political factors. Nixon shamelessly stimulated the American economy before the 1972 presidential election. He 'used the power of his office to ensure the best possible economic climate in 1972, indifferent to the havoc his decisions wreaked on the health of the economy'.[124] Indeed, 'after the 1970 [congressional] election he told his advisers, the "economy *must* boom beginning 7/72"'.[125] Similarly, under pressure from falling growth figures, the 1972 British budget reversed course and was 'highly reflationary'.[126] Commodity prices soared; excluding oil, the increase was 24 per cent in 1972 and 68 per cent in 1973, more dramatic than the 48 per cent of 1950. Food prices 'owed something to special factors . . . the running down of American grain stocks to feed the Russians, but it was essentially a speculative boom of the classical kind . . . . As ever, it reflected buoyant world markets and political tensions; as ever it was fuelled by an excess of world liquidity. Fear of inflation played a part, helping to make those fears come true'.[127]

Muldoon's 1972 Budget was also based on some of these premises. It would be unfair to describe it simply as an expansionary Budget motivated by the election due at the end of the year. All the government's advice, and all indicators to the middle of the year, were that the economy had slowed considerably even as overseas reserves went healthily into surplus thanks to the international commodity boom (and, indeed, as demand for imports fell). Farm export prices were poor in 1971, building and capital investment had declined, business confidence was low and real wage growth had slowed. Unemployment around 5000 was regarded as unacceptable. In short, deflationary policies had succeeded a little too well.[128] The surplus in the overseas account and an unprecedented inflow of overseas capital meant that the money supply was growing fast, and Treasury warned of the inflationary consequences, advising that the 1972 Budget should cautiously stimulate the production of goods and services by fully implementing the recommendations of the McCarthy Commission on social welfare, and giving a temporary income tax rebate. There should be little other stimulation except for a modest incentive to manufactured exports.[129]

The government had established the McCarthy Commission in 1969 to comprehensively review social welfare 30 years after the 1938 Social Security Act. Like similar reviews in other western countries, the commission focussed on relative, rather than absolute poverty (not in itself a new approach) and declared that benefit levels should ensure that all citizens could participate in the life of the community. However, it must be stressed that real hardship had emerged as the welfare system failed to keep up with need. Certainly the commission had no fear that increasing benefits would encourage idleness or dependency.[130] Lang warned that implementing the full range of McCarthy recommendations would alone cost at least $77m annually, 'a net increase in purchasing power [that is] . . . massive by any standards. . . . there is a school of thought . . . which considers that not much more than the implementation of the social security package is required' to stimulate demand. If a 10 per cent income tax rebate were made permanent as Muldoon contemplated, that would cost $110m annually and the overall deficit before borrowing would be between $230m and $280m, compared to a 1971 deficit of $90m.[131]

Muldoon was besieged by National MPs pitching for all manner of subsidies, grants, and incentives for manufacturers and farmers, for increased benefits and greater public spending on infrastructure, especially in rural areas.[132] The Budget was less cautious than Treasury had advised; indeed, Muldoon notoriously declared he'd 'spent the lot,' a comment possibly directed in part at his own colleagues.[133] Muldoon increased public spending by 16 per cent, made the income tax rebate permanent, and gave more generous farm support and incentives or allowances for plant, machinery, and export expansion. The Budget implemented the McCarthy recommendations in full, increasing social welfare expenditure by a third; whatever the electoral attractions of such a course, it also reflected the then-strong liberal and progressive strand in National thinking. The Budget certainly stimulated the economy, but did not have the same effect on the National Party's political fortunes, for the election at the end of November saw a landslide Labour victory.[134]

Conclusion

National had governed New Zealand for 12 years. They had been years of significant economic change, but the radicalism was understated because of the government's preference for cautious and incremental reform. It has suited commentators on the left and right to characterise the Holyoake years as years of drift, to observe that 'his greatest feat as a Prime Minister was the slowing down of every process which, if speedily dealt with, might have represented change and political harm'.[135] Bassett wrote that the Holyoake government 'will be remembered more for the opportunities lost than for those it seized'.[136] Such characterisations are unfair, even though Holyoake did prefer to avoid drama and therefore sometimes missed the chance to motivate and shape public opinion. To focus on Holyoake in this way, however, ignores the fact that economic policy is made by many actors in the public service and in central banking, to say nothing of the private sector. Holyoake and his ministers had to and did respond to a changing world, particularly the British move into Europe and the faltering of American economic hegemony. One can identify a broad consensus about the direction in which economic policy needed to go during the 1960s. The deficiencies of the British market were evident before 1960, and the search for export market and commodity diversification was a bipartisan affair. Equally, there was more bipartisan agreement than rhetoric allowed on the need for industrial development for all three reasons of employment promotion, import substitution, and export diversification. There was frequent recognition of the need to defer some present consumption in the interests of greater investment for productivity growth, although this precept was often approached in a manner that owed something to St Augustine's prayer for the virtue of chastity – 'but not yet'. And although there were differences of emphasis, there was consensus that the state should have the dominant role in providing social services.

Yet the differences between Labour and National mattered. National undoubtedly treated farmers more generously than Labour would have, and Labour would probably have been more directive in developing manufacturing. Whether Labour could have worked out an incomes policy remains unknown. It has become the conventional wisdom to attribute National's defeat in 1972 to the effluxion of time. There is some truth in that, but the economic difficulties of the preceding five years had taken their toll. Moreover, of course, 1972 represented a generational shift, with young voters enrolling in unprecedented numbers. The optimism that accompanied the Labour victory was an optimism based on continuing relative affluence, and necessarily, on the impossibility of predicting that an economic crisis of almost unprecedented severity was imminent.

Chapter 7

Crisis 1973–77

The long global postwar boom ended in 1973–74, and the New Zealand economy fell into the worst crisis since the Great Depression, a crisis that was all the more severe for its suddenness. The New Zealand economy had slowed in the first half of 1972 but recovered fast. When Labour came to office at the end of November 1972, the party believed that circumstances allowed rapid expansion of social services. Labour's biggest problem during 1973 was managing inflation in a booming economy. The crisis of 1974 was triggered by the first oil shock, when Middle Eastern oil exporters quadrupled the price of crude oil. Industrial economies rapidly fell into recession, and New Zealand's pastoral export prices fell precipitously while oil prices drove import spending upwards.

The general pattern since 1945 had been prosperity and growth. Economic confidence crashed just as many other dimensions of the postwar world were also changing. The rapid population growth of the postwar years slowed as birth-rates fell and marriage ages began slowly to rise again. Immigration was tightened. Some profound shifts were beginning in gender roles, conjugal relationships and lifestyles that challenged many of the assumptions of 1950s and 60s social policy. Although Māori birth-rates had dropped to the average, the sheer numbers of young Māori women who had been born during the 1940s and 50s meant that the Māori population continued to grow fast during the 1970s. Many Māori had moved into the towns and cities after 1956, and Pacific peoples, immigrating to New Zealand in increasing numbers since 1960, were also becoming a significant part of the population. Often Māori and Pacific workers were in low-paid occupations; a once white urban working-class now became culturally diverse. Economically and socially, New Zealand was changing profoundly in the 1970s.

Among the casualties of the recession was the Labour government. While Labour struggled to manage the recession in ways that would not unduly disadvantage those on lower incomes, the complexities of crisis management escaped many voters. Robert Muldoon led the National Party back into office at the end of 1975, promising to rapidly restore economic prosperity. Muldoon applied policies of severe deflation in his first 22 months as Prime Minister, but from the end of 1977 he moderated these policies and his approach became increasingly inconsistent.

Both Labour and National sought to build an export-led recovery while managing the transition costs. In that sense there was strong continuity in the years since 1966. Both Labour and National sought to buy time; both found the crisis far worse than imagined. Both agreed that mass unemployment was unacceptable. Yet there were continuing differences. Labour shielded the low-paid from severe retrenchment; National was not so inhibited and their tilt towards farmers and manufacturers, and business generally, was more than rhetorical.

Labour: From Boom to Bust

Labour's election victory was decisive, but perhaps the electorate was 'more bored, and irritated, than genuinely discontented' in 1972.[1] National had lost only a relatively small proportion of its 1969 vote, and even at the time one scholar thought Labour's 'handsome majority . . . [did] not reflect a massive shift in public attitudes'.[2] Yet the new government enjoyed considerable support as it seemed to offer a fresh and modernising approach; the new Prime Minister Norman Kirk personified a vigorous and compassionate nationalism. Kirk, born to working-class parents in 1923, left school at the age of 12 and followed a variety of manual occupations. With his quick intelligence and absorbent mind he became well-read, if occasionally suspicious of liberal middle-class intellectuals. Elected to Parliament in 1957, he displaced Nordmeyer as party leader in 1965. To the extent that Kirk reflected on economic matters, as a sympathetic scholar has observed, he regarded a stronger sense of national identity as a prerequisite to engaging in a world where trade competition was fierce and New Zealand would need to be aggressively marketed.[3] Kirk's vision of nationhood was compelling, but he 'failed . . . in being unable to offer an adequate economic component to that vision' other than prosperity, fair shares all round and a generous level of social services.[4] While the poverty of his youth clearly shaped Kirk's views, he had little appreciation that economic policy, especially after 1973, involved hard choices.[5]

The new finance minister, Bill Rowling, had fewer illusions. Rowling, the first trained economist to hold the position, represented a rural South Island electorate, and shared Kirk's memories of the Depression, reinforced by a family background in the Labour Party. Despite later caricatures of him that portrayed his mild manners as weakness, Rowling was a tough and determined politician.[6] Kirk reputedly distrusted Rowling, as the latter had supported Nordmeyer in 1965 and possessed a master's degree.[7] Rowling rapidly won the respect of Treasury officials; Henry Lang described him as 'the best Minister I ever worked for. . . . a strong man with a clear philosophy and high moral values. . . . and he had absolute integrity'.[8] Labour's economic approach in the early 1970s was consistent with the direction laid down by Nordmeyer in the late 1950s. Export diversification, more intensive agricultural and pastoral farming, and industrial development had become bipartisan after 1960. Labour in 1972 promised, in general terms, to move faster, provide additional finance and public assistance, continue industrial protection and emphasise regional development. Saving and investment would be encouraged. The impression was that Labour would enact policy more vigorously and decisively, with some attention to redistributing wealth and income.[9]

Inflation was the government's first problem. An international commodity boom from the middle of 1972 meant high export earnings and substantial overseas reserves.[10] The Organisation for Economic Co-operation and Development later referred to 'collective mistakes in demand-management'. After the end of Bretton Woods, each government had stimulated its own economy without considering the extent to which the combined effect of national policies was 'mutually reinforcing. While no country took expansionary steps that seemed excessive by its own historical standards, the fact that all took steps together was probably one reason why there emerged an unwanted buoyancy of demand and the subsequent commodity price-rise'.[11] Imported raw materials also increased in price, and exporters had money to spend.[12] Inflationary pressure also came from the high rate of marriage and family formation: 1971 was the peak year for marriage numbers, which meant demand for land, houses, and consumer durables. The government continued to encourage immigration; while this expanded the labour force, it further added to demand.[13] Muldoon's 1972 Budget had also stimulated the economy, particularly by implementing the McCarthy Commission reforms in social welfare.[14]

To manage inflation the government continued price control and revalued the currency twice (once by default in February 1973 by not devaluing when the United States did and once explicitly in September). The effect was to reduce exporters' incomes and therefore the money supply, and to cheapen imports. During 1973 the government also limited meat and fish exports in order to service domestic demand, and loosened import licenses.[15] Yet at the same time, the government's economic and social agenda was ambitious. As Lang wryly put it, the 1973 Budget was to put 'emphasis on human values . . . the milk of human kindness should flow freely'.[16] The Budget increased health and education spending significantly, relaxed the criteria for family benefit capitalisation in housing and reduced income tax for the majority while increasing it for the highly paid.[17]

Labour intended to encourage further expansion in manufacturing and thought it desirable to spread manufacturing through the regions. Under the minister, Warren Freer, the department of Trade and Industry oversaw regional councils in 'priority areas' and allotted such support as freight subsidies, skills training and interest-free loans for plant and machinery. The Development Finance Corporation, which Labour nationalised, reinforced this approach. The National government had intended to phase quantitative import controls out after 1973 and rely solely on tariff protection, believing that this would not only allow 'steady industrial development, increasing manufacturing exports, and full employment' but would also 'encourage competition, efficiency, and reasonable prices'.[18] Labour reversed this policy, evidently preferring the fine-tuning possibilities of import licensing; many manufacturers, too, were wary of a change to tariff protection.[19] To divert investment from property to more productive enterprise, and restrain inflation in land values, Labour imposed a property speculation tax, payable where investment properties were sold within two years from purchase. It would become very unpopular with a vocal minority.

The government accompanied its greater commitment to manufacturing with reduced support for farming. Rowling and Treasury thought that high prices for farm exports in 1973 presented a rare opportunity for cutting subsidies on fertiliser and development inputs. Even without subsidies, farm development expenditure was tax-deductible, and Labour had quickly established the Rural Bank as a state-owned agency for farm financing.[20] More generally, some subsidies might 'simply pay farmers to do what they are doing already' and Treasury had 'some doubts whether the farmers need any inducement beyond the normal market information'.[21] Rowling cut the $43m farm subsidy bill by about two thirds.[22] Trade development, of course, was more important than ever, and the government joined the OECD, principally in order to strengthen relationships with Western Europe and other industrialised states. National would not in practice have dissented from Labour's trade initiatives, which were to extend markets in Latin America, East Asia, China (Kirk having recognised the People's Republic in December 1972), Eastern Europe and the Middle East.[23]

A general air of prosperity continued into the later part of 1973. The government could feel that it had made a good start on enacting its manifesto. Then, on Yom Kippur, 6 October, Egypt and Syria attacked

Israel. The war lasted three weeks; Israel initially suffered reverses before being rescued by American weaponry. In retaliation, Arab oil-producing states imposed an oil embargo and sharply increased the price. The oil shock was only the final event in the causal chain of global recession. Volatility in currency markets following the collapse of the Bretton Woods system of pegged exchange rates did not help trade. Rapid growth in productivity in the major industrial powers, evident for 20 years or more, was tailing off. The uncertainty caused by the oil shock contributed to political and economic instability around the world.[24]

It was of course not immediately obvious that there had been a fundamental change. As late as April 1974 the Reserve Bank thought that despite inflationary pressures, shortages and uncertainty regarding oil, 'for the economy in general the immediate future looks reasonably good' with export diversification giving particular cause for optimism.[25] Treasury was more pessimistic, although it saw the downturn as little different in nature from 1957, 1960 or 1966, where rapid expansion had been followed by a crash. Normally the slowdown would have been gradual into 1975, but a number of factors made likely 'rather severe and protracted difficulties. We face a serious deterioration in our terms of trade, heavy upward pressure on prices and wages, and the prospect of a further massive increase in Government expenditure. This combination of factors could produce a critical balance of payments situation'.[26] Treasury therefore thought the 1974 Budget had to reduce demand, although not so much as to deter essential investment, which should be supported by borrowing in the following two years. Importing should be discouraged by tighter controls and by allowing prices to rise.[27] Continued price and wage control would be essential 'for the foreseeable future if stability and full employment are to be maintained'. As time passed, options narrowed and the 'longer corrective measures are delayed, the more severe the ultimate adjustment process will have to be', with significant unemployment the almost inevitable result.[28]

Rowling sought to maintain employment while encouraging adjustment. His 1974 Budget increased short-term debt to maintain public spending. Manufacturing received more assistance with scientific, technical and market research, and it would be encouraged to become more competitive through reduced protection. Farm subsidies increased slightly. Rowling sought also to maintain the government's social policy agenda, particularly by increasing housing expenditure (this, of course, would assist in maintaining employment). Overall public spending rose by 18 per cent, although revenue had risen by 20 per cent.[29] The situation deteriorated rapidly through the winter, however. Inflation reached double figures. The major industrial economies went into deflation, and demand for New Zealand exports dropped. As import prices rose, New Zealand's terms of trade index fell by 23 per cent in the year to June 1974, wiping out all the benefit of increased production. With soaring oil prices and the large quantity of imports ordered at the height of the boom, the record overseas surplus of $347m in the year to May 1973 became a record deficit of $993m in the year to March 1975.[30] Treasury officials had to pin extra sheets of paper to the wall to draw the graph of precipitously declining overseas reserves 'until the deficit literally hit the floor'.[31]

Labour: Managing the Crash

Kirk had been in failing health and died at the end of August 1974. By some accounts, to the end he remained suspicious of and unhelpful to his finance minister, who was often and unfairly portrayed as a bloodless technocrat, without emotional connection to the traditions of the Labour Party.[32] The party caucus, however, elected Rowling to replace Kirk and finance in turn went to Bob Tizard, a former history lecturer who had shadowed the portfolio before the 1972 election. Rowling and Tizard would co-ordinate policy well, but they had an appalling inheritance. Labour's approach to the recession was, first, to maintain employment and ensure that those on lower incomes did not experience undue hardship; second, to encourage a continuing reorientation towards exporting; and third, as a necessary condition of the first two, to control inflation.

As the economy moved into recession, an incomes policy became even more important than it had been in the boom. Kirk had vocally denounced the National government's approach in 1972 and promised to restore free wage bargaining; the unions expected nothing less. As one backbencher observed, wage-led inflation was 'a problem which we had brought on ourselves to some extent'.[33] The FOL president, Tom Skinner, had reassured Kirk that the FOL would work for stable industrial relations.[34] The government at first, and with little success, relied on Skinner's assurances, with the incentives of price control, tax cuts, and a three-year freeze on charges for government-provided services.[35]

In June 1973 the government's lenient approach collapsed and the Labour cabinet showed itself at least as willing as its National predecessor to impose wage restraint. A new boilermakers' award in March had increased minimum wages by around 10 per cent. Their union demanded that the increase be applied to actual as well as minimum rates. After prolonged industrial action, an independent arbitrator, C. H. Benney, found in favour of the union. The Benney decision flowed through many trades. In August the government imposed a general wage increase of 8.5 per cent capped at 14.5 cents per hour and reduced by any earlier wage increase given since February. The government also specified that the term of all awards and agreements would be enforced, and imposed a month-long price freeze.[36] The regulations, intended to be a temporary expedient, 'marked the beginning of four years of continuous statutory control of wages and prices' as the economic situation became increasingly difficult.[37]

When ministers began to discuss a new approach to wages, in January 1974, oil prices had quadrupled. The Cabinet Committee on Policy and Priorities warned that there were essentially two ways to control inflation: unemployment or an incomes policy, which would have to be mandatory rather than advisory, as well as flexible and generally acceptable.[38] It was a difficult specification at the best of times. In April 1974, with inflation breaking 10 per cent, Cabinet agreed on Wage Adjustment Regulations that gave a 9 per cent General Wage Order, with an additional 2.25 per cent negotiable in specific cases. There would also be benefit increases and a new Higher Salaries Commission for senior public sector salaries. The total was more generous than some ministers had hoped, but was based on Skinner promising he could 'obtain union acceptance of this, and . . . ensure that the subsequent wage bargaining would give rise to moderate increases'.[39] Despite Skinner's promise, the FOL was unimpressed, demanding a return to free wage bargaining and publicly doubting the efficacy of price controls. The employers professed themselves 'staggered' by the wage increases, and farmers and manufacturers were also unhappy.[40]

When Tizard took over Finance in September 1974, Treasury advised that if borrowing was to work, domestic demand had to be tightly constrained and inflation rigidly controlled in order to free up money for the investment 'required [for] continuing growth in employment opportunities'.[41] Constraining domestic demand while protecting the low-paid meant capped wage increases. On 13 December 1974 Rowling announced a package of measures. There would be an increase of four per cent on the first $75 of weekly gross wages. Benefits would increase, and housing finance would prioritise low and medium income earners. To encourage employment, the government would make additional farm development finance available, the Reserve Bank would increase its deposits with the trading banks to increase investment funds, and company taxpayers could defer payment. Rowling noted that the four per cent in addition to an earlier increase meant that everyone earning

$10,000 or less 'would be more than fully compensated' for the year's inflation and he warned quite bluntly that 'If we cannot contain rises in money incomes, we face recession and unemployment'.[42] Even the trade unions appeared persuaded.[43]

Matters were no easier in 1975. The Budget, Lang warned, would have to deliver 'restraint in aggregate demand through appropriate monetary and fiscal policies, and a break in the wage-price spiral through a successful incomes policy' if the government was to have a hope of 'restoration of a manageable balance of payments situation, maintenance of full employment and control of inflation'. Public spending had increased much more than provided for in 1974; the pre-borrowing deficit was $400m and looked likely to increase to $1100m. This trend had to be reversed if the government wished to avoid 'a situation where we might have to borrow abroad on terms which involve the lenders dictating our economic policies. As the recent UK Budget makes clear the priorities of lenders would be different from ours, notably in the field of full employment'. The government faced hard choices and Lang, 'fully aware of the difficulties . . . [had] tried to select those that interfere with the least number of sacred cows'.[44]

Some sacred cows survived the Budget. Spending on housing, health and education all increased: social policy and employment again intersected. Tizard significantly increased taxation on petrol and duty on imported electronic and optical goods, cosmetics and jewellery. He left food subsidies and post, rail and electricity charges unchanged despite officials' recommendations; Cabinet felt bound by its 1972 commitment to not increase government charges during the parliamentary term.[45] To encourage wage restraint, Tizard reduced taxes on modest and low incomes while increasing them on higher. Wage increases, again, would be capped; 'only the lower paid together with the beneficiaries can be fully compensated for estimated price rises in the first half of this year'.[46] Farmers received additional price support, reduced government charges, extended fertiliser bounties, and additional funding for the Rural Bank.[47] A new Industries Development Commission would encourage reorganisation, structural change, and efficiency in manufacturing, while regional development measures would expand.[48]

Tizard had claimed in his Budget that the economy had come through the recession 'with a minimum of damage'.[49] Ten weeks after the Budget, the government was forced to accept that 'the recovery has been longer delayed and weaker than expected' and devalued the dollar by 15 per cent, having already devalued by 6.2 per cent in September 1974.[50] The 1975 devaluation appeared to be sudden, but Muldoon had been talking up the prospect earlier in 1975.[51] In the first week of

July 1975 Lang suggested to his deputy, Noel Lough, that devaluation should be done quickly to minimise speculation and maximise the advantages. Tizard agreed that work should be done on the issue, but did not commit himself. By the middle of the month, with Federated Farmers demanding huge subsidies, officials' opinion firmed, and on 23 July Treasury and Bank officials and Colin Moyle, the Minister of Agriculture, agreed on a 20 per cent devaluation. Rowling and Tizard noted that price rises associated with 20 per cent would be a problem for incomes policy.[52] A secret paper from the Bank and Treasury on 29 July noted that 'terms of trade [were] about as bad as those of the 1930s'. Early recovery was increasingly unlikely; importing had to be deterred and exporting encouraged, and the combined alternatives to devaluation were complex and amounted virtually to a siege economy.[53] Eventually the figure of 15 per cent was agreed. With floating rates overseas, the New Zealand dollar had appreciated significantly against other currencies, and Rowling emphasised the need for a 'sizeable transfer of real incomes back to farming', as farmers had taken the brunt of the recession and exporting needed further encouragement.[54]

The Muldoon Victory, 1975

The economic situation was extremely serious by late 1975. Muldoon had replaced Marshall as National leader in July 1974, and a business magazine summarised the government's political problem:

> the biggest thing National has going for it is the economy. The Muldoon message is getting through; Mr Rowling and Mr Tizard have conceded that they were over-optimistic last year, and the borrowing goes on. The fact that a good many economists believe that this Government . . . has really done none too badly in human terms is largely irrelevant. Economic messages are not easy to put across, and Muldoon has the great art of simplifying issues into terms of their lowest common denominator.[55]

'None too badly in human terms' meant that unemployment remained below 5000, but Muldoon's 'lowest common denominator' amounted to attributing the entire blame for the country's economic difficulties to Labour's mismanagement, along with a good deal of red-baiting and various other appeals to prejudice; 'Labour's moderate social democracy was portrayed as akin to Stalinist communism'.[56] National's 1975 manifesto included a list of unexceptionable intentions regarding savings, investment, and price stability. Unsurprisingly, Muldoon promised farmers increased export incentives, and reassured manufacturers that import liberalisation would be tightly controlled.

Muldoon accused Labour of having 'destroyed . . . prosperity, dissipated our reserves, trebled the rate of inflation . . . and turned New Zealand into an international mendicant. . . . economic policy [will be] very largely devoted to restoring New Zealand's shattered economy'.[57] Implicitly, therefore, a degree of fiscal restraint was foreshadowed.

National convincingly won the 1975 election, and Muldoon took the finance portfolio for himself. As even his sympathetic biographer observes, he should not have, given the contrast between the broad overview required of a Prime Minister and the detailed work required in finance. 'It was an arrogant presumption on Muldoon's part that any person could do both jobs and equally presumptuous to judge that no one else in the caucus was capable of doing one of them'.[58]

Muldoon's relationship with Treasury was complicated by his antipathy to Henry Lang. They had worked together well enough between 1967 and 1972, but by 1975 Muldoon's attitude had changed (famously, Lang observed to a colleague after they had briefed the Prime Minister that 'My father said nothing in this world was perfect. But you have just met a perfect bastard').[59] Muldoon apparently maintained that Lang offered his advice too forcefully and tried to make policy rather than merely advise on it (perhaps Muldoon resented Lang's evident respect for Rowling).[60] Lang's diary details the breakdown of the relationship. Although at their first post-election meeting Lang 'was received most cordially', within a few days Muldoon 'returned to his more normal abrasive manner'. The two had sharp differences over superannuation. Lang, quite properly, did not attempt to obstruct Muldoon's intention to replace Labour's scheme with his own, but, equally properly, his advice emphasised the difficulties of winding up the Labour scheme and the inflationary effect of returning contributions. Muldoon 'was impatient with administrative delays . . . His ignorance was exceeded only by his breathtaking arrogance'.[61] What probably damaged the relationship beyond repair was Muldoon releasing the confidential Treasury briefing on the economy, with a covering press release that misrepresented the document. Lang was outraged that his confidential advice had been enlisted in political controversy.[62]

Treasury described a grave situation, with the 'worst terms of trade for a generation'. Inflation, the government deficit, and private consumption all needed to fall in order to allow export-oriented investment. A 'firm incomes policy' was necessary 'to prevent any improvements being cancelled out by increased demand for imports'. Government charges should be reviewed and some increased, spending controlled, and subsidies maintained but not increased.[63] Muldoon's accompanying press statement was crude political propaganda, claiming that a 'situation even more serious than he had predicted during the general election campaign . . . was disclosed in a report furnished . . . by the Secretary to the Treasury'. The report, said Muldoon, 'exposed the shallowness of the soothing electioneering statements on the economy made by . . . Labour. . . . [who had] squandered their inheritance and burdened the country with massive debts'.[64] Quite apart from involving a most senior public servant in political controversy, Muldoon's statement was simply untrue. Treasury had said that the 'sharp increase in the rate of growth of Government expenditure was justifiable in 1975–76 as a temporary expedient' in order to mitigate the oil shock and the recession, but public spending would need to be controlled if an export-led recovery was not to be undermined by rampant inflation.[65]

Treasury stressed that the crisis required long-term solutions. Citizens needed to accept the necessity of change, and a consensus on the direction of change had to be shaped. Given the welfare state and public services, citizens had to understand that only economic growth could provide the necessary funding, and growth entailed making choices. Investment for export growth meant forgoing present consumption; saving had to be encouraged, and subsidies, incentives, and protection reviewed in order to give more space to market forces. Managing the upswing part of the cycle had to be improved in order to minimise importing and inflationary blowouts.[66] This prescription differed only in its strength and urgency from a lot of advice over the previous 20 years. To broaden the range of advice, Muldoon established within the Prime Minister's Department an Advisory Group of officials on temporary secondment. The head of the Prime Minister's Department, and of the Advisory Group, was Bernard Galvin, who had been a senior official in Treasury and to which he would return as Secretary in 1980.[67] Muldoon appears to have been unconcerned about senior officials' own political views (other than Lang) and treated them with 'courteous formality. . . . Although few of them liked him, most senior Treasury officials respected Muldoon's intelligence and work habits'.[68] At least, they did in 1976; later, there would be rumblings of discontent.

Muldoon's initial approach to the crisis was a stronger version of 1967: a sharp attack on public spending by reducing subsidies and increasing charges for state-provided goods and services. Treasury had advised increasing government charges (particularly rail, post and telecommunications) by a total of $234m and reducing subsidies by $11m. The respective decisions were for $292m and $22m, which Lang privately thought 'a good deal too deflationary and unemployment is likely on a much larger scale than we had previously contemplated'.

The price rises would also make an incomes policy much harder to achieve.[69] For Muldoon, though, the priority was domestic deflation to reduce the budget and trade deficits and free up resources for export growth. Savings, he hoped, would be encouraged by deregulated interest rates.[70] Exporters would be assisted through further incentives and through intensified trade diplomacy.

In presenting the 1976 Budget, Muldoon identified four major problems: inflation, the current account deficit, the fiscal deficit and unemployment. He noted that dealing with any one in isolation exacerbated the others, and accepted that New Zealand faced 'the most dangerous economic situation . . . since the depression of the 1930s'.[71] Muldoon sought to reduce domestic demand further, especially for imports, and imposed more duties on tobacco and imported alcohol, and new sales taxes on outboard motors, radios, televisions and machinery except that required for exporters. Given the non-essential nature of these items, Treasury agreed.[72] Likewise Muldoon and Treasury agreed that continuing farm support was justified as 'in the foreseeable future the greater part of New Zealand's export income will continue to be derived from pastoral and other agricultural products'.[73] Farmers got suspensory loans and tax deductions for livestock increase, as well as tax allowances for new machinery and greater fertiliser subsidies. Muldoon rationalised assistance to manufacturing industries, making it more selective and oriented to exporting, and replaced a progressive company tax with a flat rate.[74] While the Budget was consistent with those of previous years in encouraging exporting, it was more explicitly deflationary. With substantial price increases in many commodities, as well as increased assistance to exporters, some thought Muldoon unduly favoured the well off. The impression would have been reinforced by the enthusiastic support Muldoon had received from some property speculators when he promised to abolish Labour's property speculation tax.[75]

A key element in National's election victory had been the promise to introduce a generous universal superannuation. In 1972, the McCarthy Commission had recommended continuing the mixture of universal and means-tested age benefits that had existed since 1938. Contrary to that recommendation, the Labour government had introduced a compulsory contributory scheme, whereby workers and employers paid into a state fund and payouts were related to earnings over the working life. For those in paid employment, the scheme promised greater security and probably a higher retirement income; it also promised an expanding pool of savings. The biggest problem was precisely that relationship to earnings over the working life; although the rate of female participation in the workforce was increasing, women still often spent lengthy periods out of the paid workforce raising children and this was particularly so for women approaching retirement age. Equal pay, moreover, was recent in the public sector and only foreshadowed in the private sector. The scheme would take decades to become fully operational.[76] Where Labour's scheme related payouts to earnings, National promised a flat rate of 80 per cent of the average wage for a married couple, at the age of 60, regardless of continuing employment or other income, and financed from current revenue. Other public spending would be constrained in order to fund superannuation; in the medium-term Muldoon believed that restored economic growth would make his scheme affordable.[77] It would be charitable to describe this as an optimistic assumption.

Justifying National superannuation, Muldoon and his social welfare minister, Bert Walker, pointed to the hardships older people had experienced ('two world wars and a depression' as the sometimes sardonic shorthand had it). Walker noted that they had been 'taxed hard to compensate for costs and for reconstruction after the second world war, and . . . their savings had been eroded by inflation'.[78] However, they also had many advantages after 1938, as some scholars have pointed out.[79] National superannuation reflected Muldoon's belief that the government should provide material security for 'decent citizens'. His own mother 'had had to survive and bring him up on her own, without any capacity to earn or pay into a funded system'.[80] Muldoon's scheme was socially progressive in that 'men and women were treated independently, as equals, regardless of their work experience'.[81] Inevitably, there would be inequities. Two thirds of those over 60 had other income, and for them National Superannuation was a considerable bonus. The one third who had no other income paid more attention to the effect of inflation on their new superannuation than to the comparison with the earlier regime, or with other western states where the relationship to the average wage differed and the age of eligibility was higher. Muldoon's scheme created a powerful and vociferous lobby of enduring significance, and superannuation (and the call that it made on the public purse) would in time become thoroughly contentious.[82]

There was a contrast, too, between the relatively generous provision for superannuitants and the rhetoric, and sometimes policy, directed at those on other welfare benefits. The Domestic Purposes Benefit, introduced in 1973 (or, more precisely, made statutory rather than discretionary) was a notable example. Fiscal and moral agendas intersected as officials drew attention to the rapidly increasing cost and numbers from 3092 in 1973 to 23,047 in 1976 (although in National Superannuation's first full year, that benefit would cost $926m, and the

DPB only $111m). The heads of Social Welfare and Treasury suggested that the DPB tempted some to precipitately terminate their marriages, and 'some single girls to keep their babies . . . again without regard to the long-term future wellbeing of their children'. In fact only a quarter of recipients were never married and few were under 20.[83] Officials did not make a recommendation, but Walker scapegoated DPB recipients, claiming that many were improperly receiving the money because they were enjoying an excess of male attention. He insisted that any woman on the DPB who engaged in sex with a man more than once a fortnight should forfeit her benefit, a provision subsequently disallowed by the Supreme Court.[84] More generally, Walker was happy to foster a moral panic, explicitly blaming solo mothers for youth delinquency. Walker's approach to the unemployed was similar; in 1976 those receiving unemployment benefit were required to collect the signatures of two employers approached for work every four weeks.[85] This sort of administratively inefficient pin-pricking contributed to an image, which no doubt suited the government, that the ordinary bloke's prosperity was menaced by feckless scroungers. Muldoon observed that 'for some people it is advantageous to remain on a social welfare benefit rather than resume a normal existence'.[86] While Muldoon never made a wholesale reduction in benefit levels, the rhetoric was not meaningless.

Muldoon and Incomes Policy

With inflation running above 15 per cent, an incomes policy remained urgent. Here, Muldoon's approach was inconsistent and counterproductive. He lavished vituperation on militant trade unionists (especially Ken Douglas and Bill Andersen, members of the Moscow-aligned Socialist Unity Party), but was willing to work with some union leaders. Indeed, Muldoon and Tom Skinner often had informal discussions over a Sunday morning drink.[87] The new Minister of Labour, J. B. (Peter) Gordon, was a South Otago farmer widely respected for common sense and a liberal disposition, but Muldoon usually dominated labour policy, to Gordon's frustration, and an incomes policy proved elusive.

Within days of taking office, Cabinet agreed that ministers should meet the FOL and the Combined State Sector Organisations and seek 'agreement to a cost of living order of 3 per cent across the board'. Treasury thought that wage adjustments should not compensate for the August 1975 devaluation, and that real wages should fall by an amount equal to the nine per cent drop in national income during 1974 (real wages had fallen by half that).[88] A capped cost-of-living adjustment would shield the lower-paid.[89] While Muldoon stressed that the government did not, 'and we will not, accept unemployment as a balancing factor in economic management' and, like Rowling, his stated intention was to share the burdens of economic adjustment rather than have them fall disproportionately on those with lower incomes, some of his policies were clearly inconsistent with the latter aim and continued capped adjustments threatened to reduce margins for skill.[90]

The government's hopes for an incomes policy rested on Skinner's control of the FOL. Muldoon got the FOL to agree to postpone the January cost-of-living adjustment, and on 26 January Cabinet issued a small flat-rate wage increase.[91] Muldoon and Skinner agreed on wishing to restore free bargaining as soon as possible, and during March Lang (on behalf of ministers) and Muldoon himself had confidential discussions with Skinner about a tightly managed general wage order.[92] Before anything was agreed, Muldoon told journalists that he was having top-level discussions with the FOL. The FOL vice president, Jim Knox, denied that this was the case, but of course once the news was out the whole executive had to be party to the discussions; Skinner's room to move was correspondingly reduced. As Lang observed, 'the general climate in the wage field has clearly deteriorated as a result of the Prime Minister's faux pas'.[93]

During April, Muldoon came to favour a lengthy wage and salary freeze and strict price controls while a new wage-fixing regime was devised.[94] This plan he did discuss with the FOL executive, indicating his wish to restore free wage bargaining once inflation was below 10 per cent. He got Skinner's support, who persuaded his reluctant colleagues.[95] The Combined State Sector Organizations, however, criticised Muldoon's 'pessimistic view of the future of the economy. . . . far too much weight is being attached to short-term balancing the books, resulting in serious and unnecessary damage to economic and social development and imposing serious hardship on the lower paid'. The CSSO accepted 'in the long term, neither the internal nor the external deficit can be sustained,' but did not favour the Prime Minister with any advice as to how those deficits might be addressed other than through severe retrenchment.[96]

On 14 May, Muldoon announced a 12-month wage freeze (rather longer than officials had thought desirable or possible) and abrogated an imminent Higher Salaries review. There would be a cost-of-living adjustment of no more than $7 per week from the end of June. As the FOL had insisted, the freeze would also apply to professional fees and charges; directors' fees and dividends would be limited. There would be strict enforcement of existing price controls. The package included employment and export incentives, further price support to encourage greater production of wool and meat, and cheap loans for local authorities, to encourage them to expand employment in public works.[97]

Despite Skinner's privately helpful attitude, a special FOL conference urged affiliated unions to take direct action against the freeze.[98] Lang attributed this to 'an alliance between the very conservative Catholic wing of the trade union movement . . . with the Communists,' put together by some unionists who had suffered 'a vindictive campaign' from Muldoon because of their public support for Rowling.[99] Muldoon had not expected such a hostile reaction and angrily asked officials why he had not been warned it would happen. He was reminded that he had been, frequently. 'However this was another example of his hearing only what he wants to hear'. The other problem with Muldoon attempting to manage incomes policy through private discussions with Skinner was that their meetings were, in Lang's view, usually 'distinguished . . . by alcohol consumption rather than clarity'.[100] The government's greater problem was that Skinner did not have Walsh's control over the FOL, and simply couldn't deliver an agreement. Moreover, while Muldoon was all too willing to indulge in aggressive rhetoric, after stiff union opposition, the government moderated the freeze in June 1976, agreeing to apply the seven per cent increase to total pay rather than ordinary time and allow renegotiation of non-monetary conditions. Muldoon also maintained much of Rowling's framework. The 1974 Wage Adjustment Regulations had established an Industrial Commission to deal with wage anomalies, and Muldoon added a Wage Hearing Tribunal to consider general wage orders. Towards the end of 1976 some unions pushed employers into the Commission, which interpreted its remit liberally, and in March 1977 the Tribunal granted a general wage order of six per cent.[101]

Imposing a freeze was one thing. Achieving an enduring incomes policy was quite another. The only common ground seemed to be that a permanent tripartite system was undesirable. Unions and employers disliked constraints on their freedom of action, and ministers regarded it as an unacceptable qualification on the sovereignty of parliament. Yet there was a contradiction in ministers and officials then claiming a broader public interest in wage fixing.[102] The FOL had proposed a return to relativities, whereby a pilot award or benchmarking case would be heard in one of the skilled trades. In the end 'after months of argument, [most] officials came down on the side of the FOL's proposal'.[103] In May 1977, with the issues still unresolved, Muldoon extended the wage freeze to August and then, despite his own doubts, accepted a return to free bargaining, provided that agreements had a life of 12 months and economic stability was the prime consideration in wage-fixing. Muldoon was powerfully motivated by the desire to reinforce Skinner against more militant unionists, but the nature of free bargaining meant it would be unlikely to take much account of broader economic issues.[104]

The return of free bargaining, predictably, meant that strategically positioned unions – meatworkers, pulp and paper workers, transport workers and boilermakers – promptly began campaigning for wage settlements well above the government's comfort level. Notoriously, Muldoon responded to one threatened strike, in the freezing industry in March 1978, by using public funds to subsidise a wage settlement over the opposition of the ministers of labour and agriculture.[105] While Muldoon disavowed unemployment, entirely genuinely, he failed to understand that many workers were finding times really hard. For all his rhetoric, though, Muldoon avoided a major confrontation with industrial labour, and his approach was 'erratic, veering from confrontation to compromise with the unions, from wage freeze to wage bargaining, from telling employers to be firm in resisting wage demands to subsidising them in paying wages which they claimed were untenable'.[106] In the end it was the worst of all worlds, and if employer and union organisations were often unhelpful, inconsistency at the highest level of government was even more so.

A Year of Transition: 1977

There were some signs of a fragile recovery early in 1977. The budget deficit was falling from 9 per cent of GDP in 1975/76; it would be 2.6 per cent two years later. Inflation was easing, although still in double digits. Farmers' incomes increased by 62 per cent in the year to March 1976 on the back of the 1975 devaluation and continued to increase in the following year. Manufacturing export earnings were also increasing. Restrained domestic demand meant that both primary and secondary export volumes had increased faster than output; in other words domestic consumers had been squeezed to increase export earnings, although international prices for foodstuffs also recovered during 1976. The immediately negative consequence of the deflationary approach was unemployment going over 5000, but Treasury was at least as worried about the possibility that increased export earnings would mean another importing binge.[107] In terms of Muldoon's declared intentions, the very tough retrenchment of 1976–77 seemed to be working. At the end of 1977, however, Muldoon would significantly ease the austerity.

Ministers and Treasury alike were understandably uncertain about how to deal with a crisis that was more severe and more prolonged than anyone had anticipated. While some Treasury thinking was beginning to move markedly towards further liberalisation, the department's advice was not always consistent. Ministers, perhaps, were unsure about what might follow austerity, and during 1977 the Cabinet Economic Committee spent a good deal of time on either further reviews or complete trivia. Advised that the current account deficit was 'precarious' in the short-term and 'dangerous' in the longer term, ministers inconclusively dwelt on the prospects for increasing exports and limiting imports, and asked officials to prepare a paper on current and future strategies for managing the balance of payments.[108] A discussion over reconciling price control and incomes policy concluded with ministers asking officials to prepare another paper on broad objectives.[109] On two occasions the Cabinet Economic Committee discussed a subsidy or grant of less than four thousand dollars to a small clothing company in Auckland.[110] Muldoon, immersed in detail, could not take a strategic view, and other ministers may have been inhibited from doing so.

As ministerial initiative began to stall, Treasury advice began to change. Noel Lough, who became Secretary at the beginning of 1977, is credited with 'demanding that more time and effort be devoted to strategic thinking' (not that Lang had eschewed that).[111] Lough encouraged a group of younger officials to argue for much greater liberalisation, and established a new division within the department. Internal Economics II was to deal with 'the constraints on economic growth, the examination of alternative strategies for improving New Zealand's economic performance . . . policies to put the preferred strategy into effect, and . . . re-examination of existing policies which appear to conflict with that strategy'.[112] Economics II would become the base of those officials most associated with policy changes after 1984.

Lough suggested that the 1977 Budget needed to emphasise growth rather than deflation. Tax reform was a particular priority; income tax accounted for 73 per cent of total revenue, increasing from 63 per cent in the early 1960s.[113] Lough thought this trend was 'increasingly being perceived as a major disincentive to personal effort' especially as rising money wages lifted wage-earners into higher tax brackets.[114] Tax reform, also, should 'assist the single income family'.[115] Treasury also suggested that the narrowing gap between benefits and wages was a disincentive to personal effort. The basic benefit had increased by 35 per cent since 1975. Average gross earnings had increased by 28.2 per cent and net earnings by 25.1 per cent, partly because of the thresholds on percentage wage increases applied since 1973. With allowable income on benefits set fairly low and causing abatement, and with relatively high benefit levels, there was, Lough said, little incentive to go off a benefit or to avoid going on one. He raised the possibility of severely low levels for the first six months of a Domestic Purposes Benefit, and for widows, unemployed and the sick.[116] Lough did not explain in what way women chose to go on a widow's benefit, nor why non-age beneficiaries should experience such reductions in order to fund a national superannuation scheme which was so generous that, in Treasury's own calculations, it would see married superannuitants better off than a single-income family, at least before the young-family rebate was taken into account.[117]

Muldoon would delay tax reform until 1978, but did reduce the DPB for the first six months, and made the young-family rebate for wage-earners much more generous (he would increasingly favour using the tax system to deliver targeted support for those supporting families on modest wages).[118] The most significant moves in the 1977 Budget were greatly increased export incentives. As well as manufacturing and traditional farming, the emerging fishing industry received generous incentives for new ships, in anticipation of the Law of the Sea 200 mile exclusive economic zone. Tourism, forestry and horticulture received similar encouragement.[119] These initiatives were directed to the medium term, and Muldoon warned that 'any relaxation of internal restraint in the near future would be irresponsible'.[120]

Four months later, relaxation was precisely what he did. However, it is unfair simply to blame the reversal on Muldoon.[121] Muldoon wavered in the face of rising unemployment, but so did his advisers. Lough warned in mid October that 'the economy shows signs of weakening in the next few months and in 1978–79 real activity will be lower than this year'. Retrenchment and falling real wages were reducing domestic consumption; Treasury feared falling business confidence, which could be averted by a 'modest general reflationary policy' of a tax cut, more funding for regional development, looser monetary policy, further export incentives and job creation through the public sector, lending to local government and subsidies to the private sector.[122] Officials initially favoured more selective reflation, but they rapidly concluded that with business confidence so fragile the government had to take visible action before Christmas. Reflation would worsen the balance of payments deficit 'but the long run costs must be weighed against the long run costs of a severe recession'.[123]

Muldoon delivered a mini-Budget on 28 October. He now admitted that increasing the economy's efficiency and focus on exporting would take time. Without 'much hope for a rapid growth in . . . exports' (as had followed 1967) the government intended to maintain spending and business confidence so as to prevent increased unemployment, 'treading a narrow path between too much and too little stimulus': between inflation and a balance of payments deficit on the one hand and unemployment on the other.[124] Muldoon announced a one-off supplementary family benefit payment of $25 per child (the weekly benefit was $3), cut income tax five per cent across the board, and increased building expenditure by $16m. He eased monetary policy, increased housing finance, and created or expanded a variety of state-funded employment schemes. Once again, he increased export incentives for farmers and manufacturers.[125] In subsequent weeks Muldoon reduced company tax, released farm income retention funds, relaxed import controls and increased housing expenditure.[126]

The 1978 Budget

Treasury's pessimism increased after the 1977 mini-Budget, and Muldoon received bleak advice as he approached the Budget in 1978 (an election year). Output, consumption, investment and employment had contracted during 1977 – very sharply from July – and the economy was virtually static. Prospects for 1978–79 were 'on balance a little brighter but still not very good'. The pre-borrowing deficit was expected to be about $935m; if that was appreciably reduced then unemployment would increase sharply, but a much higher deficit was unacceptable. The government had very little room to move and could do little more than hold the line, particularly as any recovery would probably provoke another balance of payments crisis.[127] Short- and long-term agendas conflicted for Treasury as much as for Muldoon. While advocating stimulation in the short-term, Treasury warned that 'the economy will continue to face a substantial balance of payments problem'. This could not be covered by endless borrowing and 'underlines the need to switch resources to internationally competitive industries while maintaining restraint on public and private expenditure'.[128]

Muldoon, in fact, did not abandon reform in 1978. Lough continued to stress 'an urgent need for personal tax reform. . . . [which was] an essential pre-requisite for a resumed growth in productivity in the private sector'. Inland Revenue agreed.[129] Muldoon wanted to limit the cost of reform to $100m, and was told that significant change required five times as much.[130] Treasury eventually proposed a package, which Muldoon adopted, costing about $300m and aimed at reducing tax on middle incomes. The key was a 'long flat step' of 38c from $4500 pa to $10000 pa (the average income was $7500). Marginal rates would rise from 48c at $10001 to 60c at $22001.[131] Nineteen tax steps were reduced to five, and Muldoon hoped that the package would moderate wage settlements.[132] The trade-off, though, was abolishing the personal rebate on the first $816 of all incomes, which substantially increased tax on incomes under $3000 and must have affected the earnings of many married women; moreover, those at the lower end of the long flat step saw very little increase in take-home pay; the benefit went to those in the middle. Increasing rebates for a sole earner with a young family was only partial compensation.[133]

Farmers continued to receive generous encouragement to increase production and export earnings. Treasury, while not disputing the principle, advised that increases in farm support had to be modest unless the budget deficit were to go over the unacceptable billion dollar mark and, with the Reserve Bank, recommended a devaluation and very moderate increase in farm support.[134] The Ministry of Agriculture recommended increasing support by $200m to a total level of $550m, which Treasury thought 'insupportable'. If that was necessary 'it is clear that we are in a position of fundamental balance of payments disequilibrium'.[135] In the end the increase was $108m. Treasury and Agriculture agreed that higher minimum prices were justified, that beef production should be encouraged, and even Treasury was prepared to accept grants of $26,000 to farmers (nearly four times the average wage) who would improve land and therefore increase production. The 1978 Budget introduced a new price support, Supplementary Minimum Prices, which would become notorious. The intention, by setting SMPs for two years ahead, was to give farmers greater certainty as to minimum income.[136]

Muldoon described the 1978 Budget as 'generous . . . but no more generous than economic realities require'.[137] In fact, the world economy was already picking up. Even in February the situation was less serious than it had seemed when he delivered the mini-Budget.[138] Export markets and the current account would continue to strengthen.[139] By late July there were clear signs of a domestic recovery with imports, retail trade, new car registrations and business confidence all increasing along with overseas reserves. The last of these was the most fragile, particularly if increased liquidity were to be translated into spending rather than investment.[140]

The 1977 mini-Budget is often described as Muldoon's retreat from economic virtue, although the condemnation usually ignores the tax cuts. One official later said that October 1977 'was the time when he stopped trying to be a statesman'.[141] It is too simplistic, though, to suggest that from October 1977 Muldoon simply abandoned economic statesmanship and devoted himself to short-term electoral considerations. Treasury counsels were divided. Jas McKenzie, in charge of Economics II, had severely criticised the 1977 Budget for unadventurousness, and for not matching the rhetoric of fiscal restraint and export development with significant action.[142] His successor at Economics II, Graham Scott, who was in the Prime Minister's Department in 1977, thought the Budget 'too tough and likely to drive the economy down'.[143] Treasury continued to give this sort of advice in the first months of 1978; officials were as concerned as Muldoon at the contracting economy. There was some evidence that the broad strategy of export incentives was working. Nor should it be forgotten that Muldoon broadly accepted Treasury advice for a significant measure of tax reform in the 1978 Budget.

Longer-Term Perspectives

One major problem with Muldoon taking finance for himself was the difficulty in finding time for strategic thinking alongside the detail of economic management. Muldoon did acknowledge the importance of longer-term thinking, and in April 1976 the government established a Task Force on Economic and Social Planning, chaired by Frank Holmes and comprising civil servants from the major economics departments. The Task Force consulted widely, and reported at some length in a document deliberately entitled *New Zealand at the Turning Point*. The very long list of individuals, organisations and companies consulted suggested that there was still a high level of commitment to the development of a national consensus.

The basic issues had not changed since 1968, or indeed 1958. As all now knew, the traditional settler economy had gone, and export diversification had to continue while efficient domestic industry needed to expand; consumption had to be sacrificed to investment. Inflation had to be addressed through a long-term incomes policy. Where the Task Force did cautiously break new ground was in emphasising the increasing diversity of New Zealand society and calling for greater involvement of women, ethnic minorities and Māori in economic and social decision-making. A permanent Planning Council followed.[144] By the end of the decade, the Planning Council's Economic Monitoring Group was reinforcing the Task Force's argument, generally advocating managed liberalisation in price and import control, a shift to indirect rather than direct taxation, reduction of the government's deficit, a managed float of the dollar and a wage-tax trade-off.[145]

Henry Lang took early retirement at the end of 1976. One of his final papers to the Cabinet Economic Committee discussed the options for the rest of the decade. He argued that since the economy was in trouble anyway, 'opportunity should be taken now to make use of the unavoidable short term hardship' and enact fundamental reform. As he had for many years, Lang advocated a 'substantial rather than marginal' shift in resources from domestic consumption to exporting. An export-led growth strategy would require that 'the whole New Zealand economy becomes more efficient' which meant a new strategy that 'places emphasis on creating the appropriate economic climate and leaving the maximum flexibility to the private sector'. Inevitably this would mean a change in relative shares of the national wealth, as exporters' incomes were allowed to grow and investment was encouraged while domestic demand and public sector growth were constrained. Reform would need to proceed on many fronts, including the labour market, transportation, 'a largely ad hoc protection system which also tends to retain resources in relatively uncompetitive industries,' and 'a price control system which rewards efficient and inefficient companies equally'. There was very little scope for further import-substituting industrialisation in any case, 'with certain exceptions such as in the energy field'. Lang's final note was cautiously optimistic: 'we have over the last thirty years developed a modern industrial sector, parts of which have become outward looking and internationally competitive and are now contributing significantly to foreign exchange earnings'.[146] The Cabinet Economic Committee endorsed Lang's analysis with little reservation, although identifying a desirable direction was much easier than working out how the transition might be managed.

Conclusion

The crisis of the mid 1970s demonstrated how the key dimensions of the postwar economy had changed. Dependence on pastoral exports, whether to Britain or a more diverse range of markets, no longer guaranteed prosperity. This had been clear since the early 1960s, and the reorientation had begun before the first oil shock. Worldwide recession after 1973 made the reorientation more urgent. On this, there was little difference between Labour and National administrations.

An increased emphasis on export-led growth in competitive world markets meant a redistribution of wealth and income in favour of exporters. As it had been since at least 1967, this was contentious because it implied reduced focus on domestic consumption and, with the imperative of managing inflation, tighter control of wages. On this point the postwar consensus was weakest, and here the fractures were most evident both in the 1972–73 boom and in the recession after 1974. The institutions of economic management were, it seems, inadequate to shape a new consensus around an economic transition.

Ministers, officials, and the sector groups were all swamped by crisis management after 1974. Labour and National governments both sought an export-led recovery, and both sought to restrain wages. There were significant differences, though. Rowling attempted to protect the low-paid during the transition and sought implicitly to maintain social cohesion. His government maintained subsidies and public spending more generally in order to protect employment and avoid sharp polarisation. Muldoon had fewer such inhibitions. He displayed scant regard for the low-paid in 1976–77, while liberally encouraging farmers and manufacturers. Even when he moderated policy in 1977 and 1978, Muldoon was motivated as much by the interests of farming and business as by concern for the vulnerable. It is clear that Muldoon and Treasury feared domestic business was getting squeezed too hard, and that an export-led recovery without a domestic sector was not worth having. Muldoon's approach, therefore, was oriented towards farming and business interests, and his aggressive rhetoric in industrial relations, and his scapegoating of some beneficiaries and of immigrant workers were all intended to secure compliance rather than consensus.

Social polarisation was unhelpful enough. Muldoon had also approached the crisis with a few simplistic notions, amounting to a reprise of the policies that had apparently worked in 1967–68. In the late 1960s, retrenchment and export incentives had been quickly followed by a short global boom, and New Zealand export earnings recovered fast. There was no such luck after 1974. Economic management and reorientation in a thoroughly stressed quasi-settler economy were far more difficult than Muldoon had led the public, and perhaps himself, to believe in 1975.

Chapter 8

Freeze: Muldoon's Second and Third Terms 1978–84

Muldoon led the National Party to an ambiguous election victory at the end of 1978, coming second in the popular vote but managing a 10-seat majority in parliament. Within two months of the election, the Iranian revolution provoked the second oil shock, which reinforced Muldoon's growing conviction that economic difficulty would be prolonged. Muldoon began his second term seeking to ensure that exports continued to grow and domestic demand remained sufficient to prevent a major downturn. The economy remained fragile. Inflation remained above 12 per cent, unemployment continued to increase, growth was negligible and the trade and budget deficits grew significantly. The following tables give these basic indicators for the decade from 1974.

Table 8.1: GDP Growth, 1974–83

Year	1974	75	76	77	78	79	80	81	82	83
+/- %	6.8	-1.1	3	-5	-0.6	0.8	2.0	3.6	-0.8	3.7

(Source: OECD, 1985, p. 80.)

Table 8.2: Unemployment, 1974–83

Year	1974	75	76	77	78	79	80	81	82	83
'000	0.7	3.1	4.9	4.1	19.8	24.9	28.8	46.7	47	76
%	0.08	0.35	0.44	0.61	1.84	1.95	2.27	3.69	3.5	5.6

(Source: OECD, 1982, p. 62; 1985, p. 83. (February; April in 1982 and 1983.))

Table 8.3: Inflation, 1974–83

Year	1974	75	76	77	78	79	80	81	82	83
%	11.2	14.6	17.0	14.4	11.9	13.8	17.2	15.4	16.1	7.3

(Source: Thorns and Sedgwick, 1997, p. 64, rounded.)

Table 8.4: Balance of payments deficit 1974–83

Year	1974	75	76	77	78	79	80	81	82	83
$m	-1129	-1400	-750	-847	-492	-683	-925	-1166	-1623	-1184

(Source: OECD, 1982, p. 65; 1985 p. 86.)

Table 8.5: Budget deficit 1974–83

Year	1974	75	76	77	78	79	80	81	82	83
$m	242	390	1002	506	694	1446	1027	1525	1818	2158

(Source: OECD, 1982, p. 64; 1985, p. 85. (figure is the borrowing requirement each year.))

The most prominent policy innovation in the second term was the complex and expensive development of energy-based industries, known as Think Big. Alongside Think Big, Muldoon shifted policy in 1979 and 1980 significantly towards a more open and less regulated economy, intensifying the reorientation to exporting and overseeing or allowing considerable restructuring of manufacturing. Muldoon was as committed as anyone to export diversification, and his government could claim some success. The common thread in the second term policies was the intention of a decisive breakout from the staples trap of the old settler economy. However, in 1982, six months into his third term and increasingly frustrated by persistent high inflation and his inability to agree with the unions on incomes policy, Muldoon imposed a comprehensive wage and price freeze, which lasted until 1984.

Until 1982, Muldoon was more of a reformer than is often appreciated.[1] The wage and price freeze, a stark contrast with the second term's managed liberalisation, has defined Muldoon's historical reputation. Muldoon himself maintained (particularly once he had lost office and was concerned with defending his record) that he sought to protect the New Zealand people from upheaval. That protection was selectively applied. True, he was always uneasy about increasing unemployment, but he was not averse to anti-welfare rhetoric and his version of the postwar consensus had never been friendly to organised labour. The real beneficiaries of Muldoon's protection were superannuitants, farmers, importers and manufacturers, but the ideological profile of New Zealand business changed after the mid 1970s; as exporting became more important and the local market less of a consideration, the politics of domestic protection were less attractive.[2] In this changing ideological climate, and because of his own increasingly erratic policymaking, Muldoon found himself at odds not only with the business lobbies but also with many influential civil servants and a younger generation in his own party.

Towards Restructuring 1979–80

In 1976 and 1977 Muldoon's policies of austerity had been directed at reducing demand in order to bring both the trade and budget deficits under control. As the recession proved far worse than expected, Muldoon had ameliorated austerity and stimulated domestic demand in the October 1977 mini-Budget and through 1978. Coming into 1979, Muldoon received a great deal of advice, sometimes contradictory. Some younger National MPs, and the business press, vociferously advocated 'more market' policies. A post-election briefing, from the heads of Treasury, the Reserve Bank, Trade and Industry and the Prime Minister's Department, advised further emphasis on exporting, liberalisation, and a 20 per cent devaluation.[3] During 1979 Muldoon would take significant steps in this direction.

In March, Treasury warned that although the domestic recovery of 1978 was fragile, when combined with the second oil shock it made another balance of payments crisis likely. That would require 'the same sort of contractionary measures that induced the crash-dive into recession taken after the 1975 balance of payments crisis' and would mean six wasted years.[4] Treasury also warned that the inflationary consequences of the budget deficit would damage exporters. Treasury suggested stabilising growth in public spending and increasing income tax to depress demand and reduce the budget deficit.[5] In May, however, thinking the domestic recovery was weak, Treasury advised cutting income taxes.[6] It was understandable that Treasury advice continued to vary. As Muldoon observed after the second oil shock, 'in today's conditions, it is not possible to set out even in a short, let alone a medium term, plans in detail for the very simple reason that basic assumptions are being changed virtually from week to week, by events which are occurring in the international economy'.[7]

Muldoon did, however, plan for the medium term in the 1979 Budget, seeking to steer between extremes. 'Some believe that by insulating the economy from the rest of the world we can pay ourselves more than we earn; others that the economy can be transformed overnight by a simple radical programme. Neither can be done'.[8] Nevertheless, he announced significant liberalisation. Muldoon had relaxed price control before the Budget, and while he disavowed dismantling import licensing and 'letting efficient industries go to the wall for the sake of a theory,' the Industries Development Commission would undertake a comprehensive review of manufacturing.[9] Overseas investment would be made much more welcome; if the 'economy is to develop on the necessary scale, we will need more direct investment, particularly that associated with advanced technology'.[10]

The most radical step was a flexible exchange rate, known as the 'crawling peg'. With export growth 'the main priority', the peg was designed to 'take account of the relative inflation movements of New Zealand against its trading partners'. While gradually devaluing the currency, it would avoid the disruption of sudden major shifts (one estimate was that a realistic one-step devaluation would be 27.5 per cent).[11] Export-led growth, Muldoon maintained, could 'only succeed if the steady shift of resources called for is not disturbed by sharp movements in internal demand'. Export incentives remained, but were simplified and more specifically linked to real gains in export earnings.[12]

To compensate for the 1977–78 easing, the Budget also reduced food subsidies and increased railway, postal and telephone charges, and delivered tighter monetary policy, raising interest rates on government stock. Benchmarking superannuation to net rather than gross average wages released the money to double the family benefit to $6 per week. Although this compensated for inflation since 1972, and Muldoon no doubt hoped that it would moderate wage claims, because the family benefit remained unindexed to the cost of living, the increase was soon eroded. Muldoon slightly reduced income-tax rates at each step, and claimed 'for approximately 90 percent of all taxpayers, the marginal rate will be 31 cents or less'.[13]

The Budget reinforced a medium-term reorientation to export-led growth. Earlier in 1979, the Reserve Bank had recommended most of what Muldoon subsequently did. The Bank later described the Budget as 'a turning point for the longer term development of the New Zealand economy. The essence of these policy initiatives was to stimulate increased production of internationally marketable goods and services; to encourage greatly increased competition and efficiency within the domestic economy; and to promote the development of New Zealand's own indigenous energy resources. . . . a significant progression in attitudes towards resolving the fundamental problems still facing the economy'.[14]

The Industries Development Commission was charged with assisting industries either to become internationally competitive or to move into activities that were competitive.[15] Treasury strongly supported this approach, and thought the IDC had to 'deal . . . with blatant distortions' under import licensing.[16] Some industries were significantly restructured (in some quarters, indeed, the IDC was known as the Industries Destruction Commission). Textiles would see reduced protection and consolidation into larger units to facilitate 'more soundly based growth in exports' transforming the high-cost, low-skill, labour-intensive nature of the industry.[17] The Government accepted the whole report.[18] Textiles employment declined by 5593, or 15 per cent, in the four years from February 1981.[19] For the vehicle assembly industry, the commission recommended reducing protection of 'one of the least efficient users of productive resources . . . the Commission has reviewed to date'.[20] Muldoon's government pushed restructuring outside the IDC as well, progressively deregulating land transport, so that by 1983 the decades-old regulations giving preference to the state-owned railways were abolished. In 1980 the government delicensed the meat industry, justifying this reform by the efficiency gains expected from competition, in an industry where many perceived that restrictive practices and collusion abounded not only in the unions but also in the freezing companies and the meat export brokers.[21] Muldoon, therefore, supported the drive for increased efficiency in manufacturing even at the cost of significant job losses.

Industry policy was inseparable from export diversification, which would require New Zealand manufacturers to become more efficient and farmers to become more flexible. Brian Talboys, foreign and trade minister from 1975 to 1981, warned that the century of prosperity which had been inaugurated by the *Dunedin*'s first shipment of frozen meat had ended. The future would be difficult: 'the white wings of the new Dunedin are not going to waft us to economic prosperity'. New Zealand needed long-term economic restructuring, breaking out of the staples trap into an economy 'more open, more internationally competitive and more export-oriented – not just in agriculture but in manufacturing, services and across the board'. Gradual and consistent reform in that direction would 'open the windows of the New Zealand economy'.[22]

Talboys observed that 'the development of a long-term overall economic relationship with Australia is vital to the future shape of New Zealand's economy', and he worked with his Australian counterpart Doug Anthony to that end.[23] The 1965 New Zealand-Australia Free Trade Agreement was only partial, although in 1973 the two governments agreed to keep tariffs against each other as low as possible.[24] The Nareen Declaration of 1978, signed by Talboys and Australian Prime Minister Malcolm Fraser, referred to 'the closest co-operation'.[25] Naturally, formalising Closer Economic Relations took time; trade diplomacy invariably does. There were several options for a new relationship, and both governments had protectionist constituencies in farming and manufacturing to placate.[26] After

Talboys retired in 1981, the Minister of Trade and Industry, Hugh Templeton, a former diplomat, took responsibility. The agreement was signed in 1982 and provided that free trade in merchandise would be progressively achieved by 1995. Scholars debate the extent of Muldoon's support, but the agreement could not have been reached without his approval, even though he and Fraser were hardly friendly. It is clear, too, that some Australian conservative politicians were at least as sceptical as Muldoon.[27]

As Muldoon famously observed, 'our foreign policy is trade'. His government worked persistently to maintain access for farm exports to both the EEC and the United States, as well as developing new markets in Asia, the Middle East and elsewhere.[28] The government believed that trade had to be a matter of long-term relationships. 'We cannot, in plain language, turn farm production off and on like a tap'.[29] Japan was, if anything, more given to agricultural protectionism than the United States and the EEC. Muldoon sought access into the Japanese market for dairy, meat and timber as the price of allowing Japan to fish in New Zealand's new Exclusive Economic Zone. After much acrimony a deal was struck in 1978.[30] The Middle East's increasing wealth presented opportunities for exporters, and it was also desirable to remain friendly with oil-exporting states. Whereas the region accounted for 0.3 per cent of exports by value in 1961, 20 years later it was 7.6 per cent.[31]

Export markets and commodities successfully continued to diversify after 1970; however, the loss of a great part of the country's British markets, if long anticipated, did harm the New Zealand economy.[32] The following tables indicate the extent of the change.

Table 8.6: Destination of New Zealand Exports, percentage of value, 1970–84

June year	UK	Aust	Japan	US	Other
1970	36	8	10	16	30
1975	22	12	12	12	42
1980	14	12	13	14	47
1984	10	14	16	13	47

(Source: NZOYB, 1985, p. 609.)

Table 8.7 Composition of New Zealand Exports, percentage of value

	1975	1984
Meat	24.9	20.0
Dairy	15.6	14.1
Wool	19.3	13.0
Total pastoral	59.8	47.1
Fish	1.3	2.8
Fruit & vegetables	2.5	4.7
Pulp, paper, paperboard	4.9	4.6
Manufacturing	13.0	23.9

(Source: NZOYB, 1976, pp. 565–77, 1985 pp. 628–30. Note that 'manufacturing', comprising categories 5–8 of the yearbook tables, has been recalculated here to exclude paper and paperboard so as to avoid double counting.)

It is difficult to argue, therefore, that Muldoon's government represented unthinking traditionalism in economic policy.[33] James Belich has overstated the case in describing Muldoon's administration as 'recolonisation's last stand'. While Muldoon was a creature of the 1950s in his social attitudes and in much of his political practice, in 1979 his government began significant restructuring in industry policy and sought, in trade policy, to accelerate the country's breakout from the old settler economy's staples trap.

Think Big

Think Big was a shorthand term for a number of capital- and energy-intensive projects developed by the state working with large New Zealand or foreign corporations. It was the government's ultimate industry policy and represented a major, if misguided, effort to break out of the staples trap. Think Big had two separate dimensions, which the government unwisely conflated: reducing dependence on imported oil and developing industries that would use apparently abundant energy. Whatever the merits of this approach in general terms, a fatal flaw was the speed with which so many costly projects were developed at the same time.

Developing the country's energy resources, especially hydroelectricity, had been a central theme in economic policy for decades. Commercial natural gas fields were discovered off the Taranaki coast in the 1950s and 60s. The Labour government had undertaken to purchase the gas for 30 years from the consortium of oil companies that, in a joint venture with the government, had the rights to the field, originally intending to use the gas for electricity generation. The first oil shock made that unattractive.[34] One National minister recalled that the 'sheer size' of the Maui field 'made it possible to establish long-term strategies for energy independence' and Labour's 'take or pay' agreement provoked National ministers to think of ways to use as much gas as possible.[35] From the end of 1978 the Minister of Energy was Bill Birch, a country surveyor who has been described as 'a doer who once he had made up his mind on a course of action pursued it with missionary zeal, never faltering, and relentlessly getting things done as quickly as possible'.[36] Birch projected that developing Maui for transport fuels and natural gas would cost $2 billion over 10 years, and save $500m annually in foreign exchange.[37] At the end of 1979 the government decided that Maui gas would be made into methanol for export and possibly to stretch domestic petrol supply, and into synthetic petrol. The Marsden Point refinery would be expanded to convert synthetic fuel into diesel and jet fuel.[38]

There was a big difference between reducing dependence on imported petroleum-based fuels and developing additional very expensive projects on the basis that there was a large surplus of electricity. The 'surplus' was in fact merely a projection that normal demand for electricity would grow more slowly than previously forecast. Indeed, some suggested the surplus was very modest, and to a large extent derived from North Island coal- and oil-burning power stations, while the rest, produced in the South Island hydro stations, could not be sent north because of the limited capacity of the Cook Strait cable.[39]

There are differing accounts of when ministers began to think in terms of industrial development using the 'surplus'. Gustafson suggests that Muldoon was 'one of the last converts' to Think Big, only persuaded by Birch at the end of 1980 that 'the creation of the energy projects led logically to the creation of manufacturing schemes to use all the new power generated'.[40] Hugh Templeton, however, recalled that 'Muldoon himself played a leading role', having become more convinced of the urgency of the situation after his annual visit to the OECD in May 1979. McKinnon suggests that the 'strategy took shape during a trip by Muldoon to Europe and the Middle East in October 1979'.[41] That Muldoon was committed to something like Think Big in 1979 was indicated by his support for the National Development Act 1979, which allowed the government by regulation to bypass normal planning procedures for projects deemed to be of national importance. Ironically, the legislation came to be seen as evidence of Muldoon's addiction to an economically centralised state, when apparently the idea came from 'more market' oriented backbenchers, on the basis that 'bureaucratic over-regulation equals stifled initiative'.[42]

The 1979 Budget and the minutes of the Cabinet Economic Committee confirm that Muldoon was thinking big before the middle of that year. The Budget noted that 'the Government is compiling a catalogue of development possibilities, with particular emphasis on those that would earn or save foreign exchange'.[43] In February 1979 Muldoon had directed officials to investigate possible uses of the electricity surplus, and in August the Cabinet Economic Committee's list included, in descending order of electricity usage, a third potline for the aluminium smelter at Bluff, a ferrosilicon smelter, a pulp-mill at Nelson, a silicon carbide plant and an ultrafine metal powders plant.[44]

Incoherent decision-making was a major problem. The projected electricity surplus to 1994 was 2000 GWh per annum, but the list of projects on the table in November 1979 accounted for over 5000 GWh. The government unrealistically observed that 'if all these developments went ahead, they would be likely to consume only a part of the surplus in the short to medium term'.[45] The Planning Council was noncommittal, noting that the projects were viable given continuing high energy prices, but advising that construction should be spread out.[46] Treasury warned that the scale of development had 'a number of implications which are of the utmost significance for New Zealand's future economic prosperity'. New power stations would have to be built in the late 1980s rather than the mid 1990s, which would mean higher electricity prices for the projects than had so far been discussed.[47] Even so, the Cabinet Economic Committee decided that an unspecified 5000 GWh package would be developed by 1984.[48] In December officials advised that the return on a ferrosilicon plant would not be attractive.[49]

In October 1979 ministers had added a second aluminium smelter to the list, to be built at Aramoana, near the entrance to the Otago Harbour, and operated by a consortium including Fletcher Holdings (New Zealand), Alusuisse (Switzerland), and CSR (Australia). Some officials worried that the consortium would demand a lower electricity price than ministers would accept, and suggested that a third potline at Bluff would be built more quickly.[50] It became clear in February 1980 that the overseas companies were not prepared to meet the government's minimum electricity price for either of the aluminium projects.[51] Within a few weeks it had also become apparent that using the Maui field for methanol and synthetic petrol limited the electricity surplus to 2000 or 3000 GWh, which would mean only the third potline and some of the smaller projects were feasible.[52] The first national energy plan was drafted in 1980 on the basis of that 2000 GWh scale of development. In August, however, ministers committed to a second smelter and 'the plan . . . on the point of being submitted to the Government Printer' was withdrawn as redundant.[53]

Ministers were increasingly driven by the political imperative of having some big projects signed off before the 1981 election. Ministers had little understanding of electricity supply. One had expected that a 5000 GWh surplus would come from hydroelectric dams in the South Island, which had never been possible. As projections changed, it seemed that even 2000 GWh would require coal-fired generation, but officials pointed out that such a quantity of coal was not available. One minister 'remarked that it was clear that there had been a lack of co-ordination among the officials involved with the subject of the proposed energy-intensive industries. It was also stated that there was a need for officials to keep Ministers fully informed of developments'.[54] Officials must have been tempted to observe that there was also a need for ministers to do some basic homework rather than making grandiose plans on the run. Ministers, indeed, grasped at straws. When officials warned that the electricity surplus was limited, Cabinet Economic Committee members argued that the aging Meremere coal-burning station 'could' be kept open past 1984; additional natural gas 'might' be discovered; the Maui B partners 'might' bring on the B platform sooner rather than later; NZ Steel 'might' begin producing its own electricity; the smaller projects in the earlier lists 'were probably not' going to happen; and, for good measure, the ministry's seven per cent margin to allow for dry years and breakdowns was 'very excessive'.[55]

Treasury warned with increasing vigour that the economics around the projects were most uncertain and that proceeding with so many at the same time was unwise. Mudoon was not willing to hear that advice.[56] The Ministry of Energy shared Treasury reservations, but Trade and Industry was more enthusiastic and likely to assume the most favourable circumstances.[57] There was growing criticism from outside the public service around the extent of overseas investment, the concessionary power prices, the scale and speed of the developments, and the secrecy and centralisation of executive power accompanying them. Few argued, though, that it was in principle undesirable for the state to guide industrial development.[58] A University of Otago economics professor, Paul van Moeseke, wrote a detailed criticism of the second smelter. The total capital outlay, he pointed out, was equivalent to the country's entire public debt, and New Zealand electricity was not cheap (if it was supplied cheaply to the smelter that would represent a large subsidy). The whole cost of the project, including its imported raw materials, made it a most inefficient way of earning foreign exchange.[59]

Electricity pricing was ministers' major problem with the second smelter; they badly wanted it but did not want to appear to be giving away electricity. At one point ministers considered burying a highly concessionary price in an export incentive, but they could not accept the consortium's insistence on a 20-year price agreement.[60] The government finally approved the second smelter at the end of September 1981, but three days later Alusuisse withdrew 'at least partly' over the electricity price.[61] World aluminium prices were falling anyway, and though the promoters tried to find another partner, they had no success.[62] In October 1982 the second smelter was 'postponed'.[63] Even so, the government pressed ahead with the Clyde Dam, which had been intended to supply the smelter. The power station was controversial on environmental and economic grounds, and Muldoon had Parliament pass legislation to override a Planning Tribunal veto. In the event, it only began generating in 1992, construction having taken considerably more time and money than specified.[64]

Alusuisse had inconveniently withdrawn from the second smelter two months before the 1981 election. The synthetic fuel plant was also proceeding slowly, and the government badly needed a Think Big success story. A month before the election, Cabinet agreed to an expansion that would increase New Zealand Steel's output fivefold. The agreement included continuing New Zealand Steel's protected status in the New Zealand market, concessionary prices for coal and electricity, and construction by a company in which the government was the majority shareholder. Treasury always regarded the project as dubious, and the extension ended up costing far more than anticipated. After 1984 the Labour government removed the company's protection, increased the price of coal and eventually sold it in something of a rush.[65]

The highly detailed management of industrial development in Think Big sat uncomfortably alongside those dimensions of industry policy, announced in 1979, which emphasised diminished protection. In the end, the completed liquid fuels projects were a synfuels plant to make natural gas into petrol, a plant to make natural gas into methanol (both in Taranaki), and expanding Marsden Point to refine diesel and jet fuel. The industrial projects were making ammonia-urea from gas in Taranaki, the third potline at Tiwai Point and the New Zealand Steel expansion. The Clyde Dam was built to provide electricity. Gustafson observes that the range of projects was so diverse that 'it is difficult to attack or defend [Think Big] as a whole'.[66] A key assumption was that oil prices would remain high. Even though they stabilised by 1981, then fell, the government's best advice was that they would increase sharply around 1986 and remain high at least until 2000.[67] Given the political situation in the Middle East, this was not far-fetched, although forecasting so far out was inherently risky.[68] Some projects cost much more than anticipated (rapid decision-making must have been a factor in this). Think Big also required heavy overseas borrowing within a short period.[69] On that point Muldoon fatally miscalculated, adding to an already large public debt just as a severe tightening of US monetary policy drove overseas interest rates up, eventually, to 20 per cent.[70]

For Bassett, the whole saga demonstrated that 'politicians were not good at picking winners' even if, as he concedes, the 'key assumption . . . was that the world price of oil would inexorably rise'.[71] Some projects had nothing to do with substituting for imported oil and required significant spending on new electricity generation; it was disingenuous to conflate those projects with others that were about substituting for imported oil. But that is not the whole story. Muldoon came out of a political economy that regarded state-supported industrialisation as justified in some circumstances at least. Quite apart from the excess of enthusiasm that attended Think Big, his successors after 1984 had no such belief. For them there was little justification either in state-supported industrialisation or in concessionary arrangements with private companies in order to foster industrialisation. Regardless of the merits of either perspective, the biggest problem with Think Big was that major and complex decisions were taken far too quickly, at least sometimes on political rather than economic criteria, with significant issues decided on the run, and the parameters changing rapidly. Just as serious a flaw was the intention to do so much so quickly, rather than spreading the projects out over a longer period.

The Budget and the Changing Climate in Treasury After 1980

Relations between Muldoon and Treasury became increasingly tense after 1980. From 1980, Bernard Galvin was Secretary; a very able protégé of Henry Lang, he had been head of the Prime Minister's Department from 1975. Some thought he had become somewhat close to Muldoon.[72] More probably he realised that the Secretary to the Treasury and the Minister of Finance cannot be engaged in open warfare. Galvin, like Lang and Lough, advocated progressive liberalisation, but Muldoon was increasingly reluctant to take such advice and became openly dismissive of economic theory.[73]

Treasury continued to have difficulty reading the economic

situation, and its advice varied through 1980. In April Galvin noted that reasonably tight policies during 1979 had reduced the budget deficit from 8.2 per cent of GDP in 1978/79 to 5.1 per cent. Although employment, consumption, and real disposable incomes had all fallen slightly, there was some new capital investment and continuing high farm expenditure, and the adjustment had been much less severe than during 1976 and 1977. It was important to 'ensure that the downward adjustment is not carried too far'.[74] A few weeks later, though, with inflation expected to remain at 15 per cent, Galvin criticised 'a strategy which gave higher priority to maintaining domestic activity and employment than to reducing inflation or the external deficit'. Treasury now thought that the crawling peg was insufficient and suggested a significant devaluation. While all options involved increased price levels 'only the exchange rate offers compensating benefits'.[75] Then in October Galvin thought 'an encouraging degree of structural adaptation is taking place. . . . Many manufacturers are taking advantage of export opportunities with the result that the weakening in domestic demand has been cushioned by production for export. Rationalisation of production, improved management and lower labour turnover are also contributing'.[76]

Galvin and Muldoon shared a belief that constant adjustments, or fine-tuning, were important in economic management. A case in point was Muldoon's November 1980 mini-Budget, which sought, as Galvin had put it six months earlier, to manage the 'downward adjustment' and consisted mostly of additional spending to relieve unemployment.[77] Some senior Treasury officials now dissented from fine-tuning, arguing that there were no soft options, and a consistent policy of reform needed to be maintained, particularly around the exchange rate, industry policy and reducing protection. The problem, according to Jas McKenzie, was that this approach was 'too strong for the Prime Minister to be able to defend himself against the charge that if this is what needs to be done, why hasn't it already been done. I accept that there is a very real political problem here but I do not think we as a Treasury can or should suggest any other line'.[78] The 1979 Budget had moved in this direction but, evidently, not far enough for some. In McKenzie's Economics II, the approach was increasingly to emphasise markets, to question the efficacy of demand management and the whole Keynesian approach, and, in the words of one official, to regard macroeconomics as 'witchcraft'.[79]

Galvin was not unsympathetic to Economics II. Approaching the 1981 Budget he pointed out that the previous five years had seen two recessions and one short-lived (and consumption-led) recovery. 'Stronger economic growth over the last year has little more than offset declines in earlier years', although the second oil shock had not been too damaging due to the tight fiscal policy in the previous two years, the success of the government's export-oriented policies and two very good farming seasons. Monetary and fiscal policy needed to remain fairly tight to facilitate export volume growth at four to five per cent annually, which would diminish unemployment in the medium term.[80] The Reserve Bank, in its public reports, encouraged the government to embed the 1979 reforms: 'much remains to be done'.[81] The Bank thought that the crawling peg needed to crawl faster, because it was linked to New Zealand inflation and thus maintained the real, as opposed to the nominal, exchange rate and so hindered adjustment.[82]

Muldoon found such advice unpalatable, and was increasingly absorbed in Think Big. The 1981 Budget was less comprehensive than usual, although it did foreshadow replacing import licensing with tariffs. More notably, Muldoon dramatically increased supplementary minimum price payments, which had been minimal since 1978 as export market prices and producer board minimum prices generally exceeded the SMP threshold. No doubt Muldoon wished to reassure farmers of the National Party's continuing solicitude for their interests.[83] In the four years from 1981, very nearly $1200m was paid out, almost all of it to sheep farmers. One study concluded that only $168m in export earnings could be attributed to SMPs.[84]

Muldoon led the National Party to another minority victory in the 1981 election, holding on with an effective majority of one seat. Treasury's briefing after the election was radical, bluntly advocating deregulation, criticising an entrenched reluctance 'to rely on market prices throughout the economy to allocate resources to the best use'. Treasury repeated the familiar criticism of income tax, and claimed that a 'system of formal and informal indexation linkages throughout the economy has developed in an attempt to ensure that the various groups – employees, producers, exporters and beneficiaries are protected against any erosion of their real incomes'[85] Moreover, 'virtually every regulation or misallocation of public sector resources has a client group that is benefitting from it [which] will resist reform'.[86] While unemployment had plateaued, Treasury thought that the recovery was temporary and any real improvement would need structural reform.

Criticisms of this nature were becoming increasingly common in both the specialist and popular literature. The Wellington geographer S. Harvey Franklin had made such comments in his 1978 book, *Trade, Growth and Anxiety,* and they were recycled through Treasury, the OECD, the Labour MP Roger Douglas, and to some extent the Planning Council.[87] In the economics literature, there was increasingly a profound scepticism about the ability of government intervention to beneficially influence economic development. Even as many younger but senior Treasury officials were expressing fundamental criticisms of Keynesian orthodoxy, the advice given to ministers was for relatively gradual, if deliberate, reform.[88] A review of taxation, the McCaw Committee, had proposed a significant shift to indirect tax. Graham Scott wrote Treasury's formal response, arguing that reform 'should be planned as a dynamic process occurring over a period of several years in order to avoid the disruption of a "tight" switch', combining a large income-tax cut and major expansion of sales tax. The task force had 'neglected to examine ways in which changes might be brought about more subtly and with less social and economic disruption'.[89] Muldoon refused to agree with the proposals; indeed, by 1983 'at any meaningful level, the relationship [between Muldoon and the Treasury] had broken down'.[90] Scott would eventually champion precisely such rapid reform as he had criticised in 1982; Muldoon made extremists out of gradualists by his prolonged intransigence.

Incomes Policy and the Freeze

Nowhere was Muldoon's intransigence more evident than in the wage and price freeze which he imposed in June 1982, and which lasted until 1984. Inflation had exceeded 10 per cent annually in every year since 1973, and although the retrenchment of 1976–77 had had some effect, the figure for 1980 was 17 per cent. The 1980 mini-Budget, Think Big and more generous SMPs had all added to inflationary pressure, and Muldoon became impatient. Quite apart from the intrinsic problems with the freeze, it was a major reversal of Muldoon's export-oriented liberalisations of 1979 and epitomised 'the excesses of Muldoon's late period that prepared the ground for the policy revolution after 1984'.[91]

Muldoon believed wages were the main cause of inflation, and he was usually reluctant to use interest rates in response. He 'viewed an increase in the nominal interest rate as a cost, whereas the [Reserve] Bank regarded it as a discouragement to borrowing and spending'.[92] Although Muldoon had deregulated interest rates in 1976, he continued to offer government stock at below-market rates, which diminished the ability of government and the Bank to use monetary policy against inflation.[93] At the end of 1981 he returned to regulating interest rates after five years of free-market operations; as the Bank warned, there were significant implications for investment and capital markets.[94]

Muldoon's difficulties in wages policy went back to his first term. In 1977 the government reinstated free wage-bargaining without any plan to mitigate its disadvantages. The Arbitration Court's terms of reference did not include tax levels and transfer payments like young family rebates, and there was 'no permanent bilateral or tripartite forum . . . to facilitate regular consultations . . . between the Government and the central labour market organisations'. Skinner had won the 1977 return to free bargaining 'largely on the assurance . . . that he would pilot the [benchmark] Metal Trades Award at a level acceptable to the Government'.[95] Skinner delivered on that, but it was more than a decade since the FOL president had been able to control the affiliated unions. Even so, many unions did moderate wage claims in 1977–78.[96]

Having stepped back from directly controlling wages, Muldoon complained when the Arbitration Court issued a 1978 wage order of seven per cent capped at seven dollars a week. The General Wage Orders Act provided that the order would not apply to workers who were not covered by an award, or to those paid above award rates who had had an increase in the last 12 months. Apparently the judge had not realised this; the unions pressed for universal application and after the usual intransigent rhetoric Muldoon caved in.[97] In January 1979 he indicated that he did not want the Arbitration Court to make a general wage order that year and would if necessary bring down regulations to suspend the Act. After much discussion, in July 1979 an ad hoc group of ministers (Muldoon, the associate finance minister Templeton, Talboys, and the new Minister of Labour Jim Bolger) recommended repealing the General Wage Orders Act in favour of a new Remuneration Act allowing the government to regulate pay and conditions. This was a complete reversal of the 1977 return to free bargaining and some officials warned that proceeding without some sort of consensus would be 'highly provocative' and industrial action would defeat the intention of the legislation.[98]

Predictably, the FOL was outraged (having already lodged a claim for a general wage order), and employer organisations were pleased. A special FOL conference authorised the executive to call a general strike if the government intervened in bargaining.[99] The climate in trade union politics had changed; Skinner had retired from the FOL presidency early in 1979. His distinctly more militant successor, Jim Knox, had been a watersider locked out in 1951 and blacklisted thereafter. Although committed to avoiding confrontation on the scale of 1951, Knox was much less inclined than Skinner to manage industrial relations over drinks with Muldoon; indeed, he increasingly 'found it impossible to disguise his deep hatred of the prime minister'.[100] Knox resented Muldoon's union-bashing rhetoric, and was deeply angered by the remorseless increase in unemployment. He was ahead of many union officials in supporting the unemployed to organise.[101]

The confrontation came over the drivers' negotiations, which reached tentative agreement on 11 per cent despite indications of prime ministerial displeasure. On 9 September Cabinet resolved to bring down regulations limiting the settlement to 9 per cent. The FOL called a general strike for 19 September; although participation was less than total it made an effective point.[102] The FOL then began negotiations with ministers; perhaps fortunately, Muldoon was overseas and Knox reached an agreement with Talboys, Bolger, and Templeton that the matter would go to the Arbitration Court. There, with two other major unions having settled between 10 and 11 per cent without a ministerial murmur, the drivers won 10.5 per cent and other provisions amounting to about what they would have got anyway.[103] The Remuneration Act was invoked a few times before being repealed after its use at the NZ Forest Products mill at Kinleith early in 1980 provoked a prolonged strike. The government eventually conceded the 20.5 per cent claimed by the unions at Kinleith, and the FOL agreed to tripartite talks on a new wage-fixing regime.[104] Once again Muldoon's approach was to indulge in intransigent rhetoric, bring on a confrontation, and then back down.

During April and May 1980 the FOL reached agreement with the Employers' Federation on a bold set of proposals. The Arbitration Court would set a minimum single adult wage, and then unions negotiate on top of that (conceptualising wages around a single adult would leave provision for families to taxation and transfer payments). There would be a shift from occupational agreements to industry agreements, inevitably breaking a lot of relativities. Treasury was unenthusiastic: the Court might set the minimum wage too high; parties could opt out; it was unlikely there would be widespread union (or employer) acceptance of a shift to industry bargaining given the strength of custom; even if there was it would take several years; and the need to bring wage inflation down was more urgent.[105] Accordingly, the government advised the parties that while it accepted the proposal in principle, it could not accept the details; both employers and the FOL replied that it was only on the details that it could be sold to their constituents. Thus 'the impetus for reform was lost'.[106] That was most unfortunate. The FOL had demonstrated some imagination in coming up with the proposals, and the Employers' Federation some courage in accepting them. Knox is often criticised for 'lack[ing] the ability and personality to work creatively and productively to find new long-term solutions to the industrial crises and the rising unemployment that were symptomatic of a deteriorating economy and an obsolete system of industrial relations and wage bargaining'.[107] Rather, it is clear that the FOL, under Knox and secretary Ken Douglas, was willing to be very constructive.

During 1980 Muldoon and Treasury pursued the idea of a wage-tax trade-off that would reduce income tax to maintain real disposable incomes without sharp wage increases. Muldoon and the officials thought it particularly important that the single-income family with children kept a reasonable position.[108] Discussions proceeded through the first months of 1981. In May the FOL conference rejected the idea, fearing that a meaningful tax cut without compensatory indirect tax increases would mean either major spending cuts or an unsustainable deficit. Muldoon described the decision as 'part of the Socialist Unity Party's continuing campaign to destroy the New Zealand economy'.[109] Notwithstanding the usual prime ministerial rhetoric, discussions continued but stuck because the FOL wanted tax rates adjusted to take account of fiscal drag; the government refused to agree to this. Moreover, the FOL wanted specific numbers included in the agreement and Muldoon insisted on reserving the quantum for his own discretion in the Budget.[110]

In early May 1982 Muldoon proposed a five per cent wage increase and tax cuts in the budget; the FOL executive and conference turned him down again. One scholar has described this decision as 'in some respects . . . surprising'.[111] Ken Douglas later said it was a mistake.[112] Pat Walsh has pointed out, though, that if the FOL leadership had accepted the trade-off without referring it to conference, the lack of membership commitment would have probably made the deal unworkable. Again, Muldoon would not commit on numbers. The FOL thought that the impact on inflation would be small, and the loss of revenue would have to be made up either by spending cuts, an inflationary deficit, or consumption taxes, which could well cancel out the benefits for the lower-paid.[113]

The real problem was 'a fundamental lack of trust between the union movement and the National Government . . . [which] was perfectly understandable. The Muldoon Administration had conducted an active anti-union campaign throughout its term in office. It had demonstrated little desire to consult with the FOL or to foster a climate of understanding and goodwill'.[114] Although Muldoon's concern about unemployment was sincere, unemployment had increased drastically since 1975, and the unions, not unreasonably, blamed government policy. Their attitude was the more understandable given the rhetoric, and the reality, of retrenchment and restructuring. Some unions, at least, actively supported unemployed workers' organisations and many had had struggles over redundancy payments.[115] The wage-tax trade-off as proposed asked too much from organised labour and offered too few guarantees.

Shortly after the FOL conference, Muldoon went overseas for an OECD meeting. Now that major industrial economies were being deflated, there was continuing low demand for New Zealand exports and therefore no windfall would rescue the economy.[116] The idea of a wage and price freeze firmed in Muldoon's mind while he was overseas, although he did not, apparently, discuss it extensively even with the Cabinet Economic Committee. Senior officials strongly opposed the idea. Graham Scott argued that it would be of little use. As well as being administratively difficult, a freeze would simply interrupt the trend and the post-freeze breakout would put matters back where they would have been anyway. High inflation was essentially due to 'the huge credit expansion since late 1980', and the current fiscal restraint and tightening of monetary policy were helping and should continue. What was missing was 'effective incomes policies to support the overall economic strategy and it is regrettable that a voluntary wage/tax bargain is not in prospect'.[117] Once again, Scott's gradualism is striking. Trade and Industry argued that a freeze could only work for a few months, and the Secretary of Labour thought that the freeze would have to be accompanied by a tax cut if the FOL was not to break it.[118]

Galvin summarised the views of the economics departments in formal advice. A freeze might only work for a very short time and if longer 'would require more and more complex and draconian administrative measures which would become less and less effective'. A post-freeze breakout was all too likely. There were 'no quick solutions to inflation . . . only a balanced and sustained approach can work if high social costs are to be avoided'. A freeze would derail the development of better fiscal strategy, tax reform, and the general but gradual liberalisation that had been progressing and should continue.[119] Worse, while Muldoon intended to reduce income tax he would not increase sales taxes to compensate, and so the budget deficit would increase. In short, Muldoon's package – a freeze, an income tax cut, no compensatory indirect tax, a higher deficit – 'involve[d] a strong fiscal stimulus, the monetary implications of which will eventually invalidate any benefits that the freeze brings to the rate of inflation'.[120] Officials advised that 'a better long-term outcome . . . could be achieved by a more orthodox (but unspectacular) economic strategy designed to improve the functioning of the price mechanism and reduce the disturbances to the economy arising from fluctuations in monetary and fiscal policies associated with excessive periods of monetary expansion'.[121]

None of the advice dissuaded Muldoon, who announced a 12-month freeze on wages, prices, rents, and professional charges on 22 June 1982. It would last until February 1984, with wages remaining all but frozen until after the July 1984 election. The freeze, in any event, was lopsided: wages had generally not increased in the six or nine months before the freeze, and exemptions applied to meat, fruit, vegetables, petrol and some other basic items.[122] Muldoon defended his actions in the 1982 Budget. Inflation, he said, was the major issue and the freeze was not only the consequence of 'union intransigence' but was 'the simplest and most equitable' alternative to the 'textbook alternatives advocated by some economists [which] would result, as in other countries, in widespread business failures and rapidly increasing unemployment'.[123] Muldoon introduced a new income tax scale, raising the lowest rate, substantially flattening the middle, and significantly raising the thresholds for each band. While this gave some relief to those on modest incomes, it also meant significant advantages for the very well paid. The cost in foregone revenue would be $890m in a full year, although increased sales taxes on alcohol and tobacco partly compensated.[124] Although Muldoon had progressively reduced income tax rates for most earners, other ministers persuaded him that wealthy professionals had considerable scope for tax avoidance through investing in primary production, taking advantage of deductions and incentives and offsetting income against farm costs, and later selling their properties at considerable capital gain. The Income Tax Amendment (No. 2) Act, 1982, addressed this issue by limiting the amount that could be offset and effectively imposing a capital gains tax. The measure, which drew howls of outrage from many well-off National supporters, was in fact driven by some of the younger 'more market' National MPs, but Muldoon wore the opprobrium.[125]

The 1983 Budget was essentially a holding pattern, with little new policy except for some public spending to reduce unemployment. As the 1984 Budget approached, officials continued to advocate a 'tough-minded' approach to expenditure.[126] They also advised that export assistance had to be reduced, not only for budgetary reasons but also because of international obligations. In turn, import protection, which was a major source of high domestic costs, would be reduced.[127] The government had agreed with manufacturers' organisations during 1983 that an export focus was paramount and that quantitative import controls would be phased out.[128] Yet Muldoon seemed to have few ideas for the 1984 Budget; a draft from early June was vague.[129]

Muldoon seemed to be losing control not only of the economy but also of himself. Where he had previously addressed officials formally, now sometimes he responded with personal abuse to advice that displeased him.[130] During 1983, Treasury noticeably abandoned a gradualist approach and the tone of advice became much more uncompromising in its 'scepticism about macroeconomic approaches such as the fine-tuning of fiscal policy, incomes policy and controlled exchange rates, and a readiness to advocate microeconomic reform as the route to efficiency'.[131] Treasury now urged strict limits on the improvements to public services, and comprehensive reviews of benefits, subsidies, and export assistance. Government trading activities should continue to move to a commercial basis; those functions that could be met by the private sector should be so met; the tax base should be broadened to increase revenue.[132] Already the 1984 briefing was taking shape in official minds.[133]

Endgame

On 14 June 1984, Marilyn Waring, a young feminist National MP, announced that she was resigning from the party and would vote against the government on sexual violence and nuclear disarmament. Waring promised support on confidence and supply, but Muldoon – generally thought to be under the influence of diabetes and alcohol – called an early election.[134] It was a desperate gamble. Not only had the Labour Party renewed itself under the leadership and peerless oratory of the Auckland barrister David Lange; much of the National Party's urban right wing had deserted in displeasure at Muldoon's increasing resort to regulation. The vehicle for their discontents was the New Zealand Party, founded and financed by the millionaire property speculator Robert Jones, who had once enthusiastically supported Muldoon. Jones had little interest in winning parliamentary seats but wished to destroy the Muldoon government.[135]

National's heavy defeat in the election on 14 July was unsurprising. During the four weeks of the election campaign, the currency came under considerable pressure. The Reserve Bank had warned in 1982 that a freeze would necessarily mean suspending the crawling peg's creeping devaluation, which would cause the balance of payments deficit to widen, exporters to be less competitive and 'speculative pressures would be built up in anticipation of a discrete devaluation. The present level of official overseas reserves is too low to withstand these pressures, and they would have to be increased', which would increase borrowing requirements and thus debt servicing.[136] That was exactly what happened, and once the election was called, the expectation of devaluation became intense. 'Holders of New Zealand currency [as always in such a situation] became anxious to bring forward purchases of foreign currency required to settle import bills and other overseas commitments. Meanwhile, those expecting to receive foreign currency payments sought to delay their conversion into New Zealand dollars'.[137] Some openly speculated, converting holdings of New Zealand dollars into foreign currency with the intention of converting back after a devaluation.[138] Despite repeated and urgent advice to devalue, Muldoon refused even to discuss the possibility. To maintain the dollar in the four weeks before the election, the Reserve Bank had to sell around $1.4 billion in foreign exchange, a year's normal trading.[139]

The situation became critical in the day or two before the election. The morning after the election, a Sunday, the Reserve Bank governor and deputy governor, the Secretary to the Treasury, and the head of the Prime Minister's Department all agreed that the foreign exchange markets had to remain closed pending devaluation and they began crisis talks with senior Labour politicians.[140] At this point the exchange crisis became a political crisis. Lange and his colleagues, particularly the likely finance minister, Roger Douglas, accepted official advice that devaluation was necessary and requested Muldoon to do so. On the basis that until the final election result was declared he was still Prime Minister, Muldoon refused. With the markets closed, Muldoon obdurate, and Lange declaiming on prime-time television, other National ministers and the Governor-General prepared to dismiss Muldoon and replace him with another caretaker who would implement Lange's request. Early on the Tuesday Muldoon conceded, and a 20 per cent devaluation was signed off the next day.[141] The Muldoon era had ended, and his successors would unravel much of the postwar consensus.

Conclusion

Nearly 30 years after he lost office, dispassionate judgements about Muldoon are still difficult. We can dispose immediately of the suggestion that he was any sort of socialist. To the extent that Muldoon espoused the postwar consensus, it was firmly within the parameters laid down by the National Party in the late 1940s. It was taken for granted that equal opportunity prevailed, and the state's responsibility was to maintain that equality. If modest prosperity were guaranteed for all, that did not place limits on individual accumulation. Transfer payments, public services and social welfare were intended to ensure security for 'decent citizens' or, in Muldoon's preferred terminology, the 'ordinary bloke'. National's version of the postwar settlement had always included maintaining domestic consumption to ensure prosperity for smaller business, and these considerations were part of the reason why Muldoon eased austerity in late 1977. Nor did he wish to see mass unemployment developing, for moral as well as economic reasons. Yet his engagement with organised labour was often counterproductive. Muldoon's 'ordinary bloke' was never an active trade unionist. It was largely in his own retrospective justifications, and in comparison with what followed him, that Muldoon was viewed as a protector of the weak and the disadvantaged (which is not to deny that he undertook many acts of private kindness).

Muldoon's biographer has emphasised that as finance minister from 1967 he 'came into a crisis situation and despite some initial apparent success never got out of it'.[142] The short crisis of 1966–67 and the much longer and more intense one from 1974 did dominate Muldoon's career, but much of what officials and other advisers regarded as the necessary response had been identified as necessary anyway. Export growth and diversification had been a major focus since the late 1950s. Particularly under National governments, this involved a fairly direct and significant shift of wealth and income to exporters, an approach that no doubt reflected the strong support for National among farmers and manufacturers.[143] In 1967 and 1976–77, Muldoon added to that a determination to limit public spending and wage increases. These policies resulted in considerable pressure on the lower-paid. Indeed, Muldoon in 1976 and 1977 enforced a conservative orthodoxy of retrenchment and wage cuts and in those years, at least, there was little evidence of 'genuine concern for the poor and powerless'.[144]

Relaxing austerity from October 1977 was not necessarily ill-judged. Cautious relaxation to maintain the domestic economy may have been preferable to allowing greater increases in unemployment. Muldoon, and his senior Treasury advisers, believed so. Relaxation did contribute to an import surge, and increased the budget deficit again. But significant factors in the budget deficit were Muldoon's very expensive superannuation scheme, and his increasing subsidisation of exporters. In the circumstances of the mid 1970s, the sudden and complete introduction of a generous superannuation scheme, funded out of current revenue, was unwise. At a stroke it doubled the spending on monetary benefits. Supporting exporters was less evidently unwise, but after 1981 SMPs became extravagant.

A professed concern for the 'ordinary bloke' did not deter Muldoon, in 1979, from the sort of liberalisation advocated by Treasury, the Reserve Bank, the business press, and some of the younger National MPs. Even energy projects fitted into the Bank's positive commentary on the policies of 1979, and they were profoundly oriented to big business and foreign investment. Muldoon, too, consistently cut income taxes from 1978 and it is strange that he receives so little credit for that.

Think Big, which dominated policy in 1980 and 1981, was imprudent. Decision-making was rushed, chaotic and driven by political imperatives. Advancing so many large projects, at the same time, and borrowing very heavily to do so was highly damaging and brought more measured ideas of state-supported development into disrepute. After 1981, increasingly preoccupied with inflation, Muldoon abruptly reversed earlier liberalisation, re-regulated financial markets, froze wages and prices, and had Parliament enact what was effectively a property speculation tax of the sort which he had vehemently opposed in 1975. Many of his wealthier supporters were no more willing to countenance such a policy in 1982 than they had been in 1975, and they turned on him with a vengeance. The freeze was a profound change of direction. 'Only during the period 1982–84 did Muldoon start to see the choice between the two positions [Keynesian and neoclassical] as a stark choice between good and evil and as a result, in the opinion of some senior advisers, committed himself totally to an anti-New Right position' – one of his own definition.[145] Until the freeze Muldoon was a capitalist restructurer, friendly to business. Treasury and the Bank were generally happy enough with his approach, and indeed much of what he did followed their advice or they approved of it after the fact.

Thinking in Treasury and the Bank changed considerably during the Muldoon years. If the general direction of advice, in favour of liberalisation and an increased emphasis on internationally competitive export industries did not change, the fervour and certainty of the tone certainly did, particularly after 1981. Senior officials had (with some success) been advocating managed and coherent liberalisation; the 1979 Budget had generally reflected their advice. They were utterly dismayed by the freeze. Many were persuaded by their experiences between 1981 and 1984 that consensual and gradual liberalisation was a dead-end, and blitzkrieg was the only option. In Roger Douglas they found a minister who shared this view. But any suggestion that Muldoon obdurately resisted the path of economic virtue as expounded by the Bank and Treasury for nine years is a gross oversimplification. The world economy changed in the Muldoon years; so did the New Zealand economy, and so did Muldoon, his ministerial colleagues, and the officials.

Muldoon, as others have argued, should never have been both Prime Minister and Minister of Finance.[146] The combined demands were too much of a contrast, the workload too great, and in the end it broke him. Muldoon would still have exercised oversight of economic policy without being minister, and perhaps with a more strategic approach. Muldoon, unfortunately, believed that he possessed unique insight into the New Zealand economy and that he alone could manage it. Perhaps also he had an unspoken belief that the New Zealand economy should bend itself quickly to his will; this impatience might explain his adoption of a succession of magic bullets: retrenchment, easing, liberalisation, Think Big and then the freeze. There were no magic bullets; the depth of the crisis after 1974 required measured reorientation and a new consensus – socially, economically and politically. Muldoon, as the most abrasive politician for a generation, was singularly ill-placed to shape that consensus.

Chapter 9

The End of the Postwar Settlement, 1984–93

Economic policy changed profoundly after 1984. The direction of reform that the Labour government elected in that year pursued – deregulation and then significant privatisation – was increasingly resented by many in the trade unions, the wider party membership and traditional Labour electorates. With Labour's disintegration and defeat in 1990, a National government extended restructuring into social policy and labour market regulation. By 1993 National, too, paid an electoral price and the pace of change slowed. The 15 years after 1984 still exert a powerful influence. Much of the success of the Labour-dominated governments led by Helen Clark between 1999 and 2008 was due to the 'rebalancing' after what Clark and her colleagues characterised as a period of extremism. The National Party's election victory in 2008 was arguably due to the party's selection of a leader who could be marketed as a post-ideological pragmatist, untainted by the baggage of the 1980s and 1990s.

The regime that emerged after 1984 contrasted fundamentally with the postwar regime. The emphasis shifted from actively developing exports and encouraging internal diversification to a belief that all that was required was getting the macroeconomic fundamentals right. Fixed exchange rates floated; the balance of payments diminished as a policy focus. If full employment had been the catchphrase in 1945, 40 years later it was price stability. Monetary policy became an increasingly important economic lever and replaced fiscal and incomes policies as the principal means of dealing with inflation. Significant dimensions of social policy were targeted according to income, which challenged social democratic notions of universalism. Inequality increased considerably. More broadly, a new international political economy, emerging since the 1960s, consolidated and, like the pre-Depression gold standard, subordinated significant dimensions of national policy to international markets.

Labour in Power 1984–87: Liberalisation

Pressure for some degree of liberalisation had been increasing after 1980. The sudden election and foreign exchange crisis epitomised

Muldoon's failure to deliver this. Lange's assessment has often been quoted: that those particular circumstances were crucial in setting Labour's course. If the election had been in late November, as usual, ministers would have 'celebrated through December, gone on holiday, come back and had a formal opening of Parliament and tried out our new seats. . . . The first Budget would have been drawn up in circumstances of great party orthodoxy and we would have had a very different Government'.[1] Jane Kelsey has suggested that 'without the exchange crisis of July 1984 . . . [t]he country's economic problems would have been subject to more leisurely assessment, and a more pragmatic response would probably have been endorsed'.[2] That counterfactual is most unlikely. Some weeks before the freeze, the Reserve Bank had warned that ending the crawling peg would provoke precisely the pressure for a large devaluation that happened in 1984, and there is no reason to imagine that if the election had occurred in November the run on the dollar would have been any less. Even if Muldoon had devalued before the election, the budget deficit and inflationary pressure would still have required urgent attention.

There had been strenuous debates within the Labour Party over economic policy after 1981. Douglas and his allies saw economic liberalisation as the means to growth, although Douglas's 'thinking on economic policy matters over the years [was] not nearly as consistent as is often assumed'.[3] Only in late 1983, for instance, did he cease to favour preferential assistance to small business and a role for the state in industrial development. Others in the party were suspicious of liberalisation, but there was no agreement on alternatives, and the debates were smoothed over in a bland and general manifesto.[4] Douglas and some of his opponents agreed however that 'consultation and consensus lead to mediocrity. A Government has to have the capacity to take bold decisions . . . for the ultimate good of the community . . . you cannot present yourself like a lump of salami and have slices taken off you by the pressure groups because you distort the whole ultimate good of the reforms you undertake'.[5]

Attempts to shape public opinion were stage-managed. The Economic Summit Conference in September 1984 was a showpiece of consensus. Business groups wanted deregulation and growth (a more user-friendly term than 'profits') rather than redistribution. Primary producers naturally advocated increased attention to exporting. Unemployment, identified as the major economic issue in Labour's pre-election material, was emphasised by community groups and the voluntary sector.[6] All agreed that permanently high employment was desirable. Where consensus disappeared was on the means by which higher growth, price stability and high employment could be achieved, and on the priority of each.[7] Douglas, at least retrospectively, regarded the summit as an opportunity to seek consent for the direction in which he already wished to go, and referred to the risk that 'a few people would come from it with heightened expectations of continued consensus and involvement'.[8]

Shortly before the summit, the government released Treasury's post-election briefing (not then normal practice). Written quickly, the briefing demonstrated the influence of younger officials and their new approach, and generally matched Douglas's own views.[9] The briefing argued for radical change, maintaining that postwar economic management had been consistently and profoundly misguided. There was less focus on the fundamental ways in which the world economy had changed since the late 1960s. The summary view was that 'we have continually failed to make the best of the circumstances we find ourselves in'.[10]

Real GDP growth since 1973 had been less than half the OECD average, which Treasury implicitly attributed to an 'unwillingness to adjust to changing external circumstances' rather than any sense that New Zealand's was a small open economy badly mauled by the recession.[11] Rowling's strategy was described as attempting to 'ride out the first oil shock rather than adjust to it'. Rowling in fact sought a managed adjustment, including domestic constraint, in line with both Treasury and IMF views of the time. Treasury was more complimentary about Muldoon's retrenchment of 1976–77, although after 1977 he had changed direction frequently and not always against Treasury advice.[12] The two oil shocks were 'estimated to have reduced New Zealand's underlying terms of trade by roughly 15 per cent each. Substantial adjustment of the real exchange rate would therefore have been expected during this period. This did not occur'.[13] In fact the real exchange rage had fallen significantly with Rowling's devaluation of August 1975 and, although it subsequently rose to pre-devaluation levels, the crawling peg dropped it again and kept it down. This may have been insufficient adjustment, but there was adjustment.[14]

Keynesian management was implicitly dismissed as 'soft options . . . [to] stimulate the economy for short-term output, income and employment gains' at the cost of inflation.[15] Budget deficits simply 'reflect[ed] an unwillingness . . . to take hard expenditure and revenue decisions, perhaps because of concerns about their possible immediate effects on employment or prices or their implications for the incomes or welfare of those benefitting from government programmes'.[16] Fiscal policy had been 'overused and ineffective in anything other than the very short run as an instrument of macroeconomic manipulation ("stabilisation") in recent years'.[17] Public spending had increased relatively and absolutely since 1970.[18] Ministers were told that assistance to industry cost $2 billion annually, but were not reminded that Muldoon had already committed to abolishing the significant SMP component. More generally industry assistance was 'linked to our inward-looking attitude to economic development'.[19] In fact much assistance to farming and manufacturing alike had, wisely or not, been intended to encourage export growth. Protected domestic industry was on notice regarding the attentions of the Industries Development Commission. Social welfare spending had increased in real terms since 1971, and while superannuation was a significant part of the reason, Treasury's much wider criticism was of 'poorly targetted . . . subsidy schemes in areas such as housing, education and medical care, where much assistance is delivered to everyone regardless of need'.[20] This was a fundamental challenge to the postwar settlement, where health and education spending were not about income support but social inclusion.[21]

More generally, Treasury advocated more transparency and openness in public discussion of policy, but that did not mean any sort of institutionalised agreements with sector groups.[22] Anticipating 'aggravate[d] pressure for wage increases' Treasury showed no enthusiasm for such negotiation, but placed considerable faith in policy consistency. So far as wages were a factor in inflation, 'the solution lies in the Government firmly making up its mind what its objectives are for monetary, fiscal and exchange rate policies for the immediate future, and making sure that these are well understood and implemented in a credible manner so that employers and employees are not likely to agree wage increases based on a mistaken view about government policy intentions'.[23] While post-freeze settlements were high, the government continued to avoid tripartite negotiations and hoped that 'unions and employers [would] become responsible for the conduct of their own relationship' in a general context of greater union responsibility for economic growth. The Industrial Relations Act 1987 encouraged unions to merge and to focus on enterprise bargaining rather than national awards.[24]

Douglas's first Budget reflected substantial agreement with Treasury, noting higher interest rates to reduce inflation, constrained public spending to reduce the budget deficit, and a 'realistic' exchange rate.[25] Most farm and forestry subsidies and assistance ended, and many government charges increased, including electricity, road user charges, and petrol tax. Superannuitants faced a 25 per cent tax surcharge on additional income over $5200 a year, which affected less than a quarter of superannuitants but provoked outrage.[26] Lower-income working families received more generous means-tested benefits, which Douglas financed by increasing the standard income tax rate from 31.5 to 33 per cent and abolishing tax exemptions on life insurance and private superannuation. The Budget was justified as simple necessity but arguably few of its provisions were inconsistent with traditional Labour priorities, although Douglas indicated that future tax reform would compensate middle and higher income earners for their increased costs.[27]

Treasury's briefing had advocated a deregulated exchange rate, but the decision to float, in March 1985, suggests that Douglas and his advisers were not always philosophically committed to a particular course of action.[28] Fixed exchange rates prevailed under the postwar Bretton Woods system, but by 1984 a fixed rate was increasingly difficult to manage; defending it before the election had cost hundreds of millions of dollars, and large discrete changes were disruptive and required complex judgements on timing and quantum. In the later part of 1984 Treasury and Reserve Bank views moved back and forth between complete deregulation and a more managed exchange rate. Douglas apparently favoured a managed rate until early March when another run on the dollar provoked him to a complete float.[29]

The combination of a floating dollar and using high interest rates to reduce inflation was unfortunate. Managing the balance of payments under a floating exchange rate was, in a new 'consenting adults' perspective, viewed as less important, so long as lenders were willing to cover a current account deficit.[30] With government stock paying 15 per cent and private rates matching, overseas lenders found New Zealand an attractive proposition.[31] Consequently the dollar rose, rapidly reversing the effects of devaluation. The 'Bank and Treasury had not anticipated the full monetary implications of a combination of devaluation and aggressive debt sales'.[32] One part of the 1984 Treasury briefing had in fact warned of exactly what happened: with a floating exchange rate and tight monetary policy 'the effect is to appreciate the exchange rate, thus squeezing the sectors exposed to foreign competition directly. This is the United States experience in the last year or two'.[33] Elsewhere, the briefing had advocated devaluation as a way of assisting the tradeable sector that would 'ease the adjustment process'.[34] The 'fundamental contradiction' between the needs of the export sector and the consequences of a tight monetary policy was, evidently, not appreciated by ministers or their senior advisers, and monetary policy torpedoed any export-led recovery.[35]

During 1985 ministers and officials worked on the flagship policies of State Owned Enterprises and tax reform. The centrepiece of tax reform was reducing the upper rates of income tax (consistent with the belief that this would give incentives to enterprise and work) and introducing a universal sales tax on goods and services that would replace existing, highly variable, sales taxes. Douglas repeatedly connected the Goods and Services Tax to funding health, education, benefits 'the social wage . . . at the heart of the Labour Government's traditional commitment to social justice'.[36] This, no doubt, reassured many Labour activists and supporters who were suspicious of a universal consumption tax because of its regressive dimensions: bearing more heavily on those on lower incomes who have little choice about spending to the limit of their income.

Treasury's briefing had criticised state enterprises for having conflicting and unclear objectives (providing both services and employment at below-market cost to the user) and a privileged position in the market. Politicians and others frequently (and with variable justification) criticised them for having little information on what they owned, the value of their assets, or even detailed accounts. During 1985 and 1986 Roderick Deane in the Reserve Bank (who enjoyed a close relationship with Roger Douglas and Deputy Prime Minister Geoffrey Palmer) and senior Treasury officials developed a new regime. The State Owned Enterprises Act 1986 required specified state enterprises to operate on the same basis as private enterprises, with boards independent from political control. Richard Prebble, a Douglas ally, became the responsible minister, and while there were severe job losses as the new companies sought to operate profitably, the government took steps to mitigate the effect of the redundancies.[37] Presumably with ministerial support, Deane 'made sure that no clause in the new legislation outlawed privatisation'.[38]

Labour in Power 1987–90: Privatisation and Disintegration

As the 1987 election approached, Lange and Douglas began to differ over the appropriate extent of further reform. It is still unclear why Douglas's views became more radical during 1987, but on tax his thinking went so far as the neo-liberal nostrum of a single flat rate levied on all incomes.[39] He began to argue for privatising the new state-owned enterprises, justified by using the proceeds to reduce debt and therefore interest payments, which would mean 'more for health, education and welfare'.[40] Labour won the August election, apparently convincingly, although there was little specific commitment to future policy.

The October 1987 sharemarket crash reinforced Douglas in his intentions.[41] While the crash was global, the New Zealand boom had been unique in its scale. In 12 months over 1985–86, 'share trading volumes had . . . increase[d] . . . almost 100 per cent, while the equivalent markets in Australia, New York and London had registered increases of 20, 30 and 30 per cent respectively'.[42] Douglas and his allies naturally regarded the boom as vindication, and there was little interest in caution or regulation, even though a good deal of the increased activity was speculative, and financed by margin trading (borrowing money to buy the shares, which then secured the loan, in the expectation of a quick capital gain) or mortgages.[43] The market had been unstable through the winter and early spring of 1987, and when the New York market dropped in mid October, small investors in the New Zealand market panicked, and on 20 October it fell catastrophically.[44] The boom in commercial property crashed with the sharemarket; banks found themselves with many bad debts and interest rates remained high, now to reflect the greater perceived risk in lending rather than high demand for money, and that intensified the squeeze on the productive and exporting sectors of the economy. A vicious circle of falling demand set in.[45]

Douglas declared that he wished to reinforce business confidence by stressing 'that further reform was in the air before any post-crash recession set in'.[46] Treasury's post-election briefing had, however, foreshadowed Douglas's agenda. Kelsey observes that if the 1984 briefing 'was about restructuring the economy [the 1987 briefing] was about restructuring the state'.[47] Whereas the 1984 briefing had described an economy in crisis, the 1987 document adopted an Olympian tone in which there was little room for debate. Highly contentious issues were treated as if there was one simple truth; significantly, and problematically, 'justice,' 'fairness' and 'equity' were treated as interchangeable terms.[48] The public sector was implicitly presented as a drain on the economy.[49] Discussion of state trading activities included a predictable and well-worn observation about confusion of objectives and even in the SOE model 'the absence of . . . market pressures . . . permits managers to give excessive weight to non-commercial objectives'.[50] Privatisation would produce maximum efficiency; even core social services such as education were regarded as inefficient because of 'the transfer costs of removing monies from families so that the government can spend it [sic] largely on their behalf; the inefficiencies of the state as a spender of other people's money in comparison with their own efficiency; the disparities between the likely state education agenda and those of families, and the difficulty of resisting centripetal and provider pressures once the family is not in direct control'.[51] That sort of thing made it all too easy to caricature Treasury officials as callow youths with neither social skills nor experience of the real world, and did the department a profound disservice.

Lange was increasingly unhappy with the direction of Douglas's thinking, and wanted to delay new policies until the Royal Commission on Social Policy had reported. Lange had convened the Commission in 1986 and some of his ministers were at least later hostile to it.[52] In any event, ministers announced, with some fanfare, a package including a flat rate of income tax, increased GST, more rigorous targeting of transfer payments, and extensive privatisation. There are still conflicting accounts of whether, or to what extent, Lange clearly opposed the package beforehand, and ministers differed, either at the time or later, about whether the package was a concept or a set of specific policies.[53] Lange would later insist that it was 'a statement of possibility rather than of firm intention'.[54]

On 28 January 1988 Lange, having come to the view that the package would not deliver what was promised, and would increase inequality to an unacceptable degree, announced at a press conference that it would not proceed. Much political damage resulted, not least because Lange had not discussed his intentions with either the full cabinet or the party caucus.[55] Controversy continues over the merits of the package and of Lange's action, and the reason for his discomfort. Bassett highlights the influence of Margaret Pope, the Prime Minister's speechwriter, and of some within the union movement and wider Labour Party. A romantic relationship was already developing between Lange and Pope, and they would later marry. It may be that Pope reinforced Lange's inclination, but Lange's attitude was consistent with a wider feeling in the Labour Party that reform had been necessary but within limits. Lange, after all, had correctly been seen as driven by a progressive Methodist social conscience, and much of his political rhetoric reflected that influence (even if, contrarily, he could display a mean streak when crossed on the campaign trail).[56]

Cabinet on 1 February 1988 resolved that the principles of the December package stood but that further work had to be done to ensure it was workable in 'equity and fiscal responsibility'.[57] One minister later said that Lange's dramatic action was unnecessary because Cabinet would inevitably have come to the conclusion the numbers didn't work.[58] The rival offices of the Prime Minister and Minister of Finance now aired their differences in the media, leaking and spinning against each other.[59] If Douglas became increasingly testy and inclined to discuss radical options in public, Lange was increasingly isolated, needing support from those more traditional elements in the party whom he had alienated with his sharp tongue and support for Douglas in the previous few years. A compromise of sorts came when the income tax scales were greatly flattened from 1 April 1988 into two steps of 24 and 33 per cent (the top rate had come down to 48 per cent when GST was introduced).[60]

The 1988 Budget announced sweeping privatisations, including Government Property Services, the New Zealand Shipping Corporation, the Tourist Hotel Corporation, the Land Corporation's financial assets, the Bank of New Zealand, Postbank, the Rural Bank, and substantial forestry assets. Others would follow before 1990, most significantly Telecom.[61] Privatisation was and remains contentious. Few if any ministers were completely opposed to it; Lange was happy to sell Air New Zealand, Railways, and the Tourist Hotel Corporation.[62] Some economists thought that privatisation was implicit in the SOE structure, or should be. Two Treasury officials who had moved into merchant banking argued that 'the attainment of the best feasible economic outcomes requires that state-owned trading organisations be transferred to private ownership in order to subject those organisations to the full range of market disciplines'.[63] For some Labour politicians, debt repayment was attractive, especially as privatisations were 'more palatable than expenditure cuts,' although Douglas later said that debt reduction was not the best argument but only the easiest one politically. Privatisation also got some risk off the government's books. 'Where critics of privatisation mourned the loss of public control of a strategic resource and the income stream it had produced, Treasury saw lids placed over bottomless financial pits'; Graham Scott commented on the efforts ministers went to in order to save relatively small sums, only to have state enterprises lose much larger sums.[64] The SOE legislation was intended to place the lids regardless, and while some at least of the SOEs would have required substantial injections of capital in order to develop, by 1989 unprivatised SOEs 'were making a significant contribution to government revenue'. There were 'major gains in productivity over the departmental structure,' and they performed well commercially, with 13 of 16 turning in a profit. Even Prebble attributed most of the improved performance to the new organisational form.[65]

Some commentators regard the worst feature of privatisation as the disregard of undertakings not to do so, such as those made by Prebble when introducing the SOE legislation in 1986: 'The Government does not regard itself as the owner . . . of the State corporations affected. The Government is the guardian on behalf of the people. No Government has the right to sell off State trading enterprises to its cronies. Government members are willing to make it an election issue'.[66] Whether they changed their minds after the 1987 election or were disingenuous before it is beside the point: if a mandate means anything, they had no such mandate for privatisation. Many voters inevitably felt deceived; privatisation contributed to what Kelsey called the 'democratic deficit' in the reform process.[67]

By the end of 1988 Lange's relations with Douglas and Prebble had broken down. After a dispute over the privatisation process, Lange removed Prebble from the SOE portfolio. Prebble then made unflattering remarks on television about the Prime Minister's mental health, which resulted in his dismissal from Cabinet.[68] A month later, after Lange refused to renew the contract of Douglas's press secretary, Douglas informed Lange that he could no longer serve in a Lange ministry and this was taken as resignation.[69] Douglas's replacement was David Caygill, a lawyer, who had fully supported Douglas and had little difficulty with privatisation. Yet Caygill followed Lange rather than Douglas in being 'not prepared to rely on the market to provide education or health' and he had no interest in major labour market deregulation.[70]

One Douglas policy that Caygill did take over was a new Reserve Bank Act. Inflation was falling and for 1988 had been projected at five per cent, which was still thought too high, although officials expected that a lower rate would be achieved within five years. Douglas wanted to achieve the lower rate by the 1990 election, and a new Governor, Don Brash, would reinforce those views. The Reserve Bank Act 1989 was based on the view that monetary policy should be limited in its ambitions to monetary matters such as the exchange rate, the quantity of money in circulation and price stability. Other policy areas like employment and investment, which had been specified in New Zealand's central banking legislation as in other countries, could not be directly influenced by monetary policy. All that monetary policy could do was 'provide a stable background for the economy – keep the machine well oiled' by creating an expectation of price stability and by itself being stable rather than erratic.[71] Monetary policy would thus only indirectly contribute to high employment and output; pursuing multiple objectives, it was said, meant that none were achieved, and removing monetary policy from political control would result in greater consistency and predictability.[72]

The new Act was a partial but significant reversal of the monetary policy regime that had prevailed since 1936. Douglas clearly wished to ensure no future minister could manipulate monetary policy as frequently and as inconsistently as Muldoon had. However, monetary policy remained subject to political control, for the Act specified that inflation targets would be agreed with the Minister of Finance and that the Governor of the Bank was accountable for achieving those targets. The other dimension in which the new Act was not a return to a pre-1930s regime was that it specified the existence of a central bank that would not be subject to competition or private shareholding. Treasury seriously advocated constituting the Bank as a State-owned

Enterprise. Unsurprisingly, the Bank was unimpressed, and managed after some time to see that idea thrown out.[73]

In August 1989 Douglas was re-elected to Cabinet and David Lange resigned as Prime Minister. Lange was a complex, gifted and flawed politician; with a phenomenally quick mind, his rapid rise in the parliamentary Labour Party meant, perhaps, that he lacked the experience that might have developed the political skills necessary to stamp his authority on the Cabinet and caucus once the easy camaraderie of 1984–86 faltered. If Lange's political persona reflected the often quoted British observation that the Labour Party owed more to Methodism than to Marxism, then a little more Marxism, or at least background in social democratic thought, might have equipped Lange better for the long haul.

Lange's political failings must be seen alongside the fact that Douglas and Prebble, in particular, had by 1987 gone far beyond the consensus for reform, and the weakness of their position is betrayed by Douglas's open advocacy of radical change without attempting to build a new consensus.[74] For Lange, making the state more efficient was one thing – acceptable and necessary; radically diminishing it was quite another. As he put it, 'people who support us are people who depend on the government. Their lives are enriched by it. Tax cuts mean little to them'.[75] On election night 1987 Lange had declared: 'we in the next three years are going to seal those gains in health and education and social welfare progress that are the hallmarks of a Labour government and a labour movement'.[76] In accepting the 1988 tax cuts and privatisations 'Lange had compromised his own political instincts to a considerable degree in order to meet his Minister of Finance halfway. But that was as far as he would allow Douglas to take the market liberal agenda'.[77] In April 1988 Lange warned Douglas that abandoning universal taxpayer-funded social services meant that many would have to 'prove their inability to pay for [services]. Those who are poor must seek for admittance to the entitlements of citizenship. They must depend not on the institutions of the state but the whim of governments. . . . That is so much in opposition to all that you and I have stood for in politics that I do not even go into the impracticalities of it'.[78] Lange had isolated the fundamental issue. He wished to modernise the postwar settlement; Douglas and his allies now wished to tear it up.

The National Government 1990–93: The Attack on Welfare and Wages

In the 15 months after Lange's resignation, the Labour government disintegrated and the National Party won a landslide victory in October 1990, with the National leader Jim Bolger campaigning more or less explicitly on the basis that reform would slow and become consensual. Just as in 1984, the incoming government was greeted with a very nasty surprise about the public finances. In 1990 it was a deficit much higher than forecast, partly due to unbudgeted decisions taken by the Labour government, but more to the near-collapse of the Bank of New Zealand, which required over $600m of public money if its bad debts were to be covered (Government Property Services required another $240m and the Development Finance Corporation $112m).[79] The BNZ was, as they now say, too big to fail, and the government was being warned about a major downgrade in its own credit rating. More generally Treasury described the economy as 'fragile', in part blaming a regulated labour market, welfare benefits, which allegedly gave too little incentive to work, and continuing high public spending, which contradicted a tight monetary policy. Treasury made no mention of the extent to which monetary policy had damaged the export sector. In that context, Treasury rhetoric about encouraging a 'strong, dynamic internationally competitive sector and businesses' might have invited some scepticism.[80]

Just as in 1984, the post-election crisis gave the incoming finance minister licence to indulge long-cherished desires. The new minister was Ruth Richardson, whose previous career had included positions as a civil servant and a legal officer for Federated Farmers. Her instincts were at least as radical as those of Treasury. Graham Scott, Secretary since 1986, described her as 'the only genuinely ideological Minister of Finance I worked for'.[81] Well before the 1990 Budget, let alone the election, 'Treasury had decided that fiscal consolidation [in plainer language, spending cuts] and labour market reform would be two principal themes of its post-election briefing. But it was difficult to make a strong case for the former on the Budget night figures'.[82] In December 1990 Richardson and Bolger announced a package of severe measures, reducing welfare benefits by between 13 and 25 per cent, and restricting eligibility. The universal family benefit was abolished. Housing assistance, defence, education, and health were all reduced; the total savings were said to be $2.3 billion, of which slightly more than half came out of the social welfare budget.[83]

Bolger spoke of the urgent requirement to reduce the government's deficit. He also stressed the need to reduce 'generous' welfare commitments, presenting the imposition of charges for core social services on all but the least well paid as a trade-off for tax cuts. He therefore intensified the language of entitlement around need rather than citizenship, and emphasised self-reliance and personal choice.[84] The 1991 Budget continued Richardson's programme, continuing privatisations, increasing targeting in social services, corporatising health services, imposing market rentals for state houses (compensated for with an accommodation supplement for beneficiaries), and abating superannuation where extra income was received. Only technically therefore was a promise to abolish the surcharge on additional income honoured. A radical revision of labour law, the Employment Contracts Act, had already been passed; it deprived unions of much of their legal status, completely decentralised the bargaining process and was intended to drive wages down. In that, at least, it succeeded.

Remarkably, in her 1991 Budget Richardson made no reference to the previous government, even by way of criticism. Her language was as if she had taken over directly from Muldoon: 'recent decades' had been characterised by 'a protected environment to support . . . domestic manufacturing . . . expansionary monetary and fiscal policies to stimulate domestic demand . . . targeting of Government assistance into areas which were believed capable of large and strategic contributions to future growth[;] pervasive use of regulations and direct controls'.[85] It was entirely a data-free observation that high debt and high tax 'burdens had sapped the initiative and the energy of New Zealand's wealth creators'. It was a gross and tendentious misrepresentation to say that there was a widespread 'assumption that all the needs of members of society can be addressed by state action'.[86] Like Douglas, like other exponents of declinist rhetoric, Richardson's intention was to pathologise the past in order to justify radical change.

Years later, Bolger would justify the 1990–91 measures as having rescued the economy from collapse. However, like Lange but more successfully, he would later argue that a point had been reached at which further reform would be counter-productive.[87] Yet Treasury had to admit in May 1991 that 'the positive effect of the savings announced in the December initiative and subsequent[ly] . . . have been almost off-set by a forecast deterioration in economic prospects and erosion of the tax base'.[88] In other words, as even a simple Keynesian analysis would have shown, reducing the income of beneficiaries and the low-paid meant reducing their spending, which was generally not discretionary. This meant reducing the earnings of traders and manufacturers who catered to their needs. Not only did the government thereby lose revenue (and that loss was intensified because of the extent to which revenue depended on the universal GST) but also spending on unemployment benefits increased as falling demand reduced employment.[89]

Table 9.1: Unemployment 1988–92

Year	1988	89	90	91	92
000	69.5	98	112.4	135.7	172.6
%	5.6	7.1	7.7	10.2	10.3

(Source: NZOYB 1995, pp. 322, 324. Unemployment numbers in thousands are from the Household Labour Force Survey, and percentages are from OECD figures.)

Scott admitted privately that the outlook in March 1991 was for 'a picture of human distress which frankly frightens me'.[90] He had earlier warned that the measures proposed for the December package ran 'the serious risk of creating pockets of serious hardship', and the benefit cuts were much more severe than Treasury had suggested in at least some advice.[91] Scott's fears were born out as inequality increased: 'between 1988/89 and 1993/94, the average weekly household income of the lowest to the highest income quintiles rose by: 0.3 percent, 2.1 percent, 4.2 percent, 8.0 percent, and 13.2 per cent respectively'.[92] The richer you were, the better you did from the reforms.

Richardson's tenure was brief and spectacular. Having won the 1993 election by the narrowest of margins, Bolger removed her from Finance; she refused all other portfolios and left parliament shortly afterwards. One of Richardson's final initiatives was the Fiscal Responsibility Act 1994, intended to ensure that no future government could leave the sort of surprise that had awaited the Bolger administration in 1990 (or, as she might have also said, Lange in 1984). The act provided that economic and fiscal updates would be published with every Budget and six months thereafter, as well as shortly before an election. The act also required 'prudent' levels of public debt, and government surpluses in the medium term; no Keynesian should have had a problem with either provision.[93] The Minister of Finance was required to note any departure from the act's principles and the expected duration of such a departure. While the act was an attempt to depoliticise fiscal policy, that was, as Treasury acknowledged, very difficult. Critics maintained that the act entrenched the Treasury view of economic management, but the language was necessarily general, and it certainly did not bind Michael Cullen, as finance minister in the Labour governments after 1999, to Treasury prescriptions, nor prevent him from describing some of them as an 'ideological burp'.

Assessing the Restructuring

The restructuring of economic and social policy between 1984 and 1992 has not been short of defenders. In 1996, a now-classic article by Lewis Evans and others justified the restructuring by 'the sustained economic upturn since 1991'.[94] That article is fairly representative of positive accounts of the restructuring, and in summary suggests that the reforms were intended to enact 'stable, credible, and mutually consistent macroeconomic policies which would assist in the efficient allocation of resources. . . . to provide stable policies rather than stabilization policies. The approach has also been characterized by attention to microeconomic efficiency when designing the macroeconomic framework'.[95] Evans and colleagues characterise the 50 years before 1984 as an undifferentiated whole that resulted in 'poor economic performance'.[96]

A key dimension of the postwar settlement had been to reduce inequality in living standards, and certainly in opportunity. The McCarthy Commission in 1972 had expressed the principle as suggesting that 'everyone is able to enjoy a standard of living much like that of the rest of the community and thus is able to feel a sense of participation and belonging to the community'.[97] In the view of critics, this meant unsustainable public spending. Evans and colleagues refer to 'the rapid escalation of social welfare which followed' and even though they correctly note that much of that increased expenditure was due to national superannuation, they do not mention that McCarthy had explicitly recommended against a scheme based on Muldoon's approach.[98] National superannuation as Muldoon conceived it did not necessarily follow from the principles of the postwar settlement. The continued growth in welfare expenditure under the fourth Labour government had, as Evans and colleagues do not mention, something to do with the significant increase in unemployment during those years. As they do say, in 'the six years to September 1991 employment fell by 5.6 percent, a fall unprecedented in New Zealand since the 1930s depression, and the unemployment rate rose from 3.8 percent to 10.9 percent'.[99] Certainly superannuation was the major component in benefit spending, but after 1984 expenditure on unemployment benefits and the domestic purposes benefit increased dramatically (it is at least plausible that the latter was to some extent attributed to disguised unemployment). Even granting that increased unemployment was a necessary cost of restructuring the economy, increased welfare expenditure should be partly regarded as a cost of the transition, not a symptom of the old regime's weakness.

Table 9.2 Major Benefit Expenditure 1984–94

	Superannuation		Unemployment		DPB		Total benefits $m
	$m	% of total	$m	% of total	$m	% of total	
1984/85	2750	66%	275	7%	460	11%	4150
1990/91	5100	58%	1400	16%	1200	14%	8780
1994	5100	58%	1500	17%	1200	14%	8850

Source: New Zealand Official Yearbook, various years.

The postwar settlement had included a fairly tightly regulated system of labour relations, although the incorporation of organised labour into policymaking was never formalised to the extent seen in Northern Europe. Evans and colleagues, discussing the Employment Contracts Act, regard labour market deregulation as self-evidently positive. The core of their analysis is that National's welfare cuts and labour market deregulation, which essentially completed Douglas's unfinished business, were followed by economic growth. This claim rests on an elementary flaw in reasoning, a fallacy known as 'post hoc, ergo propter hoc,' or, 'after that, therefore because of that': in other words, if B follows A, then A caused B. Some economists, as we noted earlier, warned that the 1990 benefit cuts would intensify the recession by depressing demand. Evans and colleagues retrospectively countered that argument by observing that 'strong real GDP and employment growth commenced from about this time. . . . 'the June quarter 1991 [was] a trough in New Zealand's business cycle'.[100] Apart from the fallacy just noted, if the three months to 30 June 1991 were the trough, it is a little far-fetched to argue that Richardson's axe produced results so quickly, given that the benefit cuts only took effect in April 1991. Nor do Evans and colleagues address the question of whether the cycle was on the up anyway, in which case Richardson may have diminished the recovery.

While Evans and colleagues identify 'some a priori evidence that the shift to the deregulated labor market under the ECA has been beneficial for labor market outcomes' in that employment started growing again after 1991, 'some a priori evidence' is simply an alternative term for the same post hoc ergo propter hoc fallacy.[101] Finally, they admit that 'it is difficult to say to what degree the reforms contributed to this outcome' of improving indicators.[102] That is a startling admission. The justification for those policies was that they were essential to economic recovery, and yet it is not at all clear what sort of contribution, if any, they made to that recovery.

Curiously for a discussion of a small economy largely dependent on primary sector exporting, Evans and colleagues give little space to export performance. Total export receipts in the year to June 1992 increased by 12.4 per cent over the previous year (in inflation-adjusted terms). The next year was less spectacular at 4.9 per cent.[103] Import spending (also in inflation adjusted terms) remained static in the two years to June 1992, but increased by 10.5 per cent in the year to June 1993.[104] On the face of it, the 'recovery' after the middle of 1991 was an old-fashioned export-led recovery that after a little time resulted in increased importing. The OECD had little to say about benefit cuts or the Employment Contracts Act but observed that the recovery had 'been led by strong export growth, especially in the non-commodity manufacturing and forestry sectors. Improved price competitiveness associated with significant gains in productivity and a lower exchange rate contributed to the turnaround. . . . The terms of trade have also had a positive influence'.[105] Export growth had begun during 1990, with strong demand in both Asia and Europe. There was notable growth in non-traditional exports 'reflecting the restructuring efforts in industry during the 1980s and an increased export orientation by New Zealand firms'.[106] These had been emphasised by governments for two decades before 1984. Apparently impressive though the recovery was, the OECD also noted that 'real GDP at the start of the current recovery was about 5 per cent below its 1985–86 level. So far, [the recovery] has just sufficed to bring real GDP back to its long-term trend'.[107]

Some scholars have disputed the positive accounts of policy change.[108] Paul Dalziel has argued that 'the New Zealand experiment did not succeed, despite achieving greater microeconomic efficiency in some industries and obtaining its intermediate objectives of price stability and fiscal balance'.[109] Where Evans and his colleagues simply compared New Zealand before and after the reforms, Dalziel attempted to use a proper counterfactual. In addition to noting the post hoc ergo propter hoc fallacy, Dalziel points out that 'simple comparison of pre-reform and post-reform outcomes is not reasonable . . . since there is no suggestion that New Zealand would have engaged in *no* reforms had it not embraced the comprehensive programme adopted after 1984'.[110]

Dalziel's counterfactual is Australia, a close neighbour and sharing many dimensions of the settler economy experience. In the 35 years after 1949 'the two economies grew at similar rates, punctuated by two large, adverse shocks to New Zealand's per capita real GDP in 1967/68 and 1977/78'.[111] Comparing per capita GDP, unemployment, and productivity growth since 1950, Dalziel finds that 'New Zealand sacrificed a large volume of real per capita GDP between 1987 and

1998 compared with Australia; that New Zealand's unemployment rate moved from well below that of Australia before 1988 to comparable values thereafter; and that labour productivity growth in New Zealand has been considerably below that of Australia since 1992, after similar rates for the previous 14 years'.[112] From 1987 until 1993, per capita growth in New Zealand was virtually non-existent or negative, while Australia continued to grow from 1987 until 1990. Australia was in a recession from then until 1993, but although both countries' growth resumed thereafter, Australian growth resumed from a much higher base and New Zealand never caught up, falling further behind from 1996 until 1999.[113] As Dalziel notes, 'the cumulative effect of this divergence is very large'.[114] One major factor was the declining rate of growth in labour productivity in New Zealand after 1991, whereas Australia continued on the upward trend, which both countries had generally shared until then.[115]

None of this is to deny that the New Zealand economy was in serious trouble by 1984. This book has argued, however, that Muldoon was distinctive in many important respects and his tenure is not an indictment of the entire postwar regime. Muldoon has rightly and frequently been criticised for unpredictable, unbalanced and inconsistent policymaking; this book suggests that his polarising politics had damaging economic consequences as well. Dalziel implicitly suggests that the much more inclusive and consultative process followed in Australia after 1983, including successive versions of an Accord between the reforming Labor government and the Australian Council of Trade Unions, had much to do with the greater success of the Australian reform process, and that more moderate reform in New Zealand would have produced better outcomes. Goldfinch has described the difference between the two approaches as that between 'crashing through' and 'bargained consensus'.[116]

Instead, Roger Douglas (for far too long abetted by David Lange) emphasised the belief that consultation and consensus-building were incompatible with comprehensive reform. Speed became a virtue, which meant that policy was little more predictable and no more measured than it had been under Muldoon. By the late 1980s the 'commitment to balanced macroeconomic policies had shifted to an obsession with achieving an inflation rate below 2 per cent. Monetary policy was being directed solely to this end, notwithstanding a major loss in international competitiveness'.[117] That was, really, little different from Treasury's 1984 complaint about the later Muldoon years, that 'a reduction in domestic inflation has been achieved at the cost of the other objectives of economic policy'.[118] The advice given to Muldoon in the late 1970s and early 1980s, of steady and consistent, if unspectacular, adjustment, could have been born in mind in the mid and late 1980s.

One consequence of Muldoon's increasing obduracy, as I have suggested, was to make zealots out of moderates. But that is only part of the story. The whole approach after 1984, as McKinnon notes, was that economic management was a purely technical matter that was only sullied by the political process; the idea 'was to insulate the activity of economic management from problematic political currents within Cabinet, Parliament and the community'.[119] In light of this elitist approach to policymaking, there is a profound irony in a Treasury official defending the downgrading of macroeconomic management in favour of increased emphasis on markets, on the basis of 'their richness. When I started at Treasury, the concept of being a Treasury person was a bright elite guy who was going to make key choices which people themselves were not equipped to make. I came back [from Harvard, in the late 1970s] with a much higher respect for the choices that people make for themselves'.[120]

With a revised version of the nineteenth century economic constitution – amounting to a comprehensive application of market principles across many sectors of public as well as private life, stringent fiscal discipline, and central banking beyond political control – economic management would, so the hope went, once again be insulated from the inconvenience of democracy, as it had been until the 1930s.[121] Or, as Evans and colleagues put it, anticipating the 1996 election, the 'process of balancing demands for economic efficiency versus rent-seeking and redistribution will be complicated by the advent of the new electoral system,' which by being proportional made capture of the policy process by a small group of ministers rather less likely.[122] It is not usually so bluntly suggested that democracy and economic efficiency are incompatible.

This is not to deny that the environment in 1984 was very different than in 1935 or 1950 or 1968. The differences have been discussed at length in this book. In a discussion of the 1990–91 policies, one economist correctly observed that 'private sector reactions [were] now much more important than they were in the 1930s to 1970s'.[123] Evans and colleagues note that one dimension of the reforms was to increase both efficiency and the predictability of policy 'by increasing the exposure of politicians to the constraints imposed by external capital markets'.[124] The power of those external capital markets had been increasing anyway, at least since the mid 1960s. To that extent, as Gary Hawke has noted, arguments about the reform process had to go beyond 'wishful thinking about the principles of the welfare state in the 1930s. The problems of the 1980s could not be solved by any simple invocation of compassion'.[125]

On the other hand, one major point of 1935 was to renegotiate

New Zealand's relationship with external capital and other markets. Particularly in 1938–39 and in 1945–53, as we have seen in some detail, those external forces dominated New Zealand economic policy, and the external environment became much more challenging after 1966 and, particularly, 1973. Much of the story of economic policymaking in New Zealand after 1935 was about negotiating the terms on which New Zealand, a small settler economy, would engage with the rest of the world. New Zealand has never been able to insulate policy from external influences, but it is legitimate to seek to negotiate those relationships if national sovereignty and political democracy have any meaning at all.[126] The pre-1930s economic constitution rested upon some strong assumptions about the inconvenience of democracy for economic management; reforming governments after the Depression in New Zealand and elsewhere sought to reconcile democracy and economic management. That reconciliation remains important in the twenty-first century.

Endnotes

Preface

1 New Zealand Treasury, *New Zealand Economic and Financial Overview 2012*, New Zealand Treasury, Wellington, 2012, p. 9. http://www.treasury.govt.nz/economy/overview/2012/nzefo-12.pdf. Accessed 23 July 2012.
2 Donald T. Brash, 'New Zealand's Remarkable Reforms,' Fifth Annual Hayek Memorial Lecture, Institute of Economic Affairs, London, June 1996. http://rbnz.govt.nz/speeches/0031201.html. Accessed 23 July 2012.
3 Luke Malpass, 'New Zealand's risky re-regulation path,' 3 November 2010, http://www.cis.org.au/media-information/opinion-pieces/article/2239-new-zealands-risky-re-regulation-path. Accessed 23 July 2012.
4 Denis Healey, *The Time of My Life*, W.W. Norton, New York, 1990, p. 383.

Chapter 1

1 Keith Sinclair, *Walter Nash*, Auckland University Press, Auckland, 1976, p. 153.
2 There is, of course, a significant literature on settler societies and their economies. A useful beginning is C. B. Schedvin, 'Staples and Regions of Pax Britannica', *Economic History Review*, 2nd ser, 43(4), November 1990, pp. 533–59. The quote is at Schedvin, p. 533.
3 This point is made in Harriet Jones, 'Introduction', in Harriet Jones and Michael Kandiah, eds., *The Myth of Consensus: New Views on British History, 1945–64*, Macmillan, Basingstoke, 1996.
4 *New Zealand Official Year Book 2000*, Government Printer, Wellington, 2000, p. 379.
5 Douglas Myers, 'New Zealand: A Window of Opportunity' in New Zealand Business Roundtable, ed., *From Recession to Recovery*, New Zealand Business Roundtable, Wellington, 1992, p. 31.
6 The Albanian parallel has been discussed by Tim Hazeldine, *Taking New Zealand Seriously: The Economics of Decency*, HarperCollins, Auckland, 1998. The Polish shipyard is dealt with by Shaun Goldfinch and Daniel Malpass, 'The Polish Shipyard: Myth, Economic History and Economic Policy Reform in New Zealand', *Australian Journal of Politics and History*, 53(1), 2007, pp. 119–138.
7 John Singleton and Paul L. Robertson, *Economic Relations Between Britain and Australasia, 1945–1970*. Palgrave, Houndsmills, 2002, p. 21.
8 Singleton and Robertson, *Economic Relations,* p. 98.
9 Singleton and Robertson, *Economic Relations,* p. 90.
10 Singleton and Robertson, *Economic Relations,* pp. 98, 90.
11 Singleton and Robertson, *Economic Relations,* p. 97.
12 Singleton and Robertson, *Economic Relations,* pp. 18–22, 25.
13 James Belich, *Paradise Reforged: A history of the New Zealanders from the 1880s to the year 2000*, Allen Lane, Auckland, 2001, p. 70.
14 Belich, *Paradise Reforged*, p. 85.
15 Belich, *Paradise Reforged*, p. 547; see also pp. 394, 425.

16 Bruce Jesson, *Only their purpose is mad*, Dunmore, Palmerston North, 1999, pp. 68–9.
17 Jesson, p. 110.
18 Jesson, p. 77.
19 Jesson, p. 70. Jesson was a perceptive commentator, but his characterisation of the business world in the 1970s and of the New Zealand political economy is overdone. After all, Thatcher and others similarly forced through radical and rapid change, and interlocking directorates were hardly specific to New Zealand. The inappropriateness of comparing New Zealand to the United States or Britain will be obvious.
20 W. B. Sutch, *The Quest for Security in New Zealand*, Oxford University Press, Wellington, 1966, p. 335.
21 Sutch, *Quest for Security*, pp. 337, 343.
22 Sutch, *Quest for Security*, p. 412.
23 Sutch, *Quest for Security*, p. 426.
24 Geoff Bertram, 'The New Zealand Economy, 1900–2000' in Giselle Byrnes, ed., *The New Oxford History of New Zealand*, Oxford University Press, Melbourne, 2009.
25 Philippa Mein Smith, *A Concise History of New Zealand*, Cambridge University Press, Cambridge, 2005, p. 155.
26 Mein Smith, *Concise History*, p. 156.
27 Mein Smith, *Concise History*, p. 157. Sinclair's arguments are made, generally, in his *Walter Nash*.
28 Mein Smith, *Concise History*, p. 177.
29 Mein Smith, *Concise History*, p. 196.
30 Mein Smith, *Concise History*, p. 205.
31 G. R. Hawke, *The Making of New Zealand*, Cambridge University Press: Cambridge, 1985, p. 176.
32 Hawke, *Making of New Zealand*, p. 204.
33 Hawke, *Making of New Zealand*, p. 205.
34 Hawke, *Making of New Zealand*, p. 299.
35 John Gould, *The Rake's Progress? The New Zealand Economy Since 1945*, Hodder and Stoughton, Auckland, 1983.
36 Gould, *Rake's Progress*, pp. 220–21.
37 John Gould, *The Muldoon Years: An essay on New Zealand's recent economic growth*, Hodder and Stoughton, Auckland, 1985.
38 Colin James, *The Quiet Revolution: turbulence and transition in contemporary New Zealand*, Allen & Unwin, Wellington, 1986; Colin James, *New Territory: the transformation of New Zealand, 1984–92*, Bridget Williams Books, Wellington, 1992.
39 Brian Easton, *In Stormy Seas: The post-war New Zealand economy*, University of Otago Press, Dunedin, 1997.
40 Easton, *In Stormy Seas*, p. 50.
41 Brian Easton, *The Nationbuilders*, Auckland University Press, Auckland, 2001, pp. 9, 11.
42 Easton, *Nationbuilders*, p. 272.
43 Michael Bassett, *Coates of Kaipara*, Auckland University Press, Auckland, 1995; Barry Gustafson, *From the Cradle to the Grave: A biography of Michael Joseph Savage*, Reed Methuen, Auckland, 1986; Gustafson, *Kiwi Keith: A biography of Keith Holyoake*, Auckland University Press, Auckland, 2007; Gustafson, *His Way: A biography of Robert Muldoon*, Auckland University Press, Auckland,

2000; Michael Bassett with Michael King, *Tomorrow Comes the Song: A life of Peter Fraser*, Penguin, Auckland, 2000; Keith Sinclair, *Walter Nash*; Mary Logan, *Nordy: Arnold Nordmeyer, a political biography*, Steele Roberts, Wellington, 2008. The major gaps to 1984 are Sidney Holland and Norman Kirk, and Bill Rowling deserves some attention as well.

44 Malcolm McKinnon, *Treasury: The New Zealand Treasury, 1840–2000*, Auckland University Press, Auckland, 2003. The role of one part of the former Industries and Commerce/Trade and Industry department, the Trade Commissioner service, is discussed in New Zealand Trade and Enterprise, *Agents abroad: the story of the New Zealand Trade Commissioner Service*, Penguin, Auckland, 2009.

45 McKinnon, *Treasury*, p. 416.

46 Michael Bassett, *The State in New Zealand 1840–1984: Socialism without doctrines?*, Auckland University Press, Auckland, 1998, p. 14.

47 Bassett, *State in New Zealand*, p. 253.

48 Recent surveys discussing the extent to which this state of affairs prevailed throughout the West include David Reynolds, *One World Divisible: A Global History Since 1945*, Norton, New York, 2000, pp. 122–31, and Eric Hobsbawm, *Age of Extremes: The Short Twentieth Century, 1914–1991*, Michael Joseph, London, 1995, ch. 9. On Britain, see Kenneth O Morgan, *The People's Peace: British History 1945–1989*, Oxford University Press, Oxford, 1990; Nick Tiratsoo, ed., *From Blitz to Blair: A new history of Britain since 1939*, Weidenfeld and Nicolson, London, 1997.

49 Bassett, *State in New Zealand*, p. 238.

50 Bassett, *State in New Zealand*, pp. 15, 22.

51 Jim Tomlinson, 'Inventing "decline": the falling behind of the British economy in the postwar years', *Economic History Review*, 49(4), November 1996, pp. 731–57, and more recently Tomlinson, *The Politics of Decline: understanding post-war Britain*, Longman, Harlow, 2000. See also Barry Supple, 'Fear of failing: economic history and the decline of Britain', *Economic History Review*, 47(3), August 1994, pp. 441–58.

52 Tomlinson, 'Inventing "decline"', p. 754.

53 Tomlinson, *Politics of Decline*, p. 3.

54 Perry Anderson, 'Origins of the Present Crisis', reprinted in his *English Questions*, Verso, London, 1992, p. 35. Wilson's phrase is often rendered as 'the white heat of the technological revolution' but the phrase is an amalgam of two distinct sentences in a 1963 speech.

55 Tomlinson, *Politics of Decline*, ch. 2; David Coates and John Hillard, *The Economic Decline of Modern Britain: The debate between left and right*, Wheatsheaf, Brighton, 1986; Sidney Pollard, *The Wasting of the British Economy: British economic policy 1945 to the present*, Croom Helm, London, 1982; Corelli Barnett, *The Lost Victory: British dreams, British reality 1945–1950*, Macmillan, London, 1995.

56 Tomlinson, 'Inventing "decline"', p. 731.

57 The capitalised term derives from E. P. Thompson's masterly critique of Perry Anderson. Thompson, 'The Peculiarities of the English', in E. P. Thompson, *The Poverty of Theory and other essays*, Merlin, London, 1978.

58 Tomlinson, *Politics of Decline*, p. 40.

59 Roger Douglas, *Alternative Budget: A personal view*, The author, Wellington, 1980, p. 2.

60 New Zealand Government, *View from the Summit: A Look at the '84 Economic*

Summit Conference, Government Printer, Wellington, 1984, p. 5.

61 Peter Clarke, *Keynes: The Twentieth Century's Most Influential Economist*, Bloomsbury, London, 2009.

62 Peter A. Hall, 'Introduction,' in Peter A. Hall, ed., *The Political Power of Economic Ideas: Kenyesianism across Nations*, Princeton University Press, Princeton, 1989, p. 6.

63 Easton, *In Stormy Seas*, p. 33.

64 Hall, 'Introduction,' p. 4.

65 D. E. Moggridge, *Maynard Keynes: An Economists' Biography*, Routledge, London and New York, 1992, pp. 453–55. Moggridge makes it clear (p. 453) that Keynes disliked the Labour Party's class politics, was something of an elitist and regarded himself as part of the educated and high-minded bourgeoisie.

66 Clarke, *Keynes*, is a useful and recent brief introduction.

67 Christopher Lloyd, 'Regime Change in Australian Capitalism: Towards a Historical Political Economy of Regulation', *Australian Economic History Review*, 42(3), 2002, p. 242.

68 See for instance Peter Gourevitch, *Politics in Hard Times: Comparative responses to international economic crises*. Cornell University Press, Ithaca, 1986, pp. 83–92.

69 Gourevitch, *Politics in Hard Times,* pp. 28–29.

70 Gourevitch, *Politics in Hard Times*, pp. 161–62.

71 Summarised by Gourevitch, *Politics in Hard Times*, pp. 28–29 and 153.

72 Schedvin is among those who adopts a narrow definition; a recent expansive study is James Belich, *Replenishing the Earth: the settler revolution and the rise of the Anglo-world, 1783–1939*, Oxford University Press, Oxford, 2009.

73 See for instance Howard J. Wiarda and Harvey F. Kline, eds., *A concise introduction to Latin American politics and development*, Westview Press, Boulder, 2007; Manuel Riesco, ed., *Latin America : a new developmental welfare state model in the making?*, Palgrave, Basingstoke, 2009.

74 Simon Kuznets, 'Level and Variability of Rates of Growth' from Kuznets, *Economic Growth of Nations: Total Output and Production Structure*, Harvard University Press, Cambridge, (Mass), 1971, p. 19. Reprinted in Bart van Ark, ed., *Economic Growth in the Long Run: A History of Empirical Evidence, volume 1,* Edward Elgar, Cheltenham, 1997, p. 179.

75 Tom Garvin, *Preventing the Future: Why was Ireland so poor for so long?* Gill and Macmillan, Dublin, 2004.

76 Belich, *Replenishing the Earth*, passim.

77 Barry Eichengreen, *The European Economy since 1945: Coordinated Capitalism and Beyond*, Princeton University Press, Princeton, 2006, p. 31.

78 Jeffry A. Frieden, *Global Capitalism: Its fall and rise in the twentieth century*, W.W. Norton, New York and London, 2007, ch.12.

79 Eichengreen, *European Economy*, p. 7.

80 Eichengreen, *Globalizing Capital: a history of the international monetary system*, Princeton University Press, Princeton, 2008: p. 92.

81 Frieden, *Global Capitalism*, p. 291

82 Frieden, *Global Capitalism*, pp. 292–96; Schedvin, 'Staples and regions'.

83 Eichengreen, *European Economy*, p. 48; also p. 129.

84 Robert M. Collins, 'The Economic Crisis of 1968 and the Waning of the "American Century"', *American Historical Review*, 101(2), 1996.

85 Eichengreen, *European Economy*, pp. 48–50, 216.

86 Barry Eichengreen, *Global Imbalances and the Lessons of Bretton Woods*, MIT Press, Cambridge (Mass), 2006, p. 38.

87 Philip B Whyman, *Third Way Economics: Theory and Evaluation*, Palgrave Macmillan:Houndmills, 2006, esp. ch. 2–3.
88 Richard Cockett, *Thinking the Unthinkable: Think-tanks and the economic counter-revolution, 1931–1983*, HarperCollins, London, 1993.
89 Michael Bassett, *Working with David: Inside the Lange cabinet*, Hodder Moa, Auckland, 2008, p. 102.
90 Anthony Giddens, *The Third Way: The renewal of social democracy*, Polity Press, Malden, Mass, 1998, esp. ch. 2. Much of this book was foreshadowed in his *Beyond Left and Right: The future of radical politics*, Cambridge, Polity Press, 1994. For a more recent discussion see Whyman, *Third Way Economics.*
91 Giddens, *Third Way*, p. 16.
92 Giddens, *Third Way*, p. 16.
93 Giddens, *Third Way*, p. 65.
94 Peter Conway, 'Industry Policy' in Srikanta Chatterjee, ed., *The New Politics: A Third Way for New Zealand*, Dunmore, Palmerston North, 1999, p. 30.

Chapter 2

1 An excellent exposition of this view is R. M. Chapman, 'From Labour to National' in W. H. Oliver and Bridget Williams, eds., *The Oxford History of New Zealand*, Oxford University Press, Auckland, 1981.
2 David Greasley and Les Oxley, 'The Pastoral Boom, the Rural Land Market, and Long Swings in New Zealand Economic Growth 1873–1939', *Economic History Review*, 62(2), May 2009, p. 331.
3 Greasley and Oxley, 'Pastoral Boom', pp. 335, 339. The more technical term which they use is 'rental values' which is 'cultivated land values de-capitalized by the mortgage rate'.
4 See, for instance, Marian Sawer, *The Ethical State? Social liberalism in Australia*, Melbourne University Press, Carlton, 2003.
5 Hawke, *Making of New Zealand*, p. 100. See also, generally, David Greasley and Les Oxley, 'Regime Shift and Fast Recovery on the Periphery: New Zealand in the 1930s,' *Economic History Review*, 55(4), November 2002, pp. 697–720.
6 A summary of the return to gold is John Philip Jones, *Keynes's vision: why the Great Depression did not return*, Routledge, London, 2008, pp. 160–65.
7 Greasley and Oxley, 'Pastoral Boom', pp. 340–41.
8 McKinnon, *Treasury*, p. 130.
9 Frieden, *Global Capitalism*, p. 18
10 Barry Eichengreen, *Globalizing Capital: A history of the international monetary system*, Princeton University Press, Princeton, 2nd ed., 2008, p. 2.
11 Eichengreen, *Globalizing Capital*, p. 2.
12 Eichengreen, *Globalizing Capital*, p. 12.
13 Greasley and Oxley, 'Regime Shift and Fast **Recovery**', p. 703. See also B. C. Ashwin, 'Banking and Currency in New Zealand', *Economic Record*, 6(3), November 1930, pp.188–204.
14 Greasley and Oxley, 'Regime Shift and Fast Recovery', p. 703.
15 Ashwin, 'Banking and Currency', pp. 198–99.
16 G. R. Hawke, 'New Zealand and the Return to Gold in 1925,' *Australian Economic History Review,* 11(1), February 1971, p. 54, note 31. See also G. R. Hawke, *Between Governments and Banks: A history of the Reserve Bank of New Zealand*, Government Printer, Wellington, 1973, pp. 26–31.

17 Eichengreen, *Globalizing Capital*, pp. 38–39.
18 Eichengreen, *Globalizing Capital*, p. 78.
19 Hawke, *Making of New Zealand*, p. 127.
20 Hawke, *Making of New Zealand*, pp. 123–25.
21 CPI changes are shown in David C. Thorns and Charles P. Sedgwick, *Understanding Aotearoa-New Zealand: Historical Statistics*, Dunmore, Palmerston North, 1997, p. 64 (Table 3.2).
22 The biographies of Savage (Gustafson), Nash (Sinclair), and Fraser (Bassett with King) all provide good examples. See also Tony Simpson, *The Sugarbag Years*, Alister Taylor, Wellington, 1974.
23 Keith Sinclair, *A History of New Zealand*, Penguin, Harmondsworth, 1969, p. 255. For the politics of the late 1920s I am much obliged to Malcolm McKinnon for discussing his forthcoming study of the Depression with me.
24 Hawke, *Making of New Zealand*, p. 158.
25 Hawke, *Making of New Zealand*, pp. 153–55.
26 P. J. O'Farrell, *Harry Holland: Militant socialist*, Australian National University Press, Canberra, 1964.
27 Bassett and King, *Tomorrow comes the Song*, ch. 8; Sinclair, *Walter Nash*, p. 76.
28 Patrick O'Farrell, 'Holland, Henry Edmund 1868–1933'. Dictionary of New Zealand Biography, updated 22 June 2007. URL: http://www.dnzb.govt.nz/. I am also grateful to Len Richardson for some recent discussions, in which he suggested that Holland was not so divorced from rethinking policy as is often assumed.
29 Bassett and King, *Tomorrow comes the song*, p. 121.
30 Gustafson, *From the Cradle to the Grave*, pp. 118, 132.
31 Sinclair, *Walter Nash*, pp. 65, 69.
32 Noel Thompson, 'Hobson and the Fabians, two roads to socialism in the 1920s', *History of Political Economy*, 26 (1994), p. 214. On Keynes, see Moggridge, *Maynard Keynes*, p. 461.
33 Summarised Bassett and King, *Tomorrow comes the song*, p. 123; see also Gustafson, *From the Cradle to the Grave*, pp. 144–46; *New Zealand Parliamentary Debates* (NZPD), 224, 1930, p. 47.
34 Walter Nash, *Financial Power in New Zealand: The case for a state bank*, New Zealand Worker, Wellington, 1925, p. 3.
35 Nash, *Financial Power*, p. 1.
36 Nash, *Financial Power*, p. 3.
37 *NZPD*, 229, 1931, pp. 710, 711 (H. E. Holland).
38 H. E. Holland, *The way out of the labyrinth: a statement of the Labour Party's policy of industrial reconstruction and rehabilitation and credit and currency reform*, Clarte Bookshop, Wellington, 1932, p. 9.
39 Sinclair, *Walter Nash*, pp. 98, 103–5, 114; Gustafson, *From the cradle to the grave*, pp. 146–48.
40 *NZPD*, 244, 1936, pp. 64–66 (Savage).
41 Bassett, *Coates*, p. 186.
42 Greasley and Oxley, 'Regime shift and fast recovery', Brian Easton, *The Nationbuilders*; McKinnon, *Treasury*.
43 I am very grateful to Malcolm McKinnon for discussing the extent to which farmers put their weight behind Coates over devaluation, a matter which will be dealt with in his forthcoming history of the Depression.
44 McKinnon, *Treasury*, p. 131.
45 Bassett, *Coates*, p. 188–91.

46 Greasley and Oxley, 'Regime shift and fast recovery', p. 703.
47 John Singleton, *Central Banking in the Twentieth Century*, Cambridge University Press, Cambridge, 2011, p. 61.
48 Brian Easton, 'Bernard Ashwin: Secretary to the Nation-building State', *New Zealand Studies*, November 1997, pp. 13–21; Bassett, *Coates*, p. 190.
49 McKinnon, *Treasury*, 124–25, 145, 149
50 Bassett, *Coates*, pp. 202–03. Bassett does suggest (p. 224) that Coates may have begun to change his mind on stimulating demand late in 1935.
51 Gourevitch, *Politics in Hard Times*, p. 131.
52 Hawke, *Between Governments and Banks*, pp. 32, 60; Paul Dalziel, 'The Reserve Bank Act: Reflecting Changing Relationships Between State and Economy in the Twentieth Century' in Brian Roper and Chris Rudd, eds., *State and Economy in New Zealand*, Oxford University Press, Auckland, 1993, pp. 77–81.
53 Singleton, *Central Banking*, p. 167.
54 quoted Sinclair, *Walter Nash*, p. 112.
55 Budget, 1936, Appendices to the Journals of the House of Representatives, (AJHR), 1936, B-6, p. 1.
56 Sinclair, *Walter Nash*, p. 122.
57 Budget, 1937, AJHR, 1937, B-6, p. 25.
58 Peter Franks, 'Predominance of Support for Moderate Policy: The formation of the New Zealand Federation of Labour, 1937', in Peter Franks and Melanie Nolan, eds., *Unions in Common Cause: The New Zealand Federation of Labour 1937–88*, Steele Roberts, Wellington, 2011.
59 Budget, 1937, p. 25.
60 The Primary Products Marketing Act, 1936, quoted Sinclair, *Walter Nash*, p. 128, and see also p. 114.
61 Budget, 1938, AJHR, 1938, B-6, p. 12.
62 Budget, 1936, p. 6.
63 Budget, 1937, pp. 1–2.
64 *NZPD*, 247, 1936, p. 326 (Sullivan). For an instructive British comparison, see Jim Tomlinson, *Democratic Socialism and Economic Policy: The Attlee Years, 1945–1951, Cambridge University Press, Cambridge, 1997.*
65 Keith Sinclair, *Walter Nash*; Elizabeth A. Hanson, *The Politics of Social Security*, Auckland University Press, Auckland, 1980.
66 This paragraph relies, generally, on Sinclair, *Walter Nash*, ch. 14.
67 Budget, 1937, p. 10.
68 Sinclair, *Walter Nash*, p. 141 and generally pp. 135–43 and 172–86.
69 Sinclair, *Walter Nash*, p. 148
70 J. V. T. Baker, *The New Zealand People at War: The War Economy*, Historical Publications Branch, Wellington, 1965, p. 77.
71 Budget 1940, AJHR, 1940, B-6, pp. 2–3.
72 Jones, *Keynes's Vision*, pp. 176–77. See also Robert Skidelsky, *John Maynard Keynes, a biography: Vol. 3, Fighting for Britain, 1937–1946*, Macmillan, London, 2001, p. 86; Moggridge, *Maynard Keynes*, ch. 24.
73 Donald Markwell, *John Maynard Keynes and international relations: economic paths to war and peace*, Oxford University Press, Oxford, 2006, p. 215.
74 A good general discussion is Baker, 1965, ch 12. See also Bassett, *State in New Zealand*, ch. 8.
75 Baker, *War Economy*, p. 301.
76 Baker, *War Economy*, p. 305, 307.
77 McKinnon, *Treasury*, p. 175.

78 Baker, *War Economy*, pp. 79, 183–84.
79 Baker, *War Economy*, p. 188
80 Baker, *War Economy*, pp. 180–90.
81 Baker, *War Economy*, pp. 79–80.
82 Baker, *War Economy*, pp. 148–49, 179.
83 Baker, *War Economy*, p. 70.
84 Baker, *War Economy*, pp. 98, 100–01.
85 Baker, *War Economy*, p. 91.
86 Thorns and Sedgwick, *Understanding Aotearoa New Zealand*, p. 79.
87 Graeme Hunt, *Black Prince: The biography of Fintan Patrick Walsh*, Penguin, Auckland, 2004, pp. 112–13; Bassett and King, *Tomorrow comes the song*, pp. 156–59.
88 Hunt, *Black Prince*, pp. 125–26.
89 Bassett, *State in New Zealand*, p. 227.
90 Quoted Bassett and King, *Tomorrow comes the song*, p. 248.
91 Baker, *War Economy*, pp. 503–19.
92 Bassett and King, *Tomorrow comes the song*, p. 268.
93 Quoted Bassett and King, *Tomorrow comes the song*, p. 271.
94 Quoted Bassett and King, *Tomorrow comes the song*, p. 272, from the *Standard*, 27 July 44.
95 There is a convenient summary in Jeffry A. Frieden, *Global Capitalism: Its fall and rise in the twentieth century*, Norton, New York and London, 2007, ch. 11.
96 Sinclair, *Walter Nash*, p. 237.
97 William Coleman, Selwyn Cornish and Alfred Hagger, *Giblin's Platoon: The trials and triumph of the economist in Australian public life*, ANU E-Press, Canberra, 2006, p. 199.
98 Coleman et al., *Giblin's Platoon*, p. 200; Gerald Hensley, *Beyond the Battlefield: New Zealand and its Allies, 1939–45*, Viking Penguin, Auckland, 2009, pp. 326–27.
99 Budget, 1944, AJHR, 1944, B-6, pp. 15–16.
100 An important study which emphasises continuities is John E. Martin, *Honouring the Contract*, Victoria University Press, Wellington, 2010.
101 Sheri Berman, *The Primacy of Politics: Social Democracy and the Making of Europe's Twentieth Century*, Cambridge University Press, Cambridge and New York, 2006, and also Berman, *The Social Democratic Moment: Ideas and Politics in the making of inter-war Europe*, Harvard University Press, Cambrige, Mass, 1998. Both the British and the Australian labour parties governed precariously in the period 1929–31, without policies equipping them to deal with the Depression, and in situations of parliamentary fragility.
102 McKinnon, *Treasury*, p. 161.
103 McKinnon, *Treasury*, pp. 152, 162.
104 McKinnon, *Treasury*, pp. 155, 206.

Chapter 3

1 John Gerard Ruggie, 'International regimes, transactions, and change: embedded liberalism in the postwar economic order', in Stephen Krasner, ed., *International Regimes*, Cornell University Press, Ithaca, 1983.
2 Fraser was notorious for living on tea and buttered toast, with cream cakes an indulgence. His wife, Janet, died shortly before the war ended. They had no

children together, but Fraser was close to Janet's son Harold Kemp, daughter-in-law Rini (a daughter of Tim Armstrong, one of Fraser's ministerial colleagues), and granddaughter Alice Kemp.

3 Logan, *Nordy*.

4 Baker, *War Economy*, p. 502.

5 Economic Stabilisation Commissioner to Minister of Stabilisation, 6 Jul 1945, T 72, 1a Economic Stabilisation Commission: appointment, minutes, etc, subseries 1, box 1a, Stabilisation Policy, vol 1. See also Notes of discussion between Joint Committee of meat and dairy industries and ESC, 13 Sep 1945, in T 72 1a Economic Stabilisation Commission: appointment, minutes, etc, subseries 1, box 1a, Stabilisation Policy, vol 1, ANZ.

6 *New Zealand Economist*, 7(1), April 1945, p. 11.

7 Organisation for National Development Survey of War-Time Controls, 1 Dec 44, T 72, 1a Economic Stabilisation Commission: appointment, minutes, etc, subseries 1, box 1a, Stabilisation Policy, vol 1, ANZ.

8 *Statutes of New Zealand*, 1945.

9 *NZPD*, 270, 1945, p. 251 (Fraser).

10 *NZPD*, 270, 1945, pp. 249, 251 (Fraser).

11 *NZPD*, 270, 1945, p. 521 (Nash).

12 Margaret McClure, *A Civilised Community: A history of social security in New Zealand, 1898–1998*, Auckland University Press, Auckland, 1998, pp. 103–08; Melanie Nolan, *Breadwinning: New Zealand women and the state*, Canterbury University Press, Christchurch, 2000, p. 202.

13 *New Zealand Official Yearbook*, 1950, ch. 3.The figures are for the year to 31 March 1947 and to 31 March 1950.

14 *New Zealand Official Yearbook*, 1950, ch. 6; 1951, ch. 6. The yearbook recorded the increase per head of total population but it seems more sensible to calculate per student and to adjust for inflation.

15 In the financial years ended March 1946 and March 1950. *New Zealand Official Yearbook* 1946, ch. 25; 1950, ch. 25.

16 Calculated from *New Zealand Official Yearbook*, 1950, ch. 25 B.

17 Condliffe's comment is J. B. Condliffe, *The Welfare State in New Zealand*, Allen and Unwin, London, 1959, p. 99.

18 Notes of discussion between Joint Committee of meat and dairy industries and ESC 13 Sep 45, in T 72 1a Economic Stabilisation Commission: appointment, minutes, etc, subseries 1, box 1a, Stabilisation Policy, vol 1, ANZ.

19 *Dominion*, 10 Aug 45, clipping in T 1 52/63/45 Budget 1945, ANZ.

20 Notes of discussion between Joint Committee of meat and dairy industries and ESC 13 Sep 45, in T 72 1a Economic Stabilisation Commission: appointment, minutes, etc, subseries 1, box 1a, Stabilisation Policy, vol 1, ANZ.

21 Notes of discussion between Joint Committee of meat and dairy industries and ESC 13 Sep 45, in T 72 1a Economic Stabilisation Commission: appointment, minutes, etc, subseries 1, box 1a, Stabilisation Policy, vol 1, ANZ

22 Bassett, *State in New Zealand*, p. 319.

23 The classic statement is Sutch, *Quest for security*, ch. 16. The enduring myth has been well-characterised by Keith Sinclair as the 'Lee-Sutch syndrome' after its principal exponents, Sutch and the renegade Labour MP, John A. Lee. Keith Sinclair, 'The Lee-Sutch syndrome : New Zealand Labour Party policies and politics, 1930–1940,' *New Zealand Journal of History*, 8 , 2 October 1974, 95–117.

24 Michal Kalecki, 'Political Aspects of Full Employment', in *Selected essays on*

the dynamics of the capitalist economy 1933–1970, Cambridge University Press, Cambridge, 1971 (originally published in *Political Quarterly*, 14, Oct–Dec 1943, pp. 322–331).

25 Tim Rowse, *Nugget Coombs: A Reforming Life*, Cambridge University Press, Port Melbourne, 2002, pp. 203–04.

26 Walsh laid his views out at some length to the 1946 FOL conference; his address is reprinted as Appendix F of Hunt, *Black Prince.*

27 See, generally, H. O. Roth, *Trade Unions in New Zealand*, Reed, Wellington, 1973, ch. 4, and Cybèle Locke, *Workers in the Margins: Union radicals in postwar New Zealand*, Bridget Williams Books, Wellington, 2012, pp. 29–31.

28 Budget 1946, AJHR 1946, B-6, p. 28.

29 Acting Sec Treas to Min Fin, 11 Jun 48, T1 61/1 Balance of Payments 1946–48, ANZ.

30 McKinnon, *Treasury*, p. 159.

31 Ministry of Works statement, AJHR, 1947, D-1 pp. 1–2, 21; AJHR, 1948, D-1, p. 3.

32 Gael Ferguson, *Building the New Zealand Dream*, Dunmore, Palmerston North, 1994.

33 *New Zealand Official Yearbook,* 1950, pp. 437.

34 Ministry of Works statement, AJHR, 1947, D-1.

35 *New Zealand Official Yearbook, 1950*, pp. 453.

36 Ministry of Works statement, AJHR, 1945, D-1.

37 *New Zealand Official Yearbook,* 1945, ch. 44; 1950, ch. 24.

38 S. R. H. Jones, 'Government policy and industry structure in New Zealand, 1900–1970', *Australian Economic History Review*, 39(3), August 1999, pp. 191–212.

39 Budget, 1945, AJHR, 1945, B-6, p. 13.

40 *New Zealand Economist*, 8(7), October 1946, p. 145.

41 Department of Industries and Commerce Annual Report, AJHR, 1946, H-44, pp. 5, 6.

42 Department of Industries and Commerce Annual Report, AJHR, 1946 H-44, p. 5. On Sullivan's career, see James Watson, 'Sullivan, Daniel Giles 1882–1947'. *Dictionary of New Zealand Biography*, updated 22 June 2007, URL: http://www.dnzb.govt.nz. Accessed 16 Feb 2010.

43 Department of Agriculture annual report, AJHR, 1947 H-29, p. 1.

44 Department of Agriculture annual report, AJHR, 1947 H-29, p.3.

45 Budget 1946, AJHR, 1944, B-6, pp. 33–38.

46 Budget, 1946, pp. 35, 38; Department of Industries and Commerce Annual Report, AJHR, 1949, H-44, p. 3.

47 These points were made in *New Zealand Official Yearbook,* 1945, p. 287.

48 *New Zealand Official Yearbook, 1945,* p. 630; Department of Industries and Commerce Annual Report, AJHR, H-44, 1946, pp. 18–20.

49 Department of Industries and Commerce Annual Report, AJHR, H-44, 1947, pp. 16, 20. See, generally, Jones, 'Government policy and industry structure'.

50 Estimates 1948–49 Company Taxation T1 52/63/47, Budget 1947, ANZ.

51 *New Zealand Economist*, 8(1), April 1946, p. 1. In 2013 terms £10,000 is about $750,000.

52 *New Zealand Economist*, 9(9), December 1947, p. 220; 9(10), February 1948, pp. 225–27.

53 *New Zealand Economist*, 7(9), December 1945, p. 168; 8(9), December 1946, p. 214.

54 Jim Tomlinson, *Democratic Socialism and Economic Policy: The Attlee years,*

1945–51, Cambridge University Press, Cambridge, 1997, p. 46.

55 Peter Clarke, *The last thousand days of the British Empire*, Allen Lane, London, 2007, Prologue.

56 Ben Pimlott, *Hugh Dalton*, Cape, London, 1985, p. 428.

57 Donald Moggridge, ed., *The Collected Writings of John Maynard Keynes, vol XXIV Activites 1944–46: The Transition to Peace*, Macmillan, London, 1979, p. 274.

58 Dalton's biographer suggests that the Chancellor 'was made uneasily aware of the tutor-student relationship'. Pimlott, *Hugh Dalton*, p. 428.

59 Pimlott, *Hugh Dalton*, p. 427.

60 Keynes, *Collected Writings*, p. 288.

61 Keynes, *Collected Writings*, vol. XXIV, p. 281.

62 The memorandum of 15 May 1945 is in Keynes, *Collected Writings*, vol XXIV. For the Indian figure, see Keynes, *CW*, vol. XXVII, p. 459–61. The proportions are from Catherine Schenk, *The Decline of Sterling*, Cambridge University Press, Cambridge, 2010, p. 39 (Table 3.1).

63 'US–UK Economic Negotiations, September 1945', in Keynes, *Collected Writings*, vol. XXIV, p. 491.

64 Clarke, *Last Thousand Days*, p. 25.

65 Robert Skidelsky, *John Maynard Keynes: a biography. Volume 3: Fighting for freedom*, Macmillan, London, 2000, p. 384.

66 Pimlott, *Hugh Dalton*, p. 429.

67 P. J. Cain and A. G. Hopkins, *British Imperialism, 1688–2000*, Longman, New York, 2nd ed., 2001, p. 625.

68 Susan Strange, *Sterling and British policy: a political study of an international currency in decline*, Oxford University Press, London, 1971, p. 60. See also Pimlott, *Hugh Dalton*, p. 431.

69 Schenk, *Decline of Sterling*, p. 45.

70 Schenk, *Decline of Sterling*, pp. 45–46.

71 Richard N. Gardner, *Sterling-dollar diplomacy: Anglo-American collaboration in the reconstruction of multilateral trade*, Clarendon Press, Oxford, 1956, pp. 219, 236–53.

72 Pimlott, *Hugh Dalton*, pp. 434, 439–40.

73 Francine McKenzie, *Redefining the bonds of Commonwealth, 1939–1948: the politics of preference*, Palgrave, Basingstoke, 2002, pp. 140–41.

74 McKenzie, *Redefining the bonds of Commonwealth*, pp. 141–42.

75 'Notes on Sterling Area Negotiations' (23 Jan 46), in Donald Moggridge, ed., *The Collected Writings of John Maynard Keynes, vol XVII Activities 1940–6*: Shaping the Post-war World: Employment and Commodities, Macmillan, London, 1979. See also Skidelsky, 2000, p. 457.

76 Gardner, *Sterling-dollar diplomacy*, p. 326; C. C. S. Newton, 'The Sterling Crisis of 1947 and the British response to the Marshall Plan' *Economic History Review*, 37(3), August 1984, p. 399.

77 Keynes, *Collected Writings*, vol. XVII, p. 449.

78 Keynes, *Collected Writings*, vol. XVII, p. 452.

79 Keynes, *Collected Writings*, vol. XVII, p. 457

80 'The Sterling Area Settlement' memo to Sir Edward Bridges, 1 Feb 1946, in Keynes, CW vol. XXVII, esp p. 458. Pimlott, *Hugh Dalton*, p. 433.

81 Keynes, *Collected Writings*, vol. XXVII, p. 459–61.

82 New Zealand Sterling Balances – note of a conversation 19 Feb 46, in Balance of Payments 1946–48, ANZ [Ref: ADRK 17391 T1 (box 410) 61/1 (R15422463)].

83 Singleton and Robertson, *Economic relations between Britain and Australasia*, p. 46.
84 Gardner, *Sterling-dollar diplomacy*, pp. 220–21, 327.
85 ATK Grant (UK Treas) to Ashwin, 1 Jul 46, in Balance of Payments 1946–48, ANZ.
86 Baker, *War Economy*, pp. 270–71.
87 Baker, *War Economy*, p. 77.
88 Schenk, *Decline of Sterling*, p. 52.
89 Only New Zealand and Australia cancelled sterling balances. Catherine R Schenk, *Britain and the Sterling Area: From devaluation to convertability in the 1950s*, Routledge, London, 1994, p. 12.
90 quoted Baker, *War Economy*, p. 527.
91 *Press*, 7 March 1947, p. 6.
92 Budget, various years 1945–49.
93 Sec State Commonwealth Relations to Minister Ext Affs 12 Aug 47, in Balance of Payments 1946–48, ANZ.
94 Nash item 1310573 Minister Ext Affs to Sec State Commonwealth Relations 22 Aug 47, Nash 131/042–619 Dollar Related Material, Nash Papers, ANZ.
95 An example of such advertising material can be seen at http://www.teara.govt.nz/en/overseas-trade-policy/3/2 (accessed 23 June 2010).
96 High Commissioner, Canberra, to Minister Ext Affs 3 Sep 47, in Balance of Payments 1946–48, ANZ.
97 Fraser to Lord Addison (PM to SecState Commonwealth Relations) 30 Sep 47, in Balance of Payments 1946–48, ANZ.
98 Nash item 1310407 High Commissioner, London, to Minister Ext Affs 8 Oct 47, Nash 131/042-619 Dollar Related Material, ANZ.
99 1310482 L C Webb to Nash 30 Oct 47, Nash 131/042-619 Dollar Related Material, Nash Papers, ANZ.
100 Minister Ext Affs to HCNZ London 15 Nov 47, Minister Ext Affs to HCNZ, London 30 Jan 48, in Balance of Payments 1946–48, ANZ.
101 Dominion 28 May 48, clipping in Balance of Payments 1946–48, ANZ.
102 Budget 1948, AJHR, 1948, B-6, p. 6.
103 High Commissioner, London, to Min Ext Affs 19 Jul 49, in Finance Minister's Conference 1949, ANZ [Ref: ADRK 17391 T1 (box 418) 61/3/5 (R15422546)]. See also Budget 1949, AJHR, 1949, B-6, p. 4.
104 Sec Treas to Minister Industries and Commerce and Acting Min Fin 17 Nov 47, in Balance of Payments 1946–48, ANZ.
105 Ashwin to Min Fin 27 Apr 48, Nash 1102/0528, ANZ.
106 Acting Sec Treas to Min Fin 11 Jun 48, in Budget 1948, ANZ [Ref: ADRK 17391 T1 (box 329) 52/63/48 (R15421940)]
107 Acting Sec Treas to Min Fin 11 Jun 48, in Balance of Payments 1946–48, ANZ.
108 Secretary of Industries and Commerce to Min IC, 11 Jun 48 'The Dollar Problem', in Nash 1102/0515, Nash Papers, ANZ.
109 Nash item 1310351 Sec IC to Min IC 11 Jun 48, Nash 131/042-619 Dollar Related Material, Nash Papers, ANZ.
110 Singleton and Robertson, *Economic relations*, p. 42.
111 Thomas W. Zeiler, *Free trade, free world: the advent of GATT*, University of North Carolina Press, Chapel Hill, 1999, p. 2.
112 McKenzie, *Redefining the bonds of Commonwealth*, p. 163.
113 McKenzie, *Redefining the bonds of Commonwealth*, pp. 188–89.
114 McKenzie, *Redefining the bonds of Commonwealth*, pp. 188, 195–96.

115 Hensley, *Beyond the Battlefield*, p. 327.
116 Sinclair, *Walter Nash*, p. 251.
117 Sinclair, *Walter Nash*, p. 246.
118 Sinclair, *Walter Nash*, pp. 244–46.
119 *NZPD*, vol. 284, 1948, p. 3493 (Nordmeyer).
120 *NZPD*, vol. 284, 1948, p. 3498 (Watts).
121 Department of Industries and Commerce Annual Report, AJHR, 1948 H-44, p. 28.
122 *NZPD*, vol. 278, 1947, pp. 604 ff (Nordmeyer)
123 Budget, 1948, AJHR, 1948, B-6, pp. 27.
124 *NZPD*, vol. 278, 1947 p. 609 (Nordmeyer).
125 *NZPD*, vol. 278, 1947, pp. 611 ff (Holland).
126 Minister IC to President, Price Tribunal 28 Nov 47, in Price Tribunal Establishment 1947–59, ANZ [Ref: AEFN 19294 ICW1534 (box 3) 301/1/10 (R16801315)].
127 What Cases are Suitable for Public Hearings (ns, nd, early 1948?), in Price Tribunal Establishment 1947–59, ANZ.
128 Director, Price Control to Secretary, Public Service Commission, 5 Aug 48, in Price Tribunal Establishment 1947–59, ANZ.
129 J. P. Lewin to Director of Price Control 5 Mar 48, in Price Tribunal Establishment 1947–59, ANZ.
130 Budget, 1946, AJHR, 1946, B-6, p. 17. Sec Treas to Min Fin 30 Mar 46, in Budget 1946, ANZ [Ref: ADRK 17391 T1 (box 329) 52/63/46 (R15421938)].
131 Budget, 1946, AJHR 1946, B-6, pp. 33–38.
132 High Commissioner, London to Min Ext Aff (For Fraser from Nash) 24 Jun 46, in Budget 1946, ANZ.
133 Sec Treas to Acting Min Fin 8 Jul 46, in Budget 1946, ANZ.
134 Budget, 1947, AJHR, 1947, B-6, pp. 14–15.
135 Budget, 1948, AJHR, 1948, B-6, pp. 14, 28–29.
136 Draft memorandum for minister, The Budget for 1948, in Budget 1948, ANZ.
137 A point also made by Gerold Krozewski, 'Sterling, the "minor" territories, and the end of formal empire, 1939–1958' *Economic History Review*, 46(2), May 1993, p. 242.
138 Twain's observation is listed in, for instance, *Bloomsbury Anthology of Quotations*, Bloomsbury, London, 2002, p. 377. Semple's is widely attributed.

Chapter 4

1 The following summary is based on relevant sections in the *New Zealand Official Yearbook* for various years.
2 We should note that the definition of 'urban' included some quite small boroughs, such as Geraldine or Waipawa, which had less than 2000 inhabitants. If all boroughs were included, the 'urban' population in the 1956 census was 62 per cent of the total; if only the 15 largest urban areas were counted, the urban population was 58 per cent of the total.
3 Barry Gustafson, *The First 50 years: A history of the New Zealand National Party*, Reed Methuen, Auckland, 1986, p. 3. Tom Brooking, 'From Tobacco Road to Pipitea St' in Margaret Clark, ed., *Sir Keith Holyoake: Towards a political biography*, Dunmore, Palmerston North, 1997, is helpful on farmer politicians.
4 Gustafson, *The first 50 years*, p. 9.
5 See, generally, Gustafson, *The first 50 years*, ch. 1.

6 Watson, James, 'Holland, Henry 1859 – 1944', *Dictionary of New Zealand Biography*, updated 22 June 2007. URL: http://www.dnzb.govt.nz.
7 Watson, James, 'Holland, Henry 1859 – 1944', *Dictionary of New Zealand Biography*, updated 22 June 2007. URL: http://www.dnzb.govt.nz.
8 Gustafson, *The first 50 years*, pp. 38–42, quotes at 42 and 41.
9 Gustafson, *The first 50 years*, p. 40.
10 Gustafson, *The first 50 years*, p. 47.
11 S. G. Holland, *Passwords to Progress*, Whitcombe and Tombs, Christchurch, 1943, p. 3.
12 Holland, *Passwords to Progress*, pp. 11–12.
13 Holland, *Passwords to Progress*, p. 4.
14 Holland, *Passwords to Progress*, p. 5.
15 Holland, *Passwords to Progress*, p. 7.
16 Holland, *Passwords to Progress*, p. 8
17 Holland, *Passwords to Progress*, p. 3.
18 Holland, *Passwords to Progress*, pp. 7–8.
19 Holland, *Passwords to Progress*, p. 1.
20 Brooking, 'Tobacco Road to Pipitea St'.
21 *NZPD*, vol 285, 1949, p. 21; vol 287, 1949, p. 1780 (Watts).
22 *NZPD*, vol 287, 1949, p. 1780 (Watts).
23 *NZPD*, vol 291, 1950, p. 2596 (Gotz).
24 Budget 1950, AJHR, 1950, B-6, p. 28.
25 *NZPD*, vol 289, 1950, pp. 11–12.
26 *NZPD*, vol. 285, 1949, pp. 161, 163, 173 (Holland).
27 *NZPD*, vol. 295, 1951, pp. 429–30 (Holyoake).
28 McKinnon, *Treasury*, pp. 185–87, 208–11.
29 Sec Treas to PM, 21 Dec 1949, Sec Treas to PM, 11 Jan 1950, in Reports to Minister of Finance 1949–1950, ANZ [Ref: ADRK 17408 T 25 (box 4) 23 (R20195503)].
30 Sec Treas to PM 21 Dec 49 (no 6626), and Sec Treas to PM 21 Dec 49, Sec Treas to PM 11 Jan 50 (no 6627), in Reports to Minister of Finance 1949–1950, ANZ
31 Sec Treas to PM 21 Dec 49 (no 6628), in Reports to Minister of Finance 1949, ANZ.
32 Survey of National Finances, in Loan Programme 1950, ANZ [Ref: ADRK 17391 T1 (box 336) 52/77/50 (R15421979)].
33 Budget 1950, AJHR, 1950, B-6; New Zealand Official Yearbook, 1950, section 25C 'Public Debt Conversion'.
34 Text of an address by Holland 'National Finances', c. Apr 50 ; Sec Treas to PM 22 Mar 50; Sec Treas to PM 24 Apr 50, in Reports to Minister of Finance 1940–1950, ANZ.
35 Budget 1950, AJHR, 1950, B-6, pp. 3–6.
36 Notes of meeting 14 May 50; PM to Newspaper Propr Assn 2 Jun 50, in Internal Loan 1950, ANZ [Ref: ADRK 17391 T1 (box 297) 44/236 (R15421700)]
37 D-G Post Office to Sec Treas 3 Jul 50, in Internal Loan 1950, ANZ.
38 Greensmith to Ashwin (in London) 16 Jun 50, in Internal Loan 1950, ANZ.
39 *The Times* (Palmerston North) 26 Jun 50, in Internal Loan 1950, ANZ.
40 Paul Goldsmith, *We Won, You Lost, Eat That: A political history of tax in New Zealand since 1840*, David Ling, Auckland, 2008, p. 10.
41 McKinnon, *Treasury*, p. 206.
42 McKinnon, *Treasury*, pp. 208–12.
43 The New Zealand Economy 1939–51, pp. 3, 44.

44 The New Zealand Economy 1939–51, AJHR, 1951, B-5, p. 34.
45 The New Zealand Economy 1939–51, p. 16.
46 The New Zealand Economy 1939–51, p. 45.
47 Michael Bassett, *Confrontation '51: The 1951 waterfront dispute*, Reed, Wellington, 1972: pp. 43, 222.
48 James W. Brodie, 'Tyndall, Arthur 1891 – 1979', *Dictionary of New Zealand Biography*, updated 22 June 2007. URL: http://www.dnzb.govt.nz/, accessed 2 Feb 2010.
49 *Book of Awards*, 1951, 51(1), pp. 9, 11.
50 John Roberts, *Listener*, 29 May 76; W. A. E. Green, J. L. Roberts, J. J. Loftus, 'An Examination of the Role of the Arbitration Court in Fixing Wage Rates in New Zealand,' typescript, Victoria University College, School of Political Science and Public Administration, 1955. I am very grateful to Peter Franks for giving me these references and a copy of the latter document.
51 *Book of Awards*, 1951, 51(1), pp. 9, 11.
52 *Book of Awards*, 1951, 51(1), p. 14.
53 Sec Treas to Min Fin 7 Feb 51, in Budget 1951, ANZ [Ref: ADRK 17391 T1 (box 330) 52/63/51 (R15421943)]; Director of Stabilisation to Min i/c Stabilisation, 30 Nov 50, Sec Treas to Min Fin 14 Dec 50, in Budget 1950, ANZ [Ref: ADRK 17391 T1 (box 330) 52/63/50 (R15421942)].
54 Apart from Bassett, *Confrontation '51*, the more recent discussions of the dispute include Anna Green, *British Capital, Antipodean Labour: Working the New Zealand waterfront, 1915–1951*, University of Otago Press, Dunedin, 2001, and David Grant, ed., *The Big Blue: Snapshots of the 1951 Waterfront Lockout*, Canterbury University Press, Christchurch, 2004.
55 Bassett, *State in New Zealand*, p. 261.
56 Budget, 1953, AJHR, 1953, B-6, pp. 25–26.
57 New Zealand Official Yearbook, 1958, ch. 19.
58 Philip Armstrong, Andrew Glyn and John Harrison, *Capitalism since World War II: The making and breakup of the great boom*, Fontana, London, 1984, p. 159.
59 Sec Treas to Min Fin 19 Apr 50, 23 Apr 50, in Balance of Payments 1948–52, ANZ [Ref: ADRK 17391 T1 (box 411) 61/1 (R15422464)].
60 Sec Treas to Min Fin 14 Dec 50, (not sent) in Balance of Payments 1948–52, ANZ; Department of Industries and Commerce Annual Report, AJHR, 1950, H-44, p. 1.
61 Sec Treas to Min Fin 17 Mar 52, in Balance of Payments 1948–52, ANZ.
62 New Zealand Official Yearbook, 1953, ch. 10.
63 J. D. Gould, *The Rake's Progress? The New Zealand Economy Since 1945*, Hodder and Stoughton, Auckland, 1982, p. 69.
64 Bassett, 1998, p. 268, and Min Ext Affs to overseas posts 11 Mar 52, in Balance of Payments 1948–52, ANZ.
65 Bassett, *The state in New Zealand*, p. 268.
66 There is a good summary in Peter Hennessy, *Never Again: Britain 1945–51*, Jonathan Cape, London, 1992, pp. 404–16; quotations from p. 409.
67 C. M. Bowden (in London) to Min Ext Affs 15 Jun 51, in Balance of Payments 1948–52, ANZ.
68 *Evening Post*, 8 Jan 52, clipping in Balance of Payments General 1950–52, ANZ [Ref: ADRK 17391 T1 (box 415) 61/2 (R15422487)].
69 Report of Working Party on Action Arising from Commonwealth Finance Ministers' Conference 6 Feb 52, in Balance of Payments 1948–52, ANZ.

70 Min Ext Affs to overseas posts 11 Mar 52, in Balance of Payments 1948–52, ANZ.
71 Catherine Schenk, *The Decline of Sterling*, p. 89.
72 Budget, 1954, AJHR, 1954, B-6, p. 5.
73 McKinnon, *Treasury*, p. 192.
74 Dir Broadcasting (Commercial Division) to L Williams, Treasury 14 Jun 50, in Internal Loan 1950.
75 Text of radio address, date attached 17 Jun 54, in Budget 1953, ANZ [Ref: ADRK 17291 T1 (box 226) 3/3/53 (R15421130)].
76 The New Zealand Economy 1939–51, p. 45.
77 The New Zealand Economy 1939–51, pp. 47–48.
78 *NZPD*, vol. 289, 1950, p. 188 (Rae).
79 New Zealand Official Yearbook, 1960. There is a slight imprecision because assisted immigrants are tabulated for the March year but net migration gain for the calendar year; thus one has to compare assisted figure for the year to March 1950 with the total for calendar 1949. See also Megan Hutching, *Long Journey for Sevenpence: An oral history of assisted immigration to New Zealand from the United Kingdom, 1947–1975*, Victoria University Press, Wellington, 1999.
80 Economic Survey 1951, p. 4.
81 Economic Survey 1955, p. 46.
82 Economic Survey 1955, pp. 35–36.
83 Report of the combined committee on the New Zealand electric power supply, AJHR, 1957, D-4A.
84 New Zealand Official Yearbook, 1958, ch. 26.
85 Economic Survey, AJHR, 1955, B5, p. 28.
86 Bassett, *State in New Zealand*, p. 265.
87 Gould, *Rake's Progress*, p. 70.
88 For example, Holland apparently disliked Fletcher Holdings, complained in 1950 about their leading position in state house construction, and asked Sir James Fletcher when his company 'was going to leave something for the little fellow'. Paul Goldsmith, *Fletchers: A Centennial History of Fletcher Building*, David Ling, Auckland, 2009, p. 134.
89 *Department of Industries and Commerce Annual Report*, AJHR, 1950, H-44, p. 13.
90 New Zealand Official Yearbook, 1951–52, ch. 9A.
91 Labour's Manifesto to NZ Manufacturers, nd (1951), Nash item 1102 0334, in Nash 1102/0310-0482, Nash Papers, ANZ. The suggestion came from a later Mayor of Auckland, D. M. Robinson: see Childswear Ltd to Nash 18 Jul 51 Nash item 1102 0347, and Nash to D. M. Robinson 24 Jul 51 Nash item 1102 0351, in Nash 1102/0310-0482, Nash Papers, ANZ.
92 Review of the Activities of the Board of Trade, AJHR, 1954, H-46, p. 15.
93 Review of the Activities of the Board of Trade, AJHR, 1954, H-46, p. 22.
94 Department of Industries and Commerce annual report, AJHR, 1950, H-44, p. 27.
95 Department of Industries and Commerce annual report, AJHR, 1951, H-44, p. 23.
96 Department of Industries and Commerce annual report, AJHR, 1952, H-44, p. 37.
97 Department of Industries and Commerce annual report, AJHR, 1955, H-44, p. 48.
98 *New Zealand Economist,* 9(9), December 1949, W. A. E. Green to Sec Treas covering letter 5 Mar 53, in Capital Issues Controls Committee, ANZ [Ref: ADRK 17391 T1 44/162/21].
99 There is a good summary in W. A. E. Green to Sec Treas, 5 Mar 1953, covering letter and also in Sec Treas to Minister, 12 Feb 1952, in Capital Issues Controls Committee, ANZ.

100 20 Feb 1953, P. L. Porter notes, in Capital Issues Controls Committee, ANZ.
101 There is a table summarising the committee's work in Capital Issues Controls Committee, 16 Jan 1952, ANZ [Ref: ADRK 17391 T1 44/162/21/3]. See also W. A. E. Green to Sec Treas covering letter 5 Mar 53, T1 44/162/21, Capital Issues Controls Committee, ANZ.
102 R. S. Deane, *Foreign Investment in New Zealand Manufacturing*, Sweet and Maxwell, Wellington, 1970, ch. 2 and 3.
103 New Zealand Official Yearbook, various years.
104 New Zealand Official Yearbook, 1958, ch. 20A.
105 Bassett, *State in New Zealand*, p. 272.
106 New Zealand Official Yearbook, 1951–52, 'Latest statistical information;' 1959, ch. 20B.
107 There is a full account in New Zealand Official Yearbook,1958, ch. 19.
108 Department of Industries and Commerce annual report, AJHR, 1957, H-44, p. 22.
109 Report on Housing, AJHR, 1954, H38, p. 6.
110 Report on Housing, AJHR, 1954, H38, pp. 13–14; 1955, H38, p. 13.
111 Report on Housing, AJHR, 1954, H38, pp. 19–20.
112 Chris Trotter, *No Left Turn: The distortion of New Zealand's history by greed, bigotry and right-wing politics*, Random House, Auckland, 2007, p. 218.
113 Paul Goldsmith, *Fletcher*, pp. 133–34.
114 Singleton and Robertson, *Economic relations*; Bassett, *State in New Zealand*; Goldsmith, *Fletcher.*
115 Singleton and Robertson, *Economic relations*, pp. 80–83.
116 Astrid Baker, 'Governments, firms, and national wealth: a new pulp and paper industry in postwar New Zealand', *Enterprise & Society*, 5(4), December 2004, p. 688. A more sceptical view is Morris Guest and John Singleton, 'The Murupara Project and Industry Development in New Zealand', *Australian Economic History Review*, 39(1), February 1999.
117 John Singleton and Paul L. Robertson are exceptions; see their *Economic Relations*, and also their 'Britain, Butter, and European Integration, 1957–64', *Economic History Review*, 50(2), 1997.
118 Economic Survey 1953, AJHR, 1953, B-5, p. 21.
119 Economic Survey 1954, AJHR, 1954, B-5, pp. 33–45.
120 Review of Trade Policy 1136D 21 Dec 56, a confidential document circulated to producer boards, in Review of New Zealand Trade Policy 1956–57, ANZ [Ref: ADRK 17391 T1 (box 424) 61/3/21 pt 1 (R15422514)].
121 Department of Industries and Commerce annual report, AJHR, 1950, H-44, pp. 19–20; 1953, H-44, p. 11; 1954, H-44, p. 8; 1955, H-44, p. 37.
122 Singleton and Robertson, *Economic Relations,* p. 110.
123 Singleton and Robertson, *Economic Relations,* pp. 111–15.
124 Officials Cttee on Economic Policy Minutes 18 Dec 56, in Review of New Zealand Trade Policy 1956–57, ANZ.
125 Chm Working Party on Econ Policy to Chm Officials Cttee on Econ Policy 18 Dec 56 (i.e. Moriarty to Greensmith), in Review of New Zealand Trade Policy 1956–57, ANZ.
126 Chm Meat Board to Chm Inter-Dept Cttee on Trade 11 Dec 56, T1 61/3/21 Review of New Zealand Trade Policy 1956–57, ANZ. It is only fair to note that Ormond later became an effective advocate of diversification: Bremer, Robert James, 'Ormond, John Davies Wilder 1905 – 1995', *Dictionary of New Zealand Biography*, updated 22 June 2007. URL: http://www.dnzb.govt.nz/.

127 Notes of meeting Meat Producers Bd and Cab Cttee Ec Policy 20 Dec 56. See also Sec Treas to Min Fin 12 Dec 56, in Review of New Zealand Trade Policy 1956–57, ANZ.
128 Minutes of meeting Producer Organisations and Cab Cttee Ec Pol 5 Feb 57, Review of New Zealand Trade Policy 1957, pt 1, ANZ [Ref: ADRK 17391 T1 61/3/21 pt 1].
129 S McLeod to Lang 14 Jan 57, in Review of New Zealand Trade Policy 1957, pt 1, ANZ.
130 *Financial Times* 20 Mar 57, in Review of New Zealand Trade Policy 1957, pt 2, ANZ [Ref: ADRK 17391 T1 61/3/21 pt 2].
131 Holyoake, opening statement 8 Apr 57, in Review of New Zealand Trade Policy 1957, pt 2, ANZ.
132 Greensmith's remarks at meeting of officials and producer organisations on NZ–United Kingdom Trade Discussions 8 Feb 57, in Review of New Zealand Trade Policy 1957, pt 1, ANZ.
133 Confidential briefing paper on Trade Discussions... London 8 April to 29 May 1957, in UK and NZ Trade Negotiations 1957–58, ANZ [Ref: ADRK 17391 T1 (box 426) 61/3/25 (R15422525)].
134 *NZPD*, vol. 311, 1957, p. 96 (Holyoake).
135 Supply and Consumption Trends in Main Supplementary Markets for New Zealand's Meat, DeptAg paper, Oct 57, in Discussions with UK Govt on Agr policy 1957, ANZ [Ref: T161/3/21/2/57 (R15422518)].
136 *NZPD*, vol. 311, 1957, p. 112 (Halstead).
137 Text of radio broadcast, nd, in Budget 1954, ANZ [Ref: ADRK 17391 T1 (box 226) 3/3/54 (R15421131)].

Chapter 5

1 Bruce Brown, 'Nordmeyer 1901–1989' in Margaret Clark, ed., *Three Labour Leaders: Nordmeyer, Kirk, Rowling*, Dunmore, Palmerston North, 2001, pp. 35–37.
2 Brown, 'Nordmeyer', p. 35.
3 Sinclair, *Walter Nash*, pp. 299–302; Mary Logan, *Nordy: Arnold Nordmeyer, a political biography*, Steele Roberts, Wellington, 2008, p. 301.
4 Quoted in Logan, *Nordy*, p. 303.
5 Economic Survey 1960, AJHR, 1960, B-5, p. 45.
6 McKinnon, *Treasury*, p. 214.
7 Easton, *Nationbuilders*, p. 259.
8 Labour Party Proposals for Social Security 7 Nov 57, in Budget 1957, ANZ [Ref: ADRK 17391 T1 (box 226) 3/3/57 (15421134)].
9 The briefing is Sec Treas to Min Fin 11 Dec 1957, in Budget 1957, ANZ.
10 The briefing is Sec Treas to Min Fin 11 Dec 1957, in Budget 1957, ANZ.
11 Sec Treas to Min Fin 12 Dec 57, in General Questions of Economic Policy 1956–58, ANZ [Ref: ADRK 17391 T1 (box 414) 61/1/9 (R15422483)].
12 Department of Industries and Commerce annual report, AJHR, 1958, H-44, p. 10.
13 Logan, *Nordy*, pp. 309–10; Draft Minutes, CCEP 20 Dec 57, in NZ Import Licensing 1952–1967, ANZ [Ref: AEFN 19294 ICW1955 (box 4) 72/1 pt 1 (R17217281)].
14 Sutch to Min IC 17 Feb 58, in NZ Import Licensing 1952–67, ANZ.

15 P N Holloway, Exchange Allocation and Import Selection, 21 Jan 58, in NZ Import Licensing 1952–67, ANZ.
16 Sec Treas to Min Fin 5 Mar 58, in Budget 1958, ANZ [Ref: ADRK 17391 T1W2412 (box 1) 3/3/58 (R11184309)].
17 Summary Estimated Effects of Increases in Indirect Taxes (nd but prob late May 58), in Budget 1958, ANZ.
18 Reserve Bank of New Zealand annual report, AJHR, 1958, B-16, pp. 7–8.
19 The term was widely used by the National Party, but coined by the uncomradely president of the Federation of Labour, Fintan Patrick Walsh. Logan, *Nordy*, pp. 320–21.
20 Logan, *Nordy*, p. 321; Easton, *Nationbuilders*, p. 181; McKinnon, *Treasury*, p. 220.
21 Economic Survey 1958, AJHR, 1958, B-5, pp. 5–7, 19, 23.
22 Budget 1958, AJHR, 1958, B-6, pp. 1–2.
23 Economic Survey 1958, AJHR, 1958, B-5, p. 22.
24 Budget 1958, AJHR, 1958, B-6, p. 3; Economic Survey 1958, AJHR, 1958, B-5, p. 43.
25 *NZPD*, vol. 317, 1958, p. 863 (Nordmeyer).
26 Economic Survey 1958, AJHR, 1958, B-5, p. 47.
27 *Press*, editorial, 8 Oct 58, clipping in NZ Import Licensing 1945–1959, ANZ [Ref: AEFN 19294 ICW1955 (box 4) 72/1 pt 2 (R17217282)].
28 EFP (E) (58) 48 Ch OCEFP to Ch Cab Cttee EFP 22 Aug 58, in NZ Import Licensing 1945–59, ANZ.
29 E (59) M.25: Cab Committee Economic and Financial Policy minutes, 27 May 59, in NZ Import Licensing 1945–59, ANZ.
30 Economic Survey 1959, AJHR, 1959, B-5, p. 35; 1960, B-5, p. 45.
31 Gould, *Rake's Progress*, p. 88.
32 The recent and very good biography is Gustafson, *Kiwi Keith*.
33 See, generally, Gustafson, *Kiwi Keith*, pp. 310–12, and Margaret Clark, ed., *Holyoake's Lieutenants*, Dunmore Press, Palmerston North, 2003.
34 Logan, *Nordy*, p. 378.
35 *NZPD*, vol. 326, 1961, p. 125 (Nordmeyer). It is difficult to assess the truth of the competing claims since the relevant budget advice files are missing.
36 Cab Ec Cttee, minutes of meeting 25 Jan 61, in Cabinet Committee on Economic Policy 1959–61, ANZ [Ref: ADRK 17391 T1 W2666 61/1/8]. See also Reserve Bank of New Zealand Annual Report, AJHR, 1961, B-16.
37 Sec Treas to Min Fin 30 Mar 62 Cabinet Committee on Economic Policy 1962, ANZ [Ref: ADRK 17391 T1 W2666 61/1/8 pt 1]. This paper was a reflection on recent Australian experience but was clearly informed by Greensmith's thoughts on recent New Zealand history as well.
38 *NZPD*, vol. 326, 1961, p. 800 (Holyoake).
39 Govr RB to Min Fin 15 May 62, in Budget 1962, ANZ [Ref: ADRK 17391 T1W2412 (box 1) 3/3/62 (R11184308)]. See also RBNZ Annual Report 1962, AJHR, 1962, B16, p. 8.
40 Sec Treas to Min Fin 24 May 63 (actually Galvin), in Budget 1963, ANZ [Ref: ADRK 17391 T1 (box 227) 3/3/63 (R15421138)]
41 Govr RBNZ to Min Fin 28 May 63, in Budget 1963, ANZ.
42 Budget, 1963, AJHR, 1963, B-6, pp. 16, 23.
43 Unsurprisingly, given the close friendship between Holmes and Henry Lang.
44 New Zealand Monetary and Economic Council (MEC), Report 1, 1961, p. 7.
45 MEC, Report 2, 1962, p. 10.
46 MEC, Report 1, pp. 43–44.

47 MEC, Report 1, p. 7.
48 Sutch, *Quest for Security*, p. 426.
49 Easton, *Nationbuilders,* ch. 7 and 10. The unsuccesful prosecution by the Security Intelligence Service in 1975, for breaching the Official Secrets Act by passing material to agents of the KGB, perhaps reinforced Sutch's reputation on the left as a scourge of the colonial-minded establishment.
50 A. M. Endres, 'The Political Economy of W.B. Sutch: Towards a Critical Appreciation' *New Zealand Economic Papers*, 20, 1986, pp. 17–40.
51 Easton, *Nationbuilders*, p. 163.
52 Endres, 'Political economy of W.B. Sutch', p. 33.
53 Endres, p. 25. A good statement of Sutch's views on this point is at p. 18–21 of his 'Programme for Growth', IDC, 1960.
54 There is little readily available material on Holloway, but see the obituary by Graeme Hunt, *National Business Review*, 6 Jun 2003, p. 38. Holloway was born in 1917 so was young for Ministerial rank; Hunt describes him as 'the smartest minister in the . . . government'. He did not contest the 1960 election, a decision attributed by Hunt to the stress of, variously, a bitter libel action he fought and won against the newspaper *Truth*, 'the general unpopularity of the Nash government' and the end of his first marriage, in 1959. The latter was 'upsetting [to] the prudish Walter Nash who deplored Mr Holloway's conduct'.
55 *NZPD*, vol. 309, 1956, p. 1123 (Holloway); vol. 319, 1959, p. 214 (Holloway).
56 John Marshall, *Memoirs vol 2: 1960 to1988*, Collins, Auckland, 1989, p. 32.
57 Budget 1960, AJHR, 1960, B-6, p. 13.
58 Budget 1962, AJHR, 1962, B-6.
59 I have discussed these developments in more detail in 'Long Slow Boom: Manufacturing in New Zealand , 1945–70,' *Australian Economic History Review*, 46(1), 2006.
60 Singleton and Robertson, *Economic relations*, pp. 86–90.
61 Malcolm McKinnon, *Independence and Foreign Policy: New Zealand in the world since 1935*, Auckland University Press, Auckland, 1993, p. 107.
62 Wolfgang Rosenberg, *Full Employment: Can the New Zealand Economic Miracle Last?* Reed, Wellington, 1960, p. 80 and, generally, ch. 8.
63 International Monetary Fund and World Bank: Implications of New Zealand Membership, AJHR, 1961, A-12.
64 McKinnon, *Independence and foreign policy*, p. 108.
65 *NZPD*, vol. 326, 1960, pp. 986–91 (Nash).
66 *NZPD*, vol. 326, 1960, pp. 1130, 1133 (Kirk).
67 *NZPD*, vol. 326, 1960, p. 1255 (Nordmeyer).
68 Min Finance to Ministers, 7 May 62, encl copy of Treasury Memorandum 52.880.5.62, 13 Apr 62, to Min Finance, reporting on discussions with IMF Mission to New Zealand 26 Mar–6 Apr 62, in Sir John Marshall Papers, Ref: 1403-173/4, Alexander Turnbull Library (ATL).
69 NZ Embassy, Washington to Sec Ex Affs 10 May 62, in Finance – IMF 1961–1967, ANZ [Ref: AEFN 19294 IC1 (box 1066) 29/7/6 pt 3 (R20945950)].
70 New Zealand Official Yearbook, 1969, ch. 26C.
71 The matter is usefully summarised in Marshall, *Memoirs, vol. 2*, pp. 15–18.
72 Neville Peat, *Manapouri Saved*, Longacre, Dunedin, 1994.
73 Ross Galbreath, *DSIR: Making science work for New Zealand*, Victoria University Press, Wellington, 1998, ch. 7.
74 Paul Goldsmith, *Fletchers*, pp. 163–67.
75 CM (57) 23 19 Jun 57, in Iron and Steel in NZ 1957–65, ANZ [Ref: AEFN

29294 ICW1843 (box 1) 60/1 pt 3 (R11821152)].

76 Commonwealth Office to High Commissioner, Wellington 17 Apr 58, in Iron and Steel in NZ 1957–65, pt 3, ANZ.

77 Minister Industries and Commerce to Cab Cttee Economic and Financial Policy, Nov 61; T M Brown to J Lewin 17 Dec 64, in Iron and Steel in NZ 1957–65, pt 3, ANZ.

78 A Case Study in the Establishment of a New Industry: Pacific Steel Ltd (IC), in Tariff and Development Board 1963, ANZ [Ref: AEFN 19070 ICW2357 (box 23) 4/1/2 pt 2 (R6191956)].

79 Goldsmith, *Fletchers*, p. 167.

80 Gen Mgr NZED to Sec IC 5 Feb 59, in Iron and Steel in NZ 1957–65, pt 3, ANZ.

81 Minister Industries and Commerce to Cab Cttee Economic and Financial Policy, Nov 61, in Iron and Steel in NZ 1957–65, pt 3, ANZ.

82 'The Economics of the Steel Industry' Statement by Dr W B Sutch, Wellington, 5 Apr 65, in Iron and Steel in NZ 1957–65, pt 3, ANZ.

83 There is a good general discussion of import-substituting industrialisation in the postwar decades by Frieden, *Global Capitalism*, pp. 306–20.

84 Galbreath, *DSIR*, pp. 189–96.'Iron and Steel – Survey of the New Zealand Requirements' P O Fairfax, 21 Feb 64, in Iron and Steel in NZ 1957–65, pt 3, ANZ.

85 Constitutional Society to PM 3 Mar 65, Holyoake to Sir Matthew Oram (president, Constitutional Society) 4 May 65, in IC 60/1 vol 3 Acc W1843 Iron and Steel in NZ 1957–65. Oram had been Speaker of the House in the first National government. Holyoake had little time for this right-wing faction, which had conspired in the late 1950s with Auckland business interests to replace him as leader of the National Party: Gustafson, *Kiwi Keith*, pp. 101–07.

86 CM 65/6/25, in Iron and Steel in NZ 1957–65, pt 3, ANZ.

87 Nash, 'Building the Future' in New Zealand Government, *Background papers: Industrial Development Conference, June 1960,* Government Printer, Wellington, 1960, p. 7.

88 Sutch, 'New Zealand's manufacturing development since 1 January 1958', in New Zealand Government, *Background papers : Industrial Development Conference, June 1960,* p. 13.

89 J. P. M. Cornwall et al, *A critique of the Industrial Development Conference June 1960*, School of Public Administration, Victoria University of Wellington, mimeo, 1960, p. 22.

90 Cornwall et al, *A critique of the Industrial Development Conference*, p. 53.

91 A. P. O'Shea, 'The New Zealand Farming Industry'; A. R. Dellow, 'The need for protection of the New Zealand market', Background Paper 23, both in New Zealand Government, *Background papers : Industrial Development Conference, June 1960.*

92 F. W. Holmes, 'International trade arrangements affecting New Zealand's exports and industrial development', Background Paper 2, New Zealand Government, *Background papers : Industrial Development Conference, June 1960*, p. 6.

93 Cornwall et al, *A critique of the Industrial Development Conference*, p. 53.

94 New Zealand Government, *The Agricultural Development Conference 1963–64*, Government Printer, Wellington, 1966, p. 5.

95 Sec IC to Chairman TDB 13 Dec 62, in Tariff and Development Board 1962, ANZ [Ref: AEFN 19070 ICW2357 (box 23) 4/1/2 pt 1 (R6191955)].

96 Stephan Haggard, *Pathways from the Periphery: T he politics of growth in the newly industrializing countries*, Cornell University Press, Ithaca, 1990, p. 10.

97 Treasury Submission Oct 62, in Tariff and Development Board 1962, pt 1, ANZ.
98 Reserve Bank Submission, in Tariff and Development Board 1962, pt 1, ANZ.
99 Associated Chambers of Commerce Submission, UK Manufacturers and New Zealand Representatives Assn Submission, in Tariff and Development Board 1962, pt 1, ANZ.
100 Federated Farmers Submission, in Tariff and Development Board 1962, pt 1, ANZ.
101 NZ Manufacturers Federation Submission, in Tariff and Development Board 1962, pt 1, ANZ.
102 Tariff and Development Board Report to the Minister of Industries and Commerce on Criteria for Industrial Development, Final report, AJHR, 1963, H-48.
103 Budget, 1963, AJHR, 1963, B-6, pp. 7–13; Budget, 1964, AJHR, 1964, B-6, pp. 3–4.
104 Marshall, *Memoirs, vol. 2*, pp. 37–38.
105 Easton, *Nationbuilders*, pp. 168–69.
106 Marshall, *Memoirs, vol. 2*; see also Easton, 'Trying to Understand Dr Sutch', http://www.eastonbh.ac.nz/?p=49, retrieved 15 Nov 2012.
107 Budget 1958, AJHR, 1958, B-6, p. 7.
108 Economic Survey 1960, AJHR, 1960, B-5, p. 47.
109 Draft Note to the United Kingdom Feb 58; HCNZ to Min Ext Affs 24 Apr 58, in UK–NZ Trade Negotiations 1957–58, ANZ [Ref: ADRK 17391 T1 (box 426) 61/3/25 (R15422525)]. See also Singleton and Robertson, *Economic relations*, p. 110.
110 Chm Officials Cttee to Chm Cab Cttee Ec Policy 24 Jan 58, 28 Jan 58, in UK–NZ Trade Negotiations 1957–58, ANZ.
111 The precise Scandinavian formula was 75 per cent of the greater of annual average of either 1936–38 or 1955–57; AJHR, 1958, A-13, p. 6. Even after leaving the Commonwealth in 1949, Ireland was not treated by London as a foreign country; this position had been urged by Fraser in 1948 in order to persuade the new Indian republic to remain in the Commonwealth. Even then it had been recognised that there was a likelihood of future difficulties in trade as a result of this approach.
112 Agricultural Discussions between the Government of New Zealand and the Government of the United Kingdom, AJHR, 1958, A-13.
113 Lord Home to Skinner 22 May 58, in Discussions with UK Govt on Agr policy 1957, pt 2, ANZ [Ref: T1 61/3/21/2/57 (R15422518)]
114 Min Ext Affs to HCNZ London 15 May 58, in Discussions with UK Government on Agricultural Policy 1957, ANZ [Ref: (R15422519)].
115 Financial Times 21 May 58, Guardian 21 May 58, in Discussions with UK Govt on Agr policy 1957, pt 2, ANZ.
116 HCNZ to Min Ext Affs 24 Apr 58, in UK–NZ Trade Negotiations 1957–58; Cab Cttee EFP 2 May 58 EFP (58) 17 in Cabinet Committee on Economic Policy 1957–1958, ANZ [Ref: ADRK 17391 T1 (box 414) 61/1/8 (R15422479)]. See also Singleton and Robertson, *Economic relations*, p. 119.
117 AJHR, 1959, A-14.
118 Singleton and Robertson, *Economic relations*, p. 121, see the negotiations as having little immediate effect.
119 Singleton and Robertson, *Economic relations*, p. 125.
120 Singleton and Robertson, *Economic relations*, p. 126.
121 Singleton and Robertson, *Economic relations*, pp. 129–33
122 New Zealand's EEC diplomacy in the 1960s is surveyed in Singleton and Robertson, *Economic*.

123 Chairman Officials' Cttee on Economic Policy to Chairman Cab Cttee on Economic Policy 15 May 61, in Cabinet Committee on Economic Policy 1959–61, ANZ [Ref: ADRK 17391 T1W2666 (box 30) 61/1/8 (R16997131)]; minutes of 7 Jun 61, in Cabinet Committee on Economic Policy 1961, ANZ [Ref: ADRK 17391 T1W2666 (box 30) 61/1/8 pt 1 (R16997132)].

124 Sec Ext Affs to Sec Treas and other heads 31 Aug 61, in Cabinet Committee on Economic Policy 1961,pt 2, ANZ [Ref: ADRK 17391 T1W2666 (box 30) 61/1/8 pt 2 (R16997133)].

125 Cabinet Committee on Economic Policy, 29 Sep 61, minutes of 26 Sep 61, in Cabinet Committee on Economic Policy 1961,pt 3, ANZ [Ref: ADRK 17391 T1W2666 (box 30) 61/1/8 pt 3 (R16997237)].

126 DG Ag to Min Ag 14 Sep 61, in Cabinet Committee on Economic Policy 1961, pt 3, ANZ.

127 Ch Off Cttee to Ch Cab Cttee 2 Jun 61, T 1, in Cabinet Committee on Economic Policy 1961, pt 1, ANZ.

128 Cabinet Committee on Economic Policy, 31 Aug 61, minutes of 22 Aug 61, in Cabinet Committee on Economic Policy 1961, pt 3, ANZ.

129 Ch Off Cttee to Ch Cab Cttee 8 Mar 62, in Cabinet Committee on Economic Policy 1962, pt 2, ANZ [Ref: ADRK 17391 T1W2666 (box 31) 61/1/8 pt 2 (R16997240)].

130 Ch Off Cttee to Ch Cab Cttee 23 Jul 62, in Cabinet Committee on Economic Policy 1962, pt 3, ANZ [Ref: ADRK 17391 T1W2666 (box 31) 61/1/8 pt 3 (R16997138)]; Ch Off Cttee to Ch Cab Cttee 18 Dec 62, in Cabinet Committee on Economic Policy 1962–63, ANZ [Ref: ADRK 17391 T1W2666 (box 31) 61/1/8 (R16997139)].

131 Ch Off Cttee to Ch Cab Cttee 8 Feb 63, 11 Feb 63, in Cabinet Committee on Economic Policy 1963, pt 1, ANZ [Ref: ADRK 17391 T1W2666 (box 31) 61/1/8 pt 1 (R16997140)].

132 Cabinet Committee on Economic Policy, 27 Jan 61, minutes of meeting 25 Jan 61, in Cabinet Committee on Economic Policy 1959–61, ANZ

133 Cabinet Committee on Economic Policy 24 Apr 63, minutes of 26 Mar 63, in Cabinet Committee on Economic Policy 1963, pt 1, ANZ. Marshall, 1989, p. 23.

134 Ch Off Cttee to Ch Cab Cttee 11 Mar 63, in Cabinet Committee on Economic Policy 1963, pt 1, ANZ.

135 Ch Off Cttee to Ch Cab Cttee 31 Jul 64 , in Cabinet Committee on Economic Policy 1964, ANZ [Ref: ADRK 17391 T1W2666 (box 32) 61/1/8 (R16997145)]. See also Cabinet Committee on Economic Policy 9 Apr 64, minutes of 2 Apr 64, in Cabinet Committee on Economic Policy 1963–64, ANZ [Ref: ADRK 17391 T1W2666 (box 32) 61/1/8 (R16997144)]. Endres suggests ('Political economy of W.B. Sutch', p. 31) that Sutch had grossly oversimplified the Swedish economist Gunnar Myrdal's warning about state support of nodal growth points like pulp and paper in New Zealand. Myrdal's concern was that such development might 'draw off capital from other sectors of the economy to such an extent that they jeopardised the balanced development . . . of the economy as a whole'. Myrdal's observations might well have applied to Think Big. They hardly applied to getting a trade agreement for forest products that were already being produced and for which markets were needed.

136 Marshall, *Memoirs, vol. 2*, pp. 24, 28 and generally chapter 3.

137 Singleton and Robertson, *Economic relations*, p. 203.

138 *NZPD*, vol. 344, 1965, pp. 2818 (Marshall), 2901 (Kirk).

139 Ch Off Cttee to Ch Cab Cttee 2 Dec 63 Acc W2666, in Cabinet Committee on

Economic Policy 1963–64; Govr Reserve Bank to Min Fin 4 May 64, Sec Treas to Min Fin 25 May 64, in Budget 1964, ANZ [Ref: ADRK 17391 T1W2412 (box 1) 3/3/64 (R11184307)].

140 Budget, 1964, AJHR, 1964, B-6, p. 17.

141 Sec Treas to Min Fin 16 Sep 64, in Budget 1964, ANZ.

142 Sec Cabinet to Min Fin 24 Sep 64 CM (64) 37, in Budget 1964, ANZ.

143 Sec Treas and Govr RB to Min Fin 6 Aug 65; Press Statement 31 Aug 65, in Balance of Payments – General Questions of Economic Policy 1963–66, ANZ [Ref: AALR 873 W3158 38 61/1/9].

144 Sec Treas to Min Fin 23 Aug 65, in Budget 1966, ANZ [Ref: T1 3/3/66].

145 New Zealand – 1965 Article XIV Consultations – Final Statement (4 Mar 66), in Finance – IMF 1961–1967, ANZ [Ref: AEFN 19294 IC1 (box 1066) 29/7/6 pt 3 (R20945950)].

146 Sec Treas to Min Fin 23 May 66, in Budget 1966, ANZ.

147 Gustafson, *Kiwi Keith*, p. 327.

148 Min Fin to Sec Treas 17 May 66, in Budget 1966, ANZ.

149 Easton, *In Stormy Seas*, p. 73.

Chapter 6

1 PM to all ministers 27 Jan 67, in Budget 1967, ANZ [Ref: ADRK 17391 T1 (box 1) 3/3/67 (R11184305)].

2 Sec Treas to Min Fin 12 Dec 66, Min Fin Memorandum to Cabinet 24 Jan 67, in Budget 1967, ANZ.

3 PM press statement 10 Feb 67, in Budget 1967, ANZ.

4 McKinnon, *Treasury*, p. 243.

5 Gustafson, *His Way*, pp. 88–90.

6 Gustafson, *His Way*, pp. 89–91.

7 Gustafson, *His Way*, pp. 136–37.

8 Gustafson, *His Way*, p. 92.

9 Gustafson, *Kiwi Keith*, pp. 329.

10 Sec Treas to Acting Min Fin 27 Feb 67; Sec Treas to Min Fin 13 Mar 67, in Budget 1967, ANZ.

11 Sec Treas to Acting Min Fin 27 Feb 67, in Budget 1967, ANZ.

12 Gustafson, *Kiwi Keith*, pp. 329.

13 Sec Treas to Min Fin 13 Mar 67, in Budget 1967, ANZ.

14 Gustafson, *Kiwi Keith*, pp. 329; see also *His Way*, pp. 92–94.

15 AJHR, B-6A, 1967, p. 4.

16 AJHR, B-6A, 1967, pp. 7–11.

17 Sec Treas to Min Fin 7 Jun 67, in Budget 1967, ANZ.

18 E. Ray Canterbery, *Economics on a New Frontier*, Wadsworth, Belmont, California, 1968, p. 81, quoted in Robert B. Parker, *John Kenneth Galbraith: His life, his politics, his economics*, Farrar, Strauss and Giroux, New York, 2005, p. 462.

19 Jim Tomlinson, *The Labour Governments 1964–70: Economic Policy*, Manchester University Press, Manchester, 2004, p. 56.

20 Devaluation of New Zealand Pound, 2 Jun 67, in Changes in exchange rate of the New Zealand Dollar 1967, ANZ [Ref: AALR 873 Acc W5427 (box 961) 61/1/24 pt 13 (R20432063)].

21 Barry Eichengreen, *Imbalances and the lessons of Bretton Woods*, MIT Press,

Cambridge, Mass, p. 9 and more generally, Eichengreen, *Globalizing Capital: A history of the international monetary system*, Princeton University Press, Princeton, 2nd edn. 2008, p. 95.

22 Devaluation of New Zealand Pound, 2 Jun 67, in Changes in exchange rate of the New Zealand Dollar 1967, ANZ.

23 Secret File 'Changes in the exchange rate 1967' – Introductory, Meeting in Mr Seath's Office 5pm Friday 29 September 1967, in Changes in exchange rate of the New Zealand Dollar 1967, ANZ.

24 Meeting at Prime Minister's House, Sunday October 1st 1967; Notes of telephone conversation Davis and Lang 2 Oct 67, in Changes in exchange rate of the New Zealand Dollar 1967, ANZ. Those present at the Sunday meeting were Holyoake, Marshall, Seath, Shand, Lang, McLeod, White (RBNZ), Coney (RBNZ).

25 Meeting in Mr Marshall's Office 4 Oct 67, in Changes in exchange rate of the New Zealand Dollar 1967, ANZ.

26 Meeting in Prime Minister's Office 5 Oct 67, and additional note 5 Oct 1967, in Changes in exchange rate of the New Zealand Dollar 1967, ANZ.

27 Meeting with Mr Muldoon (at his home) 3 pm Sunday 8 Oct 67, in Changes in exchange rate of the New Zealand Dollar 1967, ANZ.

28 Before becoming a minister, Muldoon had aggressively passed on accusations from his 'manufacturing friends' to Jim Moriarty, the Secretary of Industries and Commerce and New Zealand's leading official in the NAFTA discussions, that Moriarty had 'sold us out'. Gustafson, *Kiwi Keith*, p. 322.

29 Meeting at Prime Minister's House, Sunday 8 October 1967 730pm, in Changes in exchange rate of the New Zealand Dollar 1967, ANZ.

30 Meeting at Prime Minister's House, Sunday 8 October 1967 730pm, in Changes in exchange rate of the New Zealand Dollar 1967, ANZ.

31 Meeting in Mr Marshall's Office 4 Oct 67, in Changes in exchange rate of the New Zealand Dollar 1967, ANZ.

32 Meeting at Prime Minister's House, Sunday 8 October 1967 730pm, in Changes in exchange rate of the New Zealand Dollar 1967, ANZ.

33 Alec Cairncross, *Managing the British Economy in the 1960s: A Treasury perspective*, Macmillan, Basingstoke, 1996, ch. 10; Schenk, *The Decline of Sterling*, pp. 157–85.

34 Meeting at Prime Minister's House, Sunday 8 October 1967 730pm, in Changes in exchange rate of the New Zealand Dollar 1967, ANZ.

35 Govr RB and Acting Sec Treas to Min Fin 8 Oct 67, in Changes in exchange rate of the New Zealand Dollar 1967, ANZ.

36 Meeting at Prime Minister's House, Sunday 8 October 1967 730pm, in Changes in exchange rate of the New Zealand Dollar 1967, ANZ.

37 Ministers' Decision (9 October 1967), in Changes in exchange rate of the New Zealand Dollar 1967, ANZ.

38 Tomlinson, *The Labour Governments 1964–70*, p. 55; see also Caincross, *Managing the British Economy,* ch. 10.

39 Notes on the devaluation 21 Nov 67, in Changes in exchange rate of the New Zealand Dollar 1967, ANZ.

40 Meeting at Prime Minister's Residence Saturday 18 November 1967 at 8pm, in Changes in exchange rate of the New Zealand Dollar 1967, ANZ.

41 Meeting held in the residence of the Prime Minister 19 Nov 67 at 8 pm; Notes on the devaluation 21 Nov 67, Changes in exchange rate of the New Zealand Dollar 1967, ANZ.

42 Devaluation announcement 21 Nov 67, in Changes in exchange rate of the New

Zealand Dollar 1967, ANZ.
43 Economic Review, AJHR, 1968, B-5, p. 30.
44 Economic Review, AJHR, 1968, B-5, pp. 31–33.
45 Eichengreen, *European Economy*, pp. 217–18.
46 Jonathan Boston, *Incomes Policy in New Zealand, 1967–1984*, Institute of Policy Studies/Victoria University Press, Wellington, 1984, pp. 1–4. Boston notes the problems of definition.
47 Pat Walsh, 'An "Unholy Alliance": The 1968 Nil Wage Order,' *New Zealand Journal of History*, 28(2), October 1994, pp. 180–81.
48 Peter Franks, 'Skinner, Thomas Edward 1909 – 1991', *Dictionary of New Zealand Biography*, updated 22 June 2007, URL: http://www.dnzb.govt.nz/ accessed 3 Feb 2010.
49 Walsh, 'Unholy alliance', pp. 181–82.
50 Book of Awards (BoA), vol. 68, 1968, p. 1294.
51 BoA, vol. 68, 1968, pp. 1294–95
52 BoA, vol. 68, 1968, pp. 1300–02.
53 BoA, vol. 68, 1968, p. 1300.
54 BoA, vol. 68, 1968, p. 1303.
55 Walsh, 'Unholy alliance', p. 184.
56 BoA, vol. 68, 1968, pp. 1334–43.
57 R. D. Muldoon, *The Rise and Fall of a Young Turk*, Reed, Wellington, 1974, p. 96.
58 Dep. Sec (Lough) to Lang and Galvin 23 Apr 70, in Cabinet Committee on Economic Policy: Balance of payments – Incomes Policy 1967–70, ANZ [Ref: AALR 873 W3158 61/1/22].
59 Sec Treas to Min Fin 29 May 70, in Budget 1970, ANZ [Ref: ADRK 17391 W2412 (box 1) 3/3/70 pt 1 (R11184301)].
60 *NZPD*, vol. 365, 1970, pp. 27–28 (Kirk).
61 See David Grant, *Man for all Seasons: The life and times of Ken Douglas*, Random House, Auckland, 2010, pp. 121–37.
62 Boston, *Incomes Policy*, p. 90.
63 Walsh, 'Unholy alliance', p. 179.
64 J. C. Averill (NZFP) to Lough 24 Mar 70, in Cabinet Committee on Economic Policy: Balance of payments – Incomes Policy 1967–70, ANZ.
65 Marshall, *Memoirs, vol.* 2, p. 115.
66 *NZPD*, vol. 365, 1970, p. 337 (Marshall)
67 Minutes of Conference on Prices, Incomes and Productivity 9 Apr 70, in Cabinet Committee on Economic Policy: Balance of payments – Incomes Policy 1967–70, ANZ.
68 Minutes of meeting between ministers and Employers' Federation 13 Nov 70, in Cabinet Committee on Economic Policy: Balance of payments – Incomes Policy 1970–71, ANZ[Ref: AALR 873 W3158 61/1/22 pt 2].
69 Boston, *Incomes Policy*, p. 97.
70 Meeting between Officials and Employers 6 Jan 71; FOL to North Island Freezing Companies 22 Dec 70, in Cabinet Committee on Economic Policy: Balance of payments – Incomes Policy 1970–71, pt 2, ANZ.
71 Precis of meeting between Employers Federation and Federation of Labour on wages problems 27 Nov 70, in Cabinet Committee on Economic Policy: Balance of payments – Incomes Policy 1970–71, pt 2, ANZ.
72 Minutes of Cab Cttee Wages and Prices 1 Feb 71, in Cabinet Committee on Economic Policy: Balance of payments – Incomes Policy 1970–71, pt 2, ANZ.

73 3 Feb 71 Minutes of meeting between employers' representatives and FOL with Minister of Labour as chairman on prices and wages, in Cabinet Committee on Economic Policy: Balance of payments – Incomes Policy 1970–71, pt 2, ANZ.
74 Recommendations from the Federation of Labour 10 Feb 71, in Cabinet Committee on Economic Policy: Balance of payments – Incomes Policy 1970–71, ANZ. [Ref: AALR 873 W3158 61/1/22 pt 3]. See also Boston, *Incomes policy*, p. 99.
75 8 Feb 71 Minutes of meeting between employers' representatives and FOL with Minister of Labour as chairman on prices and wages, in Cabinet Committee on Economic Policy: Balance of payments – Incomes Policy 1970–71, pt 2, ANZ.
76 There is a convenient summary in Boston, *Incomes policy*, p. 101.
77 Minutes of Cab C Wages and Prices 13 Feb 71, in Cabinet Committee on Economic Policy: Balance of payments – Incomes Policy 1970–71, pt 3, ANZ.
78 Sec Labour, Sec IC, Sec Treas to Chairman Cab Committee Wages and Prices 12 Feb 71, in Cabinet Committee on Economic Policy: Balance of payments – Incomes Policy 1970–71, pt 3, ANZ.
79 Boston, *Incomes policy*, pp. 103, 109–10.
80 Boston, *Incomes policy*, p. 104.
81 Dep Sec Treas to PM, Dep PM, Min Fin, Min IC, Chairman Cab Committee State Services 21 Jan 72, in Cabinet Committee on Economic Policy: Balance of payments – Incomes Policy 1970–71, ANZ [Ref: AALR 873 W3158 61/1/22 pt 5].
82 Cab Office to Min Fin 27 Jan 72, Cabinet Committee on Economic Policy: Balance of payments – Incomes Policy 1970–71, pt 5, ANZ.
83 Press Statement: Stabilisation 14 Feb 72, in Cabinet Committee on Economic Policy: Balance of payments – Incomes Policy 1970–71, pt 5, ANZ.
84 Sec Treas to Chairman, Cabinet Committee on Economic Policy 24 Feb 72, in Cabinet Committee on Economic Policy: Balance of payments – Incomes Policy 1970–71, ANZ [Ref: AALR 873 W3158 61/1/22 pt 6].
85 Press Statement Draft: Stabilisation 23 Mar 72; Cab Ec Cttee 23 Mar 72 draft of regulations, in Cabinet Committee on Economic Policy: Balance of payments – Incomes Policy 1970–71, pt 6, ANZ.
86 Boston, *Incomes policy*, pp. 110–11.
87 See, for instance, Sec Treas to Min Fin 9 Jun 67, inBudget 1967, ANZ.
88 New Zealand Government, *Report of the proceedings of the National Development Conference, plenary session, 27–29 August, 1968*, Government Printer, Wellington, 1968, p. 47.
89 New Zealand Government, *Report of the proceedings of the National Development Conference, plenary session*, pp. 9, 103.
90 Budget 1969, AJHR, B-6, 1969, p. 4.
91 Budget 1969, AJHR, 1969, B-6; Budget 1970, AJHR, 1970, B-6.
92 Goldsmith, *Fletchers*, pp. 200–01, suggests that the burden on non-exporting companies and on individuals became insupportable.
93 Sec Treas to Min Fin budget report 39 12 Jun 70; Sec Treas to Min Fin 22 May 70, in Budget 1970, ANZ; Budget 1970, AJHR, B-6, 1970.
94 Sec Treas to Min Fin budget 27 Apr 71, in Budget 1971, ANZ [Ref: ADRK 17391 W2412 (box 2) 3/3/71 (R11184298)].
95 Sec Treas to Min Fin budget 27 Apr 71, in Budget 1971, ANZ.
96 Merwyn Norrish, quoted Gustafson, *Kiwi Keith*, p. 307.
97 Belich, *Paradise Reforged*, p. 425.
98 Belich, *Paradise Reforged*, pp. 433–35.

99 Singleton and Robertson, *Economic relations*, p. 213.
100 *NZPD*, vol. 372, 1971, p. 1525 (Marshall).
101 Gustafson, *Kiwi Keith*, p. 303.
102 Peter Aimer, *Wings of the nation : a history of the New Zealand National Airways Corporation, 1947–78*, Bush Press, Auckland, 2000, ch. 7.
103 This paragraph and the preceding draw on Gustafson, *Kiwi Keith*, ch. 15, especially pp. 292–98 and 308.
104 Gustafson, *Kiwi Keith*, p. 295.
105 Eichengreen, *Globalizing Capital*, and Eichengreen, *Global Imbalances and the lessons of Bretton Woods*, MIT Press, Cambridge, Mass, 2006.
106 Diane B. Kunz, *Butter and guns: America's Cold War economic diplomacy*, Free Press, New York, 1997, p. 196.
107 Eichengreen, *Globalizing Capital*, p. 121.
108 Eichengreen, *Global Imbalances*, p. 20. The dilemma is known as the Triffin Dilemma, after Robert Triffin.
109 Eichengreen, *Global Imbalances*, p. 22.
110 Eichengreen, *Global Imbalances,* pp. 57–58.
111 Eichengreen, *Global Imbalances*, pp. 16–18.
112 Kunz, *Butter and guns*, p. 192.
113 Quoted Francis J. Gavin, *Gold, dollars, and power: the politics of international monetary relations, 1958–1971*, University of North Carolina Press, Chapel Hill, 2003, p. 194.
114 Schenk, *Decline of Sterling*, pp. 317, 319.
115 Kunz, *Butter and guns*, p. 192.
116 The partial exculpation of Nixon is implied by Frieden, *Global Capitalism*, pp. 340–46; the aggression is emphasised by Eichengreen, *Exorbitant Privilege: The Rise and Fall of the Dollar and the Future of the International Monteary System*, Oxford University Press, New York, 2011, p. 59.
117 Eichengreen, *Global Imbalances*, pp. 16–18.
118 Kunz, *Guns and butter*, pp. 208–13; Eichengreen, *Globalizing Capital*, pp. 126–32.
119 Eichengreen, *Globalizing Capital*, p. 132.
120 Budget 1972, AJHR 1972, B–6, p. 6.
121 Reserve Bank annual reports, AJHR, B-16, 1972 and 1973.
122 Catherine Schenk and John Singleton, 'Basket Pegs and Exchange Rate Regime Change: Australia and New Zealand in the Mid-Seventies' *Australian Economic History Review*, 51(2), 2011, p. 128. As the authors note at p. 129, 'Although 10 currencies were in the initial basket, four dominated: sterling at 40 per cent, the USD at 18 per cent, the AUD at 20 per cent, and the Yen at 11 per cent',
123 Andrew Britton, *Monetary Regimes of the Twentieth Century*, Cambridge University Press, Cambridge and New York, 2001, p. 152.
124 Kunz, *Guns and Butter*, p. 182.
125 Kunz, *Guns and Butter*, p. 201.
126 Nick Tiratsoo, '"You've Never Had it So Bad"? Britain in the 1970s' in Tiratsoo, ed., *From Blitz to Blair: A new history of Britain since 1939*, Weidenfeld and Nicolson, London, 1997, p. 166.
127 Britton, *Monetary regimes*, pp. 152–53.
128 Reserve Bank annual report, AJHR, B-16, 1972.
129 Sec Treas to Min Fin 12 May 72, in Budget 1972, ANZ [Ref: ADRK 17391 W2412 (box 2) 3/3/72 (R11184296)].
130 McClure, *Civilized Community*, pp. 164–75.

131 Sec Treas to Min Fin 12 Jun 72, in Budget 1972, ANZ
132 Gustafson, *His Way*, pp. 124–25.
133 Margaret Hayward, *Diary of the Kirk Years*, Cape Catley, Queen Charlotte Sound, 1981, p. 47.
134 Budget, 1972, AJHR, B-6, 1972, and McClure, *Civilized Community*, p. 175 for the welfare increase.
135 Robert Chapman, 'From Labour to National', p. 365.
136 Bassett, *State in New Zealand*, p. 323.

Chapter 7

1 Steven Levine and Alan McRobie, *From Muldoon to Lange: New Zealand elections in the 1980s*, MCEnterprises, Rangiora, 2002, pp. 9–10.
2 John Roberts, 'Who Won, Who Lost?' in Brian Edwards, ed., *Right Out: The inside story, Labour victory 1972*, AH & AW Reed, Wellington, 1973, p. 246.
3 Easton, *Nationbuilders*, p. 183.
4 Easton, *Nationbuilders*, p. 190
5 Jim Anderton, 'Kirk and Rowling: Recollections and Significance', in Clark, ed., *Three Labour Leaders*, p. 54.
6 John Henderson, 'Bill Rowling: The Man and his Politics' in Clark, ed., *Three Labour Leaders*. Jim Anderton, indeed, described Rowling as the toughest politician he ever knew – high praise from that quarter.
7 Jim Eagles and Colin James, *The Making of a New Zealand Prime Minister*, Cheshire, Wellington, 1973: p. 27. See also Warren Freer, *A Lifetime in Politics: The memoirs of Warren Freer*,Victoria University Press, Wellington, 2004, pp. 118–20.
8 Henry Lang to Glen Rowling, 9 November 1995, in Lang Papers, Alexander Turnbull Library, MS 99–032–1.
9 New Zealand Labour Party, 1972 Election Manifesto.
10 Reserve Bank annual report, AJHR, B-16, 1973.
11 OECD 22 Nov 73 Follow-up to Discussion on Inflation at Ministerial Level 6–8 Jun 73, in New Zealand Economy Incomes Policy 1973–74, ANZ [Ref: AALR 873 (box 59) T61/1/22 pt 9 (R16681841)].
12 Jeffry A Frieden, *Global Capitalism: Its fall and rise in the twentieth century*, Norton, New York and London, 2007, pp. 354–65.
13 Michael Bassett, *The Third Labour Government: A personal history*, Dunmore, Palmerston North, 1976, p. 54.
14 Sec Treas to Min Fin budget report 5, 13 Apr 73, in Budget 1973, ANZ [Ref: ADRK 17391 T1 (box 2) 3/3/73 (R11184293)].
15 Oral Statement by PM Press Conference 9 Sep 73, in New Zealand Economy Incomes Policy 1973 74, ANZ.
16 H G Lang, 25 May 73, note on Budget Text, in Budget 1973, ANZ.
17 Sec Treas to Min Fin budget report 34 25 May 73, in Budget 1973, ANZ.
18 McKinnon, *Treasury*, p. 255.
19 AJHR, 1973, G-14 T&I Ann rept, pp. 15–17; *NZPD*, vol. 382, 1973, pp. 879–80 (Gair); McKinnon, p. 260.
20 Sec Treas to Min Fin br 12 9 May 73, in Budget 1973, ANZ.
21 Min Ag to Min Fin 30 May 73, Sec Treas to Min Fin budget report 49 1 Jun 73, in Budget 1973, ANZ.
22 Budget 1973, AJHR, 1973, B–6, p. 21.

23 McKinnon, *Independence and Foreign Policy*, p. 215; NZOYB, 1975, s. 22,
24 Frieden, *Global Capitalism*, pp. 364–72.
25 Reserve Bank annual report 1974, AJHR, 1974, B-16, p. 5.
26 Sec Treas to Min Fin budget report 1 13 Mar 74, in Budget 1974, ANZ [Ref: ADRK 17391 T1 W2412 (box 3) 3/3/74].
27 Sec Treas to Min Fin budget report 1 13 Mar 74, Sec Treas to Min Fin budget report 21 27 Apr 74, in Budget 1974, ANZ.
28 Sec Treas to Min Fin budget report 21 27 Apr 74, in Budget 1974, ANZ.
29 Budget 1974, AJHR, 1974, B-6.
30 Reserve Bank annual report, AJHR, 1975, B-16, pp. 4–5.
31 McKinnon, *Treasury*, p. 248. There is a useful survey of exchange rate movements at http://intl.econ.cuhk.edu.hk/exchange_rate_regime/index.php?cid=35 (accessed 17 Nov 2009).
32 John Henderson, *Rowling: The Man and the Myth,* Australia and New Zealand Book Co, Auckland, 1981, p. 100. For a strongly anti-Rowling account see Tony Garnier, Bruce Kohn and Pat Booth, *The Hunter and the Hill: New Zealand politics in the Kirk years*, Cassell, Auckland, 1978.
33 Bassett, *Third Labour Government*, p. 35.
34 Boston, *Incomes Policy*, p. 118.
35 Ch Off Cttee to Ch Cab Ec Cttee 13 Feb 73, Sec Treas to Min Fin 4 Jun 73, Cabinet Economic Committee, New Zealand Economy Incomes Policy 1972–73, ANZ [Ref: AALR 873 (box 59) T61/1/22 pt 8 (R16681840)]; Minutes of Cabinet Economic Committee 11 Oct 73, in New Zealand Economy Incomes Policy 1973–74, ANZ.
36 Boston, *Incomes Policy*, pp. 122–29, 139.
37 Boston, *Incomes Policy*, p. 136.
38 Minutes Cabinet Cttee on Policy and Priorities (CCPP), 6 Mar 74, New Zealand Incomes Policy 1974, ANZ [Ref: AALR 873 (box 59) T61/1/22 pt 10 (R16681842)]; paper from officials to Chairman CC PP, Prices and Incomes Policy (Dec 73), in New Zealand Economy Incomes Policy 1973–74, ANZ.
39 Minutes of CCPP 10 Apr (for quotes) and 17 Apr Prices and Incomes 19 Apr 74, statement by Acting PM Watt, in New Zealand Incomes Policy 1974, ANZ.
40 Telegrams 22 Apr 74 Lang to Rowling (in Tokyo), New Zealand Incomes Policy 1974, ANZ.
41 Chairman Off Ec C to Ch CCPP 5 Nov 74, New Zealand Incomes Policy 1974–75, ANZ [Ref: AALR 873 W3158 (box 59) T61/1/22 pt 11 (R16681843)]; McKinnon, pp. 249–50, ANZ.
42 Press Statement Prime Minister 13 Dec 74, New Zealand Incomes Policy 1974–75, ANZ.
43 Boston, *Incomes Policy*, p. 155.
44 Sec Treas to Min Fin budget report 21 21 Apr 75, in Budget 1975, ANZ [Ref: ADRK 17391 T1W2412 3/3/75].
45 Sec Treas to Chm, Cab Cttee Policy and Priorities budget report 45 7 May 75, in Budget 1975, ANZ; Budget 1975, AJHR, 1975, B-6, pp. 4–6.
46 Sec Treas to Min Fin budget report 61 16 May 75, budget report 65 21 May 75, in Budget 1975, ANZ; Budget 1975, AJHR, 1975, B-6, p. 27.
47 Sec Treas to Min Fin budget report (br) 37, 41 6 May 75; budget report 53, 55, 56, 13 May 75, in Budget 1975, ANZ; Budget 1975, AJHR, 1975, B-6, p. 12.
48 Budget 1975, AJHR, 1975, B-6, pp. 7–9.
49 Budget 1975, AJHR, 1975, B-6, p. 1.
50 Speech by the Prime Minister 10 Aug 75, in Post 1975 Budget Economic Measures,

ANZ [Ref: ADRK 17391 T1W2412 (box 4) 3/3/75/2 (R11184257)].

51 H G Lang, Devaluation: A Case Study 10 Aug 1975 (date 13 Aug 75), in 1975 Devaluation, Lang Papers, 99-032-1/04, ATL. The irony was that Muldoon would accuse his successor as finance minister, Roger Douglas, of doing the same in 1984; Gustafson, *His Way*, p. 387.

52 H G Lang, Devaluation: A Case Study 10 Aug 1975 (date 13 Aug 75), in 1975 Devaluation, Lang Papers, 99-032-1/04, ATL.

53 Gov RB and Sec Treas to Min Fin 29 Jul 75; Draft Summary Possible Worst Outcome Contingency Plans 28 Jul 75, in 1975 Devaluation, Lang Papers, 99-032-1/04, ATL.

54 Press Statement by Prime Minister 10 Aug 76, in 1975 Devaluation, Lang Papers, 99-032-1/04, ATL.

55 *New Zealand Economist*, September 1975.

56 Gustafson, *His Way*, p. 170.

57 'Economic Policy', in New Zealand National Party, *1975 General Election Policy*.

58 Gustafson, *His Way*, p. 174.

59 Easton, *Nationbuilders*, p. 269.

60 Gustafson, *His Way*, p. 179.

61 Lang's diary of the transition, 2 Dec 1975, p. 2, 5 Dec, pp. 7–8, in 1975 Change of Government, Note for file 2 December 1975, Lang Papers, 99-032-1, ATL.

62 Lang's diary of the transition, pp. 14–16, Lang Papers, 99-032-1, ATL.

63 Economic Strategy. Secret. Prepared for Hon R D Muldoon 2 Dec 1975, pp. 1–3, Lang Papers, 99-032-1, ATL.

64 Press statement Hon R D Muldoon 12 Dec 1975, Document M, in Change of Government, Note for file 2 December 1975, Lang Papers, 99-032-1, ATL.

65 Economic Strategy Secret, Prepared for Hon R D Muldoon 2 Dec 1975, p. 3, Lang Papers, 99-032-1, ATL.

66 Dep Sec Treasury to Min Fin 17 Dec 75, and attached paper 'Structural Problems of the New Zealand Economy', in 1975/76 Change of Government – General Reports, Lang Papers, 99-032-1/03, ATL.

67 Gustafson, *His Way*, pp. 179–89 is the general source for this paragraph.

68 Gustafson, *His Way*, p. 187.

69 Lang's diary of the transition, 16 Dec 75, pp. 19, 22, Lang Papers, 99-032-1, ATL.

70 John Singleton, with Arthur Grimes, Gary Hawke and Frank Holmes, *Independence and Innovation: The Reserve Bank of New Zealand, 1973–2003*, Auckland University Press, Auckland, 2006, pp. 48–50.

71 Budget 1976, AJHR, 1976, B-6 p. 3.

72 Sec Treas to Min Fin budget report 48, 3 Jul 76, in Budget 1976, ANZ [Ref: AALR 873 W5427 (box 13) 3/3/76 pt 1 (R20429416)].

73 DG Ag&Fish and Sec Treas to Min Fin, Min Ag&Fish budget report 22, 25 Jun 76, in Budget 1976, ANZ.

74 Sec Trade &Industry and Sec Treas to Min T&I and Min Fin budget report 60, 8 Jul 76, in Budget 1976, ANZ.

75 Sec Treas to Min Fin budget report 20, 25 Jun 76, 3/3/76, in Budget 1976, ANZ.

76 McClure, *A Civilized Community*, pp. 190–91.

77 Gustafson, *His Way*, pp. 237–38; Hugh Templeton, *All Honourable Men? Inside the Muldoon Cabinet, 1975–1984*, Auckland University Press, Auckland, 1995, p. 46; McClure, *A Civilized Community*, p. 192.

78 NZPD, vol. 415, 1977, p. 4005 (Walker), quoted Gustafson, 2000, p. 238.

79 In particular, David Thomson, *Selfish Generations? The Ageing of New Zealand's Welfare State*, Bridget Williams Books, Wellington, 1991.
80 Templeton, *All Honourable Men*, p. 44.
81 McClure, *A Civilized Community*, p. 191.
82 McClure, *A Civilized Community*, pp. 193–95
83 Director-General Social Welfare and Sec Treas to Min SW and Min Fin budget report 71, 11 Jul 76, in Budget 1976, ANZ.
84 Melanie Nolan, *Breadwinning: New Zealand women and the state*, Canterbury University Press, Christchurch, 2000, pp. 272–88.
85 *NZPD*, vol. 404, 1976, p. 1196; vol. 410, 1977, p. 522.
86 Muldoon, *Muldoon*, Reed, Auckland, 1977, p. 215.
87 Gustafson, *His Way*, p. 250.
88 CM 75/50/22 Cabinet 15 Dec 75; Dep Sec Treas to Min Fin 8 Jan 76, Cabinet Economic Committee, in New Zealand Incomes Policy 1975–76, ANZ [Ref: AALR 873 W3158 (box 60) T61/1/22 pt 12 (R16681844)]; Boston, *Incomes Policy*, p. 167.
89 Dep Sec Treas to Min Fin 9 Jan 76, Cabinet Economic Committee, in New Zealand Incomes Policy 1975–76, ANZ.
90 Acting Perm Head PM Dept to Sec Treas 19 Dec 75, Cabinet Economic Committee, in New Zealand Incomes Policy 1975–76, ANZ; Boston, 1984, p. 165.
91 Acting Perm Head PM Dept to Sec Treas 19 Dec 75; CM 76/2/26 26 Jan 76, Cabinet Economic Committee, in New Zealand Incomes Policy 1975–76, ANZ.
92 Lang's diary of the transition, 16 Feb 76, p. 32, 4 March 76, p. 37, 10 Mar 76, p. 38, and p. 42, Lang Papers, 99-032-1, ATL.
93 Lang's diary of the transition, 1 Apr 76, p. 45, 7 Apr, p. 50, Lang Papers, 99-032-1, ATL.
94 PM to Chairman Off Ec C 8 Apr 76, Cabinet Economic Committee, in New Zealand Incomes Policy 1975–76, ANZ. It should be noted that Peter Franks and Melanie Nolan, *Unions in Common Cause*, p. 44, state that Muldoon's discussions with Skinner 'were not clandestine . . . and were accepted by the FOL executive'. Whether this was always true is open to doubt. Gustafson, unfortunately, is silent on the point.
95 H G Lang, Confidential note for file 8 Apr 76; Lang to Lorimer 26 Apr 76, Cabinet Economic Committee, in New Zealand Incomes Policy 1975–76, ANZ.
96 Combined State Services Organisations to PM 28 Apr 76, Cabinet Economic Committee, in New Zealand Incomes Policy 1975–76, ANZ.
97 Statement by the Prime Minister 14 May 76, Cabinet Economic Committee, in New Zealand Incomes Policy 1975–76, ANZ. See also Boston, *Incomes Policy*, pp. 169–70.
98 Boston, *Incomes Policy*, pp. 170–71.
99 Lang's diary of the transition, 1 June, pp. 71–72, Lang Papers, 99-032-1, ATL.
100 Lang's diary of the transition, 1 June, pp. 72–73, Lang Papers, 99-032-1, ATL.
101 Boston, *Incomes Policy*, pp. 166, 171–73. There is a convenient summary in NZOYB, s. 32.
102 See, generally, Boston, *Incomes Policy*, pp. 166–78, and also Ch OEC to Ch CEC 10 Dec 76, in Cabinet Economic Committee 1976–77, ANZ [Ref: AALR 873 W5427 (box 917) 61/1/8 pt 30 (R20431908)].
103 Boston, *Incomes Policy*, p. 178, and pp. 177–80.
104 Boston, *Incomes Policy*, pp. 180–82; Gustafson, *His Way*, p. 252.
105 Gustafson, *His Way*, pp. 253–54. It is not clear whether Muldoon was aware that

in the mid 1940s the freezing industry had also been subsidised in this fashion: Hunt, *Black Prince*, p. 233.

106 Gustafson, *His Way*, p. 254.

107 E (77) M 10 Part III Minutes 29 Mar 77, in CEC Agendas Minutes Submissions 1977, ANZ [Ref: AALR 873 W5427 (box 918) 61/1/8 pt 31]; Sec Treas to Min Fin budget report 1, 14 Apr 77, Sec Treas to Min Fin budget report 17, 26 May 77, in Budget 1977, ANZ [Ref: AALR 873W5247 (box 14) 3/3/77 pt 2 (R20429422)]; McKinnon, Treasury, p. 251.

108 E (77) M 19 Pt V Minutes of 24 May 77, in CEC Agendas Minutes Submissions 1977, ANZ [Ref: AALR 873 W5427 (box 918) 61/1/8 pt 33 (R20431911)].

109 E (77) M18 Pt VI 17 May 77, in CEC Agendas Minutes Submissions 1977, ANZ [Ref: AALR 873 W5427 (box 918) 61/1/8 pt 34 (R20431912)].

110 E (77) M 37 Pt I Minutes 27 Sep 77 and E (77) M36 Pt III Minutes 20 Sep 77, in CEC Agendas Minutes Submissions 1977, ANZ [Ref: AALR 873 W5427 (box 919) 61/1/8 pt 35 (R20431913)].

111 McKinnon, *Treasury*, p. 284.

112 McKinnon, *Treasury*, pp. 284–85; the brief for Internal Economics II is quoted by McKinnon from 'An Introduction to the Treasury', John Martin papers.

113 Sec Treas to Min Fin budget report 16, 7 Apr 78, in Budget 1978, ANZ [Ref: AALR 873 W5427 (box 15) 3/3/78 pt 1 (R20429427)].

114 Sec Treas to Min Fin budget report 30, 11 Jun 77, in Budget 1977, ANZ.

115 Sec Treas to Min Fin budget report 2, 14 Apr 77, in Budget 1977, ANZ.

116 Sec Treas to Min Fin budget report 4, 18 Apr 77, in Budget 1977, ANZ.

117 Sec Treas to Min Fin budget report 9, 10 May 77, in Budget 1977 ANZ.

118 Budget 1977, AJHR, 1977, B-6, pp. 31, 39.

119 Budget 1977, AJHR, 1977 B-6, pp. 12–17; Templeton, *All Honourable Men*, pp. 67–69.

120 Budget 1977, AJHR, 1977, B-6, p. 4.

121 Templeton, *All Honourable Men*, pp. 91–92.

122 Sec Treas to Min Fin 14 Oct 77, in Mini-Budget October 1977, ANZ [Ref: AALR 873 W5427 (box 14) 3/3/77 pt 1 (R20429420)].

123 Permanent Head PM Dept, Governor Reserve Bank, Sec Treas to Min Fin 11 Oct 77; PH PM Dept, Govr RB, Sec Treas to Min Fin 21 Oct 77, in Mini-Budget October 1977, ANZ.

124 AJHR, 1977, B6A, pp. 3–4.

125 AJHR, 1977, B6A.

126 Budget 1978, AJHR, 1978, B-6, p. 5.

127 Sec Treas to Min Fin budget report 15, 7 Apr 78, in Budget 1978, ANZ

128 Ch OEC to Ch CEC 28 Oct 77, in E (77) M41 Pt VII Minutes of 1 Nov 77, in CEC Agendas Minutes Submissions 1977, ANZ [Ref: AALR 873 W5427 (box 919) 61/1/8 pt 36 (R20431914)].

129 Comm IR and Sec Treas to Min Fin budget report 4, 20 Mar 78, in Budget 1978, ANZ.

130 Sec Treas to Min Fin budget report 5, 20 Mar 78, in Budget 1978, ANZ.

131 Sec Treas to Min Fin budget report 16, 7 Apr 78, in Budget 1978, ANZ.

132 Budget 1978, AJHR, 1978, B-6, p. 40.

133 Budget 1978, AJHR, 1977, B-6, pp. 37–39.

134 Sec Treas to Min Fin budget report 15, 7 Apr 78, in Budget 1978, ANZ.

135 Sec Treas to Min Fin budget report 15, 7 Apr 78; Sec Treas to Min Fin budget report 17, 7 Apr 78, in Budget 1978, ANZ.

136 Sec Treas to Min Fin budget report 51, 15 Apr 78; Sec Treas GM Rural Bank

and DG Ag Fish to Min Fin Min Ag budget report 52, 15 Apr 78; Sec Treas and DG Ag Fish to Min Fin Min Ag budget report 53, 15 Apr 78; Sec Treas and DG Ag Fish to Min Fin Min Ag budget report 55, 15 Apr 78, in Budget 1978, ANZ; Budget 1978, AJHR, 1978, B-6, pp. 15–21; R L Sheppard and J M Biggs, 'Supplementary Minimum Prices: a production incentive?' AERU Discussion Paper no. 63, Lincoln College, June 1982, pp. 11–12.

137 Budget 1978, AJHR, 1978, B-6, p. 44.

138 Ch OEC to Ch CEC 24 Feb 78, in E (78) M5 Pt III Minutes 28 Feb 78, in CEC Agendas Minutes Submissions 1978, ANZ [Ref: AALR 873 W5427 (box 920) 61/1/8 pt 38 (R20431916)].

139 E (78) M 16 Pt IX Minutes 16 May 78, in CEC Agendas Minutes Submissions 1978, ANZ [Ref: AALR 873 W5427 (box 920) 61/1/8 pt 39 (R20432020)].

140 Ch OEC to Ch CEC 26 Jul 78, in CEC Agendas Minutes Submissions 1978, ANZ [Ref: AALR 873 W5427 (box 921) 61/1/8 pt 41 (R20432022)].

141 John Yeabsley, quoted McKinnon, *Treasury*, pp. 251–52.

142 Staff in Confidence For Laking from McKenzie 21 July 77, in Mini-Budget October 1977, ANZ

143 McKinnon, *Treasury*, p. 252. See also Templeton, *All Honourable Men*, p. 92.

144 Task Force on Economic and Social Planning, *New Zealand at the Turning Point*, Government Printer, Wellington, 1976.

145 New Zealand Planning Council, Economic Monitoring Group, reports, 1–5, 1978–83.

146 Ch OEC to Ch CEC 3 Dec 76, in CEC Agendas Minutes Submissions 1976–77, ANZ [Ref: AALR 873 W5427 (box 917) 61/1/8 pt 30 (R20431908)].

Chapter 8

1 For instance, Gustafson, *His Way*, pp. 4–5 'not a radical reformer. . . . took time to get used to new ideas. . . . made stability his highest, indeed overriding goal'.

2 Brian Roper, 'A Level Playing Field? Business Political Activism and State Policy Formulation' in Brian Roper and Chris Rudd, eds., *State and Economy in New Zealand*, Oxford University Press, Auckland, 1993.

3 McKinnon, *Treasury*, pp. 274–75.

4 8 Mar 79 Budget 1979/80 Economic Strategy – Secret, in Budget 1979, ANZ [Ref: AALR 873 W5427 3/3/79].

5 8 Mar 79 Budget 1979/80 Economic Strategy – Secret; Sec Treas to Min Fin budget report 4 16 Mar 79, in Budget 1979, ANZ.

6 Sec Treas to Min Fin budget report 64, 21 May 79, in Budget 1979, ANZ.

7 Muldoon, *New Zealand Herald*, 3 May 79, quoted Gustafson, *His Way*, p. 270.

8 Budget 1979, AJHR, 1979, B-6, p. 3.

9 Budget 1979, p. 5.

10 Budget 1979, p. 4.

11 Colin James, 'Muldoon offers party series of half-measures', *National Business Review, 27 June 1979, p. 1.*

12 Approaching the 1979 Budget, the farm lobby wanted subsidies and grants for roading, boarding school fees, adverse weather, and contractors' services. Sec Treas and DG Ag to Min Fin Min Ag budget report 44, 11 May 79, in Budget 1979, ANZ.

13 Budget 1979, p. 24. On the family benefit, McClure, *A Civilised Community*, p. 200.

14 Annual Report of the Reserve Bank, 1980, B-16, p. 4; see also B-16, 1979.
15 Sec Treas and Sec T&I to Min Fin budget report 75, 26 May 79, in Budget 1979, ANZ.
16 Sec Treas to Min Fin budget report 34, 10 May 79, 3/3/79 Budget 1979; Sec Treas to Min Fin budget report 29, 21 May 80, in Budget 1980, ANZ [Ref: AALR 873 W5427 3/3/80].
17 Industries Development Commission (IDC), *The New Zealand Textile Industry Development Plan 1976–1986: General Principles*, Report 9, August 1979, pp. 85–92.
18 'Govt faithfully implements IDC textile plan', *National Business Review, 25 Feb 80, p. 26.*
19 Industries Development Commission, Interim Report on the Review of the Textile Development Plan, Report 26, 1985, pp. 11, 69.
20 Industries Development Commission, *The N.Z. Motor Vehicle Industry Development Plan*, Report 21, 1983, p. xiv.
21 *NZPD*, vol. 433, 1980, p. 3532 (MacIntyre). A succinct discussion of perceptions at the time is in Sandra Martin, *The Fortex Story*, Dunmore Press, Palmerston North, 2004.
22 *New Zealand Foreign Affairs Record*, 26(5), Jul–Sep 1976, pp. 7–10.
23 John Henderson, 'New Zealand in a Changing World: The Talboys Speeches', *New Zealand International Review, Jan–Feb 1978, p. 10.*
24 Philippa Mein Smith, 'Did Muldoon really "go too slowly" with CER?', *NZJH*, 14(2), October 2007, p. 164.
25 Mein Smith, 'Did Muldoon really "go too slowly"', p. 166.
26 Templeton, *All Honourable Men*, p. 131.
27 Mein Smith; Gustafson pp. 263, 273. See also Templeton, *All Honourable Men*, ch. 13, 17; McKinnon, *Independence and Foreign Policy*, pp. 217–19.
28 *New Zealand International Review*, May–Jun 1977, p. 8.
29 *New Zealand Foreign Affairs Record*, 26(4), Apr–Jun 1976, p. 9.
30 This paragraph is largely based on McKinnon, *Independence and Foreign Policy*, pp. 213–24.
31 Ted Woodfield, 'Marketing in the Middle East', *New Zealand International Review, Mar–Apr 1983, p. 22. See also McKinnon, Independence and Foreign Policy, p. 221.*
32 Shane Brownie and Paul Dalziel 'Shift–Share Analysis of New Zealand Exports, 1970–1984', *New Zealand Economic Papers*, 27(2), 1993, p. 247.
33 Gould, *The Muldoon Years*, p. 41, emphasised the success that Muldoon could claim in trade diversification.
34 Warren Freer, *A Lifetime in Politics: The memoirs of Warren Freer*, Victoria University Press, Wellington, 2004, p. 170.
35 Templeton, *All Honourable Men*, p. 123, and generally pp. 123–27.
36 Gustafson, *His Way*, p. 281.
37 W. F. Birch, *Energy Strategy '79*, Government Printer, Wellington, 1979, p. 7.
38 Gustafson, *His Way*, pp. 281–82.
39 Geoffrey Bertram and Keith Johnston, *Electricity in New Zealand: is there a surplus to sell?*, Development Information Group, Wellington, 1980, pp. 2–4.
40 Gustafson, *His Way*, p. 283. Gustafson relies on Winston Peters, then a first-term backbencher, for some of these points.
41 Templeton, *All Honourable Men*, p. 123; McKinnon, *Treasury*, p. 280.
42 The backbenchers mentioned were Doug Kidd and Ian McLean. Colin James, 'The state shall be mightier than the sword', *National Business Review, 17 Oct 79, p. 2.*

43 Budget, 1979, AJHR, 1979, B-6, p. 4.
44 E (79) M 33 Pt V Minutes 28 Aug 79, in CEC Agendas 1979, ANZ [Ref: AALR 873 W5427 (box 924) 61/1/8 pt 49 (R20431950)].
45 Birch, 1979, p. 39.
46 NZ Planning Council, *Implications of New Energy Developments, Wellington, 1979.*
47 Ch OEC to Ch CEC 22 Nov 79, in CEC Agendas 1979, ANZ [Ref: AALR 873 W5427 (box 925) 61/1/8 pt 52 (R20431930)].
48 The ministers voting included Muldoon and some others of the old guard – Agriculture minister Duncan MacIntyre, Lance Adams-Schneider (Trade and Industry), and David Thomson (State Services), as well as the younger Hugh Templeton (Revenue), Jim Bolger (Labour), and Derek Quigley (Works), and Birch, who may not have voted, E (79) M46 Pt III Minutes 27 Nov 79, in CEC Agendas 1979, pt 52, ANZ.
49 E (79) M47 Pt VI Minutes 4 Dec 79, E (79) M47 Pt VII Minutes 4 Dec 79, in CEC Agendas 1979, pt 52, ANZ.
50 E (79) M41 Pt I Minutes 24 Oct 79, in CEC Agendas Minutes Submissions 1979, ANZ [Ref: AALR 873 W5427 (box 924) 61/1/8 pt 51 (R20431929)]; see also Gustafson, *His Way*, p. 284.
51 E (80) M5 Pt V Minutes 5 Feb 80, in CEC Agendas 1979–1980, ANZ [Ref: AALR 873 W5427 (box 925) 61/1/8 pt 53 (R20431931)].
52 E (80) M11 Pt II Minutes 1 Apr 80, in CEC Agendas 1980, ANZ [Ref: AALR 873 W5427 (box 925) 61/1/8 pt 54 (R20431932)].
53 Ch OEC to Ch CEC 14 Aug 80, in E (80) M30 Pt II Minutes 19 Aug 80, in CEC Agendas 1980, ANZ [Ref: AALR 873 W5427 (box 926) 61/1/8 pt 57 (R20431935)].

54 E (80) M14 Pt II Minutes 22 Apr 80, in CEC Agendas 1980, ANZ [Ref: AALR 873 W5427 (box 926) 61/1/8 pt 55 (R20431933)].
55 E (80) M26 Pt II Minutes 22 Jul 80, in CEC Agendas 1980, pt 57, ANZ.
56 McKinnon, *Treasury*, p. 282.
57 E (80) M26 Pt II Minutes 22 Jul 80, in CEC Agendas 1980, pt 57, ANZ.
58 Bertram and Johnston, *Electricity in New Zealand*; Gustafson, pp. 286–88.
59 Paul van Moeseke, 'Aluminium smelting in New Zealand : an economic appraisal,' Department of Economics, University of Otago, Economics Discussion Papers no. 8008, 1980.
60 E (80) M39 Pt IV Minutes 21 Oct 80, in CEC Agendas 1980, ANZ [Ref: AALR 873 W5427 (box 927) 61/1/8 pt 60 (R20431938)]; E (81) M8 Pt III Minutes 10 Mar 81, in CEC Agendas 1981, ANZ [Ref: AALR 873 W5427 (box 928) 61/1/8 pt 63 (R20431941)].
61 Gustafson, *His Way*, p. 285.
62 Gustafson, *His Way*, p. 285.
63 E (82) M39 Pt V Minutes 19 Oct 82, in CEC Agendas 1982, ANZ [Ref: AALR 873 W5427 (box 932) 61/1/8 pt 76 (R20431977)].
64 John E. Martin, ed., *People, politics and power stations: electric power generation in New Zealand*, 1880–1990, Bridget Williams Books, Wellington, 1991, ch. 14. The various schemes, and public protest, are also discussed in Michael Bagge, 'Dams Dividing Democracy' in Tony Ballantyne and Judith A. Bennett, eds., *Landscape/Community: Perspectives from New Zealand*, University of Otago Press, Dunedin, 2005.
65 Gustafson, *His Way*, pp. 285–86; Easton, *Nationbuilders*, pp. 233–37.

66 Gustafson, *His Way*, p. 287.
67 E (81) M28 Pt IV Minutes 28 Jul 81, in CEC Agendas 1981, ANZ [Ref: AALR 873 W5427 (box 929) 61/1/8 pt 66 (R20432072)].
68 McKinnon, *Treasury*, p. 280.
69 Gustafson, *His Way*, pp. 286–87.
70 Jeffry A. Frieden, *Global Capitalism: Its fall and rise in the twentieth century, Norton, New York and London, 2007,* pp. 372–74.
71 Bassett, *State in New Zealand*, p. 366.
72 This is implied by some officials cited in McKinnon, *Treasury*, p. 302.
73 McKinnon, *Treasury*, pp. 310–11.
74 Sec Treas to Min Fin budget report 2 22 Apr 80, in Budget 1980, ANZ.
75 Sec Treas to Min Fin budget report 40 9 Jun 80, in Budget 1980, ANZ.
76 Ch OEC to Ch CEC 17 Oct 80 in E (80) M39 Pt V Minutes 21 Oct 80, in CEC Agendas 1979–80, pt 60, ANZ [Ref: AALR 873 W5427 (box 925) 61/1/8 pt 60 (R20431938)].
77 AJHR, 1980, B-6A.
78 C J McKenzie to Lough and Scott 20 May 80 secret, in Budget 1980, ANZ.
79 Rob Cameron, quoted in McKinnon, *Treasury*, p. 287.
80 Sec Treas to Min Fin budget report 5, 5 May 81, in Budget 1981, ANZ [Ref: AALR 873 W5427 3/3/81].
81 B-16, 1981, pp. 6–7
82 John Singleton, with Arthur Grimes, Gary Hawke and Frank Holmes, *Independence and Innovation: The Reserve Bank of New Zealand, 1973–2003, Auckland University Press, Auckland, 2006,* p. 85.
83 R. L. Sheppard and J. M. Biggs, 'Supplementary Minimum Prices: a production incentive?', AERU Discussion Paper no. 63, Lincoln College, June 1982, pp. 1–2, 13.
84 G. R. Griffith and T. P. Grundy, 'The Supplementary Minimum Price Scheme: a Retrospective Analysis', AERU Research Report no. 191, Lincoln College, January 1988, pp. 5, 32.
85 Ch OEC to Ch CEC 4 Dec 81, in E (81) M41 Pt II Minutes 8 Dec 81, in CEC Agendas 1981, ANZ [Ref: AALR 873 W5427 (box 930) 61/1/8 pt 69 (R20431955)].
86 Quoted Bassett, *State in New Zealand*, pp. 363–64.
87 S. Harvey Franklin, *Trade, Growth and Anxiety: New Zealand beyond the welfare state*, Methuen, Wellington, 1978; see also Michael Bassett, *Working with David: Inside the Lange cabinet, Hodder Moa, Auckland,* 2008, p. 70, and OECD, Economic Surveys: New Zealand March 1980, pp. 19, 26.
88 McKinnon, *Treasury*, pp. 287, 302.
89 Sec Treas to Min Fin budget report 8, 4 May 82, in Budget 1982, ANZ [Ref: AALR 873 W5427 3/3/82].
90 McKinnon, *Treasury*, p. 306.
91 Singleton et al, *Independence and Innovation*, p. 35.
92 Singleton et al, *Independence and Innovation*, p. 40.
93 Singleton et al, *Independence and Innovation*, p. 58.
94 Reserve Bank annual report, 1982, AJHR, B-16, pp. 8, 11.
95 Boston, *Incomes Policy*, p. 196.
96 Boston, *Incomes Policy*, pp. 197–98.
97 'Industrial Relations Chronicle', *New Zealand Journal of Industrial Relations*, 3(3), December 1978, pp. 91, 92.
98 Boston, *Incomes Policy*, p. 204.

99 Boston, *Incomes Policy*, p. 204.
100 Franks, Peter, 'Knox, Walter James 1919 – 1991', *Dictionary of New Zealand Biography*, updated 22 June 2007. URL: http://www.dnzb.govt.nz/. Knox, who had diabetes, was often unwell and could become particularly irascible when his blood sugar was low, although there is little suggestion this damaged the discharge of his responsibilities. Sonja Davies, *Marching On*, Random House, Auckland, 1997, pp. 22, 36.
101 This point is made in Locke, *Workers in the margins.*
102 Boston, *Incomes Policy*, pp. 206–07.
103 Colin James, 'Government opts for sanity on wage front,' *National Business Review, 3 Oct 79, p. 11; Boston, Incomes Policy*, pp. 206–07
104 Boston, *Incomes Policy*, pp. 209–10
105 Boston, *Incomes Policy*, pp. 211–13.
106 Boston, *Incomes Policy, p. 214*
107 Gustafson, *His Way*, p. 344.
108 Sec Treas to Min Fin 5 Jun 79, in Budget 1979, ANZ.
109 'Chronicle', *NZJIR*, 6(2), August 1981, pp. 114–15.
110 Boston, *Incomes Policy*, pp. 217–18, 225. See also 'Chronicle', *New Zealand Journal of Industrial Relations*, 6(2), August 1981, p. 115.
111 Boston, *Incomes Policy, p. 227.*
112 Gustafson, *His Way*, p. 347.
113 Pat Walsh, 'Myth and reality in industrial relations: moderates, militants and social contracts', *New Zealand Journal of Industrial Relations*, 7(2), August 1982, pp. 79–80.
114 Boston, *Incomes Policy*, p. 227.
115 Locke, *Workers at the Margins*, ch. 3.
116 Templeton, *All Honourable Men*, p. 164; McKinnon, *Treasury*, pp. 302–03.
117 Outline of Paper on the Return to Wage/Price Controls 28 May 82, in Budget 1982, ANZ.
118 Sec T&I to Sec Treas 28 May 82, Sec Lab to Sec Treas 28 May 82, in The Prime Minister 28 May 82 Inflation, in Budget 1982, ANZ.
119 Sec Treas to Min Fin 30 May 82, in Budget 1982, ANZ.
120 Sec Treas to Min Fin 18 Jun 82, in Budget 1982, ANZ.
121 Sec Treas to Min Fin Anti-Inflationary Policy 30 May 82, in Budget 1982, ANZ.
122 Grant, *Man for All Seasons*, pp. 22–122.
123 Budget 1982, AJHR, 1982, B-6, pp. 2–3.
124 Sec Treas to Min Fin budget report 41, 24 Jun 82, in Budget 1982,. Budget 1982, AJHR 1982, B-6, pp. 32–34.
125 Gustafson, *His Way*, pp. 334–35; Paul Goldsmith, *We Won, You Lost, Eat That: A political history of tax in New Zealand since 1840*, David Ling, Auckland, 2008, p. 283.
126 Sec Treas to Min Fin budget report 9 12 Apr 84, in Budget 1984, ANZ [Ref: AALR 873 W5427 3/3/84]. This was drafted by Scott, who was increasingly influential.
127 E (84) M3 Pt III Minutes 8 Feb 84, in CEC Agendas 1984, ANZ [Ref: AALR 873 W5427 (box 935) 61/1/8 pt 85 (R20431963)]; E (84) M11 Pt VI Minutes 10 Apr 84, in CEC Agendas 1984, ANZ [Ref: AALR 873 W5427 (box 936) 61/1/8 pt 86 (R20431964)].
128 AJHR, G-14, 1984–85, p. 17.
129 Sec Treas to Min Fin budget report 70, 8 Jun 84, in Budget 1984, ANZ.
130 McKinnon, *Treasury*, pp. 304–05.

131 McKinnon, *Treasury, pp. 287–88.*
132 Sec Treas to Min Fin budget report 4, 4 May 83, in Budget 1983, ANZ [Ref: AALR 873 W5427 (box 20) 3/3/83 pt 1 (R20436235)].
133 E (83) M36 Pt V Minutes 27 Sep 83, in CEC Agendas 1983, ANZ [Ref: AALR 873 W5427 (box 935) 61/1/8 pt 83 (R20431961)].
134 Hensley, *Final Approaches*, p. 262.
135 The sequence of events for the 1984 election is widely discussed. Gustafson, *His Way*, ch 21, is a useful summary.
136 Sec Treas to Min Fin 30 May 82, in Budget 1982, ANZ.
137 Singleton et al, *Independence and Innovation*, p. 64.
138 Gustafson, *His Way*, p. 385.
139 Michael Bassett and Judith Bassett, *Roderick Deane: His Life and Times, Viking, Auckland, 2006, p. 112.*
140 Gustafson, *His Way*, p. 388.
141 Bassett, *Working with David*, pp. 101–05.
142 Gustafson, *His Way*, p. 92.
143 David G. Pearson and David Thorns, *Eclipse of Equality*, George Allen and Unwin, Sydney, 1983, pp. 54–59, identify a shift away from consensus in 1967.
144 Gustafson, *His Way*, p. 356.
145 Gustafson, *His Way*, p. 357.
146 Some will reasonably ask me to nominate an alternative finance minister. Brian Talboys seems the obvious candidate.

Chapter 9 Endnotes

1 Colin James and Nikitin Sallee 'Lange's hands still steady two years further on', *National Business Review*, 11 Jul 1986, quoted Colin James, *New Territory: The transformation of New Zealand*, Bridget Williams Books, Wellington, 1992, p. 149.
2 Jane Kelsey, *The New Zealand Experiment: A world model for structural adjustment?*, Auckland University Press/Bridget Williams Books, Auckland, 1997, pp. 348–49.
3 W. Hugh Oliver, 'The Labour Caucus and Economic Policy Formation, 1981 to 1984' in Easton, ed., *The Making of Rogernomics*, Auckland University Press, Auckland, 1989, p. 13. Oliver's is an admirable study of the situation up until 1987.
4 Oliver's argument emphasises the influence firstly of Treasury and secondarily of Muldoonism; Bassett, *Working with David*, has provided helpful details on what Douglas and others were reading.
5 Simon Sheppard, *Broken Circle: The decline and fall of the fourth Labour government*, PSL Press, Wellington, 1999, p. 9 quotes Stan Rodger on the evils of consultation and consensus. The issue is generally discussed in Oliver, 1989.
6 New Zealand Government, *View from the Summit: View from the Summit: a look at the '84 Economic Summit Conference*, Government Printer, Wellington, 1984; Paul Dalziel 'The Economic Summit: What People Were Thinking' in Easton, ed., *Making of Rogernomics*, pp. 54–61.
7 Dalziel,'The Economic Summit', p. 63.
8 Roger Douglas and Louise Callan, *Toward Prosperity*, David Bateman, Auckland, 1987, p. 80, quoted Dalziel, 'The Economic Summit', p. 53.
9 New Zealand Treasury, *Economic Management*, Treasury, Wellington, 1984, p.

iii. See also McKinnon, *Treasury*, p. 313.

10 *Economic Management*, p. 104.

11 *Economic Management*, p. 104.

12 *Economic Management*, p. 105. For the IMF see Margaret Garritsen de Vries, *The International Monetary Fund 1972–1978: Cooperation on Trial, Volume 1: Narrative and Analysis*, International Monetary Fund, Washington, 1985, pp. 306–15.

13 *Economic Management*, p. 159.

14 Reserve Bank of New Zealand, 'Key Graphs: Real exchange rate', http://www.rbnz.govt.nz/keygraphs/Fig8b.html, accessed 13 April 2013.

15 *Economic Management*, p. 140

16 *Economic Management*, p. 136

17 *Economic Management*, p. 177 and generally pp. 173–77.

18 *Economic Management*, p. 195.

19 *Economic Management*, p. 196

20 *Economic Management*, p. 197.

21 See also Geoff Bertram, 'Middle class capture: a brief survey' in *The April report, volume III, part two, Future directions: associated papers; report of the Royal Commission on Social Policy. Te Komihana a te Karauna mo nga Ahuatanga-a-iwi*; Government Printer, Wellington, 1988.

22 *Economic Management*, p. 130–33

23 *Economic Management*, p. 141.

24 Brian Easton, *The Commercialisation of New Zealand*, Auckland University Press, Auckland, 1997, p. 78. Simon Sheppard, *Broken Circle: The decline and fall of the fourth Labour government*, PSL Press, Wellington, 1999, p. 9 quotes the minister of labour on the evils of tripartism.

25 Budget 1984, AJHR, 1984, B-6, pp. 4–7.

26 Michael Bassett, *Working with David: Inside the Lange cabinet*, Hodder Moa, Auckland, 2008, p. 121.

27 Budget 1984, AJHR, 1984, B-6, p. 24.

28 *Economic Management*, pp. 157–63; see also Michael Bassett and Judith Bassett, *Roderick Deane: His Life and Times*, Viking, Auckland, 2006, p. 131.

29 Easton, 'From Run to Float', pp. 101–13

30 See, for instance, Paul Dalziel, 'National's Economic Strategy' in Jonathan Boston and Paul Dalziel, eds., *The Decent Society? Essays in response to National's economic and social policies*, Oxford University Press, Auckland, 1992. The term 'consenting adults' is in Stephen Bell and John Quiggin, 'Beyond Stop/Go?: Explaining Australia's Long Boom', *Journal of Australian Political Economy*, 61, 2008, pp. 71–72. A key article is John Pitchford, 'A Sceptical View of Australia's Current Account and Debt Problem', *Australian Economic Review*, 22(2), 1989, pp. 5–14.

31 John Singleton, with Arthur Grimes, Gary Hawke and Frank Holmes, *Independence and Innovation: The Reserve Bank of New Zealand, 1973–2003*, Auckland University Press, Auckland, 2006, pp. 96, 108.

32 Singleton et al, *Innovation and Independence*, p. 109.

33 *Economic Management*, p. 137, quoted in Paul Dalziel, 'The rhetoric of Treasury: a review of the 1990 briefing papers', *New Zealand Economic Papers*, 25(2), 1991, p. 261.

34 *Economic Management*, p. 309, quoted Dalziel, 'The rhetoric of Treasury', p. 261.

35 'Fundamental contradiction' is Dalziel's term, 1991, p. 261.

36 Budget 1985, AJHR, 1985, B-6, pp. 12, 14.

37 Stephen Jennings and Rob Cameron, 'State-owned enterprise reform in New Zealand', in Alan Bollard and Robert Buckle, eds., *Economic Liberalisation in New Zealand*, Allen and Unwin, Wellington, 1987, pp. 123–26; Bassett, *Working with David*, pp. 188–89; Bassett and Bassett, *Roderick Deane*, pp. 139, 146–8.
38 Bassett and Bassett, *Roderick Deane*, p. 160.
39 Paul Volcker, who as chairman of the Federal Reserve had inaugurated the high interest rates of 1979, observed that 'the more starry-eyed Reaganauts argued that reducing taxes would provide a kind of magic elixir for the economy. . . . some of their arguments made me wonder why we bothered to collect taxes at all'. Quoted in Jeffry A. Frieden, *Global Capitalism: Its fall and rise in the twentieth century*, Norton, New York and London, 2007, p. 379.
40 Bassett, *Working with David*, p. 247.
41 This paragraph relies on David Grant, *Bulls Bears and Elephants: A history of the New Zealand Stock Exchange*, Victoria University Press, Wellington, 1997, ch. 9.
42 Grant, *Bulls Bears and Elephants*, p. 285.
43 Grant, *Bulls Bears and Elephants*, pp. 328–37.
44 Grant, *Bulls Bears and Elephants*, p. 314.
45 Colin James, *New Territory: The transformation of New Zealand, 1984–92*, Bridget Williams Books, Wellington, 1992, ch. 13.
46 Bassett, *Working with David*, p. 308.
47 Kelsey, *The New Zealand Experiment*, p. 57.
48 New Zealand Treasury, *Government Management*, Treasury, Wellington, 1987, vol. 1, p. 31.
49 *Government Management*, vol. 1, p. 75.
50 *Government Management*, vol. 1, p. 100.
51 [51] *Government Management*, vol. 1, pp. 137–38.
52 Sheppard, *Broken Circle: The decline and fall of the fourth Labour government*, PSL Press, Wellington, 1999, pp. 39–48, and generally see Robert Chapman, A political culture under pressure: The Struggle to Preserve a Progressive Tax Base for Welfare and the Positive State', *Political Science*, 44(1), 1992, pp. 1–27.
53 Bassett, *Working with David*, pp. 328–32; David Lange, *My Life*, Viking, Auckland, 2005, p. 247. Bassett perhaps fudges the status of the package, but Lange was not alone in his view. Compare Bassett, *Working with David*, pp. 336, 354. See also McKinnon, *Treasury*, p. 337.
54 Lange, *My Life*, p. 248.
55 Bassett, *Working with David*, pp. 333–53.
56 Bassett, *Working with David*, p. 271 for an example of the mean streak.
57 Bassett, *Working with David*, p. 352.
58 The minister was David Caygill: Sheppard, *Broken Circle*, p. 61.
59 Sheppard, *Broken Circle*, pp. 65–66.
60 Bassett, *Working with David*, ch. 14; in 1986 Lange had referred to party traditionalists as 'economic neanderthals' with views little different from Muldoon's; see McKinnon, *Treasury*, p. 331.
61 Budget 1988, AJHR, 1988, B-6, pp. 13–14.
62 Goldfinch, *Remaking New Zealand and Australian economic policy: Ideas, institutions and policy communities*, Victoria University Press, Wellington, 2000, p. 107.
63 Jennings and Cameron, 'State-owned enterprise reform', p. 152.
64 McKinnon, *Treasury*, p. 372; for Douglas, see Kelsey, *New Zealand Experiment*,

p. 136.

65 Lewis Evans, Arthur Grimes and Bryce Wilkinson with David Teece, 'Economic Reform in New Zealand 1984–95: The Pursuit of Efficiency' *Journal of Economic Literature*, 34(4), 1996, pp. 1874–75.

66 *NZPD*, vol. 474, 30 Sep 1986, p. 4731 (Prebble), quoted Jane Kelsey, *The New Zealand experiment: a world model for structural adjustment?* Auckland University Press, Auckland, 1995, p. 128.

67 Kelsey, *The New Zealand Experiment*, ch. 12.

68 Bassett, *Working with David*, pp. 430–35.

69 Bassett, *Working with David*, pp. 445–55.

70 McKinnon, *Treasury*, p. 342.

71 Milton Friedman, 'The Role of Monetary Policy' *American Economic Review*, 58(1), February 1968, pp. 1–17, quote at p. 13.

72 Singleton et al, *Independence and Innovation*, p. 134.

73 Singleton et al, *Independence and Innovation*, p. 5.

74 See Roger Douglas, *Unfinished Business*, Penguin, Auckland, 1993, ch. 10.

75 Quoted in Bassett, *Working with David*, p. 252.

76 Sheppard, *Broken Circle*, p. 35.

77 Sheppard, *Broken Circle*, p. 79, who gives more credit to Lange for trying to maintain a working relationship than does Bassett.

78 Lange to Douglas 22 April 1987, quoted Sheppard, *Broken Circle*, p. 32.

79 Dalziel, 'National's Economic Strategy', pp. 25–27.

80 Dalziel, 'The rhetoric of Treasury', pp. 263–66, quote at 265.

81 Quoted McKinnon, *Treasury*, p. 349.

82 McKinnon, *Treasury*, p. 347.

83 J. B. Bolger, Ruth Richardson, W. F. Birch, *Economic and social initiative, December 1990: statements to the House of Representatives*, Wellington, 1990, p. 50.

84 Bolger, Richardson and Birch, *Economic and social initiative*, pp. 11–12.

85 Budget 1991, p. 34.

86 Bolger, Richardson and Birch, *Economic and social initiative*, p. 17. I owe the phrase 'data-free observation', or DFO for short, to a former colleague at Lincoln University, Dr Eric Scott.

87 Bolger, 'Opening Remarks' in Margaret Clark, ed., *The Bolger Years*, Dunmore, Palmerston North, 2008.

88 Quoted McKinnon, *Treasury*, p. 350.

89 This was outlined by Dalziel, 'National's Economic Strategy'. I should emphasise that I do not regard Professor Dalziel as peddling simple analyses: only that even a non-technical discussion makes this point.

90 Quoted McKinnon, *Treasury*, p. 351.

91 Quoted McKinnon, *Treasury*, p. 354.

92 Evans et al, 'Economic Reform in New Zealand', p. 1882.

93 The Act is summarised by McKinnon, *Treasury*, pp. 356–58, 406–08.

94 Evans et al, 'Economic Reform in New Zealand'. This article has been described as one of 'two authoritative studies [which] have been particularly important in promoting [the success of the reforms] for economists outside New Zealand'. Paul Dalziel, 'New Zealand's Economic Reforms: An Assessment,' *Review of Political Economy*, 14(1), January 2002, p. 32.

95 Evans et al, 'Economic Reform in New Zealand', pp. 1862–63.

96 Evans et al, 'Economic Reform in New Zealand', p. 1860.

97 Quoted Evans et al, 'Economic Reform in New Zealand', p. 1877.

98 Evans et al, 'Economic Reform in New Zealand', p. 1878; Report of the Royal Commission on Social Security, AJHR, 1972, H-53, pp. 207, 214.
99 Evans et al, 'Economic Reform in New Zealand', p. 1880.
100 Evans et al, 'Economic Reform in New Zealand', p. 1861.
101 Evans et al, 'Economic Reform in New Zealand', p. 1880.
102 Evans et al, 'Economic Reform in New Zealand', p. 1880.
103 *New Zealand Official Yearbook, 1994*, p. 472.
104 *New Zealand Official Yearbook, 1994*, p. 477.
105 OECD *Economic Surveys, New Zealand, 1994*, OECD, Paris, 1994, p. 11.
106 OECD, *Economic Surveys*, p. 15.
107 OECD, *Economic Surveys*, p. 11.
108 For instance, Kelsey, 'The New Zealand Experiment; some contributions' in Brian Roper and Chris Rudd, eds. *State and Economy in New Zealand*, Oxford University Press, Auckland, 1993; Boston and Dalziel, eds., *Decent Society?*; Brian Easton, *In Stormy Seas.*
109 Dalziel, 'New Zealand's Economic Reforms', pp. 43–44.
110 Dalziel, 'New Zealand's Economic Reforms', p. 34.
111 Dalziel, 'New Zealand's Economic Reforms', p. 35
112 Dalziel, 'New Zealand's Economic Reforms', p. 33.
113 Dalziel, 'New Zealand's Economic Reforms', fig. 2, p. 37.
114 Dalziel, 'New Zealand's Economic Reforms', p. 38.
115 Dalziel, 'New Zealand's Economic Reforms', fig. 7, pp. 41–42.
116 Goldfinch, *Remaking New Zealand and Australian economic policy*, ch. 9.
117 Dalziel, 'New Zealand's Economic Reforms', pp. 23–24.
118 *Economic Management*, p. 106, quoted in Dalziel, 'The rhetoric of Treasury', p. 266–67.
119 McKinnon, *Treasury*, p. 314.
120 Rob Cameron, quoted McKinnon, *Treasury*, p. 287.
121 This account of the ideal economic constitution is essentially that of McKinnon, *Treasury*, p. 316.
122 Evans et al, 'Economic reform', p. 1893.
123 Gary Hawke, quoted McKinnon, *Treasury*, p. 353.
124 Evans et al, 'Economic reform', p. 1863.
125 Gary Hawke, 'Bliss at dawn – social policy in the first term of the Lange Government' in Margaret Clark, ed., *For the record: Lange and the fourth Labour Government*, Dunmore, Palmerston North, 2005, pp. 117–18
126 This argument owes something to Joseph Stiglitz, 'Interview', in Brian Snowdon, *Conversations on growth, stability and trade: an historical perspective*, Edward Elgar, Northampton, Mass, 2002, esp pp. 403–07.

Bibliography

ARCHIVAL SOURCES: ARCHIVES NEW ZEALAND

TREASURY

Budget Advice

Budget 19** (1945–52) [ADRK 17391 T1 52/63/**]Reports to Minister of Finance 1949–1950 [ADRK 17408 T 25 (box 4) 23 (R20195503)].

Budget 19** (1953–75) [ADRK 17391 T1 3/3/**] Budget 19** (1976–84) [AALR 873 W5247 3/3/**].

Cabinet Committee on Economic Policy, Cabinet Economic Committee

Cabinet Committee Economic Policy 19** (1957–58) [ADRK 17391 T1 61/1/8].

Cabinet Committee on Economic Policy 19** (1959–64) [ADRK 17391 T1 W2666 61/1/8].

Cabinet Economic Committee Agendas Minutes Submissions 19** (1976–84) [AALR 873 W5427 61/1/8].

Stabilisation

T72

1a Economic Stabilisation Commission: appointment, minutes, etc

subseries 1 box 1a

Stabilisation Policy vol 1

T72

subseries 1

box 1b: Stabilisation Policy vol 3

Economic Stabilisation Commission - Minute Book 1950–1952 [ADRK 17435 T72 (box 132) (R20528586)].

Economic Stabilisation Commission - Minute Book 1947–1949 [ADRK 17435 T72 (box 133) (R20528587)].

Economic Stabilisation Commission - Minute Book 1943–1946 [ADRK 17435 T72 (box 134) (R20528588)].

Ministerial Memoranda 1942–1949 [ADRK 17435 T72 (box 130/142) (R20528578)].

Price Control [ADRK 17435 T72 (box 96) 4/2/1/-4/3].

Balance of Payments

Balance of Payments 1946–48 [ADRK 17391 T1 (box 410) 61/1 (R15422463)].

Balance of Payments 1948–52 [ADRK 17391 T1 (box 411) 61/1 (R15422464)].
Balance of Payments General 1950–52 [ADRK 17391 T1 (box 415) 61/2 (R15422487)]. Commonwealth Finance Ministers Conference 1949 [ADRK 17391 T1 (box 418) 61/3/5 (R15422546)].
Balance of Payments UK general 1949–50 [ADRK 17391 T1 (box 427) 61/4/1 (R15422531)].
Balance of Payments UK general 1950–51 [ADRK 17391 (box 427) T1 61/4/1 (R15422532)].
Balance of Payments and sterling area 1951–53 [ADRK 17391 (box 427) T1 61/4/1 (R15422533)].
Review of New Zealand Trade Policy 1956–57 [ADRK 17391 T1 (box 424) 61/3/21 pt 1 (R15422514)].
Review of New Zealand Trade Policy 1957 (part 1) [ADRK 17391 T1 (box 424) 61/3/21 pt 1 (R15422515)].
Review of New Zealand Trade Policy 1957 (part 2) [ADRK 17391 T1 (box 424) 61/3/21 pt 1 (R15422516)].
Discussions with UK Government on Agricultural Policy 1957 [T1 61/3/21/2/57].
UK-NZ Trade Negotiations 1957–58 [ADRK 17391 T1 (box 426) 61/3/25 (R15422525)].
Discussions with UK Government on Agricultural Policy [T1 61/3/21/2/58].
Balance of Payments – General Questions of Economic Policy 1963–66 [AALR 873 W3158 38 61/1/9].
Balance of Payments General Questions Economic Policy 1966–67 [AALR 873 W3158 38 61/1/9 (R16681698)].
Changes in the exchange rate of the New Zealand Dollar 1967 [AALR 873 W5427 (box 961) 61/1/24 pt 13 (R20432063)].
Balance of Payments Officials Cttee 1967–78 [AALR 873 W3158 (box 28) 61/1/1].
Balance of Payments Cab Ec Cttee 1968 vol 3 Jun-Sep [AALR 873 W3158 (box 32) 61/1/8].
Balance of payments – Incomes Policy 1967–76 [AALR 873 W3158 61/1/22].

General Economic Policy

Economic policy general questions 1952–56 [ADRK 17391 T1 (box 414) 61/1/9 pt 1 (R15422482)].
General Questions of Economic Policy 1956–58 [ADRK 17391 T1 (box 414) 61/1/9 (R15422483)].
Capital Issues Control Policy 1951–60 [ADRK 17391 T1 44/162/21 pts1–18].

Loans

Internal Loan 1946 [ADRK 17391 T1 (box 297) 44/223 (R15421690)].
Internal Loan 1948 [ADRK 17391 T1 (box 297) 44/229 (R15421696)].
Internal Loan 1949 [ADRK 17391 T1 (box 297) 44/232 (R15421698)].
Internal Loan 1950 [ADRK 17391 T1 (box 297) 44/236 (R15421700)].
Internal Loan 1951 [ADRK 17391 T1 (box 298) 44/237 (R15421701)].
Loan Programme 1948–52 [ADRK 1731 T1 52/77/**].

INDUSTRIES AND COMMERCE

Minute Book 1944–1946 [AEFN 19257 IC69 1 (R6280930)].
Minutes July 1945–October 1945 [AEFN 19205 IC 44 (box 16) (R17701209)].

PERSONAL PAPERS

Walter Nash Papers.

ALEXANDER TURNBULL LIBRARY

Sir John Marshall Papers MS Papers 1403.
S.G. Holland Papers MS Papers 1624.
Henry Lang Papers MS Papers 99-032.

PUBLISHED OFFICIAL SOURCES

Birch, W. F., *Energy Strategy '79*, Wellington, 1979, p. 3.
Bolger, J.B., Ruth Richardson, W.F. Birch, *Economic and Social Initiative, December 1990: Statements to the House of Representatives*, Wellington, 1990.
Book of Awards, various years.
Industrial Development Conference, Background Papers, June 1960, Government Printer, Wellington, 1960.
Industries Development Commission (IDC), *The New Zealand Textile Industry Development Plan 1976-1986: General Principles*, Report 9, August 1979.
Ministry of Energy, *Goals and Guidelines: An Energy Strategy for New Zealand*, Ministry of Energy, Wellington, 1978.
New Zealand Government, *Background papers: Industrial Development Conference, June 1960.*
New Zealand Government, *The Agricultural Development Conference 1963–64.*
New Zealand Government, *Report of the Proceedings of the National Development Conference,* plenary session, 27–29 August, 1968.
New Zealand Monetary and Economic Council, Reports, various years.
New Zealand Official Year Book, Government Printer, Wellington, various years.
New Zealand Planning Council, Economic Monitoring Group, reports.
New Zealand Treasury, *Economic Management*, Treasury, Wellington, 1984.
New Zealand Treasury, *Government Management*, Treasury, Wellington, 1987, 2 vols.
Task Force on Economic and Social Planning, *New Zealand at the Turning Point*, Government Printer, Wellington, 1976.
View from the Summit: A Look at the '84 Economic Summit Conference, New Zealand Government, Wellington, 1984.
Appendices to the Journals of the House of Representatives, annually. In particular:
Budget (B-6)
Economic Survey (B-5)
Department of Industries and Commerce Annual Report (H-44)
Reserve Bank of New Zealand Annual Report (B-16)
New Zealand Parliamentary Debates.

SECONDARY SOURCES

Aimer, Peter, *Wings of the Nation: a History of the New Zealand National Airways Corporation, 1947–78*, Bush Press, Auckland, 2000.

Armstrong, Philip, Andrew Glyn and John Harrison. *Capitalism since World War II: The Making and Breakup of the Great Boom*, Fontana, London, 1984.

Ashwin, B. C., 'Banking and Currency in New Zealand', *Economic Record*, 6(3), November 1930, pp.188–204.

Baker, Astrid, 'Governments, Firms, and National Wealth: a New Pulp and Paper Industry in Postwar New Zealand', *Enterprise & Society*, 5(4), December 2004, p 688.

Baker, J. V. T., *The New Zealand People at War: The War Economy*, Historical Publications Branch, Wellington, 1965.

Baker, J. V. T. and H. G. Lang, 'Economic Policy and National Income', New Zealand Official Yearbook, 1950.

Ballantyne, Tony and Judith A.Bennett, eds., *Landscape/Community: Perspectives from New Zealand*, University of Otago Press, Dunedin, 2005.

Barnett, Corelli. *The Lost Victory: British dreams, British reality 1945-1950*, Macmillan, London, 1995.

Bassett, Michael, *Confrontation '51: The 1951 Waterfront Dispute*, Reed, Wellington, 1972.

Bassett, Michael, *The Third Labour Government: A Personal History*, Dunmore, Palmerston North, 1976.

Bassett, Michael, *Three-Party Politics in New Zealand, 1911–1931*, Historical Publications, Auckland, 1982.

Bassett, Michael, *Coates of Kaipara*, Auckland University Press, Auckland, 1995.

Bassett, Michael, *The State in New Zealand 1840–1984: Socialism Without Doctrines?* Auckland University Press, Auckland, 1998.

Bassett, Michael, with Michael King, *Tomorrow Comes the Song: A life of Peter Fraser*, Penguin, Auckland, 2000.

Bassett, Michael, *Working with David: Inside the Lange Cabinet*, Hodder Moa, Auckland, 2008.

Bassett, Michael and Judith Bassett, *Roderick Deane: His Life and Times*, Viking, Auckland, 2006.

Belich, James, *Paradise Reforged: A History of the New Zealanders from the 1880s to the Year 2000*, Allen Lane: Auckland, 2001.

Berman, Sheri, *The Social Democratic Moment: Ideas and Politics in the Making of Inter-War Europe*, Harvard University Press, Cambrige, Mass, 1998.

Berman, Sheri, *The Primacy of Politics: Social Democracy and the Making of Europe's Twentieth Century*, Cambridge University Press, Cambridge and New York, 2006.

Bertram, Geoffrey and Keith Johnston, *Electricity in New Zealand: is There a Surplus to Sell?*, Development Information Group, Wellington, 1980

Bollard, Alan and Robert Buckle, eds., *Economic Liberalisation in New Zealand*, Allen and Unwin, Wellington, 1987.

Boston, Jonathan, *Incomes Policy in New Zealand 1968–84*, Institute of Policy Studies, Wellington, 1984.

Boston, Jonathan and Paul Dalziel, eds., *The Decent Society? Essays in Response to National's Economic and Social Policies*, Oxford University Press, Auckland, 1992.

Britton, Andrew, *Monetary Regimes of the Twentieth Century*, Cambridge University Press, Cambridge and New York, 2001.

Brownie, Shane and Paul Dalziel, 'Shift-Share Analysis of New Zealand Exports, 1970-1984' *New Zealand Economic Papers*, 27(2), 1993.

Cain, P. J. and A. G. Hopkins, *British Imperialism, 1688–2000*, Longman, New York, 2nd edition, 2001.

Cairncross, Alec, *Managing the British Economy in the 1960s: A Treasury perspective*, Macmillan, Basingstoke, 1996, p. 180.

Capling, Ann, *Australia and the Global Trade System: From Havana to Seattle*, Cambridge University Press, Cambridge and New York, 2001, pp. 17–18.

Cassis, Youssef, *Capitals of Capital: a History of International Financial centres, 1780-2005*, Cambridge University Press, Cambridge, 2006.

Chapman, Robert, 'A Political Culture Under Pressure: The Struggle to Preserve a Progressive Tax Base for Welfare and the Positive State', *Political Science*, 44 (1), 1992, pp. 1–27.

Chatterjee, Srikanta, ed., *The New Politics: A Third Way for New Zealand*, Dunmore, Palmerston North, 1999.

Clark, Margaret, ed., *Sir Keith Holyoake: Towards a Political Biography*, Dunmore, Palmerston North, 1997.

Clark, Margaret, ed., *Three Labour Leaders: Nordmeyer, Kirk, Rowling*, Dunmore, Palmerston North, 2001.

Clark, Margaret, ed, *Holyoake's Lieutenants*, Dunmore Press: Palmerston North, 2003.

Clark, Margaret, ed., *The Bolger Years*, Dunmore, Palmerston North, 2008.

Clarke, Peter, *The Last Thousand Days of the British Empire*, Allen Lane, London, 2007.

Clarke, Peter, *Keynes: The Twentieth Century's Most Influential Economist*, Bloomsbury, London, 2009.

Coates, David and John Hillard, *The Economic Decline of Modern Britain: The Debate Between Left and Right*, Wheatsheaf, Brighton,1986.

Cockett, Richard, *Thinking the Unthinkable: Think-tanks and the Economic Counter-Revolution, 1931–1983*, HarperCollins, London, 1993.

Coleman, William, Selwyn Cornish and Alfred Hagger, *Giblin's Platoon: The Trials and Triumph of the Economist in Australian Public Life*, ANU E-Press, Canberra, 2006.

Collins, Robert M., 'The Economic Crisis of 1968 and the Waning of the "American Century" *American Historical Review*, 101(2), April 1996, pp. 396–422.

Cornwall, J. P. M. et al, *A Critique of the Industrial Development Conference June 1960*, School of Public Administration, Victoria University of Wellington, mimeo, 1960.

Crafts, Nicholas and Gianni Toniolo, eds., *Economic Growth in Europe Since 1945*, Cambridge University Press, Cambridge, 1996.

Dalziel, Paul, 'The Rhetoric of Treasury: a Review of the 1990 Briefing Papers', *New Zealand Economic Papers*, 25(2), 1991.

Dalziel, Paul, 'New Zealand's Economic Reforms: An Assessment,' *Review of Political Economy*, 14(1), January 2002.

Davies, Sonja, *Marching On*, Random House, Auckland, 1997.

de Vries, Margaret Garritsen, *The International Monetary Fund 1972–1978: Cooperation on Trial, Volume 1: Narrative and Analysis*, International Monetary Fund, Washington, 1985.

Douglas, Roger, *Alternative Budget: A Personal View*, The author, Wellington, 1980.

Douglas, Roger and Louise Callan, *Toward Prosperity*, David Bateman, Auckland, 1987.

Douglas, Roger, *Unfinished Business*, Penguin, Auckland, 1993.

Eagles, Jim and Colin James, *The Making of a New Zealand Prime Minister*, Cheshire, Wellington, 1973.

Easton, Brian, ed., *The Making of Rogernomics*, Auckland University Press, Auckland, 1989.

Easton, Brian, *In Stormy Seas: The Post-War New Zealand Economy*, University of Otago Press, Dunedin, 1997.

Easton, Brian, 'Bernard Ashwin: Secretary to the Nation-building State', *New Zealand Studies*, November 1997, pp. 13–21

Easton, Brian, *The Commercialisation of New Zealand*, Auckland University Press, Auckland, 1997, p. 78.

Easton, Brian, *The Nationbuilders*, Auckland University Press, Auckland, 2001; McKinnon, 2003.

Edwards, Brian, ed., *Right Out: The Inside story, Labour Victory 1972*, AH & AW Reed, Wellington, 1973.

Eichengreen, Barry, *Global Imbalances and the Lessons of Bretton Woods*, MIT Press, Cambridge, Mass, 2006.

Eichengreen, Barry, *The European Economy since 1945: Coordinated Capitalism and Beyond*, Princeton University Press, Princeton, 2006, p. 7.

Eichengreen, Barry, *Globalizing Capital: A History of the International Monetary System*, Princeton University Press, Princeton, 2nd edn 2008, p. 2.

Endres, A. M., 'The Political Economy of W.B. Sutch: Towards a Critical Appreciation' *New Zealand Economic Papers*, vol. 20, 1986, pp 17–40.

Evans, Lewis, Arthur Grimes, Bryce Wilkinson and David Teece, 'Economic Reform in New Zealand 1984–95: The Pursuit of Efficiency'*Journal of Economic Literature*, 34(4), December 1996.

Ferguson, Gael, *Building the New Zealand Dream*, Dunmore, Palmerston North, 1994.

Franklin, S. Harvey, *Trade, Growth and Anxiety: New Zealand Beyond the Welfare State*, Methuen, Wellington, 1978.

Freer, Warren, *A Lifetime in Politics: The Memoirs of Warren Freer*,Victoria University Press, Wellington, 2004.

Frieden, Jeffrey A, *Global Capitalism: Its Fall and Rise in the Twentieth Century*, W. W. Norton, New York, 2006.

Friedman, Milton, 'The Role of Monetary Policy' *American Economic Review*, 58(1), February 1967.

Galbreath, Ross, *DSIR: Making Science Work for New Zealand*, Victoria University Press, Wellington, 1998.

Gardner, Richard N, *Sterling-Dollar Diplomacy: Anglo-American Collaboration in the Reconstruction of Multilateral Trade*, Clarendon Press, Oxford, 1956.

Garnier, Tony, Bruce Kohn and Pat Booth, *The Hunter and the Hill: New Zealand Politics in the Kirk years*, Cassell, Auckland, 1978.

Garvin, Tom, *Preventing the Future: Why Was Ireland So Poor for So Long?* Gill and Macmillan, Dublin, 2004.

Giddens, Anthony, *Beyond Left and Right: The Future of Radical Politics*, Cambridge, Polity Press, 1994.

Giddens, Anthony, *The Third Way: The Renewal of Social Democracy*, Polity Press, Malden, Mass, 1998.

Goldfinch, Shaun, *Remaking New Zealand and Australian Economic Policy : Ideas, Institutions and Policy Communities*, Victoria University Press, Wellington, 2000.

Goldfinch, Shaun and Daniel Malpass, 'The Polish Shipyard: Myth, Economic History and Economic Policy Reform in New Zealand', *Australian Journal of Politics and History*, 53(1), March 2007, pp.119–138.

Goldsmith, Paul, *We Won, You Lost, Eat That: A Political History of Tax in New Zealand Since 1840*, David Ling, Auckland, 2008.

Goldsmith, Paul, *Fletchers: A Centennial History of Fletcher Building*, Auckland, David Ling, 2009.

Gould, John, *The Rake's Progress? The New Zealand Economy Since 1945*, Hodder and Stoughton, Auckland, 1983.

Gould, John, *The Muldoon Years: An Essay on New Zealand's Recent Economic Growth*, Hodder and Stoughton, Auckland, 1985.

Grant, David, *Bulls, Bears, and Elephants: A History of the New Zealand Stock Exchange*, Victoria University Press, Wellington, 1997.

Grant, David ed., *The Big Blue: Snapshots of the 1951 Waterfront Lockout*, Canterbury University Press, Christchurch, 2004.

Greasley, David and Les Oxley, 'Regime Shift and Fast Recovery on the Periphery: New Zealand in the 1930s', *Economic History Review*, 55(4), November 2002.

Greasley, David and Les Oxley, 'The Pastoral Boom, the Rural Land Market, and Long Swings in New Zealand Economic Growth 1873–1939', *Economic History Review*, 62(2), May 2009.

Green, Anna, *British Capital, Antipodean Labour: Working the New Zealand Waterfront, 1915–1951*, University of Otago Press, Dunedin, 2001.

Griffith, G. R. and T. P. Grundy, 'The Supplementary Minimum Price Scheme: a Retrospective Analysis', AERU Research Report no. 191, Lincoln College, January 1988.

Guest, Morris and John Singleton, 'The Murupara Project and Industry Development in New Zealand', *Australian Economic History Review*, 39(1), February 1999.

Gustafson, Barry, *The First 50 years: A History of the New Zealand National Party*, Reed Methuen, Auckland, 1986.

Gustafson, Barry, *From the Cradle to the Grave: A Biography of Michael Joseph Savage*, Reed Methuen, Auckland, 1986.

Gustafson, Barry, *His Way: A Biography of Robert Muldoon*, Auckland University Press, Auckland, 2000.

Gustafson, Barry, *Kiwi Keith: A Biography of Keith Holyoake*, Auckland University Press, Auckland, 2007.

Haggard, Stephan, *Pathways from the Periphery: The Politics of Growth in the Newly Industrializing Countries*, Cornell University Press, Ithaca, 1990.

Hawke, G. R. 'New Zealand and the Return to Gold in 1925,' *Australian Economic History Review*, 11(1), February 1971.

Hawke, G. R. *The Making of New Zealand*, Cambridge University Press: Cambridge, 1985.

Hayward, Margaret, *Diary of the Kirk Years*, Reed and Cape Catley, Wellington and Queen Charlotte Sound, 1981.

Henderson, John, *Rowling: The Man and the Myth*, Australia and New Zealand Book Co, Auckland, 1981.

Hennessy, Peter, *Never Again: Britain 1945–51*, Jonathan Cape, London, 1992.

Hensley, Gerald, *Final Approaches*, Auckland University Press, Auckland, 2007.

Hensley, Gerald, *Beyond the Battlefield: New Zealand and its Allies, 1939–45*, Viking Penguin, Auckland, 2009.

Hobsbawm, Eric, *The Age of Extremes: The Short Twentieth Century, 1914–1991*, Michael Joseph, London, 1995.

Hocking, Jenny and Colleen Lewis, eds., *It's Time Again: Whitlam and Modern Labour*, Circa Books, Melbourne, 2003.

Holland, H. E., *The Way Out of the Labyrinth : A Statement of the Labour Party's Policy of Industrial Reconstruction and Rehabilitation and Credit and Currency Reform*, Clarte Bookshop, Wellington, 1932.

Holland, S. G., *Passwords to Progress*, Whitcombe and Tombs, Christchurch, 1943.

Hunt, Graeme, *Black Prince: The Biography of Fintan Patrick Walsh*, Penguin, Auckland, 2004.

James, Colin, *The Quiet Revolution: Turbulence and Transition in Contemporary New Zealand*, Allen & Unwin, Wellington, 1986.

James, Colin, *New Territory: The Transformation of New Zealand*, Bridget Williams Books, Wellington, 1992.

Jesson, Bruce, *Only Their Purpose is Mad*, Dunmore, Palmerston North, 1999.

Jones, John Philip, *Keynes's Vision: Why the Great Depression Did Not Return*, Routledge, London, 2008.

Jones, S. R. H., 'Government Policy and Industry Structure in New Zealand, 1900–1970', *Australian Economic History Review*, 39(3), August 1999.

Kalecki, Michal, 'Political Aspects of Full Employment', in *Selected Essays on the Dynamics of the Capitalist Economy 1933–1970*, Cambridge University Press, Cambridge, 1971.

Kelsey, Jane, *The New Zealand Experiment: A World Model for Structural Adjustment?* Auckland University Press, Auckland, 1995.

Kunz, Diane B., *Butter and Guns: America's Cold War Economic Diplomacy*, The Free Press, New York, 1997.

Lange, David, *My Life*, Viking, Auckland, 2005.

Levine, Steven and Alan McRobie, *From Muldoon to Lange: New Zealand Elections in the 1980s*, MC Enterprises, Rangiora, 2002.

Logan, Mary, *Nordy: Arnold Nordmeyer, a Political Biography*, Steele Roberts, Wellington, 2008.

Maddison, Angus, *The World Economy: Historical Statistics*, OECD, Paris, 2003.

Markwell, Donald, *John Maynard Keynes and International Relations: Economic Paths to War and Peace*, Oxford University Press, Oxford, 2006.

Marshall, John, *Memoirs vol 2: 1960 to1988*, Collins, Auckland, 1989.

Martin, John E., ed., *People, Politics and Power Stations: Electric Power Generation in New Zealand, 1880–1990*, Bridget Williams Books, Wellington, 1991.

Martin, John E., *Honouring the Contract*, Victoria University Press, Wellington, 2010.

Martin, Sandra, *The Fortex Story*, Dunmore Press, Palmerston North, 2004.

McClure, Margaret, *A Civilised Community: A History of Social Security in New Zealand, 1898–1998*, Auckland University Press, Auckland, 1998.

McKenzie, Francine, *Redefining the Bonds of Commonwealth, 1939–1948: the Politics of Preference*, Palgrave, Basingstoke, 2002.

McKinnon, Malcolm, *Independence and Foreign Policy: New Zealand in the World Since 1935*, Auckland University Press, Auckland, 1993.

McKinnon, Malcolm, *Treasury: The New Zealand Treasury, 1840–2000*, Auckland University Press, Auckland, 2003.

Mein Smith, Philippa, *A Concise History of New Zealand*, Cambridge University Press, Cambridge, 2005.

Mein Smith, Philippa, 'Did Muldoon Really "go too slowly" With CER?', *New Zealand Journal of History*, 14(2), October 2007.

Moggridge, D. E., *Maynard Keynes: An Economists' Biography*, Routledge, London and New York, 1992.

Moggridge, Donald, ed., *The Collected Writings of John Maynard Keynes*, Macmillan, London, various dates.

Morgan, Kenneth O., *The People's Peace: British History 1945–1989*, Oxford University Press, Oxford, 1990.

Muldoon, R. D., *The Rise and Fall of a Young Turk*, Reed, Wellington, 1974.

Nash, Walter, *Financial Power in New Zealand: The Case for a State Bank*, New Zealand Worker, Wellington, 1925.

New Zealand Business Round Table, ed., *From Recession to Recovery*, New Zealand Business Round Table, Wellington, 1992.

Newton, C. C. S., 'The Sterling Crisis of 1947 and the British Response to the Marshall Plan' *Economic History Review*, 37(3), August 1984.

Nolan, Melanie, *Breadwinning: New Zealand Women and the State*, Canterbury University Press, Christchurch, 2000.

O'Farrell, P. J., *Harry Holland: Militant Socialist*, Australian National University Press, Canberra, 1964.

Oliver, W. H. and Bridget Williams, eds., *The Oxford History of New Zealand*, Oxford University Press, Auckland, 1981.

Parker, Robert B., *John Kenneth Galbraith: His Life, His Politics, His Economics*, Farrar, Strauss and Giroux, New York, 2005.

Pearson, David G. and David Thorns, *Eclipse of Equality*, George Allen and Unwin, Sydney, 1983.

Peat, Neville, *Manapouri Saved*, Longacre, Dunedin, 1994.

Pimlott, Ben, *Hugh Dalton*, Cape, London, 1985.

Pollard, Sidney, *The Wasting of the British Economy: British Economic Policy 1945 to the Present,* Croom Helm, London, 1982.

Reynolds, David, *One World Divisible: A Global History Since 1945*, Norton, New York, 2000.

Riesco, Manuel, ed., *Latin America: A New Developmental Welfare State Model in the Making?*, Palgrave, Basingstoke, 2009.

Roper, Brian and Chris Rudd, eds., *State and Economy in New Zealand*, Oxford University Press, Auckland, 1993.

Roth, H. O., *Trade Unions in New Zealand*, Reed, Wellington, 1973

Ruggie, John Gerard, 'International Regimes, Transactions, and Change: Embedded Liberalism in the Postwar Economic Order', in Stephen Krasner, ed., *International Regimes*, Cornell University Press, Ithaca, 1983.

Sawer, Marian, *The Ethical State? Social Liberalism in Australia*, Melbourne University Press, Carlton, 2003.

Schedvin, C. B., 'Staples and Regions of Pax Britannica', *Economic History Review* 2nd ser, 43(4), November 1990.

Schenk, Catherine R., *Britain and the Sterling Area: From Devaluation to Convertability in the 1950s*, Routledge, London, 1994.

Schenk, Catherine R., *The Decline of Sterling: Managing the Retreat of an International Currency 1945–1992*, Cambridge University Press, Cambridge, 2010.

Schenk, Catherine and John Singleton, 'Basket Pegs and Exchange Rate Regime Change: Australia and New Zealand in the Mid–Seventies', *Australian Economic History Review*, 51(2), 2011.

Sheppard, R.L. and J M Biggs, 'Supplementary Minimum Prices: A Production Incentive?', AERU Discussion Paper no. 63, Lincoln College, June 1982.

Sheppard, Simon, *Broken Circle: The Decline and Fall of the Fourth Labour Government,* PSL Press, Wellington, 1999.

Simpson, Tony, *The Sugarbag Years*, Alister Taylor, Wellington, 1974.

Sinclair, Keith, *A History of New Zealand*, Penguin, Harmondsworth, 1969.

Sinclair, Keith, 'The Lee-Sutch Syndrome: New Zealand Labour Party Policies and Politics, 1930–1940,' *New Zealand Journal of History*, 8, 2 October 1974.

Sinclair, Keith, *Walter Nash*, Auckland University Press, Auckland, 1976.

Singleton, John and Paul L. Robertson, *Economic Relations Between Britain and Australasia, 1945–1970*, Palgrave, Houndsmills, 2002.

Singleton, John with Arthur Grimes, Gary Hawke and Frank Holmes, *Independence and Innovation: The Reserve Bank of New Zealand, 1973–2003*, Auckland University Press, Auckland, 2006.

Skidelsky, Robert, *John Maynard Keynes: a Biography. Volume 3: Fighting for Freedom*, Macmillan, London, 2000.

Snowdon, Brian, *Conversations on Growth, Stability and Trade: AnHistorical Perspective*, Edward Elgar, Northampton, Mass, 2002.

Strange, Susan, *Sterling and British Policy: A Political Study of an International Currency in Decline*, Oxford University Press, London, 1971.

Supple, Barry, 'Fear of Failing: Economic History and the Decline of Britain', *Economic History Review*, 47(3), August 1994.

Sutch, W. B., *The Quest for Security in New Zealand*, Oxford University Press, Wellington, 1966.

Temin, Peter, *Lessons From the Great Depression*, MIT Press, Cambridge, Mass, 1989.

Templeton, Hugh, *All Honourable Men? Inside the Muldoon Cabinet, 1975–1984*, Auckland University Press, Auckland, 1995.

Thompson, Noel, 'Hobson and the Fabians, Two Roads to Socialism in the 1920s', *History of Political Economy*, 26 (1994).

Thorns, David C. and Charles P. Sedgwick, *Understanding Aotearoa-New Zealand: Historical Statistics*, Dunmore, Palmerston North, 1997.

Tiratsoo, Nick, ed., *From Blitz to Blair: A New History of Britain Since 1939*, Weidenfeld and Nicolson, London, 1997.

Tomlinson, Jim, 'Inventing 'Decline': The Falling Behind of the British Economy in the Postwar Years', *Economic History Review*, 49(4), November 1996.

Tomlinson, Jim, *Democratic Socialism and Economic Policy: The Attlee Years, 1945–51*, Cambridge University Press, Cambridge, 1997.

Tomlinson, Jim, *The Politics of Decline: Understanding Post-War Britain*, Longman, Harlow, 2000.

Tomlinson, Jim, *The Labour Governments 1964–70: Economic Policy*, Manchester University Press, Manchester, 2004.

Trotter, Chris, *No Left Turn: The Distortion of New Zealand's History by Greed, Bigotry and Right-Wing Politics*, Random House, Auckland, 2007.

van Ark, Bart, ed., *Economic Growth in the Long Run: A History of Empirical Evidence, volume 1*, Edward Elgar, Cheltenham, 1997.

Walsh, Pat, 'Myth and Reality in Industrial Relations: Moderates, Militants and Social Contracts', *New Zealand Journal of Industrial Relations*, 7(2), August 1982.

Walsh, Pat, 'An Unholy Alliance: The 1968 Nil Wage Order', *New Zealand Journal of History*, 28(2), October 1994.

Waring, Marilyn, *Counting for Nothing: What Men Value and What Women are Worth*, Allen and Unwin, Wellington, 1988.

Whitwell, Greg, *The Treasury Line*, Allen and Unwin, Sydney, 1986.

Whyman, Philip B, *Third Way Economics: Theory and Evaluation*, Palgrave Macmillan, Houndmills, 2006.

Wiarda, Howard J. and Harvey F. Kline, eds., *A Concise Introduction to Latin American Politics and Development* Westview Press, Boulder, 2007.

Zeiler, Thomas W., *Free Trade, Free World: The Advent of GATT*, University of North Carolina Press, Chapel Hill, 1999.

Index